Smart Flexibility

Smart Flexibility

Moving Smart and Flexible Working
from Theory to Practice

ANDY LAKE

Routledge
Taylor & Francis Group

LONDON AND NEW YORK

First published in paperback 2024

First published 2013 by Gower Publishing

Published 2016 by Routledge
4 Park Square, Milton Park, Abingdon, Oxon OX14 4RN

and by Routledge
605 Third Avenue, New York, NY 10158

Routledge is an imprint of the Taylor & Francis Group, an informa business

British Library Cataloguing in Publication Data
Lake, Andy.
  Smart flexibility : moving smart and flexible working from theory to practice.
  1. Flextime.
  I. Title
  331.2'5724-dc23

Library of Congress Cataloging-in-Publication Data
Lake, Andy.
  Smart flexibility : moving smart and flexible working from theory to practice / by Andrew Lake.
     p. cm.
  Includes bibliographical references and index.
  ISBN 978-0-566-08852-0 (hbk)
  1. Flextime. I. Title.
  HD5109.L355 2013
  331.25'724--dc23

                                                                    2012029738

ISBN: 978-0-566-08852-0 (hbk)
ISBN: 978-1-03-283813-7 (pbk)
ISBN: 978-1-315-60937-9 (ebk)

DOI: 10.4324/9781315609379

Contents

List of Figures

List of Tables

About this Book

This books aims to provide a guide for managers in implementing what I am calling 'Smart Flexibility' in their organisation in a business-focused way.

The approach to the subject is informed by five key ideas. The first is that the time for 'evangelising' about the benefits of flexible working is all but over. The point is how to achieve these benefits in the real world. So the main area that people are interested in now is about the practicalities. Hence the title of the book, *Smart Flexibility: Moving Smart and Flexible Working from Theory to Practice*.

The second key idea is that 'flexible working' needs to be implemented in ways that are progressive, business-focused and hit a range of benefits across the Triple Bottom line. It's great to offer family-friendly options to staff. But it's not enough. Working smarter and more flexibly needs to be central to corporate strategy, not a bolt-on to help those with caring responsibilities and to be generally nice to employees.

The third key idea is that implementing Smart Flexibility does not fall within a single specialism. Though flexible working projects may often be led by HR, Property or IT professionals, successful implementations are interdisciplinary. To achieve benefits across a broad front of increasing efficiency, improving agility, reducing costs, increasing employee satisfaction, widening opportunity and improving environmental performance requires coordinated action and getting everybody on board.

This integrated approach includes technology changes, culture change and physical changes back at the office, as well as facilitating new locations of work. That's why in this book there are sections covering issues such as office layout, desks and storage. How things change 'back at the office' is an important ingredient of making Smart Flexibility a success.

The fourth key idea is that for Smart Flexibility to succeed, there has to be a robust empirical basis for change. Achievements have to be measurable. In some quarters flexible work and work-life balance are seen as being somewhat fluffy concepts, incapable of measurement and likely to add to company costs. If the approach is woolly, the outcome may indeed be fluffy. So it is important at the outset to establish metrics. It's time to put some grit in the fluff, so to speak.

A fifth key idea is that we're in an age of transition. The world is changing fast. The old ways are becoming increasingly less credible. But with the pace of change in technologies and the often slow pace of behavioural and cultural change in organisations, we're only in the early stages of transformational change in the way we work, and in the ways we think organisations should operate.

Within the book there's also an additional focus on change in the government sector. This is not only because I have done a fair amount of work in the sector, but also because the need to change is particularly acute in the current economic crisis. I also believe that changes to national and local government can be particularly beneficial, and relate to wider benefits that new ways of working can deliver for society.

There is no alternative to change. The issues are around whether we do it well or do it badly.

This is not an academic book as such, though I hope the reader will find it has a sound academic underpinning. Academic research into new ways of working by its nature tends to lag a few years behind what companies are actually doing at the leading edge of business transformation. While this book references appropriate research and hopefully throws up some new ways of looking at things, it is not primarily concerned with theoretical models or proposing new concepts. Except when making a specific historical reference, I've tried to ensure that most of the studies referred to are dated within the last five or six years.

By focusing on what companies and public sector bodies are actually doing in the real world, my hope is to paint a lively and informative picture of how organisations are making the most of the new opportunities for Smart Flexibility, and the techniques for doing likewise in your own organisation.

The book focuses on larger organisations – private, public and voluntary sector – as these have a commonality of interest. They face a different set of issues from the micro-business and the home-based self-employed. We do include references to smaller businesses that are growing in smarter ways, where it illustrates aspects of smart and flexible working that have a wider importance.

So the book is written for a corporate audience – that is, it is not written to provide advice to the individual employee seeking more flexibility or for guidance on how to run a home-based business. There are numerous other resources out there to provide advice for the latter market. The guidance provided in these pages is for the manager in a large organisation managing teams of employees on a smarter and more flexible basis, or providing the corporate facilities, resources and policies to enable them to do so.

The book is based on 18 years of implementation work and related research. Working inside organisations, reporting on the changing world of work for *Flexibility.co.uk*, and carrying out research for a range of government agencies on the impacts of new ways of working, I've had the opportunity of seeing what works well and what does not. The book also benefits from the collective experience and wisdom of the Smart Work Network, a collaboration network for large organisations implementing smart and flexible working. I've tried to crystallise that experience in these pages in a framework that I hope is helpful for managers seeking to implement more advanced forms of flexible work.

Smart Flexibility: Moving Smart and Flexible Working from Theory to Practice 'does what it says on the tin'. Chapters 1 and 2 briefly outline the context, principles and drivers – the reasons why companies are interested in becoming flexible and how the world is changing to make it both possible and desirable. Chapters 3 to 12 focus on the practicalities with case studies to show how forward-looking companies and public sector organisations are adapting to the challenge and gaining the benefits.

In Chapter 13, there is a look at the wider impacts on the world and how organisations can dovetail their strategies for Smart Flexibility with wider environmental and social benefits. Finally, in Chapter 14, there's a brief look forward to what might be next on the horizon, in the continuing story of Smart Flexibility evolution.

I hope you find the book both useful and enjoyable, and that it helps you on your journey as you help your organisation to modernise and succeed in the new world of work.

Note on the Case Studies

I've included in this book 10 case studies of organisations that are embedding Smart Flexibility in their working practices – though they may call it by various other names. Five are from the private sector, and five from the public sector. The achievements or approaches of several other organisations are mentioned, with references to where you can follow up for more information.

There are, of course, other companies and public sector organisations out there on a similar track. The ones included here illustrate various aspects of leading practice in implementing Smart Flexibility, whether it's the use of technologies, innovative working environments, or techniques for cultural change. There are many things we can learn from each of them. One thing they have in common is, each in their own way, adopting an integrated and strategic approach to achieving Smart Flexibility benefits across a number of fronts.

Several of the people I spoke to in the course of the interviews described it as a 'journey', involving a lot of learning and sometimes mistakes on the way. I don't think any of them would describe their journey as being at an end: there are always next steps and a key principle is about being adaptable and being open to the future.

For more case studies, and a bit more detail on some of the cases included in the book, it's worth checking the *Flexibility* website at www.flexibility.co.uk/cases.

About the Author

Andy Lake is editor of *Flexibility*, the online journal of flexible work at www.flexibility.co.uk, which he has edited since 1994. A graduate of Selwyn College, Cambridge, Andy has over 18 years' experience of implementing smart working, working with large UK organisations and international clients.

Andy has run or participated in numerous research projects funded by the UK government, the European Commission and private companies, specialising in particular in the impacts of new ways of working on business location, land use and transport.

Through the participation in international research projects, publications and requests to present at conferences and run workshops around the world, Andy has built up a very large network of contacts in the field of flexible working. His experience spans the business, government, media and academic sectors.

He is also coordinator of the Smart Work Network (www.smart-work.net), a network of 170 larger companies and public sector organisations that collaborate in developing their flexible working programmes.

Acknowledgements

Having been working in the field of flexible working for some 18 years now, there are debts that I owe to many people who have influenced my thinking over the years and who are too numerous to name. These include leading exponents with whom I have been in contact, as well as people directly involved in implementation projects whose insights into the practical issues have provided great food for thought.

For the past five years I have also been running the Smart Work Network, a peer collaboration network for people in large organisations implementing smart and flexible working. The open discussions we have around the issues facing these organisations have helped to crystallise some of my thinking around the appropriate solutions, and have helped me to develop several of the workshop tools described in the book, and which I have used in workshops with client organisations.

Particular thanks go to the friends and colleagues who have taken the time to review the text: Tim Dwelly of the Live/Work Network, Lynette Swift from Swiftwork, Bob Crichton of HOP Associates, change management expert John Gracey, Bridget Hardy of Integrans Consulting and Richard Graham of the Government Property Unit. I would also like to thank the team at Gower for their highly professional help and support throughout the process of taking the book to publication.

I would also like to extend special thanks to everyone who supported me in producing the case studies: David Fletcher (Birmingham City Council), Adrian Rathbone of TelerealTrillium and Hayley Walton of Customer Plus (also for the Birmingham City Council case study), Sue Skinner (Britvic), Dave Dunbar (BT), Jill Pritchard and Linda Robertson (Fife Council), David Robinson (Hertfordshire County Council), Christiane Perera (OAC), Caroline Oldham (Ofsted), Paul Clark, Norma Pearce and Carly Read (Plantronics), Carmel Millar, Morag Dowds, Jennifer Aitken and Carol Cammiss (Surrey County Council), Neil Stride and Jo Smith (Vodafone). Thanks also to Bill Fennell of Actium Consult for permission to use data from the Total Office Costs Survey.

One thing all these contributors share is a passion for and commitment to the new ways of working. This has been energising for me, and I'm sure it must be inspiring for those they help in implementing smart and flexible ways of working.

Finally, I'd like to thank my wife Jan for her encouragement, patience and support over the two and a half years it's taken to complete the work. This support has been invaluable as she's badgered me to 'go back into your little room and change the world', as she puts it. If the world of work does change a little bit faster and a little bit more coherently as a result of people using *Smart Flexibility*, then these are the people who should take a big share of the credit.

Prologue: What's in a Name?

That the world of work is changing is undeniable. But how should we refer to the new and flexible working practices that are evolving?

There are many words and phrases used to describe the changes: Flexible Working, New Ways of Working, Agile Working and Smart Working are the most commonly used phases. For aspects of the new ways that use technology to work beyond the workplace there are words and phrases like Telework, Telecommuting, eWork, Location Independent Working, Workshifting and several others besides.

And sometimes flexible working is presented as being synonymous with 'Family Friendly Working' to emphasise the role of these new ways in assisting work-life balance. Often these are linked with options like maternity and paternity leave. Though this is quite a dominant mode of thought in some of the HR literature, academic research and some government policy areas, it is really too narrow and lacks sufficient business focus to be widely accepted.

So at the outset, I think I should begin by outlining what I mean by the term Smart Flexibility.

Flexible Working and Smart Working

'Flexible working' in an organisation encompasses:

- A range of flexible working practices.
- Changes to the way work is carried out and services are delivered.
- Changes to the environments in which work is carried out.

Flexible working practices typically fall into three areas:

- *Flexible time options* – such as flexitime or variable hours, compressed working week (doing five days' work in four, or ten days' in nine, and so on), annualised hours, part-time working, job share, term-time working.
- *Flexible location options* – such as mobile working, home-based working, working seamlessly from other company sites or from client-sites, working from local 'workhubs'.
- *Flexible contract options* – working with contract staff, agency staff, freelancers, teams of associates.

These options, of course, are often combined – for example, having staff working at different times and in different locations, or having 'virtual teams' combining permanent staff and associates or contractors working in a range of locations.

'*Smart Working*' is a term currently in vogue to describe the range of changes enabled by greater flexibility combined with greater use of information and communication technologies (ICT). This combines flexible work options with changes to the way work is organised and delivered, in particular streamlining processes using ICT. This is often necessary to liberate the business from the constraints of place, time and paper and allow staff to work more flexibly.

Working environments will also change. Typically this involves moving away from both cellular offices and serried ranks of workstations in open-plan offices. These are replaced by desk-sharing solutions, plus touch-down areas for mobile staff, project areas for teamwork and break-out areas for informal meetings. Remote offices – including home offices – may be part of the new working environment. The place where you work assumes less importance, and for many staff the office is the network.

How It All Fits Together – Smart Flexibility

Though some people have attempted it, I don't think it's possible to make sharp distinctions between terms such as Flexible Working, New Ways of Working, Agile Working and Smart Working. There are not hard and fast but rather overlapping definitions in what is a fluid and fast-changing world. All these terms in most instances can be used interchangeably, because in practice they are talking about the same thing.

Where people sometimes try to draw a line is between what they see as the more technology-enabled forms and the more family-focused forms, or between the more business-focused and the more employee-choice-focused forms. To me these distinctions are not always especially helpful.

What we have is a broad canvas of evolving working practices and changes to the way businesses operate. Changes to technology, processes and management thinking are crucial to these, as well as a wide range of other social changes that I'll be looking at in Chapter 1.

These changes can all be characterised as increasing flexibility, whether for the employee, the organisation, or both. They can also be characterised as being 'smart', in that they are supported by a range of smart innovations that enable the organisation to operate in smarter and more flexible ways.

Figure P1.1 sets out three overlapping areas of innovation:

1. 'Flexible Working' as often somewhat narrowly conceived in HR policies, that is, a range of employee choices around where and when to work that can be requested by employees.
2. Business Transformation activities – at least the ones that have a particular impact on or relationship with changing the way we work.
3. Work Anywhere possibilities, which describe forms of flexible working that critically depend on technology-enabled business transformation.

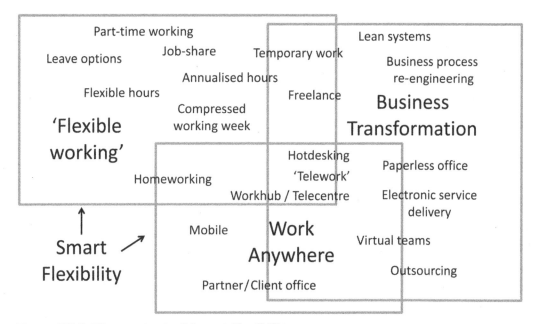

Figure P1.1 The context of Smart Flexibility

This book is about looking at all the forms of working involved and the directions one needs to take to maximise the benefits. 'Smart Flexibility' is a composite term which I hope signifies this combination of flexible and smart (or agile) working practices.

'Smart Flexibility', then, is about all the forms of working that fit into the 'Flexible Working' and 'Work Anywhere' boxes. And in implementing it in a comprehensive and strategic way, it really has to be strongly grounded in a strong understanding of the business transformation opportunities that underpin it.

Smart Flexibility is also about delivering measurable benefits across the 'Triple Bottom Line': benefits for business, for people and for the environment.

So to take Smart Flexibility from theory to practice is not just about coming up with the right policies and practices. It requires an integrated approach that looks at people, property and technology, and needs to be grounded in a strong understanding of the business needs of the organisation and of the wider context of economic, social and environmental change.

And that's what this book is about – working more flexibly, and working smarter to make your business and the world a better place.

1 *Changing Work in a Changing World*

It is not the strongest of the species that survive, nor the most intelligent, but the ones most responsive to change.

Charles Darwin

The world of work is changing. Some of the largest and most successful organisations in the world now give their employees the freedom to work from wherever they want, and whenever they want, as long as it's good for the business. If the work gets done, and customer needs are met, that's good. Even better is that the new working times and locations can be used to improve productivity, meet customer needs better and at the same time reduce costs.

The world of work is changing for organisations across all sectors. We are perhaps not surprised to hear that companies in the field of IT and telecommunications are doing this, or companies with large numbers of knowledge workers. But across all sectors new working practices are being introduced – financial services, manufacturing, construction, health services and emergency services: no sector is excluded.

Our case study in Chapter 5 of soft drinks company Britvic shows that intelligent deployment of smart and flexible working practices can bring benefits across sectors. The argument that 'this can't work in our sector' just doesn't wash.

Government organisations are also going down this route. Many have a creditable record in introducing flexible work options to meet employee aspirations for a better work-life balance, and to create a more level playing field for people with caring responsibilities. The next step that some have taken is to use Smart Flexibility to reduce the cost base of government operations and make government services more agile. Many more will go down this path over the next 10 years, faced with the imperative to increase efficiency and in particular reduce property costs.

All sectors are feeling this imperative to change. In this chapter we take a look at why this is so, and why standing still really isn't an option.

The Old Ways of Working – and Their Value

The terms 'new ways of working', 'flexible working', 'agile working' or 'smart working' and of course Smart Flexibility imply that we need to move away from older, less flexible, less smart, more traditional ways of working that are now past their sell-by date. The organisational model that we need to change is one based on factory methods – herding people together and marshalling resources in significant concentrations in order to manage them better and to achieve economies of scale.

One mustn't forget that these 'old' ways provide a model that has been highly successful and has achieved unprecedented prosperity, at least in the developed world. Although it may in the end be futile, resistance to change is quite natural. The old model is a tried and tested one, and one in which today's managers have made successful careers.

In historical terms, however, the old model is one of fairly recent vintage, emerging from the Industrial Revolution. Having offices organised on factory lines with regimented desks and a production-line approach to processes is even more recent.

This kind of regimented organisation of working life was exacerbated in the twentieth century by the dominance of 'collectivist' approaches to social organisation, in both the capitalist West and the communist East. The regimentation of mass activity to achieve improved results is evident in approaches not only to industrial organisation, but also to mass transit systems, public health reform and public education, plus of course military organisation and strategy in two world wars and the conflicts of the Cold War era. The influence of having three generations in uniform in the twentieth century cannot be exaggerated in terms of setting the norms for workplace organisation and behaviour.

By the last quarter of the twentieth century, nearly everyone who worked in the developed world was an employee, rather than being self-employed or having other variations of pre-industrial work relationships. Work for most people had become a place you go to as much as the activity you undertook. Long-term job security had become far more attainable, and the 'job for life' became the dominant expectation, backed up by solid pension schemes.

A job for life, and 9–5 working for most people. The world of work seemed a well-ordered and simple place compared to the ferment we have today. Of course, it wasn't so simple. There were always self-employed people, people working all hours in small businesses, people working shifts, people moonlighting with second jobs, people doing part-time, term-time, casual or seasonal work. But we all knew what was normal, and there was a consensus in public policy that the best jobs to create were full-time, permanent jobs for life with regular hours.

How and why did this consensus slip away?

Reflections on the History of Work – How We Got to Where We Are Now

There has been a growing realisation that work doesn't have to be organised in this way. Even in 1900, despite more than 100 years of Industrial Revolution already, most work was not in factories or offices even in the UK, the most industrialised nation. The home was still the centre of much enterprise and employment, whether one's own home or working in domestic service. Living and working in the same premises was still a normal way of working, at all levels of society. Seasonal work and contract working were also much more common than they are today.

Looking back before the Industrial Revolution, some commentators have even suggested there was no such thing as a job – only work (for example, Bridges 1995). This is, of course, not exactly true. But there is a point to be made about jobs back then on the whole being much more fluid and less defined than in the modern world with its bureaucratic/regulatory payroll and taxation systems.

Even so, more or less as far back as records go there is evidence of people having jobs, in the sense of paid, regular employment for a single employer. That seems to be more or less an inevitable part of running large-scale, complex organisations. Initially these tended to be palaces, temples and armies, then moving into other areas of administration – in the beginning was the public sector, perhaps. Then over the centuries, similar models are adopted in trading, banking and manufacturing.

Regular, paid jobs, however, were in the minority and much coveted. Other work may have been more flexible, but carried with it the flexibility of earning or not earning, surviving or starving. So it is no wonder that security and stability became highly prized. Generally, apart from a minority of adventurers and entrepreneurs, people are unwilling to risk trading security and stability for greater autonomy and control over their working lives. The experience of periods of substantial unemployment and the evils that arose from them underlie the consensus between employers and employed about the need for security and stability in the labour market and the workplace. For the post-war generations with 'jobs for life', regular hours, improving working conditions, health insurance and the prospect of comfortable retirement this was not a bad deal. And much better than anything their fathers or grandfathers had experienced.

So one has to be wary of approaches to new ways of working that romanticise the past. Questioning the collectivist approaches to the organisation of work should not mean reviving some kind of romantic 'artisan workshop' ideal or 'two acres and a cow' idyll. These utopian themes are common to both late nineteenth-century 'Merrie England' socialism and the late twentieth-century 'telecottage' movement.

People want flexibility, and they want autonomy – but they also want to be secure and be sure that they have the means to provide for their families. Can we have it all? Both flexibility and autonomy on the one hand, security and stability on the other?

According to Dan Pink, in his 2001 work *Free Agent Nation*, the increased wealth and security we generally enjoy in the western world is leading more people to seek work that gives greater meaning to their lives. This is behind the rise of 'free agent' working, people who are freelancers or starting small, often home-based, businesses (Pink 2001).

The rise of freelancing and contract work is part of the picture of the changing world of work. It is not the major focus of this book, except insofar as it provides options for large organisations and the people working in them. But it's worth noting that similar aspirations motivate employees who want to stay as employees but also aspire to more freedom in the way they work. This is having a significant impact on corporate life.

It is also worth reflecting on the fact that in ancient, medieval and early modern times, 'corporate' life was often more mobile than it is today. This is not so much in terms of having field workers operating nomadic styles of work – though there certainly were plenty of such people. Rather it is in terms of *the whole corporate centre being peripatetic*. Where the emperor or general or business owner went, so did much of the central apparatus of the organisation: advisers, secretaries, clerks, scribes (and their paperwork), security staff and organisers for the household, plus entertainers of various kinds too, perhaps.

The concept of carrying your office with you is making a return. We can all be our own king, queen or general, though for better or for worse we don't have the same kind of retinue. We may not have scribes, runners and cooks in attendance, but we do have laptops, BlackBerrys and ready meals. Such is progress, and the tools we need for ownership of our working lives.

Working 9–5 is, however, a modern invention. And a regular 8-hour – or less than 8-hour – day has been the culmination of campaigns and legislation to protect workers from exploitation and to ensure a better quality of life. In the 1890s, this was a distant dream for workers, a dangerous fantasy as far as most business owners were concerned. We have gone beyond this, and a recent report for the New Economics Foundation has recommended a universal 21-hour working week as a default standard (NEF 2010).

Having a 7- or 8-hour continuous working day with most people working at the same time is, though convenient and reliable, an artificial and inefficient norm for working practices. And in recent decades there have been many changes in the wider world that have exposed weaknesses in the model.

The Context of Work is Changing – Nine Trajectories of Change

The way we work is always changing. The 'where', 'when' and 'how' of our work arises from a combination of factors relating to power relationships, access to resources, levels of prosperity, available tools and technologies, mobilities, social systems, cultures and, somewhere down the line, individual preferences.

Social change and changes in markets create new contexts in which organisations have to function. The ability to adapt to new contexts is crucial to a company surviving. It presents challenges, but also can create opportunities to do things better.

The following nine trends provide the context for change in moving towards more flexible working practices.

Trend 1: Lean Organisations, Re-Engineering and Outsourcing

To some extent, the old industrial ways of working were already living on borrowed time by the 1980s. Lean production techniques and business process re-engineering (BPR) meant that companies were questioning the ways they operate, and the resources they need – including the human resources.

In the ensuing struggles and debates, the word 'flexibility' was associated with creating more flexible labour markets, greater use of contractors, agency workers and outsourcing. For some, particularly on the political left and in the trade union movement, this gave flexibility a bad name. 'Whose flexibility?' was the key question, and many felt that these kinds of labour flexibility being introduced were mainly in the interest of the employer, not the worker (for example, Purcell et al. 1999).

The issues and the political positioning around this that we saw in the UK in the 1980s and 1990s remain current in some continental European countries where unions have a more dominant position and remain very suspicious of flexible working. They fear the erosion of hard-won working rights.

BPR, as the name suggests, is about changing processes and the advent of new information, and communication technologies (ICT) have a central role in this. Implementing integrated enterprise-wide IT systems and systems to connect with customers and suppliers forms part of the picture. The progressive elimination of paper from processes, and moves towards electronic service delivery, are all part of re-engineering processes to cut out waste and increase efficiency.

However it's interesting that for the most part in companies re-engineering themselves that the approach to working practices has remained entirely traditional. Some work may be outsourced – outsourced to people working in traditional ways, only for a different employer. Work became much more electronically based, but the need for employees to commute to a fixed workplace to work with these systems was rarely questioned. The reasons for this are more cultural than technological. And it's still going on in many large organisations.

Many organisations now have programmes of business transformation (the current preferred and slightly less contentious term), rethinking and redesigning work processes and workflow, aiming to eliminate wasteful processes, reduce costs and outsource non-core activities. In principle this should help to focus activity on core objectives and delivering value to customers. New technology solutions are central to implementing these.

The challenge now, which greater flexibility in working practices can address, is to leverage greater value from the huge IT investments involved. This means challenging not only business process design, but also the assumptions about property, facilities, travel, working time, working culture and management techniques that form the context for reforming business processes.

Trend 2: More Women in the Workplace

From the 1960s, ever increasing numbers of women in the workplace led to a rise in 'non-standard' or 'atypical' working arrangements such as part-time work and term-time working. There has been a strong association between flexible/atypical and 'family friendly' working practices.

Work-life balance *for the individual* is brought more sharply into focus when both partners in a family work. Before the 1970s there was a kind of consensus, whether fair or not. The man was the breadwinner, and the woman was the homemaker and primary carer for the children. In this way families managed the home-work interface, and had *between them* a balance. There was a man's territory, and a woman's one.

Though some people think we should return to these ways, most of us do not. But we haven't entirely found the solution. 'Can women have it all?' ask the women's magazines, referring to having a successful career and a great family life. Can men?

Gender stereotyping and genderist assumptions still pervade many of the debates and even the regulations about flexible working. Introducing measures to help combine caring responsibilities and work is seen by many campaigners as a key way to help women in their careers (Fawcett Society 2009). Is this, in its own way, sexist? Or is it realistic and pragmatic? It starts from where we are, and looks to flexible working as a way to achieve greater equality between women and men.

The fact is that women are far more likely to work part-time, term-time and have start and finish times to align with caring responsibilities. The evident benefits of this and of having a more diverse workforce provide a key element of the context for the growth of flexible working. And a concern for women's equality in employment has also spurred legislation by governments on flexible working and parental leave arrangements, which we will return to in the next chapter when considering drivers for companies to introduce Smart Flexibility.

Trend 3: Demographic Change

The age structures of society are also changing. We are moving from a three-generation society to a four-generation society. People live longer. And increasingly they also either need or want to work for longer. Or, if they are a reasonably well-off baby boomer, they may want to half-retire earlier and continue to half-work or work intermittently until they choose to stop.

Currently around a third of the UK population is over 50. This is going to rise to half the population some time over the next 20 years, according to current estimates. Around half of the children born around the world in 2009 will live to be 100.

At age 65 men can now expect to live for a further 21 years, and women for a further 23 years. And amongst other effects, this is creating major challenges to pension provision. The trends are clear. But what does it mean for the workforce, and for the nature of work?

There has been a lot of focus on 'dependency ratios', that is, the number of people who are not economically active compared to the number of people who are working, paying tax and national insurance. The long and short of it is that people are living too long, and not enough people are working to support them. Short of a *Logan's Run* type of solution – that is, vaporising people before they get too old – what are the solutions?

First of all, there are many things wrong with the 'long and short of it' view expressed in the last paragraph, and with a misunderstanding of the concept of a 'dependency ratio'. Though there are of course real issues of health and social care for older people, in general people are living longer because they are fitter and healthier rather than because we are spending a fortune on propping them up. For all the problems, today's pensioners are healthier and wealthier than at any time in history.

Today's older people are also more likely to have people depend on them than to be dependent on others. Today's grandparents are increasingly a 'sandwich generation', with older, frailer parents perhaps as well as children and grandchildren that they support in many ways. They are also the most likely to be undertaking voluntary work. To a significant extent, society depends on the labour and spending of its older citizens.

Increasingly, we are also depending on their continuing to work past pensionable age. While think tanks and politicians wrestle with the issues, the flow of the river of work into retirement has already burst its banks. People are increasingly working beyond pensionable age – some because they have to, and some because it's what they want to do. What many don't want to do, however, is follow the old patterns of working flat out in the old ways up to the point when they stop working altogether. 'All or nothing' is not acceptable to increasing numbers of older workers.

There are many high profile people working into their 70s or 80s – monarchs, popes, politicians, high court judges, heads of international sporting bodies, self-made millionaires, writers and celebrities, for example. However, it's easier for the rich and famous to carry on and do what they want in old age than for the rest of us. Money and status are important, it seems. For those of us with more modest means or lower status, the attitudes and policies of employers and the impact of tax and pensions regulations mean that it's altogether a more difficult proposition.

Even so, the trajectory of change is, and must be, towards blurring the hard divide between work and retirement. And some demographers and sociologists anticipate a 'baby boomer effect' as that generation reaches retirement age. They will revolutionise their own 60s as much as they revolutionised the 1960s. They will continue to be demanding consumers, innovating socially and economically in their approach to older age. And this may be in terms of employment, semi-employment, investing and enterprise.

Michael Moynagh and Richard Worsley (2004) have said that we are moving from lives that are divided 'horizontally' to lives that are divided 'vertically'. By this they mean that in the past, the norm was to divide our lives into clear phases based on age: from childhood to education, to work, through marriage and parenthood, and then to retirement. The 'vertical' divisions of life mean that transitions, or the options for transition, may be available throughout a longer life: into and out of work, back into and out of education, into and out of marriage, then maybe back into marriage again at some point. Like an ageing boxer in need of ready money, perhaps we will flex in and out of retirement as need or preference arises. The work/non-work interface is then not only about retirement, but also about choice.

According to a recent report by PWC, 'extending working lives is a social and fiscal imperative' and 'Employers in all sectors … need to develop solutions to overcome barriers to flexible and later working that can benefit both companies and their employees including the potential changing nature of the job role and career trends as the employee grows older' (Hawksworth et al. 2010). Government, meanwhile, has accepted the logic of this by abolishing the default retirement age, effective in 2011 in the UK.

A survey by the Department for Work and Pensions found that around half of workers aged 30 to 69 would consider working part-time after they retire, but only 10 per cent would like a full-time job (DWP 2004). Flexible working (especially reduced-time, home-based, or temporary contracts), and self-employment are the natural ways for older people to work in the ways that suit them. The main challenge we face now is not the acceptability of the concept, but how to remove the barriers to this.

Trend 4: Individualism and Personal Autonomy

It's not possible to get through the weekend's TV without being exhorted in Hollywood films and the inescapable talent shows that 'you've got to follow your dreams!' The generations surviving conflict and rebuilding nations in the last century knew the opposite: you had to get real and moderate your dreams. But for baby boomers and the subsequent generations X, Y and Z who have grown up with the safety net held high beneath them, realising their dreams and becoming who they want to be is a key motivator.

For the aspirational society we live in the first few basic levels in Maslow's hierarchy of needs can be taken as given, for the majority. We've got food, shelter, clothing, no worries. It's seeking the higher levels of happiness and self-actualisation that drive us. There is a lot to debate and critique about such trends, no doubt. And sooner or later we might be in for some kind of Malthusian reality-check, though heaven forbid.

What is important, though, is that this urge to self-actualisation and the resistance to external control that goes with it are reshaping the way we look at organisations and employment. As mentioned above in our brief tour of the history of work, people are seeking more autonomy in their lives. They are impatient with the lowest-common-denominator collectivist solutions of the twentieth century. They want to shape their world around themselves, rather than be shaped.

This manifests itself in having two, three or even four different careers in a working life. To be a 'company man' in the 1950s mould, or to desire a 'job for life' strikes many people as being somehow inauthentic, even if not expressed in so many words.

At a deeper level, however, what is actually happening is that in all areas of life people are more individualistic and crave more autonomy. It's about the decline of collectivist mentalities and the rise of individualism. It's why 8 out of 10 people choose to drive cars rather than ride in buses. It's why we now have multi-channel TV rather than a schedule largely dictated by the state, and why we have choice over our utilities providers. It's why self-help books sell millions. And it's why employees like to choose employers who enable them to balance their lives better and pursue interests outside work.

From some standpoints, we live in an age that is too individualistic and self-indulgent, that is seeing the breakdown of families, institutions and all the old certainties and solidarities. The rapid changes in society and attitudes appears to be a kind of fragmentation, to the point where some think that society itself is breaking down.

It is of course possible to be too gung-ho either way when looking at these kinds of trends. There is a multitude of different attitudes and aspirations running side by side and sometimes in conflict with each other. Collectivist mindsets still abound, though are no longer so dominant. But few would dispute that the choices are greater, and the possibilities more extensive for being oneself rather than fitting into someone else's groove.

There is also an associated trend of what might be called the democratisation of aspiration. What I mean by this is that groups formerly marginalised, disadvantaged or discriminated against can now 'dare to dream' like the rest of us. For the most part, this means aspiring to be able to have the same opportunities to do things as everyone else. So it's about a woman's aspiration to have a place in the board room, a parent's aspiration to balance work and family life, or an older employee's aspiration to keep on working or to start up a 'sunset business'.

For many people with disabilities or long-term health conditions, the traditional workplace is a disabling environment. The need to commute to it can be an additional hurdle to overcome. Smart Flexibility is a facilitator of the aspiration to work for people with mobility disadvantages, who are unable to work long periods at one time or who need either regular or intermittent medical treatment.

Society as a whole now accepts this equality of aspiration, even if we're not always sure how to facilitate it in practice. It is no coincidence that in many organisations it is the Equal Opportunities and Diversity people who are the ones pushing for the introduction of flexible working practices to overcome disadvantage in the workplace. And I would say, 'More power to their elbow!' even though I also say throughout the book that an equalities approach or a work-life balance approach is not sufficient to achieve the range of benefits that Smart Flexibility can provide.

Trend 5: Blurring Boundaries

Boundaries between home and work are changing. This is only in part down to business-related reasons. It also reflects changing personal preferences with aspirations for a better work-life balance, as outlined in our fourth trend above. And the fact that new technologies mean that we can work in new ways also makes a difference.

The boundaries are blurring because the nature of work is changing. We are leaving behind the Industrial Age – at least in the developed world. And with it we are leaving behind the imperative to separate the domestic environment from the dirty, smelly and hazardous world of industrial work, and the economies of scale of the centralised office.

Other changes are taking place, shifting not only the places of work but also the times when work takes place. The accelerated emergence of global markets and an increasingly integrated world economy mean that the traditional 9–5 is not an option for organisations that need to compete or interact internationally.

At the same time we see the stubborn development of a 'long hours culture', particularly in the UK. It is not clear that people are necessarily doing anything very useful in these extra hours 'at work' – but all the same the evidence is there to show that we are using our 'time budgets' differently.

The headline figures on hours worked also mask more subtle trajectories in the evolution of new ways of working. During both our working time and our wider life we are much more likely to be doing – or attempting to do – several tasks simultaneously.

Sociologists of work have for some time been talking about a basic distinction between people who are 'integrators' and people who are 'separators' in terms of managing the interface between home and work (Nippert-Eng 1996, Kossek and Lautsch 2008). The rigid boundary between home and work is fading. Integration and separation describe psychological rather than geographical approaches – a home worker can be a separator, and an office worker can be an integrator. It's about how you intertwine or separate the tasks and concerns of work and life outside work. Either way, the boundaries tend to be less hard-edged than in the old days.

Organisations have also changed. Concern for employees' well-being, 'benefits' such as workplace crèches or childcare vouchers take employers into territory that was once the preserve of the employee's home life.

Trend 6: Globalisation

The acceleration of globalisation in the past few decades is having a profound impact on our lives, from the food we eat to the times and places that we work. New technologies from the telegraph to the Internet, from steamships to jet planes, have played their part in overcoming the constraints of distance and enabling us to work closely with people from all over the planet. The old ways are not suited to working in an integrated way with colleagues and customers all over the world.

Flexibility in working time is needed to work effectively across time zones. Individuals cannot work 24/7, but there is a need for companies to do so and to marshal their employees and subcontractors to cover around the clock as needed.

And with the need to work in collaborative virtual teams across the world, the precise work location of members of the team reduces in importance. Employees also need to be able to work when they are travelling around the globe, and to work as effectively as when they are 'in the office'.

The impetus to more flexible work arrangements from globalisation does not only affect corporates. Smaller businesses can access global markets using the power of the

Internet, and will be more successful if from the outset they incorporate flexible working practices and flexible organisational models.

Globalisation is a process stretching back well before the Internet. But there is no doubt that modern telecommunications and computing are having a profound effect. Being able to do 'business at the speed of light' and to cope with rapid market changes requires organisations to be increasingly agile, and this provides an impetus to adopt flexible working practices.

Globalisation is also having an impact in the way that new models of working can be rapidly imitated across the world. Yesterday's innovation in Silicon Valley can be today's practice from London to Tokyo.

Perhaps above all it is the competitive pressures arising from globalisation that are driving the impetus for change. Companies need to be more agile, quicker to adapt to competition in the market and to seize new opportunities, wherever they may arise.

Trend 7: Beyond Industrialisation

The nature of work has also been changing in the UK, with the decline of manufacturing, the development of a service-dominated economy and in recent decades the emergence of the 'knowledge economy'.

While flexible working has been developing in parallel with these trends, too often people make easy – and mistaken – assumptions about the relationship between flexible work and different sectors or different kinds of jobs. It tends to be seen as something more for the service sector or knowledge economy than for traditional industries like manufacturing or construction. While the knowledge economy may be based on bits and bytes, some sectors are irreducibly involved with 'lumps and bumps'.

But these distinctions between sectors are increasingly artificial and misleading. Manufacturing today is very different from manufacturing in the 1950s. Factories are far more automated and need fewer people to operate them. By comparison with the last century, far more of the people working for, or subcontracted to, a manufacturing company will be in occupations with high information content: design, procurement, logistics, research, sales, marketing, HR, administration and many managerial and professional functions.

In historic terms, we are probably only just at the beginning of these changes. Developments in artificial intelligence, robotics and nanotechnology over the coming decades will utterly transform our concepts of manufacturing and production. The boundaries between the knowledge economy and the manipulation of physical artefacts will blur.

Those whose roles are *intractably* site-specific or focus on the handling of physical objects are increasingly in a minority, even in a manufacturing-focused industry. This will particularly be the case in a company that outsources production to another country, while employees in the UK deal with the more creative and information-rich components of work.

'This type of job can't be done flexibly' is increasingly a prejudice rather than an objective observation. There is usually some kind of flexible work that is possible, even if the tasks involved mean that not all flexible options are possible.

Trend 8: Information and Communication Technologies

The availability of new ICT is having a transformative impact on society – on the ways we communicate, the way we socialise, the way we access services, the way we buy products, the products we buy and the way we work.

Letter-writing has all but disappeared. Texting and social networking have had a profound effect on behaviours and the way people interact, meet and arrange to meet. Online shopping, initially treated with scepticism by many, is having a major impact on the way we consume and on the nature of the products that we buy. Bookshops and record shops are closing almost every day, and high street stores find that online sales make up an ever greater proportion of turnover.

This is also having impacts on mobility and on 'activity spaces', that is, the places we choose to do what we do. Places we used to go to are now often online spaces we visit. And things we used to buy as physical products are increasingly 'dematerialised' as online products or services. Sectors such as the entertainment, newspaper and advertising industries are being transformed by new media.

Though the process is slow for cultural reasons, the same technologies are bound to have an impact on working practices. Computers and Internet access are introduced to workplaces as productivity tools, but in due course their use has a subversive impact on the workplaces they are brought into. They undermine the need to work in a particular place.

Technological change outside the workplace often runs ahead of change inside the workplace. For many young people, using webcams and social networking are commonplace at a time when many IT departments still ban their use, standing Canute-like against the tide. Desktop videoconferencing and business use of instant messaging and social networking technologies are on their way, sooner or later. Most of our case study organisations are already doing it. And these technologies will impact on the way we work, the places we work, and how geographically distributed teams work with each other. Leading companies including the case studies in this book are already deploying them.

The technology tools we use on a daily basis also interact with, and bring changes to, the spaces where we use them and the furniture, fittings and services that characterise those spaces. As computers and phones become smaller and more portable, screens become more versatile and wireless technologies are deployed, everything we assume about the configuration of the office is open to question.

This is only the beginning. A theme of this book is that in using technologies for Smart Flexibility, we're very much in a transitional era. What will we see over the next 10 years? Vastly increased use of video, increasingly immersive environments for meetings, new virtual environments for collaboration and for storing information, holographic technologies, reliable speech recognition technologies, extensive use of sensing and tracking technologies … and many innovations we can't yet envisage.

What is certain, though, is that many applications that will transform the way we work will be developed initially as consumer technologies rather than specifically for business use. The pace of change, however, is also constrained by public policy and the effective monopoly position of the providers of telecommunication services such as broadband.

Eyes tend to glaze over when conversations get into the technological details. But the details make a difference. In 2009 the UK Department for Business published a report called 'Digital Britain'. This spectacularly unambitious document juggled the interests of existing telecoms and broadcast providers into a dismal fudge, and called it a strategy for our digital future. Amongst other things this proposed an aspiration to achieve a universal 2 Mbps (megabits per second) Internet download speed for all homes in Britain. Upload speeds in this view should stick around 0.5 Mbps. What is particularly remarkable about a report produced by the Department for Business, is that there is not a single mention of the word 'enterprise', or self-employment; no mention of home-based business, nor remote working and no understanding at all of the changing patterns of work. The inference is that we should all be passive consumers, rather than producers of digital content or entrepreneurs running businesses from home.

Fortunately, other countries such as South Korea are setting the pace, with services up to 100 Mbps, and to be fair BT and Virgin Media here are starting to roll out premium services heading towards this. If you are reading this book a few years after its publication, all this may seem impossibly quaint. Some commentators feel that Internet speeds are a red herring – we can do most of what we need to do with the pretty modest speeds we have now. This is wrong.

Imagine a time a few years hence when we all have access to a zillion zettabits per second. Unlimited broadband. When there are no constraints on the amount of data that can be zipped around between anyone and everyone. It will be transformative. The applications will develop for interaction between workers (and friends, and families – not to mention producers and consumers, and 'prosumers') that not only facilitate what we do now, but will create new contexts for sharing activities and experiences.

We think the pace of change is great at the moment with the technologies we have. But *this is only the beginning*.

No doubt it's worth pausing for a while and questioning why we have embarked on this headlong rush for innovation, change, progress. There may be the occasional backlash, where we seek moments of escape to lead a simpler, less techno-full life. However, the great engine of progress, as they would have said in Victorian times, is steaming ahead – it doesn't look like coming to a halt in the foreseeable future.

Trend 9: Global Warming and Environmental Awareness

After talking about the unstoppable engine of progress, we should move on to the environmental impacts of that engine.

The global climate may have been changing for more than a century, but it's only in the last few years that it has moved to centre stage in public policy and the media. It's now an inescapable fact of life, especially if you read scientific journals or *The Independent* newspaper where in every edition the climate makes the headlines. Politicians who formerly saw the environment as a fringe tree-hugging issue now compete with each other for green virtue and carbon taxes.

There are increasing amounts of regulation and legislation forcing organisations to look to their environmental performance – and there is sure to be more coming soon. The environment is clearly on the agenda.

In paperback thrillers, Hollywood blockbusters, and international development conferences, it is almost a given that big corporations, hand-in-glove with corrupt governments, make it their daily business to despoil the environment in search of quick profits.

I daresay there is some truth under the clichés. In real life, there is another side to the story too. Since the 1960s there has been a growing awareness of the environmental impacts of the ways in which we live and work, and it has become embedded in our educational systems – in the curriculum, in our textbooks, even in the fiction we are given to read.

I might be accused of naivety in saying this, but for the generation of corporate managers, civil servants and politicians who are coming through now, concern for the environment is not mere lip-service or cynical self-interest. While activists and green politicians may lay claim to a monopoly of wisdom or righteousness, in reality there would be no change if there were not in fact a much broader movement of understanding across people in all walks of life – not least in management.

The impacts of production, business processes, buildings operation, transport, travel and working practices are in fact of great concern to organisations. Often these concerns find their way into policies for Corporate Social Responsibility. Maybe it is not enough, or not of sufficient priority. But that is not the point here.

The point is that the trend of awareness has developed to a stage where proposals for Smart Flexibility can and often do strike a chord with the environmental awareness of senior managers, who are sharply aware of the imperatives to reduce the corporate environmental footprint.

As yet, though, the actual benefits that flexible working practices can have are not well understood by senior managers and public policy makers. It is easier to grasp concepts relating to 'greening the office', intelligent buildings, reducing emissions and so forth – essentially engineering solutions – than it is to grasp the impacts of the interdisciplinary field of Smart Flexibility, and the associated behavioural and cultural changes.

The environmental product pitch goes like this: 'use that bit of kit and your energy consumption is x. Use our new bit of kit and your energy consumption will be one tenth of x. And you'll save money'. It's easy to grasp, and there doesn't seem to be an obvious downside.

By contrast, the environmental impacts of flexible working seem to come packaged in 'maybes' and concerns about the possible downsides. Well, it could reduce travel for employees and make them happy. But what will it do for business travel? How can I manage them if I can't see them? Will their performance improve? Will they be isolated?

This is a theme I will return to later in Chapter 13. There is an acceptance of the importance of improving environmental performance, and an increasing receptiveness to innovate to achieve this. But in terms of accepting sustainability arguments for Smart Flexibility, the gatekeepers of change want some facts to back up the argument, and reassurance that it won't cost the earth to save the planet.

What is the Evidence for Increasing Flexibility?

These trends are all factors in the growth of Smart Flexibility. But what actual evidence is there that flexible working is on the up?

There are many indicators that the world of work is indeed changing. According to the government, there are around 15 million flexible workers in the UK – roughly half the workforce. And flexible work options are offered by some 95 per cent of employing organisations (BERR 2007b) – though how developed and how truly flexible that 'flexibility' is remains open to question.

Part-time work has been growing steadily, in large measure connected to the increasing number of women in the workforce. In August 2012 there were 8.07 million part-time workers out of a working population of 29.5 million – 27.4 per cent of the workforce. Three-quarters of part-time workers are women, but the number of male part-timers has risen by 10 per cent over the recession, with the number of women rising by 3 per cent.

Most people who work part-time do so because they want to. Only a quarter of male part-timers say that they are working part-time because they could not find a full-time job, and 10 per cent of women.

Flexible working time arrangements are also becoming more common. These include flexible hours/flexitime, compressed working week, term-time working and annualised hours. According to Social Trends 2010, in 2009 there were 4.8 million full-time employees with a flexible working time arrangement – 22.5 per cent (ONS 2010). Twenty-seven per cent of part-time workers also have another kind of flexible working time arrangement. The most popular form by far is flexible working hours, though part-time workers are more likely to combine part-time working with term-time working than are full-time workers. Table 1.1 below gives a more detailed breakdown.

Part-time work is itself generally considered a form of flexible working, so we see here the combination of different forms of flexibility in a tailored blend.

Data from the UK Labour Force Survey shows a continued rise in the number of people working mainly from home. At the end of 2011, 13.1 per cent of the workforce (3.8 million people) worked mainly at or from home. This is a 24 per cent increase since 2001 (Live/Work Network, 2012). Some 19 per cent of the workforce sometimes (more than once a month but less than half the week) work from home during working hours. Sixty per cent of the self-employed now work mainly from home. They make up two-thirds of all homeworkers. The number of employees who work mainly at home lags behind, and makes up only 5 per cent of employees.

Table 1.1   Flexible working time arrangements

	Men (%)	Women (%)	All (%)
Full-time employees			
Flexible working hours	10.9	15.3	12.6
Annualised working hours	4.9	4.9	4.9
Term-time working	1.2	6.7	3.3
Four-and-a-half-day week	1.2	0.5	0.9
Nine day fortnight	0.5	0.4	0.4
Any flexible working pattern	19.0	28.1	22.5
Part-time employees			
Flexible working hours	8.6	10.3	9.9
Term-time working	3.6	11.6	9.9
Annualised working hours	3.3	4.6	4.3
Job-share	1.0	2.1	1.9
Any flexible working pattern	18.4	29.6	27.1

If we take together the 27 per cent of the workforce who work part-time, the 22.5 per cent of full-time employees who work flexibly, and the 5 per cent who work from home, allowing for some overlap with home-based work and other forms of flexibility we are looking at around just over 50 per cent of employees who do not work a standard office-based 9–5. This isn't counting in shift workers and temporary workers. There should be a clear message for employers and managers in here: it's not unusual.

What we have is a situation where we have a 45 per cent block of employees who work in 'traditional' ways and who set the tone and the mindset for how employees should work. But the exceptions are starting to outnumber the rule by some way.

Businesses are now much more likely to be run from home. A survey of small business by the then Department for Business, Enterprise and Regulatory Reform found that 41 per cent of all businesses were home-based, and that 51 per cent of start-ups begin at home (BERR 2007a). For a long time these home-based businesses have been under the radar, with economic development policies and business support efforts focusing almost exclusively on businesses operating in separate business premises.

The number of people who work at home using computers and telecommunications – 'teleworking' – has been growing at around 13 per cent per year since the mid-1990s, according to official figures. As computing and the use of the Internet become ubiquitous, the distinction between teleworking and other forms of homeworking is becoming increasingly artificial. The old forms of offline homeworking, such as stuffing envelopes or sewing, have been in retreat for some time. And many craft-based forms of traditional homeworking now use ICT for dealing with orders, marketing and purchasing. Social Trends puts the numbers of teleworkers (a subset of homeworkers as a whole) at 10 per cent of the UK workforce in 2009 (Randall 2010). The percentage of homeworkers who are classed as teleworkers is steadily rising as the technologies used become ubiquitous.

A series of surveys into work-life balance have been conducted by the Department for Trade and Industry (DTI) in the UK. The most recent at the time of writing is the Third Work Life Balance Survey, conducted in two parts: for employees (DTI 2007) and for employers (BERR 2007b). (In case the references are confusing, the DTI was subsequently rebranded as BERR and then BIS, a symptom of the endemic 'restructuritis' in the UK public sector.) The survey findings are summarised in Table 1.2 overleaf.

The Employers Survey looked at six kinds of flexible working practice: part-time working, job-sharing, flexitime, compressed working week, temporarily reduced working hours and regular home-working. The survey found that 95 per cent of employing organisations said that at least one kind of flexible working practice was available in their organisation; 85 per cent said that at least one of these arrangements had been used in the past 12 months.

One of the things highlighted by the survey is that there is a difference of perception between how employers see the availability of flexible working patterns and their take-up, and how employees see them. The third column shows the percentage of organisations where the working practice is taken up by at least one person – it isn't an estimate of the number of people doing it.

If the employer survey is correct, then clearly many employees are not aware of the options that are in principle available in the company. For all the flexible working options surveyed, employers are far more likely than employees are to say it is available. Availability doesn't mean that take-up of any option will be significant.

Table 1.2   Surveys of flexible working patterns

FW practice	WLB employer survey		WLB employee survey	
	Availability (% of orgs)	Take-up (% of orgs)	Availability (% of orgs)	Take-up (% emps)
Part-time	92	79	69	26
Job-share	59	15	47	6
Temporary reduced hours	74	22	54	10
Term-time working	n/a	n/a	37	13
Compressed working week	41	11	35	8
Flexible hours	55	25	53	26
Annualised hours	n/a	n/a	24	6
Homeworking	26	15	23	10

Note: n/a = not asked.

I have some reservations about the methodologies of such surveys and the limited samples employed. However, what they show, along with the other evidence cited in this section, is that flexible working is very much on the workplace map.

We will see in later chapters evidence from workplace surveys that there is considerable unmet demand for flexible working. And we'll also see how many companies and public sector organisations are taking further steps to extend flexible working.

Recognising the Capacity for Flexibility

Progress towards greater flexibility is often hindered by assumptions about what types of job can be undertaken more flexibly. People say for example that flexible working is not appropriate in *this* sector or for *that* kind of job. Such assumptions are often lagging behind the actual trends of change in the world of work. A number of our case studies, for example at Britvic, illustrate how flexible working can be introduced and make a difference in industries where at first sight it would seem not to be an option.

Often the capacity for flexibility is not recognised, and models of working practice that are traditional for the sector endure without being questioned. Even when new technologies are introduced, the opportunities to modernise work styles are not recognised. For example, companies may introduce new electronic systems for service delivery, or for internal management processes, but still require all staff to turn up every day at the same time and for the same hours as if nothing had changed.

This is one of the main themes of this book: *understanding how to recognise the context and the opportunities for introducing flexible working practices.*

Evolution and Resistance

The way organisations are run has only started to evolve. Flexible working practices when introduced are typically seen as exceptions from an office-based nine-to-five norm.

Resistance to change is often strong amongst middle managers, and the scope for change often narrowly conceived.

Psychologically, this makes sense. Managers have progressed in their careers by doing things in a certain way, have developed certain professional competences, and have a degree of comfort in doing things in familiar ways. Moreover, their sense of worth and success as managers may be bound up in the way they do things. As a result, they can be sceptical of calls to operate in unfamiliar and – to them – unproven ways.

On the other hand, the role of being a manager requires innovation: an openness to look for better and more efficient ways of working, and to manage more effectively.

Herein lies the challenge. Other forms of change, involving company reorganisations or process change, do not necessarily challenge the fundamentals of managing people and places. Moving to flexible working can introduce a whole new set of challenges that may take even the best managers out of their comfort zone.

Flexible working can be, and often is, introduced in a partial or piecemeal way that does not change the nature of the organisation. Introduced in an integrated way, it contributes to the evolution of the organisation.

That makes it sound like a choice – evolve or not. In the longer term, it isn't a choice. The other factors such as competitive pressures, new technologies and employee aspirations are forcing the pace. Trying to freeze working practices in a mid-twentieth century mould is, effectively, to choose organisational failure.

Recession and Retrenchment

At the time of writing (early 2012), we are trying to emerge from the worst recession since the 1930s. Even though we may appear to be emerging from recession, we will certainly be heading for a period of adjustment that will see significant increases in unemployment as companies and public sector employers streamline their operations.

The public sector in particular has been charged with achieving huge savings to meet the costs of bailing out the banks and addressing the structural deficit, and this is leading to tens of thousands of redundancies as posts are cut. The challenge is to cut costs while maintaining services to the public. The way to do this is to, as far as possible, cut central costs, drive down waste and increase productivity while leaving outward-facing operations intact.

New working practices have a role to play in this, in particular where the costs of delivering services can be reduced by using new technologies and where the costs of property are reduced. I am not confident that public sector bodies are good at doing this – usually it is those in internal-facing roles who are more skilful at building empires and keeping them safe from cuts.

And for the hundreds of thousands who lose their jobs, new ways of working potentially offer the chance to build new companies with a much reduced cost base compared to traditional companies, or to become interims or freelancers (as many in fact are doing). In the coming years we should hope to achieve the twin goals of supporting public services with a smaller public sector, and creating the conditions for a more entrepreneurial society. The only way to do this is if flexible working is at the heart of it. If we don't embrace flexibility, it will be a long road to recovery.

The Changing World

This then is the context for developing Smart Flexibility – a rapidly changing world that to some extent provides a 'following wind', or several following winds that to a large extent are driving change without clearly defining what those changes should be. Taking the road to Smart Flexibility is to provide a coherent framework for change, embracing the positive aspects of these larger trends.

We have seen that change is happening in the world of work, that a range of flexibilities is growing. But they tend to lack business focus, and are still considered anomalous by many managers, and encounter scepticism and resistance.

So having identified the trends, we next need to explore the specific business drivers for change and the benefits that well directed change should achieve.

2 *Drivers for Smart Flexibility*

The previous chapter covered the context of the changing world of work. Many of the drivers for moving to flexible work are implicit in these changes. In this chapter we focus more specifically on the drivers that motivate organisations to introduce smart and flexible working practices.

These drivers stem on the one hand from the advantages of particular identified benefits, and on the other from external factors such as technological and public policy changes. The main drivers can be summarised as:

- *Business drivers*: reducing property costs, reducing absenteeism, improving recruitment and retention, getting closer to customers, increased productivity, reducing business travel, reducing resource consumption, maximising benefit from ICT investments.
- *Employee drivers*: better motivation and morale, improved work-life balance, more diverse workforce, reduced commuting, greater autonomy.
- *Sustainability drivers*: reduced travel, reduced energy consumption, reduced resource use; more vital communities, repatriating spending to local communities, more local work opportunities.
- *Technological drivers*: using technology to overcome geographical constraints, the ability to 'untether' the workforce, moving work to people – not people to work, using technology to gain a competitive edge, becoming 'paper-free' and developing an 'e-culture'.
- *Legislative and public policy drivers*: legislation introducing the right to request flexible working, awareness-raising and behaviour-changing campaigns supporting flexible working, specific requirements for example, to introduce a company travel plan to get planning permission for expansion; programmes aimed at public sector employers under the umbrella of the efficiency agenda or transformational government.

Driver 1: Achieving the Business Benefits

Companies that adopt smarter working practices are typically motivated by the need to find new solutions to familiar problems, such as reducing overheads, being more productive and recruiting the best people.

It is often the case that introducing flexible working is a response to a particular issue, such as not being able to recruit enough of the right people for a particular job, or the aspiration to have more women return to work for the company after maternity leave. Sometimes it is coupled with an imperative to reduce office space.

However, it is not so common to find companies that have a comprehensive vision of transforming their organisation based around smarter and more flexible working.

A key motivator for introducing flexible working has been to improve recruitment and retention. Banks like First Direct have incorporated flexible working – particularly flexible time options – into their organisational model from the outset, while others such as Barclays have exemplary flexible working policies that focus on equality and diversity. First Direct achieve a 90 per cent return rate of women coming back to the company after maternity leave. Their flexible hours options are also tightly integrated with business objectives as a telephone- and Internet-based bank in having staff available to work at the same time that their customers want to contact them.

The AA (Automobile Association) breakdown recovery service has introduced virtual call-centre working. A key motivator for this was the difficulty in recruiting staff to work in their call centres for the evening peak. Setting up home-based call-centre working has enabled them to tap into a pool of reliable recruits who are willing to work at this time so long as it does not take them away from their homes. On the employer side, it has the benefit of cutting back on the amount of office space they need (case study on www. flexibility.co.uk).

This ability to reduce office overheads is a key driver for organisations both large and small. There are two trends at work here:

- Consolidation into less space.
- Spaceless growth.

Many large organisations are realising that their property is substantially underused, and want to 'sweat the assets' more effectively. One of the reasons why buildings are underused is that with new technologies staff are more mobile, and they often work from other places without the need to return to the office. But what is true for mobile workers, can also be true for many other employees too. Using the new technologies and with the right supportive framework for flexible working, large numbers of their employees can be set free to work from wherever and whenever is most appropriate.

So 'consolidation into less space' doesn't mean working in fewer places – on the contrary, it involves working in many more places than before. It means working in fewer places that are fixed costs for the organisation. Property costs are usually the second highest fixed costs for a company, after salaries. The more they can be trimmed, the better for prioritising front-line operations.

BT is probably the largest flexible working company in the UK, and has perhaps done more than any to try to quantify the benefits to them. BT reports a range of measurable business benefits, detailed in the case study in this chapter.

In the public sector, Ofsted, the education inspection agency, has led the way in implementing flexible working, and has the largest home-based workforce of any department or agency in the public sector. The radical move was a positive response to the need to expand when absorbing the early years childcare inspection service, previously run by local councils. It would have been an easy option in one sense to build more offices to accommodate the additional inspectors. Instead, the organisation adopted a model of spaceless growth, requiring all inspectors to work from home (OGC and DEGW 2008, and see case study in Chapter 9).

It is not only large organisations that can benefit. OAC plc is a company that has adopted a similar growth model. OAC has been able to grow the business, grow the numbers of staff, increase the number of services provided and increase geographical coverage in the UK without having offices at all. It is a completely virtual company. Advanced technology provides the surrogate for the office. See the case study in Chapter 7.

Business benefits can therefore stretch across a range of measures, and it is unwise to take a narrow approach. Flexible work is often seen as a 'nice to have', a benefit to give the staff if you can afford it. This is because flexible working is often conceived narrowly, as a family-friendly measure to help out with childcare. Adopting such an approach will yield few or no business benefits.

Comprehensive and strategic approaches are preferable, that is, approaches that aim to achieve benefits on a broad front. If as a work-life balance measure, staff are working at different times, or from home, then it makes sense to address the property and technology issues too to maximise the benefits all round. Companies, however, need to be wary of words like 'holistic' on the lips of a workplace change consultant. There may be a hidden subtext of 'let's turn this into a bigger and more lucrative project'.

Changing many things at the same time is challenging. But it is also less costly than edging along bit by bit, with each element of flexibility not delivering its full range of potential business benefits.

A key business benefit of flexible working comes from maximising the return from other technology investments. Large organisations often invest huge sums of money in their IT infrastructure to enable the integration of internal company business processes for sourcing and managing supplies, and for delivering services electronically to customers. Substantial savings are promised from these enterprise systems. These arise from improved efficiency, improving the flow of information and eliminating or reducing paper. And they should make processes leaner and more responsive.

However, at board level there is a constant refrain when the next bid for IT investment comes in: 'What happened to the savings we were promised from the last big chunk of money you asked for?'

When these systems are introduced and people are retrained to use them, key assumptions often remain unchallenged about the times and location of work and about the culture of work. Last week people sat at a desk and pushed paper around. This week they sit at the same desk and pretty much replicate that process on a screen. An opportunity for further savings and increased agility has gone begging.

Similarly, people who used to go out and provide customer service are replaced by people who sit at a desk in the office and do so by telephone. The wisdom of having people commute thousands of miles each year to sit in expensive premises to use computers and telephones simply has to be challenged.

The same technologies used for changing work processes can also be used to change radically the times and locations of work – saving money and boosting productivity into the bargain.

Driver 2: Addressing Employee Aspirations

Employees want more flexibility at work. This is related to our Trend 4 in the last chapter, the growth of individualism and an increased emphasis on personal autonomy. That people do want more flexibility is demonstrated repeatedly in workplace surveys and public opinion polls. (We provide further evidence of this in Chapter 5.)

Employees want more flexibility – but in itself that is not the best business reason for providing it. However, if meeting employee aspirations for more flexibility can also deliver business benefits then there is every reason to aim for benefits on this part of the Triple Bottom Line.

In public policy and in HR thinking there is a strong focus on work-life balance (WLB). The UK government, for example, back in 2002 initiated a Work-Life Balance Challenge Fund, which paid for specialist consultants to work with companies who put in bids to receive money to take their company policies and practices forward, and help their staff achieve a better balance. The results for the companies concerned have generally been very positive, and we include several case studies where the introduction of WLB measures has had very positive results for both employees and employers.

A term that was current before WLB and is often – mistakenly – used interchangeably with it is 'family friendliness'. Workplaces sought to become more 'family friendly' by introducing measures targeted at people with children and family caring responsibilities. Indeed, the current legislation in the UK on WLB is really based on 1990s ideas of family friendliness, rather than a comprehensive approach to WLB.

Approaches to family-friendly policies at work usually seek to address particular time management problems that people may have when they become parents. Options such as moving to part-time work or term-time working are about achieving a kind of balance by altering the scheduling of the division between home and work. This is only one limited aspect of the more aspirational factors involved in the current trend towards having a better WLB.

Around 30 per cent of the workforce have children under the age of 16. That leaves out of the equation the other 70 per cent of us without children, or whose children have grown up. Yet we have other aspirations. We have more things to do in an increasingly complex, demanding and opportunity-filled world.

What are the other things people want to do apart from go to work and spend time with their family? Here are a few:

- Enjoy a dedicated pastime or hobby.
- Do something in the way of public service, like be a school governor or magistrate, or volunteering at the local hospital.
- Learn something – for fun, or for career.

So the problem with a predominantly family-friendly approach is that it is designed to react to certain issues that some sections of the workforce experience at certain stages of life, and provide a limited range of responses. It doesn't address the wider issues around trends towards more autonomy and choice in society, nor wider issues of WLB, and it does not take full advantage of the strategic opportunities offered by smarter working.

Flexible working has become strongly associated in the HR and recruitment literature with becoming an 'employer of choice'. An era of full – or nearly full – employment played a role in this. Competition for the best staff and retaining skilled staff became key issues at a time when it seemed the balance of choice was swinging in the direction of employees. The recession may have swung it back a bit the other way. But in the longer term, employers want to be able to choose the best – and probably the most choosey – people to recruit.

A quick skim through the 'Careers' section on the websites of large employers will find that flexible working and WLB are often promoted as key selling points for potential recruits. However, though it is important, WLB is not the only factor of importance to employees. What people value is being more in control of one's own work, as is being treated as a mature person capable of being trusted with good decision-making.

So there are benefits for the employer too in enabling employees to meet their aspirations and work more flexibly:

- To keep the best staff.
- To recruit the best staff.
- To have more satisfied staff, who will then be willing to go the extra mile for their employer.

Driver 3: The Sustainability Imperative and the Triple Bottom Line

'Can homeworking save the planet?' was the somewhat tongue-in-cheek title of a recent think tank report from the Smith Institute (Dwelly and Lake 2008). A number of eminent authorities from the worlds of business, central government, planning, housing and transport gave their views on the ways in which new ways of working are affecting our domestic and work lives, and how public policy should respond in terms of planning the shape of our future communities. The report includes new data on the environmental impacts of flexible working practices and its capacity to reduce work-related travel.

Flexible working is getting firmly on the agenda, and the potential environmental benefits are being recognised and debated.

But when people talk of sustainability in the context of business, sceptics prepare themselves for spin cycles of 'greenwash' and hogwash. In the end, for business it's all about profits. And for government it's all about image and votes, isn't it?

An informed scepticism is always in order for testing the reality and robustness of claims to environmental virtue and achievement. However, the significant adjustments that some companies are making to the way they do business are evidence that the issues are taken seriously, even if in the end no one is really doing enough and some initiatives fail to deliver.

Companies are being driven to clean up their act by a mixture of legislation, public pressure and increasing awareness of their corporate social responsibility (CSR). Any organisation – private, public or voluntary sector – that coordinates the activities of large numbers of people and the consumption, production and distribution of significant resources has an impact on the environment. And it will have a key role to play in trying to ensure these impacts are as benign as possible.

But moral persuasion and legislative compliance are drivers that on the other hand can prompt corporate resistance and evasion, and are not sufficiently effective levers for change. Much more persuasive are business-focused arguments and evidence that cleaning up the way we do business has competitive advantages.

Doing more with less is a key driver for business success, and essentially this is what getting green is all about. It shouldn't be about red tape and about targets, monitoring and reporting. It should be about reducing the physical resources required to carry out the organisation's mission. This is the third part of the 'triple bottom line'.

The environmental benefits of smarter working come in three main areas:

- Reducing the amount of work space needed by each worker, and therefore reducing the resources required to build and service this space. Aggregated, this means over time a reduced requirement for society to build more offices.
- Reducing the amount of travel of each worker – both commute travel and business travel.
- 'Dematerialising' processes and products – doing things electronically rather than physically.

In Chapter 13 we add some numbers to this – numbers that greatly impact the financial bottom line. Within these parameters, the business bottom line and the environmental bottom line are intrinsically linked in win-win situations.

That's not to say that on their own such measures are going to save the planet. If these measures improve company performance, 'doing more with less' raises the question of the overall impacts of everyone 'doing more'. At the end of the day, economic growth will have environmental costs. No one who wants to run a business or run a country is looking seriously at reversing economic growth, though arguably this may in the end be the only way to save the planet. Considering these larger philosophical and political issues is way beyond the scope of this book, so we'll have to 'bracket' them for the time being, though they may be coming back to bite us 20 years from now.

In the meantime, by using smarter and more flexible ways of working, each individual organisation can do what it does at significantly reduced environmental cost. This is what is in their capacity to do, and they should do it.

Driver 4: Technological Trajectories of Change

Central to the changes in the new world of work are changes in technology. Organisations are changing how they do things because now the technologies and systems are available to make this possible.

The applications that are making a difference are all based on new ICT. Telecommunications have of course been with us for over 170 years, including the telephone which has been with us for over 130 years. Computing has been a growing facet of managing organisations for some 60 years and the personal computer has been with us for around 30 years. Combining telephony and computing are Internet and mobile phone technologies, and this trajectory of digital convergence has been having a dramatic impact on business since the 1990s.

The new ICT have been adopted by organisations because they offer opportunities to meet certain perennial business objectives:

- To do things faster.
- To organise things more effectively.
- To overcome the barriers of distance.
- To work better with customers and suppliers.

- To cut the costs of doing things.
- To do new things that previously would have been prohibitively costly to attempt.
- To harness, analyse and process information essential for competitiveness and for starting new ventures.

This is to say that *it is not the technology, per se, that is the driver*. Rather it is the underlying business objectives that effective use of technology can serve. However, this is sometimes forgotten, and acquiring new technologies can sometimes become an end in itself.

We have seen trajectories of change over the past 100 years or so in the introduction and use of technology that can be summed up as:

- *Previously limited or elite access to technologies moving towards ubiquitous access* – for example, a company having just one or two phones, then phones for privileged people according to role or status, and now phones for everyone; having one computer and specialist computer operators, then moving to having almost everyone using them.
- *Technology becoming smaller and more portable* – both phones and computers and devices that combine the two.
- *Converging of technologies* – mobile phones now run computer operating systems, and computing devices are used for a range of communication applications, including standard and feature-rich telephony.
- *Technology applications that are first used in a different context find their way into a business context* – for example, the Internet and email were first developed in military and higher education contexts, but are now essential to business. Texting, instant messaging and social networking are currently important social applications, but are now finding their way much more into business as a new generation enters the workforce.

As technology becomes more prevalent, personal and portable, new possibilities emerge in the way work is done.

But before getting too gung-ho about the transformative capabilities of technologies, we need to reflect. New technologies themselves do not make a revolution. Change does not happen overnight. Our first instinct, in fact, is to do the familiar things with new tools.

For example, it is often said in popular history books and programmes that the introduction of the printing press radically altered society, leading in Europe to new ways of thinking, mass literacy and democracy. Yet for the first 200 years or more, the main uses of books were just as before – religious texts, government propaganda and recording financial information (accounts and taxes). A lot of other social and economic change needed to occur before the printing technologies could really step up and play their part in changing the ways we live and work.

Likewise when the automobile first came on the scene, it was conceived largely as a horseless carriage, and led to a boost in the order books of coach-makers. The power and the range of choices that cars would provide to individuals and governments took time to bed in, and their impacts on society evolved over the course of a century.

An interesting image can serve as a parallel for how some organisations use the new technologies. The first tanks in the First World War were seen as big motorised cannons, moving along with infantry at walking pace, an innovation in the context of trench warfare tactics. It took another two decades before the emphasis on their use shifted to mobility, and tanks were to add a significant new dimension to warfare.

So, for your organisation, do the new technologies simply reinforce and support the old ways of doing things? Or have they radically changed the way you do things, offering increased agility and new, faster routes to achieving your objectives?

That will be the first and last military metaphor in this book! But I hope it makes the point. It takes time for genuinely new ways of doing things with new technologies to emerge. People find it hard to step out of their old habits and structures of thinking to envisage genuinely different applications based on new technologies.

And with ICT we are still very much in an age of transition. The new technologies are really only in their infancy, and it is hard for us to see what is on the horizon, or indeed round the corner in terms of tangential or unexpected uses.

A few years ago the levels of ICT-enabled remote working that some companies operate today were inconceivable. Despite concerns often expressed by those unfamiliar with the practices involved, it is quite possible to work securely with full access to one's work systems and telephony network from pretty much anywhere that you can get an Internet connection (see Chapter 7 for more details).

However, there is more to come. Much more. Specialist applications that currently 'require' people to come into the workplace will become footloose as pretty much unlimited bandwidth enables us to instantly transfer vast amounts of data to each other over the networks. Bill Gates calls it 'business at the speed of light', though I guess he does have better kit and connection than most of us.

So what's coming up on the horizon that we need to take notice of and prepare for?

Technologies for collaboration will continue to evolve and contribute to changing the ways in which we work. Various forms of teleconferencing are now commonplace in many businesses. The most useful form at present is audio-conferencing – basically having a telephone call involving more than two participants. This is having a big impact in reducing travelling for meetings and enabling collaboration with people across the globe in much more effective ways.

Videoconferencing is available, and effective, but is far from a ubiquitous application as yet. Once bandwidth and familiarity issues have been addressed, however, it will be on a desktop near you in the next 10 years or so. It's starting to happen now with applications like Citrix GoToMeeting, Microsoft Lync and similar applications that combine video communications with working on shared documents.

But there is more to come. 'Telepresence' systems are starting to come on stream. These much more closely replicate the vibe and ambience of real-life meetings, which it seems conceptually and psychologically we cannot yet do without.

There will be more, for sure. Enhanced abilities to work jointly together on applications and 3D imaging of products – and each other – will come on stream. Initially this will be using studio systems, and will be too expensive for most. In due course it will become affordable, to be used in meeting rooms and perhaps ultimately find its way to desktop and portable systems.

In principle, these types of things will bring us closer to 'the real thing', meaning traditional ways of face-to-face working. But there is bound to be a point in the future when these technologies and working practices are ubiquitous and psychologically comfortable. This is the point at which we forget what 'the real thing' was. The new thing is then the real thing.

This is some way off. To use the analogy of the motor car, by comparison we are now around the year 1900. At the moment we mostly base our use of the new technologies around old ways of working. And there's a man walking in front of the car with a red flag, warning everyone of the dangers and telling us to take it slowly. Today the dangers being flagged up are: 'What about security? What about teamwork? What about social isolation?' All real issues, but ones to which there are already known and practical solutions. Habits of the past and fear of the new combine to create an unwillingness to embrace the future.

The basic changes needed to progress, to unleash the full power of the technology drivers, are mainly ones of mindset and culture.

Drive 5: Legislative and Public Policy Changes

In the UK and in many other countries, all employing organisations are required by law to at least consider flexible working if any of their eligible employees wants it.

A series of legislative initiatives in the UK have established a 'right to request' flexible working. Introduced in the Employment Act 2002 and modified in the Work and Families Act 2006, this initially gave parents of children under the age of 6, of disabled children under 18 and carers of dependent adults the right to request flexible work. Employers have a duty under law to consider such requests and not to refuse them 'unreasonably'. These acts also introduced or altered other family-friendly measures, mainly to do with maternity and paternity leave.

In May 2008, as a result of a government review led by Imelda Marsh, HR Director of Sainsburys, it was announced that the 'right to request' would be extended to parents of all children aged 16 and under. These recommendations were adopted and came into force in April 2009. Further measures to extend the right to all employees are part of the Modern Workplaces consultation, which hasn't yet reported as we go to press.

This approach correctly identifies that the workforce has been changing, and continues to change. It is becoming more diverse. A higher proportion of women now work, and the changing age structure of the workforce means that the future workforce will contain more older workers. Social attitudes are changing too, and employees have different aspirations that affect the balance they wish to achieve between work and the rest of their lives.

As a result of the legislation many organisations now have a policy for flexible working that sets out how to respond to official requests for flexible working. This is a long way, though, from being a real flexible working policy.

The key problems with both the legislation and the reactive approach it encourages are:

- The initiative for suggesting flexible work options and the responsibility for justifying them lies with the individual employee.
- Managers are expected to make decisions in the absence of a coherent framework that relates flexible work options to business objectives.
- Policy is, in effect, made on an ad hoc case-by-case basis.
- Eligibility for flexible working is based on personal circumstances, rather than appropriateness for the work in question.

- Eligibility for flexible working applies to certain groups of employee and not to others, even though they may be doing the same kind of work.
- This approach reinforces the notion of flexible work as the exception, rather than a legitimate mainstream approach.
- For sceptical employers, it can reinforce a preconception that flexible working is all about red tape and additional costs that have no business merit.

I can't recommend this kind of reactive approach! It runs the risk of being unstrategic, and lacks business focus. It may also be discriminatory when applied only to parents, even though that is what the law supports.

If the benefits of flexible work are to be realised, then it is *essential to adopt an approach that is strategic and comprehensive*. It should offer an appropriate range of flexible work options, and see that they are properly resourced, managed effectively and apply to all employees subject to the constraints of the tasks they undertake in their work.

The legislation and the impacts of the associated tribunal decisions are nonetheless a significant driver towards flexibility, albeit one that can drive organisations to adopt unstrategic and ineffective approaches to flexible working.

The legislative initiatives are the fruit of a significant change in the political mindset operating across all three of the main parties in the UK and also the trades unions.

Back in the 1980s and 1990s, the Conservatives resisted 'Scandinavian' approaches to family-friendly legislation. It was seen as more red tape that would tie up employers and impose costs that would affect competitiveness. The political left, on the other hand, resisted flexibility as basically being all about exploitation – an attitude one still sees on the political left in places like France and Belgium. The emphasis then on flexible labour markets and changing working practices was interpreted as being about breaking collective agreements, using more temporary and part-time workers, reducing union power and basically putting workers at the mercy of employers.

In the new millennium the new Conservatives warmly support flexible working, and the political left champions greater flexibility. In an interview with *Flexibility* magazine back in 1994 the then General Secretary of the TUC, John Monks, insisted that flexibility was a temporary fashion that would be reversed when full employment returned:

> For unions, we have to ask whether it [flexible working] is an inevitable process, because of world competition. Or is it the product of high levels of unemployment? That is, people have to accept what they get because there are plenty of other people around ... Our preferred way of looking at it is that a return to full employment will lead to a return to full-time, core employment. This can be encouraged with minimum wage legislation and tax regimes.
>
> Basically I see it all as negative. There may be benefits for women. But for the average and below average worker there is little choice involved.
>
> People need to be careful about becoming teleworkers. They miss out on social life at work, and we worry about the health and safety aspects, and about employers getting away from overhead costs. We would be keen to see homeworkers get good legal advice.
>
> I anticipate that as levels of employment increase, the pendulum will swing back in favour of the worker, and we'll see the reversal of current trends. (Monks 1994)

This was a remarkably negative assessment. And 100 per cent wrong. As almost full employment returned in the 1990s and continued through to the current recession, flexible working in fact increased. As we saw in Chapter 1, unprecedented levels of prosperity and workforce participation are strongly associated with the rise of new ways of working.

The next time I saw John Monks was around 2001, when he was giving a speech at a conference on Flexible Working, extolling its benefits for workers and families. This is no criticism – far from it. In many ways his change of heart is quite typical of the times.

What had happened in the meantime? It is hard to pin down a Damascus moment. 'New Labour' had perhaps transformed the agenda, and government ministers such as Patricia Hewitt and Harriet Harman were placing flexible working strongly within an equalities and diversity agenda, issues on which unions are strongly committed. Also by this time several unions had policies for 'best practice' home-based working. In fact they often employ regional staff who work from their own homes. The notion of WLB was also taking root, and found a champion in the Department of Trade and Industry.

Flexible working – variously understood – is now supported in principle by a range of government departments and agencies: the Department for Business (the old DTI), Government Equalities Office, Department for Transport, Regional Development Agencies, Transport for London and Business Link all have roles in promoting it.

This enthusiasm from government agencies does not necessarily persuade private sector companies and may even worry them at times. It can also fail to convince when government agencies talk the talk but don't walk the walk in terms of their own working practices. As we will see in Chapter 12, the government sector is in fact making continuing if somewhat uneven progress towards greater flexibility.

So legislation has promoted flexibility, rather than seeking to curtail or control it, as many on the left advocated in the 1990s. But the legislation has been in the British tradition of 'permissive legislation' – creating a framework that people can opt in to, with many an exemption and loophole. Some might call it a fudge. But I tend to regard it as a kind of benign Trojan Horse. It may only apply to a third of the workforce, but they will open up the gates for the rest of us.

What next? The current legislation helps eligible people already in a job, but is of no use to people out of work or applying to work in another company. One option up for discussion at the time of writing is that people with caring responsibilities will have the right when applying for jobs to suggest alternative working arrangements.

That would involve further legislation. But probably more powerful will be the impact of precedent. It will become harder for employers to insist that certain roles or tasks cannot be done on a flexible basis when all around them will be examples of other people doing just that.

Another area that in due course could see new public policy drivers or even legislation is around older workers and phased retirement. As the issues become more pressing, with the abolition of the default retirement age and with probable continuing changes to statutory pension age, new approaches to choice of working patterns around retirement seem increasingly likely. Forward looking companies would do well to make positive moves in this direction.

Smart Flexibility Integral to Future Management

It is a combination of factors that have driven the progress of flexibility in the workplace. There is impetus from above, from below and from outside.

And there is more to come. The report *Management 2018*, from the Chartered Management Institute sought the views of a wide range of top managers and academics. They found a strong belief that managers will have to adapt to ever greater amounts of flexibility (CMI 2008). Managers will be managing much more diverse and dispersed groups of employees, associates and freelancers, who will make up 'an increasingly flexible and transient workforce' that is 'multi-generational, multi-cultural, and remote'. This is only one of a number of reports flagging up similar changes.

In one sense, John Monks was right when he saw flexible working as a fashion. Since the turn of the Millennium, flexibility has indeed started to become fashionable. It is the style of working that is being watched and imitated. The workplace futurists offered their haute couture of wacky working in the 1980s and 1990s. Now the most practical of the concepts and designs have made their way from the conference catwalks to an office near you. This is the way people work – copying what they think is good and adapting it to their own circumstances. This is no temporary fad – far from it.

What makes it an enduring trend are the tangible and measurable benefits involved in smarter forms of flexible working. Knowing exactly what benefits you want to achieve and how to quantify them are the subject of the next two chapters as we move from the theory to the practicalities.

CHAPTER **3** *Developing a Strategic Approach*

In the last section there was a strong warning against developing a reactive approach to flexible working. To do so will not deliver benefits on a significant scale. It could actually increase costs and cause resentment. Resistance to change often stems from poor and partial implementations.

I have enormous admiration for those people who develop a flexible or smart working initiative without the full support of the organisation. It is possible sometimes to muddle through from local initiatives and pilots to the point where the principles are adopted by the organisation. But it is much better to get the buy-in from the top and adopt a comprehensive and strategic approach to doing it well and setting out to achieve the full benefits.

Developing a Comprehensive Strategy for Smart Flexibility

A Smart Flexibility strategy is a strategy for changing working practices based on a clear understanding of what benefits the changes are intended to achieve.

An integrated Smart Flexibility Strategy will seek to achieve benefits in four key areas:

- Increasing organisational effectiveness.
- Reducing the costs of being an organisation.
- Improving the motivation and well-being of employees.
- Improving environmental performance.

Changing the ways people work can bring about substantial improvements in each of these areas.

In each of these four areas an organisation needs to ask itself:

- 'How can we take advantage of new ways of working to improve performance?'
- 'What kind of flexibility in particular will help to achieve these benefits?'
- 'What other strategies do we have that may help or hinder the implementation of a flexible working strategy – and how do they need to change or evolve?'

Getting senior managers to work through these questions will tease out key issues for the organisation, and also highlight areas where there are knowledge gaps and where there is a need for developing greater awareness about new ways of working.

Table 3.1 summarises the key areas of improvement.

Table 3.1   Linking benefits to activities

Area of benefit	Particular benefits	Areas of activity	Linkages that need aligning
• Effectiveness • Increased effectiveness	• Getting closer to customers • Improved productivity • Agility – responsiveness to market	• Mobile and remote working • Increasing virtual team-working • Changing hours of working • Reforming processes	• IT strategy • Electronic service delivery plans • Procurement strategy
• Costs • Reduced cost of operation	• Reduced property costs • Reduced travel costs • Reduced absenteeism • Reduced staff turnover	• Desk-sharing • Creating flexible work environments • Storage reduction • Collaboration technologies • Remote working • Work-life Balance programme	• Accommodation strategy • Company travel plan • Recruitment strategy
• Workforce • Employee motivation, loyalty and development	• Increased staff satisfaction • Increased staff loyalty • Reduced work/life conflicts/stress • Improved recruitment • Empowered employees with new skills	• Applying the range of flexible working options • Culture change programme • Training	• HR strategy • Recruitment strategy • Equal opportunities and diversity strategy • Communication strategy • Organisational development strategy
• Environment • Improved environmental performance	• Reduced business and employee travel • Reduced environmental footprint of premises • Reduced resources consumed	• Promoting flexible work-styles • Supporting virtual collaboration • Culture change programme • Developing an 'eCulture' – eliminating paper processes	• Environmental strategy • Corporate social responsibility strategy • Initiatives on greening the office and greening IT

The second column in Table 3.1 summarises the key business benefits of flexible working. All these benefits are measurable – an important factor that we will return to in the next chapter.

The third column – 'Areas of activity' – outlines the areas of flexible working practice and the key associated activities that need to happen to achieve the benefits. In practice, there is a good deal of overlap between the activities within each section. For example, remote working, including home-based working, relates to each area of benefit. To take another example: having more flexible working hours is important for increasing effectiveness, for dealing with absence, recruitment and retention issues, and for staff satisfaction. It has relatively little impact compared to remote working on issues such as property reduction and environmental performance – though it does have some (see Chapter 6).

The fourth column identifies key strategic linkages. Existing strategies may be to some extent supportive of new ways of working. It is more likely, however, that due to its interdisciplinary nature, introducing Smart Flexibility will impact across a range of strategies.

In some cases a strategic approach will augment existing strategies and policies, adding new dimensions to them. This is most likely to be the case with equal opportunities and diversity strategies and environmental or corporate social responsibility strategies.

In the case, though, of property/accommodation strategies, it is quite likely that modernising working practices will pose some challenges. Perhaps the organisation has an accommodation strategy predicated on the provision of 1:1 desks, and assumptions built around increasing or reducing numbers of staff. The introduction of desk-sharing and remote working will mean that the underlying assumptions about the relations of floor space to headcount will need to be changed.

Accommodation strategies will also feed back into Smart Flexibility strategy. The process of building the business case for change will almost certainly highlight current levels of under-occupancy and the capacity to reduce floor space requirements.

Given the role that new technologies have in facilitating flexible working, it is surprising how often IT strategies are significant obstacles to innovation in working practices. IT managers can sometimes be resistant to adapting to any strategy they haven't thought of themselves. If flexible working hasn't been included in the current IT strategy, you can be sure it will be painful to graft it on: a new strategy that does include it is a must – plus allocation of the necessary resources.

Having highlighted the need to be aware of linkages with other strategies, it would be a mistake to try and get all the strategies aligned before moving on with developing smart working. In many organisations, that would create too much delay, and possibly in-fighting as well. It's an iterative process: developing the vision, making it clear that there will be change, getting the interdisciplinary team together and then getting them to offer what they can to the process, and seeing how the various other strategies can contribute and how they need to be modified en route.

This process will bring some interesting challenges, and requires people to think and to gain new skills and insights outside their traditional specialisms.

Identifying the benefits and relating the benefits to particular activities in this way can be a useful part of awareness-raising work for senior managers, and forms a key element in developing the vision for the change process and for understanding the kind of organisation that will be there once working practices have changed.

Incorporating Smart Flexibility Principles

At the strategic level there needs to be a statement about the underlying principles on which new ways of working will be based. In this section I am taking a 'maximal' approach to introducing Smart Flexibility – where flexibility becomes the norm and the organisation is open to maximising the opportunities for flexibility.

This maximal approach to Smart Flexibility is about taking a comprehensive and strategic approach to working practices, and is based on the following principles:

- Work takes place at the most effective locations.
- Work takes place at the most effective times.
- Flexibility becomes the norm rather than the exception.
- Everyone is, in principle, considered eligible for flexible working, without assumptions being made about people or roles.
- Employees have more choice about where and when they work, subject to business considerations.
- Space is allocated to activities, not to individuals or on the basis of seniority.
- The costs of doing work are reduced.
- There is effective and appropriate use of technology.
- Managing performance focuses on results rather than presence.
- Smart/flexible working underpins and adds new dimensions to diversity and equality principles.
- Work has less impact on the environment.
- There are positive impacts on the 'Triple Bottom Line' – benefits for the business, the individual and for the environment.

These principles are powerful statements to galvanise the reform of working practices, and to act as the touchstone when settling debates. For example, when making judgements about where and when people should work, in the final analysis it's all about where is most effective do get the work done. When considering whether managers should retain their personal offices, it's a lot easier to make the call if the strategy has clearly set out a principle that overrides egoism and power-plays.

These principles impact on investment decisions too. When, for example, decisions are to be made to invest in new technologies for remote working or for videoconferencing, the tests are: does it reduce the costs of doing work (for example, by releasing office space)? Does it mean that work has less impact on the environment (for example, by reducing travel?) Does it help us to be more effective (for example, by increasing productivity or getting closer to customers)?

The answers are not necessarily self-evident. To say 'yes' to all these questions because you support flexible working may be to indulge in wishful thinking. The secondary question in each case is 'By how much?' It could be that the investment in videoconferencing technologies won't reduce travel significantly: adding all this kit may actually increase the environmental impact of working. Other solutions for collaboration may have a greater impact, or it may be that other changes have to be in place before it can make the impact you want. So in practice individual *decisions must be supported by the evidence as well as the strategy.*

Beyond the principles, any flexible working strategy will need to set out the goals that are to be achieved by modernising working practices, and set out the targets and timescales that should be adhered to. In the following chapters we will look at how to go about setting meaningful targets.

Interdisciplinary High-Level Team

Getting everyone on board at senior level is vital for making the strategy workable. One of the themes of this book is that for Smart Flexibility to work it has to be approached on a broad front – because the benefits are intertwined across several areas of interest and across a range of disciplines. For this reason it is essential to establish at the outset a high-level interdisciplinary team to drive forward the change programme and oversee the individual projects within the organisation.

Who should be on the team may vary from one organisation to another. But it should contain senior representatives from HR, Property, Facilities, IT and Finance as well as senior managers from directorates undergoing change.

The role of this group is not to have endless meetings dealing with all the details of introducing new working practices. Their role is to establish the vision, drive the process forward, set expectations and see that the necessary resources are allocated. They will oversee the process as a whole and keep it on course, monitor progress against the strategic objectives, and they will also have a role in breaking through any logjams that occur.

Beneath this high-level board will sit action-oriented project teams whose job is to deliver the new work styles and associated facilities and resources against agreed timescales.

The high-level team has to demonstrate commitment to the principles and take a lead in setting an example. I know of several implementations that have run into trouble where senior managers have not walked the walk. In two cases that I know of, they arbitrarily undid their flagship executive, shared smart working environment and retreated to private offices, while still requiring others to get on with implementing space-sharing.

So *the senior team has to set up an example.* This can be done in many ways, according to circumstances. The HR literature is full of examples of senior managers working flexibly. This can be by working from home a day a week – or by enabling their support staff to do so. Moving to desk-sharing if others are doing so is another way – some options for doing this are set out in Chapter 6.

Making a song and dance about it is also very valuable, to communicate the key messages. For example, the communications team can write up a case study on the director who works from home one day per week, volunteers on school sports day, has a job-share remote working PA, has cut his or her storage by 80 per cent, cut business travel by 30 per cent, and is in closer touch with staff by desk-sharing on the office floor whenever he or she can.

So, however sceptical some people may be about flexible working, one thing they shouldn't be able to do is accuse senior management of hypocrisy.

Senior Management Awareness-Raising

Getting senior managers all on board and singing from the same hymn sheet normally doesn't just happen. It is probable that there are some enthusiasts for change amongst the senior team, but it is unlikely to be all of them. And even amongst those who are enthusiasts, it is probably the case that they are not aware of the range of possibilities and the range of benefits achievable. Few will be experts in flexible work. And why should they be? Each person will have their own expertise, and it is pulling these together in the context of change that is required.

So an essential part of the process is to work with senior managers to widen their horizons about flexible work, so they can understand better the possibilities for change. This requires openness to new ideas. One problem is that for many people 'flexible working' may already be pigeon-holed in one way or another.

It's good to incorporate awareness-raising into management away days, where a good amount of time can be reserved exclusively for open and candid exploration of the options and issues, with less pressure to move on to other business.

Nothing persuades quite like the business case, so presentations showcasing the achievements of other organisations are invaluable, and benchmark data about costs and benefits. The aim is to increase and deepen understanding about what is possible, and about the nature of the commitment that is needed to achieve change.

Considering the possibilities and the issues in their area of responsibility, whether HR, Property, IT or an operational department, is a key part of awareness-raising, and it helps to move beyond the abstract and consider hard practical issues at the exploratory stage. Often there are already initiatives within the organisation that are not properly understood, or which have been constrained by lack of awareness at senior levels. Involving those who have been running the initiatives can help to deepen understanding.

Awareness-raising is not a one-off event, but a process of continuous engagement as the strategy is developed.

Agreeing the Vision

Introducing flexible working in a strategic way is a transformative process. So it is important to have a clear view of what is to be transformed and what the change will achieve. This will vary from one organisation to another, according to their wider strategic aims and circumstances.

The vision will be about the kind of organisation they wish to become, the benefits they wish to achieve, the new working culture they wish to develop, the new values they wish to promote and the ways in which they intend to achieve all this,

Many of the 'Smart Work Principles' set out earlier in this chapter are likely to be part of the agreed vision, and we would expect words like 'empowering' 'trust-based' to be in there as well as 'agile', 'efficient' and 'effective'. For more on the cultural aspects, see the components of a Smart Flexibility working culture in Chapter 8.

In the box below is the Vision Statement of Hertfordshire County Council's smart transformation programme, called 'The Way We Work'.

HERTFORDSHIRE COUNTY COUNCIL – VISION STATEMENT

The Way We Work is about creating a customer-centred organisation which maximises the potential of its staff, is efficient in the use of resources, and optimises its use of new technology.

The Way We Work will help us achieve our aim of making Hertfordshire an even better place to live.

We will measure success in achieving our objectives against our core values:

Our Customers
- Are kept at the centre of everything we do
- Receive essential quality services where and when they are needed

- Benefit from joined up service delivery
- Are confident that we give good value for money

Our Staff

- Deliver a quality, cost effective service
- Have the skills, confidence and opportunity to work in new ways
- Work jointly with colleagues
- Work flexibly to provide responsive services
- Achieve their own work-life balance
- Are informed in an open way about changes
- Are positively supported through change

Our Resources

- We will secure efficiency in working practices and service delivery
- Remove duplication and unnecessary bureaucracy
- Make effective use of new technology
- Provide services from efficient and fit-for-purpose facilities

Our Partners

- Work with us to deliver seamless services
- Secure the benefits of joined up and customer-centred working
- Ensure efficiency in the delivery of high quality services
- Are engaged with us in enabling these changes and benefits to be delivered

The first sentence here sums up the intention of the change programme: 'The Way We Work is about creating a customer-centred organisation which maximises the potential of its staff, is efficient in the use of resources, and optimises its use of new technology'. The remainder clearly sets out in very summary form the key elements of change that are envisaged. It makes the links between business efficiency, new ways of working, work-life balance and customer service. New technologies and new working environments are to be key enablers.

As we will see when looking at a more detailed case study of Hertfordshire's change programme (Chapter 12), they have really walked the walk as well as setting out an eloquent vision.

For a commercial company, there might be more emphasis on increasing sales, or fostering creativity or innovation through new ways of working. Another organisation might put a greater emphasis on sustainability – cutting back on travel and greening working practices. It all depends on the starting point and the nature of the organisation.

The example here is of a very comprehensive approach to transformation through smart and flexible working. For various reasons an organisation might be attempting a less all-embracing project. For example, Company A may be quite satisfied with its flexible working arrangements, which have been developed from a work-life balance perspective. But it realises that its buildings are under-used and not fit for the kinds of use that their more mobile workforce now requires. So the change programme focuses very much on developing smart working environments. There's still a need for an agreed vision, even if it is more narrowly focused.

Company B has the contrasting situation – one I've come across several times. They've introduced flexible work environments, but the culture hasn't moved in the same direction. There's no sense of direction about how working practices should change or about managing flexible working. The change programme here will need a different vision.

I can hear some groans of scepticism as I write this. In the UK especially, people tend to be cynical about having visions and missions in the workplace. Empty words and management-speak!

It's no doubt true that vision statements and mission statements are often found pompously oscillating in the range between platitude and pie-in-the-sky, or floundering between cliché and hypocrisy. But the importance of establishing a clear vision when taking a strategic approach to Smart Flexibility is like this:

a) The process of getting to the vision is itself vital, bringing all the relevant parties to the table to agree the vision. Once the top managers have signed up to it, it greatly reduces the 'wriggle room' for recidivists later on.
b) Once set out, it acts as a spur to get things done and can unlock the necessary resources and consents.
c) It leaves no one in any doubt that change will come, and that it comes with blessing and authority from the highest level.
d) It produces part of the yardstick for measuring success – have we achieved these things we set out to do?

External Support

Depending on the level of expertise to be found in the organisation, it is usually advisable to bring in some external support to assist in the awareness-raising, if not in the strategy development as a whole. There is a growing number of companies that can offer the necessary expertise in this interdisciplinary field.

But there are also some caveats. Some companies may offer excellent advice and guidance, but also have products to sell at the end of the day – technologies in particular. So when engaging outside support, it's necessary to go in with eyes open, watching where impartial advice starts to shade into a sales pitch for a particular product or service.

What external advice can bring in particular is experience of implementations in other organisations. They may also be able to facilitate introductions to other companies, where you can hear from people who have travelled along the same road and see how they have put it into practice.

Similar insights can be gained by attending conferences and networking events looking at the issues.

Sometimes external advisers are brought in to provide an impartial and objective viewpoint, where it is felt an internal voice lacks clout or is too likely to get mired down in internal politics. The external voice validates a programme that might otherwise lack internal validity or credibility. That's fine, up to a point. But consultants who take on this kind of job often find themselves landing in a can of worms. Introducing Smart Flexibility in a dysfunctional organisation often requires going back to basics on strategy, leadership and culture in order to facilitate sensible changes.

Weak Management Is the Greatest Enemy of Change

Once the senior management have agreed the strategy and vision, it's time for the rest of the organisation to get the message, starting with the rest of the managers. We look in Chapter 5 and Chapter 9 at the issues for management training.

At the outset, though, there is a clear need for all managers to be motivated and be ready to support the changes. These are the people who in many cases will be at the sharp end of change, arranging and approving the flexible working patterns that will be put into practice in their departments and teams. Many of them will be involved in detailed planning of new working environments, liaising with the relevant departments to procure the necessary resources, motivating their own staff and dealing with any hostility and opposition.

So managers need to be sure where they stand, fully aware of the new strategy, the new targets being set and the expectations put on them to succeed. Their role is pivotal.

Nothing undermines change like weak management. Weakness can come from two directions: their own management weaknesses, such as being indecisive or being too keen to be liked by everyone; or from lack of clear support and guidance from above. I've known managers who felt as if they have been hung out to dry when trying to implement new ways of working in fractious departments.

I've also know middle managers who have strong and well-evidenced plans for change, but in a 'kick-ass' corporate culture are too afraid to force the pace of change and challenge that culture. While the top level was groping towards a strategy, there was an intermediate layer strongly wedded to management by presence and fearful of loss of control.

So managers need to feel empowered to bring about the changes that the strategy requires, and know they will have the resources, tools and top-level support to get the job done.

Championing Change and Offering Support from the Centre

Once the strategy is in place it will be necessary to have a mechanism for taking it forward. Unless someone has a clear and specific responsibility to champion and initiate the change programme, the danger is that it will fall by the wayside, be diluted by competing interests and resistance, or fall victim to bickering between departments.

The worst of all worlds is to have an ineffective champion. To get anything done in an organisation one needs a power-base. Smart Working falls across departments. It needs top-level backing, or strong roots in a powerful department and the ability to access significant budget.

It is most effective to have a programme manager who has the resources to provide practical support to departments undergoing change. One approach is to have a small corps of experienced change envoys who can be sent out to departments to help them through the changes, transferring skills in the process.

The important thing is that managers and staff making the changes throughout the organisation know that they will be helped and supported throughout the process, that there is a coherent strategy, and that senior management is entirely serious about making a success of it.

Communicate the Strategy

A key part of making the change programme work is to let people know about it, and to reinforce the message at every possible opportunity. When communication is poor, it is easy for rumours and misinformation to undermine change. If the word gets around that 'it's all about cost-cutting', for example, it will be an uphill battle after that to capture hearts and minds. Any talk after that about employee benefits or environmental benefits from flexible working will just be seen as spin.

Though one doesn't want to get bogged down in branding, it is definitely worth having an identifiable brand name for the strategy and change programme. Brands you might have come across include Smart Work, SMART Work, Work Wise, Wise Work, Workabout, Workstyle, The Way We Work (TW3), [Company name] Works, Office of the Future, Agile Working, Modern and Flexible Working … Here's a challenge to all readers to come up with something really inventive and unique!

If nothing else, the brand will make it clear that this is a programme with official endorsement, and it identifies a single programme of activity embodying clear aims and values. As the change programme moves on, there will be many more things to communicate: news, plans, updates on the roll-out so far, consultation exercises, new policies and protocols for new ways of working. Having agreed mechanisms for communication and avenues for dialogue are essential for the change programme to succeed.

Avoiding Bureaucracy and Delay

Strategies should be dynamic models for action, always ready to evolve and adapt to new circumstances. Too often, the drawing up of a strategy involves a long sequence of reports and meetings, and the result is a document that is past its sell-by date by the time it is agreed. It's not possible to iron out all the details at the inception stage. There should be plenty of opportunities to debate, discuss, and consult on detail as the strategy is implemented, as we'll see in the chapters ahead.

The Route Map to Smart Flexibility

At one of the meetings of the Smart Work Network we discussed the starting point for flexible/smart working initiatives, and how the overall process of introducing Smart Working should ideally be constructed. Figure 3.1 on the next page is a route map we developed out of these discussions.

In this chapter we've been looking at the 'Setting out' stage. Part of this stage of setting out is being conscious of the road you are embarking on, and what lies on the road ahead.

It's worth reflecting on what your organisation has done. Often, as we found, the starting point is in small pilots and departmental initiatives. For many, writing a policy is the starting point – whereas on our route map it's pretty much one of the last things: codifying the change. Often writing a policy is a compliance measure: complying with the legislation. Other organisations have just plumped in with a selection of flexible working options, evolved from their situation and preferences, or individual cases. A

| Setting out | Getting real | Options and impacts | Getting underway | Managing change |

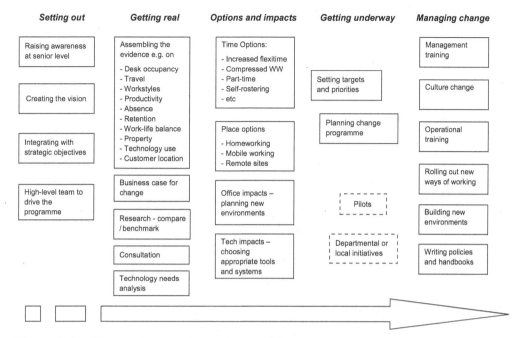

Figure 3.1   The route map to smart working

quick search on the Internet will throw up a few hundred organisational policies for flexible working. Almost none of them are strategic documents.

In some ways, these are fine as tentative first steps, though many people have told us of the difficulty of scaling up a successful project. One of our case studies on Flexibility. co.uk is of Islington Council, where an integrated approach was developed over time, successfully scaled up from a departmental initiative with a lot of learning on the way. So it is possible. But in the end there will need to be a process that looks something like our route map if the whole organisation is to be transformed.

The key characteristics of this approach are having a clear vision, strong leadership, an evidence-based approach, a comprehensive approach to achieving quantified benefits, and a strongly managed approach to rolling out the changes to people, property and technologies.

STRATEGIC IMPLEMENTATION OF AGILE WORKING AT BIRMINGHAM CITY COUNCIL

'Working for the Future' is the programme transforming Birmingham City Council's workplaces and introducing agile working. As the UK's largest local authority, once it is complete it will be the largest implementation of Agile Working in the sector.

On the property side the aims are ambitious: reducing from over 1 million sq ft (92,900 m²) in the Central Administrative Buildings (CAB) portfolio to circa 650,000 sq ft (60,400 m²) of space. This is being achieved by reducing the back office estate from 55 properties to eight while enabling around 9,000 people to work from 6,500 workstations.

This involves the disposal of circa 30 freehold surplus properties and the relinquishment of 19 leased buildings together with investing in a prestigious new building and undertaking major refurbishments at a number of the retained office locations.

This rationalisation and the introduction of Agile Working is on course to reduce annual revenue running costs from in excess of £19 million to around £11 million per year and over the life of the project delivering over £100 million of net efficiency savings.

The process for delivering the change has been based on the extensive gathering of evidence – space utilisation surveys, occupier surveys and analysis of the work undertaken in each part of the Council. Using this data and working with managers, 'work families' were modelled to identify the opportunity and scope for implementing Agile Working. At the same time, there was a strong engagement process with senior managers to establish the vision, policy and standards for future working and use of property in the Council.

Birmingham has taken the approach of identifying several different work styles to help with planning for accommodation and technology needs. These works styles are: Office Worker, Access Point Worker, Mobile Worker, Field Worker and Home-worker. The Home-worker category is split into three: Occasional, Regular and Full-time, although the numbers of full-time home-workers are minimal.

The provision of settings within the office space reflects the greater mobility and flexibility, with workstations located in 'team zones' allocated at an average ratio of 7 workstations to 10 staff, a variety of multi-function rooms, break-out spaces and refreshment and relaxation areas. Desk-sharing is on a 'team neighbourhood' basis which helps to support team identity. There are no single-person offices in any of the new spaces, though a handful remain in 'legacy buildings' where there are constraints on altering the internal layout. Storage has been driven down, and there is a clear desk policy to maximise the opportunity for shared use of desks.

Technology at desks is either a PC or laptop, a large screen and a VoIP phone. A soft phone facility is loaded on to each PC. Remote connectivity solutions include 3G and Netmotion (VPN). Instant messaging and video conferencing to desktop and meeting rooms is being rolled out on an as-needed basis.

There have been challenges, mainly arising as a consequence of major change within the public sector. According to Adrian Rathbone, Enabling Agile Working Lead at the Council, 'Although we've had a very clear vision, we've had to work very closely with Service Areas to align and develop evolving operational needs within the agreed strategy. To deal with this it's been essential to have a good governance structure in place from the beginning. A Property Champion is assigned to each service to work through their needs with them and help them through the changes. And now we can see that it's working, we're seeing an integral change in the behaviours of staff'.

David Fletcher, Head of Corporate Landlord at Birmingham City Council, has been at the heart of the transformation and recognises the change. 'Employees really appreciate the new spaces they are working in. They have embraced the flexibility and trust that comes with this and are able to do their job more effectively'.

CHAPTER 4

Building the Business Case for Smart Flexibility

What counts in business is what can be counted. If not entirely true, it's still a good principle to have in mind. What you count, how you count it and how you interpret it once you've counted it underpin any good business decision. This is certainly the case with introducing Smart Flexibility. *All the business benefits highlighted so far are measurable.* This applies to both the hard measures (like property costs) and the softer measures (like work-life balance).

Most flexible working implementations that fail to deliver the benefits – or just simply fail – do so at least in part because there were inadequate metrics at the outset.

Others may succeed or fail – but no one actually knows, because no one put the metrics in place to measure if there have been any benefits.

What Should Be Measured?

To move flexible working successfully from theory to practice, there needs to be a business case built on robust evidence. The evidence base should cover:

- What people do.
- Where they do it.
- Property and facilities costs.
- Space occupancy levels.
- Travel and travel costs.
- Interaction with customers, suppliers, partners, and so on.
- Teamwork and interaction with colleagues.
- What technologies they use.
- How much storage they use.
- Number and usefulness of meetings.
- What issues employees face.
- Current flexible working practices.
- Attitudes to other possible flexible working practices.
- Attitudes to current working environments.
- Preferences for future working environments.
- Issues in recruitment, retention and absence.
- Potential work-life balance benefits.

Some of this data will already be recorded, such as property, facilities and travel costs. But often this kind of information is not kept in a way that is useful to a change programme. For example, trying to find out what are the total costs per workstation in a building or a department can prove to be surprisingly problematic.

In the following sections we take a hard look at the main areas of costs that need to be counted in for building the business case for flexible working, and measuring the results of change.

What are the Real Costs of Giving Everyone a Desk at Work?

The real costs of a workstation (desk) in an office comprise the whole range of expenditure on rent, business rates, furnishings, decoration, heating, lighting, ventilation, water, maintenance, IT, telephony (etc) divided by the number of workstations that are accommodated there. In the UK, these range from around £3,900 per workstation in an older office in Leicester to over £16,000 per workstation in the most expensive areas of London. The average for central London is around £10,400 per workstation, and £5,700 for the rest of the UK (Actium Consult 2012).

In a traditional office, each workstation is allocated on a one-person-to-one-desk basis. So measuring the cost of individual workstations is the same as measuring the costs of the office per worker. That is something that changes when desk-sharing is introduced.

In traditional one-desk-to-one-employee office set-ups, many desks are unoccupied for much of the time. This means that working desks harder is one area where substantial savings can be made when people are enabled to work more flexibly.

Desk-sharing is often controversial. People are often reluctant to give up what they see as being their personal space in the office (see Chapter 6). Levels of desk-sharing are often the subject of fierce debate. Should the ratios be 8 desks for every 10 people, which seems to have become a kind of default standard in the public sector? Or 7 to 10? Or 1 to 2? Or 1 to 4? 1 to 10 even?

Decisions are too often the result of guesswork, compromise or office politics. But there are more scientific approaches to establishing the levels required. These involve understanding actual average space usage, understanding peak demand, and understanding how enabling people to work more effectively away from the office will impact demand.

Auditing Space Use

I have come across attempts to understand space occupancy needs that have been based on attendance records – who has 'swiped in' over the past month, for example. This is plainly inadequate, as it does not touch on whether desks are actually used at particular times of the day.

Other approaches involve having managers or team leaders assess their needs and estimate how much their staff are in the office. These always result in overestimates of occupancy.

The only way to get accurate information is actually to measure how desks and other spaces are occupied on a 'live' basis. There are two effective ways to do this:

1. Have small teams of people going round with a clipboard or handheld device recording how space is used at periodic intervals. The more frequent the measurements, the more accurate the record will be.
2. Use sensor technology that can detect when people are at their desks, and in more sophisticated implementations wearing 'Star Trek'-like tags to record movements in the office.

Perhaps the first option sounds a little bit 'Time and Motion', but the aim is to measure the productivity of the desk or room, not the productivity of the person. Sometimes people don't realise this, and during a study will rush back to their desk, like a naughty kid caught loitering when the teacher comes into class. There's an important point here. Occupying a desk is not an indication of personal productivity, or of doing your job, or of corporate virtue – or even of being in the right place for that matter. All these things are often assumed by both managers and staff, however. For field staff or for a manager, *not* being at your desk could be a better indication of productivity and corporate virtue.

The second option sounds a bit Big Brother, although people do adjust to the surveillance involved just as they do with daily exposure to CCTV cameras and in TV reality shows. The major issue is that it's considerably more expensive for a one-off audit than the 'roaming scouts' techniques. It does give real time information, so is arguably more accurate. And it can give more in-depth information about movements in the office and occupation hotspots, which can greatly help in office redesign. But it won't pick up what people are doing at a desk.

The following two figures are from a space utilisation audit in a large organisation, using a scouts-and-PDAs technique for data capture. It's from a department where about a third of employees have a mobile work style. Their role is to be out and about with customers (external or internal) and partner organisations.

The dark grey areas on the chart show the percentage of desks that are occupied – that is when someone is actually sitting there. The light grey shows when the desk has been recorded as 'claimed', that is, unavailable for someone else to work there due to work in progress (not just a coat slung over the back of the chair or a computer left on). In this case, average desk occupancy between 9 a.m. and 5 p.m. is 39 per cent, 44 per cent if the light grey temporary non-occupation time is included.

Though most managers know that desks are often empty, few accurately predict the extent of the under-occupancy. Around 30–35 per cent is about the average occupancy you will find for managers and 35–40 per cent (similar to this case) for professionals in a traditional working organisation. Mobile professionals may be there for less than 25 per cent of the time.

There is nothing wrong with this. If you found that your team of salespeople or social workers were in the office for 80 per cent of the time, then that would be something to worry about. These figures indicate that they are probably out of the office doing what they should be doing – working with customers and clients (though that is not the whole story of their working day, as we shall see).

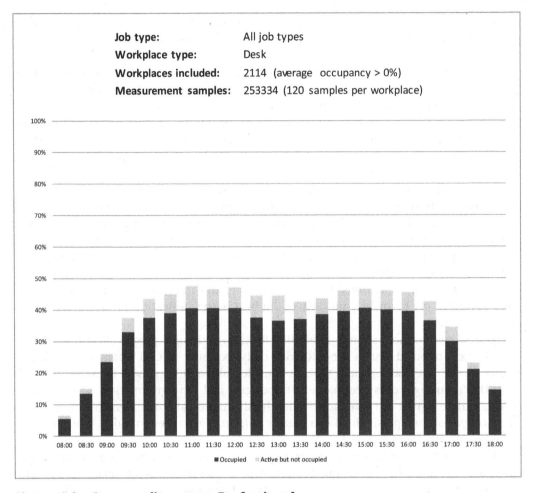

Job type: All job types
Workplace type: Desk
Workplaces included: 2114 (average occupancy > 0%)
Measurement samples: 253334 (120 samples per workplace)

Figure 4.1   Space audit output: Professionals

Note: Average occupancy – based on 183012 workplace samples, 0090–1200, 1400–1700:

   – 39 per cent in-use and occupied.
   – 45 per cent including temporarily unoccupied.

Source: HOP Associates, www.hop.co.uk.

But if they are out of the office most of the time, what is the value of having desks individually allocated to them? And more to the point, of spending so much money on the space required for this?

What about the administrators – information processors, secretaries, receptionists? They'll be there most of the time, won't they? The answer is – not as much as people think. The figure on the following page shows occupancy by admin and support staff in the same department.

In this organisation, staff were asked in workshops to guess the percentage of time admin staff were typically in the office. Most guessed round the 80 per cent to 90 per cent mark. There was general disbelief that in this case it did not rise above 60 per cent during the 9–5 period. Of course, there are peak times when occupancy is higher. But you

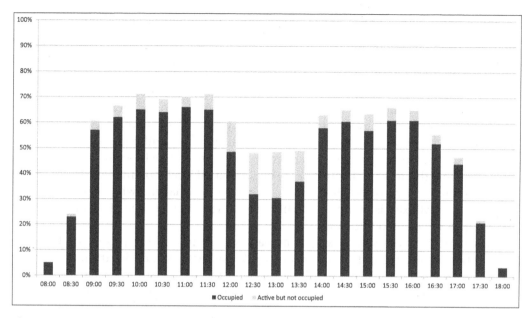

Figure 4.2   Space audit output: Admin staff

don't often see a peak over 70 per cent. Even if you knock the lunch break out of such calculations, the average only rises two or three percentage points.

Perceptions of staff and managers are often coloured by their personal perceptions, which are necessarily limited to the areas immediately around them. The supervisor of a small team of eight people will say that all her staff were in the office and at their desks at 10 a.m. yesterday. But not all teams in the organisation will have those peaks at the same time. So where are they all when they are not at their desks?

Well, at a basic level there is staff annual leave and sickness absence, which together amount to more than 10 per cent of working time. Then there are people who work part-time, but have a desk each. There are posts unfilled. It can be quite an eye-opener to senior staff how many of these there are, and how many middle managers are hoarding empty desks as a way of earmarking space for future expansion. Then there are people who have got time off in lieu, working flexitime, working occasional days at home. This is even before getting to the point of considering operational reasons for people being away from their desks, such as meetings (internal or external).

Any organisation of over 100 people with individually assigned desks that says it has average occupancy of 80 per cent or more is either deluded, or is not measuring accurately. They may be talking about peak occupancy. But even peak occupancy rarely tips 60 per cent in a large traditionally organised company.

Where Is Everybody and What Are They Doing?

These are, one might think, rather obvious questions: 'Where is everybody and what are they doing?' Unfortunately, the answers are not so obvious. At least, in no organisation I've ever worked with have people had the answers ready to hand.

It's surprising what organisations don't know about themselves, given the amount they invest in all kinds of management and monitoring systems. Actually, many organisations fail at step one, when you ask 'How many people work here?' Leaving aside the obligatory droll response of 'About half', one often finds the serious answers are not always more enlightening. Departmental managers, Payroll, HR and Facilities will come up with different answers. Often wildly different. So sometimes it's only when a reorganisation, relocation or smart working project kicks in that employers find out who is working for them, which department they are in and what building they are based in.

So the usual answer to the 'How many?' question is: 'We'll get back to you'. It's interesting that this tends to happen at the departmental level too. Interviews with senior managers bring many insights, but how many people do what and where tends not to be among them. Ball-park is best hope at this level, at least at first time of asking. But they can delegate someone to find out.

Structured interviews with senior managers help to build a picture of how the organisation works, the different styles of work, and with whom departments interact internally and externally. They also help to build the picture of how smart work is at the moment, what the appetite is at senior level for greater flexibility, and where further awareness-raising is necessary.

Some methodologies put great store by getting managers to slot their staff into categories based on mobility, along the lines of whether they are fixed, flexible, mobile, very mobile or in some special category that means they need access to very particular places when they are doing a particular part of their job. For a critique of this approach, see Table 6.2 in Chapter 6. The big risk in this approach is that it depends on an arbitrary judgement by someone at a senior level who may not really know the role very well, or understand the potential to repack the tasks in the job more efficiently to create new flexibilities.

To find out what people do and where they do it, the best way is to ask them. This can be a snapshot in a staff consultation. Or it can be in the form of an activity diary or Day In the Life or Week In the Life (DILO or WILO) survey, which are more onerous and intrusive, but also more likely to be accurate. Figure 4.3 shows a breakdown of activities of a team of field workers.

This team is spending just over 30 per cent of their time at the office, most of that at their desks. Working at home tends to happen when they start the day from home and go straight to a meeting. Otherwise, they are dependent on returning to the office for access to systems and information.

A quarter of their time is spent travelling, and travelling is indeed necessary for their work. But it is increased by their using the office as a base to go to meetings.

The aim of a project to get them working more flexibly would be to:

a) Increase their time away working with clients.
b) Reduce their time spent travelling.
c) Doing this mainly by taking their desk time away from the office, and enabling them to do this kind of work wherever they happen to be.

The purpose of coming into the office will change for these employees. It will be for collaborative activities, rather than desk work in the future. The success of this project will crucially depend on having good technologies for mobile and remote working.

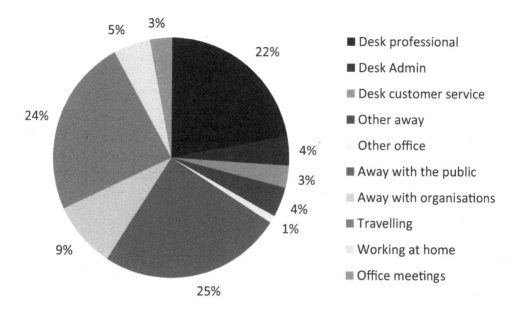

Figure 4.3   Time and place of activities

Can this team go completely virtual? Can they become home-based, like the people at OAC or Ofsted? Those are judgements to be made when considering the nature of their work and the wider context of the organisation. The question to ask is: if we were starting from scratch, what arrangements would we be making?

This team already spends more than two-thirds of its time away from the office. Currently the fact that they need to use the office base injects inflexibilities and inefficiencies into the pattern of work. The amount of time in the office can be at least halved. So what is the value of the office base? It's historic, it's comfortable – but is it necessary?

A few words of caution about measurement. People tend to overestimate the amount of time they spend at their desks, people opposed to greater flexibility especially so, and simply asking the questions can stimulate the fear of loss of territory. So in analysing the results, it's always wise to cross-check with the space audit to measure the gap between perception and reality.

People also underestimate the amount of time they spend travelling, as this seems to count against their productivity. And they don't report the amount of time they spend doing nothing – it's a question you can't easily ask without provoking strike action.

For planning any moves to Smart Flexibility, this kind of information is vital. It provides a baseline, helps in the planning of new ways of working, and will help in measuring their impacts.

Outline Storage Audit

At first site auditing storage wouldn't seem to have a lot to do with flexible working. But the relationship is intimate and practical, in two respects:

1. Nothing tethers people to unproductive working practices like needing to access files and physical materials. Getting rid of paper is vital to untethering the workforce to worksmarter and more flexibly.
2. All that storage takes up place on the office floor. It's a very expensive use of prime office space, and it needs to be reduced to a minimum both to save costs and make way for new collaborative flexible working environments.

At the stage of building the business case, getting an overview of the scale of the issues and the potential for reduction is required. There are more details about this in Chapter 6.

Measuring Travel

How much people travel can be picked up in part through this process. The advantage of this is that it ties travel into particular patterns of working. In any organisation, though, there will also be other ways of recording travel, through reimbursement of expenses, fleet records, centrally booked travel, and so on. These provide the big picture of company travel, and it's something chief finance officers are always looking at to find ways of reducing costs. Pulling together all this information is not always easy, but it is worth doing it and having the picture broken down by department and team, to measure the impacts of change.

Many companies responded to the recession by introducing a travel freeze. This can be very painful on the front line and can damage productivity as well as save money. Working more flexibly and using collaboration technologies are part of the solution, and part of building the business case for change includes targeting reductions in business travel and quantifying the costs of alternative solutions.

Business travel is one part of work-related travel. Commuting is the other part, and employers should be concerned about this too. Measuring employees' journeys to and from work and targeting reductions in them forms a legitimate part of the business case for Smart Flexibility. This is in two respects:

1. Both business travel and commuting should be counted in when looking at the environmental footprint of working practices.
2. Reduced commuting as an employee benefit is part of the 'sell' to gain buy-in from staff.

There is another financial consideration too when looking at the impacts on reduced commuting. This relates to whether expenses should be paid to staff when they work from home. For most staff savings from reduced commuting will considerably outweigh any increases in domestic bills for heating and electricity.

Auditing Technology Provision and Use

Using new technologies has a key role to play in the strategic implementation of Smart Flexibility. The technologies and processes that people use currently play a key role in either tethering people to traditional working styles or liberating them to work smarter. So it's important at the outset to have an appraisal of what people use, and what has to change. From this the costs of both change and future support can be calculated.

Technology audits can throw up some unexpected results. In one organisation I worked with it emerged there were 1.5 computers per member of staff. This was down to the haphazard ways that laptops were handed out, under authority from middle managers. And the great majority of laptops were, of course, issued to managers. In some cases managers were also kitted out with a computer at home, and so in effect had three sets of office equipment: home, mobile and office.

Telephony needs to become more flexible to support flexible working. Inflexible telephones anchor people not only to the office but to particular desks. Simply providing mobile phones or smart phones, as tends to happen when people first become mobile, can be an expensive solution. More integrated solutions are needed that allow people to be mobile in the office and beyond, and as far as possible operate seamlessly as part of the corporate telephony network. We look at the range of solutions in Chapter 7.

Part of the technology audit will be looking at existing telephony and IT contracts, what they support, what they don't, and what the scope is for innovation.

A close look at existing processes is also needed. It may be that paper-based processes are a brake on flexibility, and investment is needed to bring them online. Or it may be that there has been substantial investment in enterprise systems that in principle could facilitate much greater flexibility, but no advantage has been taken of this potential. In any case, the point of the investigation is to identify the levels of investment needed to set up the technology platform that will support Smart Flexibility.

Before setting out on this audit, it's important to have a clear vision of the future ways of working in the organisation. If the vision is not clear, proposed changes will sooner or later run into the buffers of existing priorities. The role of those carrying out the audit is not to see to what extent the existing technology strategy can support flexible working and stop there. The point is to see how both the strategy and provision need to change to maximise the benefits from flexible working. That tends to mean asking some uncomfortable questions, challenging assumptions and occasionally treading on some toes.

Auditing processes is not only a preparation for getting existing processes online to be available to people who may in future work remotely. If everyone thinks the systems are not fit for purpose already, making them available for remote access has limited value. It's an opportunity for rethinking what is being done, how it's being done, where it's being done and who is doing it.

It's sometimes assumed that the basic equation for costs when implementing flexible work is property and travel costs go down, and ICT costs go up. But this is not necessarily so. Unpacking the way work is done and repackaging it more effectively in a Smart Flexibility context can bring substantial savings too, leveraging additional value out of IT investments.

Measuring Existing Flexible Work Practices ...

How flexible are organisations before they start to get serious about flexibility? Usually this is another unknown. Organisations usually know the range of flexible work options available, but probably don't have an accurate picture of the actual take-up, unless perhaps it is very small.

Sometimes the take-up of different options is very uneven. One department may have a large number of part-time posts, while another may have none. Bearing in mind that 27 per cent of jobs in the UK are part-time, it ought to be a surprise when there are no part-time posts in any department. Lack of flexible work options can be associated with problems in recruitment or retention, gender imbalances, or age imbalances with a lower than average number of parents in the workforce.

These kinds of issues are best picked up through a specially designed Smart Flexibility survey. It's not sufficient to tack a few questions on to the annual staff satisfaction survey. It needs to be much more targeted and focused on the information needed for changing working practices.

... and Measuring Demand for Flexibility

Understanding what kinds of flexibility employees are looking for is essential for planning the implementation of Smart Flexibility. And there is no better way than asking them.

Sometimes employers are very hesitant about doing this. They fear letting the genie out of the bottle. They worry about raising expectations that they feel the organisation can't – or possibly won't – fulfil. They don't want to ask a question when possibly they don't want to hear the answer. When senior managers take this kind of defensive approach, it's worth delving a little bit deeper and trying to find out why.

Probably underlying it are assumptions that changing the ways of working will be disruptive, and there may be a reluctance to believe the possible benefits. Questions within a structured interview process may elicit resistance from managers, expressed in fears about the impacts on teamwork, on performance management and on costs. Sometimes underlying these concerns are personal fears of losing private offices, and the status that goes with it, and of weak management skills becoming exposed.

This is why awareness-raising amongst senior management is such an important part of the process at the outset. If you get to a stage of detailed investigation, and senior managers are trying to block key aspects of it, there's sure to be more trouble ahead. To compromise for the sake of pacifying a recalcitrant manager or two is recklessly short-term, and has to be avoided. But if he or she has signed up to the shared vision, this shouldn't be a problem.

It's important to be clear about the consequences of limiting the investigation. If you don't ask about the kinds of flexibility that people want and which could be operationally practicable, there's a crucial slice of evidence missing for future planning. For example, knowing the extent to which people could work away from the office, or work in the office but at different times, is crucial for future space planning. It's important to know this when projecting the amount of new technology investment that is needed.

Asking the question doesn't necessarily mean you are going to implement every form of flexible working, and it's perfectly possible to make this clear during the consultation process. But as full an exploration as possible is necessary. With that evidence it is possible to build scenarios looking at a range of options, examining the costs and benefits of each.

In the next chapter we take a look in more detail about gathering this evidence.

What Kind of Space Would You Like to Work In?

The process of building the business case also involves canvassing views about current working environments and preferences for the future. Asking people their views on the best and worst features of their present working environment throws up a multitude of useful insights.

I can more or less guarantee that top of the list in any survey for most liked features will be 'colleagues'/'interaction with great colleagues' and so forth. Top of the list for worst features will be aspects of the physical environment such as poor air quality, temperature control, toilets, and so on, whichever happen to be the case. And after that will be 'distractions', or as some people put it 'disruptive/noisy colleagues'. So – people good, people bad: it depends on who they are and what you are trying to do at the time.

I find people are open and honest when they are genuinely consulted about their working environments, and about how they think they should change. They enjoy being involved in aspects of redesigning their working environments, and will say what they think they need. Of course they are not unanimous, and will ask for contradictory features, and a few may ask for things that are contrary to the aim of the Smart Flexibility project – such as for more storage, or for a private office for their team.

And apart from the office, there will also be feedback about where else people want to work, or feel they could work more effectively if they had the tools.

So out of all this should come a picture of the types of spaces and facilities that people need in order to work effectively in the future, and that is important for assessing the levels of investment needed.

Factoring in Productivity Increases

Flexible working tends to be more productive, though productivity can be quite slippery to measure. We take a closer look at this in Chapter 10. Examples of the types of implementations where productivity increases may be a particular focus include:

- Moving telephone-based customer services or data processing onto a home-based footing: differences in productivity can be examined on a historic basis and also compared with office-based performance.
- Introducing flexible hours working in the context of changing hours of operation to meet customer requirements better.
- Setting up field workers to work more effectively on the road, so as to increase customer contact time.
- Moving processes online to reduce the time taken (an element of change that supports most forms of flexible working).
- Improving team performance by introducing collaboration technologies and techniques, for better cohesion of distributed and virtual teams.

Establishing metrics at the outset is crucial to evaluating the success of the project. Many evaluations of flexible working are done on the basis of asking employees and managers if productivity has increased. This can be valuable, but it's also possible to set 'harder' metrics in place as part of the business plan, and setting targets as part of the justification for investment. This is the approach being taken by Fife Council (see the case study in Chapter 10).

There can be headcount issues in here too. If you've streamlined internal processes, the same work can be done more efficiently by fewer people. If home-based customer-service staff are answering 20 per cent more calls, is it time to reduce headcount in this area, or an opportunity to expand sales and marketing operations?

Recruitment, Retention and Absence

Some organisations introduce flexible working specifically to deal with problems in staff recruitment and retention, or with staff absence. These are areas where the existing situation should not be too hard to discover, and where improvements can be measured fairly easily.

Organisations like the AA and the East Riding of Yorkshire Council have introduced home-based working specifically to deal with recruitment problems, and have succeeded in reducing staff turnover. Ensuring staff loyalty, especially in hard-to-fill roles, has immense business value. The Chartered Institute of Personnel and Development calculates that the average cost of recruitment in the UK is £7,500 for senior managers and £2,500 for other employees (CIPD 2011a). Though this has dipped over the last couple of years, it's still a substantial cost. And when normal economic times return after the downturn, we can expect these costs to rise again.

Absenteeism usually falls when flexible working is introduced. Average absence rates in the UK are 5.7 days per year per employee in the private sector, and 9.1 in the public sector (CIPD 2011b). The average 7.7 days per year means a loss to the UK economy of 220 million working days and £19.5 billion. The median figure is £673 per worker per year, £800 in the public sector. It doesn't take long to do the maths to work out the potential savings in an organisation if absence is a problem.

The East Riding of Yorkshire Council introduced home-based working in its benefits department to reduce staff turnover and sickness. According to the Audit Commission (Audit Commission 2006a), by doing this they reduced staff turnover from 35 per cent a year to 10 per cent, and sickness absence from 8 per cent to 3.4 per cent. In the process they saved £104,000 over three years while at the same time achieving service improvements.

Halving absence rates to achieve below national average rates is a legitimate target to have within a flexible working project. The biggest growth area in reported reasons for absence is in stress-related mental health issues, and flexible work can help in this regard, particularly if coupled with a positive approach to well-being in the workplace.

Flexible working also helps people work when they are not feeling a hundred per cent but know they are still well enough to do some work. Nine hours or more out the house and sniffling and coughing through the day is too much to take, but they still want to work. It's also the case that some parents feel compelled to 'throw a sickie' when their kids are ill or when there is a childcare crisis, even if it means their struggling to work at another time when they really are ill. Allowing the flexibility to put together alternative arrangements helps to cut sickness absence, though of course flexible working cannot be a regular substitute for proper childcare, or for essential sick-leave.

MEASURING THE BENEFITS AT BT

BT is one of the pioneers of flexible and smart working in the UK. What makes BT especially valuable as a case study is not only the track record of developing new ways of working, but the fact that for many years now the figures that appear in their case studies are audited internally and externally.

Their journey into flexible working began around 1990 with the introduction of flexible working on a limited basis. In the early 1990s they became an advocate of teleworking, and I remember their producing one of the first online calculators for mileage and emissions reduction from home-based working. They also ran some of the earliest corporate teleworking pilots in Europe.

BT stepped up the pace of migrating to smarter working in the late 1990s with their Options 2000 programme. By 2005 they had reduced desks in central London from 10,000 to 3,000 and cut the number of BT offices in central London from 23 to just 5. The company's headquarters in the City of London was transformed with new open areas, meeting rooms and 1,600 shared workstations to accommodate not just people who worked there every day, but also 8,000 mobile employees who use the space for meetings and hotdesking on a daily basis.

This is interesting as a comparator for many organisations that are only now beginning to take smarter working to this kind of level. However, time doesn't stand still and BT has moved forward with its BT Workstyle model, which has been picked up by many other organisations. This identifies five separate flexible work-styles:

- Team Desk Worker (the employee shares a desk, and the default work style for the majority of employees).
- Allocated Desk Worker (the employee has his or her own full-time desk space).
- Mobile Office Worker (based at a specific BT building no more than one day on average per week and does not need dedicated office space).
- Occasional Home Worker (contractually based at a BT building and works from a flexi-desk or a team zone but regularly works from home).
- Home-Based Worker (the employee is equipped with a broadband connection, PC and related equipment at home).

Today, 65,000 of BT's 94,000 employees work flexibly in some way. The benefits to the business (and employees) are considerable:

- Property-estate cost savings of £590 million per year within 5 years of the Workstyle programme.
- Annual travel cost savings of £30 million.
- Absenteeism is reduced by 63 per cent among flexible employees.
- Flexible employees are 20 per cent more productive than their office-based counterparts.
- BT post-maternity leave retention rate is 98 per cent compared with the UK average of 47 per cent.
- Conferencing removes the need for 1.5 million return journeys per year, saving BT people equivalent of 1,800 years of commuting.
- Reduced consumption of 12 million litres of fuel a year (=54,000 tonnes of CO_2).

- CO_2 emissions reduced by 58 per cent between 1996 and 2008 (with the aim to reduce them by 80 per cent in 2016).
- Business resilience in the event of transport disruptions, pandemics or adverse weather.

BT is now preparing to move on to a third wave of flexible working. Worksmart 2015 is a major global programme, with a group board-level focus, that will take flexible working to the next stage. Involving every business function – property, people, technology and security – Worksmart 2015 will further transform working practice at BT.

Worksmart 2015 carries on with the transformational focus of earlier programmes but delivers a much greater focus on introducing much more flexible practices into those areas where flexible working has not traditionally been applied. This shifts the emphasis away from home and mobile working, practices which are already very well established within BT, and towards flexible working and desk-sharing for those employees who work full-time in the office. Until now, BT has had good success in supporting those people who work 100 per cent of their time at a desk to adopt some form of flexible working, but the next stage will see a much more structured move to completely unallocated desking throughout the organisation.

Dave Dunbar, Head of BT Workstyle, is a passionate advocate of flexible working. According to Dave, 'Flexible working is absolutely central to BT's competitiveness. Flexible working – at every level of seniority – is routine, not the exception. Not only does it help us to keep on improving our cost base and productivity but it brings important personal benefits, such as a better work-life balance and underpins the resilience of our business in turbulent times'.

Work-Life Balance – Can You Measure It?

Using Smart Flexibility as a way to deal with recruitment, retention and absence problems is, to a large degree, about enabling employees to balance their lives better, reducing stress and work-life conflicts, and stimulating greater loyalty and motivation into the bargain. But can you actually measure work-life balance itself?

The hard measures are those outlined above, to do with recruitment, retention and absence, and also productivity which we look at in more depth in Chapter 10. Softer metrics can be developed to measure work-life balance in a non-monetised way by looking at the impacts on staff satisfaction and staff engagement, and asking specifically about employees' perceptions of their work-life balance and conflicts. Using surveys before and after change, asking staff to rate statements such as 'I enjoy my job', I enjoy working for my company', I feel stressed at work' (and so on), can measure any improvements. This can subsequently be monitored on an annual basis to see if your Smart Flexibility and/or work-life balance programmes are having an impact.

If improved staff satisfaction with their work-life balance is accompanied by improvements in the hard business measures, then there is a positive correlation worth making a song and dance about in company communications.

One-third of non-manual employers report that stress is the most common cause of absence, and this can also be monitored to see if flexible working is having an impact in reducing it. And around 40 per cent of employers put home/family issues in their top five reasons for absence in 2011. So there are issues around health and absence that relate to work-life balance that can be monitored.

Benefits, Costs and Return on Investment

From gathering evidence in these categories, it's time to build the business case. You've got benefits that can be measured, and you've got a clear baseline about where you are starting from. And you've got a clear idea of costs. Table 4.1 summarises the main areas of costs and benefits. From these it should be possible to get a clear picture of the return on investment.

It's possible that, seeing the scope of this, some people thinking about Smart Flexibility may want to run a mile. It's all too much, and a long way from introducing a few flexible working options to make staff happy. At the outset, I said this is an approach to maximise the benefits by achieving wins on as many fronts as possible.

For some organisations, some parts of it may not be seen as being relevant or crucial. It may be they don't want to change to flexible working environments or move to desk-sharing, though they are interested in improving productivity, reducing travel, and reducing absence and staff turnover. Or it may be that their focus is primarily on becoming more mobile and using property much more effectively, while being less concerned about recruitment and retention.

Even so, an investigation of all the issues is worth doing to see if there are areas for improvement that have not initially been considered. A more comprehensive approach is more likely to deliver the benefits, and to create a more robust business case for change.

Table 4.1   Benefits and costs of implementation

Main areas of benefit	Main areas of costs
– Property disposal – Facilities costs reduction – Productivity improvements – Travel reduction – Reduced environmental footprint of work – Recruitment/retention – Absence reduction – Work-life balance	– Refurbishment or new build – Facilities costs – Technology kit and infrastructure – Culture change – Continuing support – Project management

CHAPTER 5 *Who Can Work Flexibly?*

'People issues' are central to Smart Flexibility, and this is the first of four chapters dealing with the human factor. This one examines the issues around who can work more flexibly, and what kinds of work can be appropriate. It also looks at the balance between the individual's aspirations for working more flexibly and the business issues around selection.

Chapter 8 looks at cultural and behavioural change, Chapter 9 looks at managing the 'Anywhere, Anytime Team', and Chapter 11 explores the issues and problems that may arise, and how to deal with them.

Do People Want to Be More Flexible?

To read some of the guides to flexible working and much of the academic research, you'd think that people are fairly evenly divided about flexible working. They list the pros and cons, and stress that flexibility isn't everyone's cup of tea. There's some truth in that, of course, but the fact is that most people do want more flexibility than traditional ways of working allow. It's like most of us are tea drinkers. We tend to take it in different ways, but there are very few who don't take it at all. (Non-British readers should take this metaphor in its cultural context!)

The same is true for flexible working. In the last chapter I stressed the importance of asking how much flexibility people want. And working in dozens of organisations, we've asked (a) whether people want more flexibility in their work, (b) how soon they want it, and (c) what kinds of flexibility they would like.

Here are the answers:

a) Usually it's only around 10–15 per cent of employees who don't want more flexibility at all.
b) The 85–90 per cent who do want more flexibility divide fairly evenly between those who want it right away or in the next year, and those who want it in the medium-to-longer term.
c) People are up for all different kinds of flexibility. The next section elaborates on this.

Usually, slightly more people want greater flexibility in their working time than want it in their place of work. In some organisations where jobs can be quite site-specific (for example, building motorways or working in a hospital), the appetite for locational flexibility is tempered by the site-specific needs of the work.

These findings can be quite shocking to senior managers, who might be expecting more resistance and who may in fact be listening to loud voices protesting against change. Possibly the voices are their own. But for people who want to push on with introducing greater flexibility, results from surveys like this are very exciting. The naysayers and the cynics are immediately put on the back foot.

There are big practical advantages in this democratic approach of consulting everyone. If you go down the focus group route of drawing together a representative sample of people to test the waters, I can more or less guarantee what the results will be. People will be asked to look at the pros and cons, and at the end will be a banal chart listing the pros and cons, the opportunities and threats, and the whole project looks much more iffy and in-the-balance than it really is.

So exercises such as focus groups need to be contextualised by seeing what the actual level of support is for change. Of course one should not ignore potential problems. But without the context, potential pitfalls can be read as insuperable obstacles to change, rather than issues where the workforce has a collective will to find solutions.

How Much Flexibility Do People Really Want?

When given a range of flexible options that employees would value for their work, they tend to favour options that give them more control over their working lives but without radically restructuring their working lives.

Table 5.1 shows the responses to having wider flexible work options in one organisation. Over 600 respondents, a mix of managers, professionals and administrative staff, gave their views on whether they would value each of the following options:

- Reduced hours (with pro-rata reduced pay).
- More flexible hours each day (for example, by starting or finishing earlier).
- More flexible choice of days worked (for example, weekends or school terms only).

Table 5.1   Preferences for different flexible working options

	Shift to part-time	More flexible hours	Flexible choice of days	Comp' working week	Office closer to home	At home 1–2 days per week	At home 3–5 days per week	Home/ office daily split
Disagree	67%	8%	21%	9%	16%	10%	30%	38%
Tend to disagree	11%	4%	7%	4%	7%	5%	25%	23%
No opinion	14%	16%	25%	15%	33%	13%	22%	18%
Tend to agree	6%	26%	21%	30%	21%	28%	8%	13%
Agree	2%	46%	26%	42%	23%	43%	15%	8%
% agree/ tend to agree	8%	72%	47%	72%	44%	71%	23%	21%

- Compressed working week (for example, full-time spread over 4-day week or 9-day fortnight).
- Working in an office closer to home for some or all of the week.
- Working at home 1–2 days per week.
- Working at home 3–5 days per week.
- Spreading each day between working at home and at the office.

The questions were posed in the format: 'Please respond to the following: "I would like to work more flexible working hours each day (for example, choose to start or finish earlier or later)"'.

In almost every implementation I have been involved in, the three most favoured options are:

- More flexible working hours.
- Compressed working week.
- Working from home 1–2 days per week.

There are a number of key observations on the responses from this survey:

- Though part-time work is the focus of many campaigns about flexible working for people with caring responsibilities, it is not so greatly in demand from people already in work. About half of those who would value this option are people over 45.
- More flexibility in working time is in high demand, even amongst those already working 'core hours' flexitime. People want to be treated as grown-ups, capable of making mature decisions about when they can start and finish their working day.
- Working at home is valued – but for 1–2 days per week, rather than the whole week for most people. This is important to remember when discussion focuses on potential problems like isolation or the breakdown of teamwork. When expressing fears, people tend to speak in all-or-nothing terms, but very few people want to work full time from home.
- In this case, the 'home/office daily split' option is not feasible for many people, as it is a London-based organisation and people tend to live far away and/or have fearsome journeys. Levels of interest in this option depend very much on the distance that employees live from work. When this option increases in popularity, the 'office nearer to home' option decreases correspondingly, because the main office is near enough for most people.
- The options can often be combined. People working flexible hours may also work at home or in local offices, and may also work part-time. Any of the flexible hours options may be combined with any of the flexible place options.

The answers to such surveys should not be treated as an *X Factor* vote, with the least popular options dropping off the end or forced to sing for survival. It is important to consider the work-style preferences of the minority as well as the majority. That few people want to reduce to part-time or split the day between home and office does not mean that it should be ruled out as an option. The fact that half those interested in moving to part-time are older workers has something important to say about aspirations for phased retirement amongst the organisation's older workers, perhaps.

So – the short answer to the question is that people want all kinds of flexibility. And they usually have a good appreciation of the business constraints and benefits too.

Who Is Most Likely to Want Flexibility?

Having said that most people would like more flexibility, it's also true that some groups of people are more likely to feel a pressing need for it. The two groups most likely to favour greater flexibility are:

a) People with caring responsibilities.
b) People with longer journeys to work.

Parents of children under 17 (that is, those covered by the UK legislation) make up about 30 per cent of the UK workforce. They are significantly more likely than non-parents to want flexible working now rather than at some future date, and are far more likely to agree, as opposed to 'tend to agree', with the flexible work options in Table 5.1. It's not hard to appreciate why this is so. It gives them greater flexibility to meet the various demands on the different fronts in their lives.

There's also a clear correlation between journey distance and the demand for flexible working, as Table 5.2 shows. This survey is from an organisation that already has flexitime and a positive approach to work-life balance, but has not as yet adopted a strategic approach to Smart Flexibility.

Options that allow people with longer journeys to organise their working time and/ or their working location so that they can avoid travelling, or avoid travelling so far, are significantly more favoured. It is not only the home-working and local office options that are proportionally more popular, but also changing the days they work and, for those who live furthest away, having a compressed working week. Having more flexible hours each day offers no great advantages for people with longer journeys.

Table 5.2   The relationship of journey time to demand for flexible working

	Shift to part-time	More flexible hours	Flexible choice of days	Comp' working week	Office closer to home	At home 1–2 days per week	At home 3–5 days per week	Home/office daily split
< 60 minutes return	11%	61%	36%	56%	24%	57%	13%	20%
60–90 minutes	9%	57%	36%	52%	31%	60%	16%	17%
90–120 minutes	3%	59%	38%	50%	39%	65%	18%	18%
> 120 minutes	10%	58%	40%	65%	62%	80%	23%	16%
All	*9%*	*60%*	*38%*	*55%*	*39%*	*65%*	*17%*	*18%*

Many studies of teleworking have shown that early adopters of telework tend to be amongst people who have longer journeys to work. They have a particular incentive to try a new approach (Lake and Cherrett 2002).

There are interesting psychological impacts that arise from the experience of longer or shorter journeys. If people are asked to respond to the statement, 'It is essential that I am present in the office every day', the answers tend to vary according to how far they live from work. Those who live closest to work are more likely to feel that their presence is essential in the office, and those who live furthest feel it is least essential every day. I'm sure this can't really be the case. What is happening is that those with short journeys are not challenged in the same way to think about going to the office that those who live furthest away do.

Conventional Wisdom – A Hotchpotch of Challengeable Assumptions

There is a great deal of conventional wisdom about what kinds of roles and people are suitable for flexible working. There are countless challengeable assumptions, all based on traditional ways of working and partial understandings of how flexible working operates.

The following extract is a quite standard example of conventional wisdom. It's taken from the US Government's *Implementation Manual for Telework* (GSA, 2001) which informed their approach to teleworking until superseded in April 2011:

> *Work may not be suitable for telecommuting if the employee needs to have extensive face-to-face contact with the supervisor, other employees, clients, or the general public; if the employee needs frequent access to material which cannot be moved from the main office; if the agency cannot provide any special facilities or equipment that are necessary; or if it would be too costly for the agency to duplicate the same level of security at the alternative workplace.*

What are the assumptions here? The work considered suitable for telework is primarily professional work, particularly knowledge work. It is the 'unsuitable work' section that is perhaps most in need of challenge. Here are some of the assumptions:

- Face-to-face contact with a supervisor, colleagues or the public has to be in person.
- Face-to-face contact has to be in the office.
- Supervisors must be in the office.
- Material will be kept in a form that necessitates regular attendance in the office.

Underlying these assumptions is a deeper assumption: that telework will be an exception from the norm, and 'normal working' will remain unchanged.

Many organisations with high levels of contact with the public have introduced home-based working so that people can be closer to the customers they serve. It's quite an astonishing assumption, in some ways, that to be close to the public, the public must come in to the office to see you.

Security is a serious issue, particularly for government organisations for whom breaches of security can be very embarrassing, and sometimes damaging too if confidential information about vulnerable people is leaked. But security is also too convenient an escape clause for people opposed to Smart Flexibility or not sufficiently motivated to think it through. All kinds of organisations dealing with secure information enable remote working, from banks to social services to intelligence agencies. There are ways to enable secure remote working. And it's often pointed out that most high-profile security lapses have come through traditional routes, like leaving a briefcase in a car, rather than from remote working.

The point of quoting this is that it is quite typical of assumptions I still come across when doing workshops with managers.

Another key assumption comes through under 'Employee Characteristics' (from *Implementation Manual for Telework* (GSA 2001)):

> *The characteristics of an employee are particularly important. The employee should be an organized, highly disciplined, and conscientious self-starter who requires minimal supervision.*

The assumption here is that remote work is unsupervised work. This is not true. And we know that most people who 'telework' do not do so for the majority of the time, so the assumption of isolation is also up for challenge. A little later in this chapter I take a closer look at the whole question of trying to specify employee characteristics, and the muddle that passes for good advice.

Which Kinds of Flexibility for Which Jobs?

The last example is one that particularly relates to home-based working. But similar ideas arise for all kinds of flexible working.

The Equalities and Human Rights Commission in the UK have thrown their weight behind flexible working, which they feel is a key factor in enabling equality. They have produced some excellent research and guidance in this field. A recent publication, dramatically entitled *Enter the Time Lords*, makes a strong case for employers to introduce more flexible working options.

They recommend considering the nature of different roles in terms of their location dependence or independence, and their time dependence or independence, as can be seen in Figure 5.1. This is one way of seeing how different kinds of jobs may have more or less flexibility. The authors have come up with some catchy sci-fi-influenced names as well, to form a basic typology.

To my mind, this is a great start for discussions. But you only have to start talking about the jobs put into each section to stimulate a whole lot of questioning. People will start to slide some of the roles into different categories, find exceptions, and mention real-life examples of organisations or individuals that do it differently.

It's About Tasks, Not Jobs

This kind of approach is great in workshops, but should be seen as the first step in awareness-raising. If you approach flexible working from the point of view of conventional wisdom about jobs, key opportunities for greater efficiency and choice will be missed.

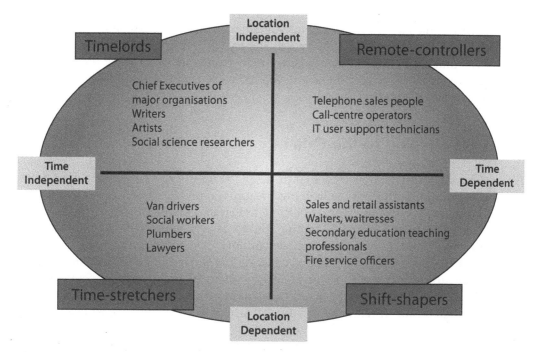

Figure 5.1   Plotting different kinds of remote working

Source: *Enter the Timelords*, EHRC, 2007.

Plumbers are on the grid as being 'Time independent, location dependent'. They have to go where the jobs are, and anyone who's waited in for a plumber knows just how time independent they can be.

But it's not wholly true, is it? Some of a plumber's jobs are extremely time-critical, especially when they are part of a project where their work fits into a particular sequence alongside other building disciplines, or when dealing with emergencies. And British Gas fitters have for some time now been cut loose from daily attendance at a depot, and use home as a base, so they have a degree of location independence. And admin, scheduling and marketing tasks associated with plumbing work are now pretty much location independent too.

In the same part of the grid as the plumbers are lawyers. Are they 'location dependent' as the grid says? Yes, they have to be in court sometimes. And yes, they have appointments with clients. But, despite the conservatism of the sector, much work can be done anywhere, anytime. The same goes for social workers. It may be a big leap for many of them to think like that, but all the same it's true.

If we think back to Figure 4.3 about the time and place of activities in the last chapter, then we know that it's necessary first to get a profile of what people do, and where and when they do it. Whether the time and location of work can change depends on:

a)   The individual task.
b)   How tasks are grouped together.
c)   How tasks are assigned between individuals.
d)   What resources are used for the task.

Dealing with whole jobs is a very blunt instrument when it comes to scoping the potential for flexibility. If you take the job you've got, and try to do it in exactly the same way but at different times and/or in different places, it may not work. But shuffle the pack a bit, rearrange the tasks you do and the media you use to do them, and suddenly you can be more flexible and more effective.

What Tethers You to the Office?

It's important to critique the factors that tie people to traditional working practices when considering what kinds of flexible working are appropriate for which role.

In traditional ways of working, people are tethered to places and time of work (a) by the need to use something, and (b) by the need to be available. Figure 5.2 illustrates the factors that can stand in the way of flexible working:

Often these factors are a combination of locational and temporal constraining factors. For example, using the paper files in the office has to be within office opening times. Similarly, being available to give instant responses to the boss means being in the same place at the same time, usually the default standard of 9–5. Or, perhaps, whenever he or she feels it's convenient for you to be in attendance.

Most of these tethering factors can be altered. Paper files can be replaced almost entirely by electronic ones, accessible anywhere, anytime. IT systems and tools should be accessible outside of the office, unless very highly specialised, for example, lab equipment. For the most part, the things that people believe can only be available in the office (for example,

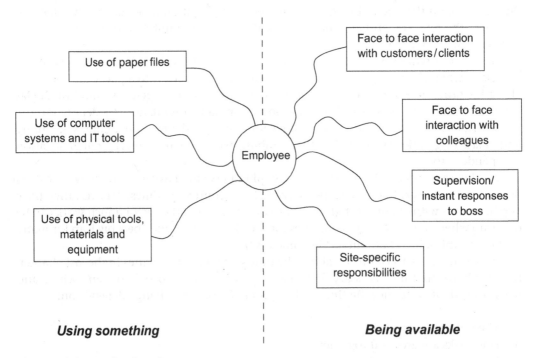

Figure 5.2   Tethering factors

particular databases or software) can be made accessible and used remotely as long as there is the will to do it.

Face-to-face interaction may be necessary. But in global teams people know that this will rarely be *physically* face to face. What is so distinctive about local teams to make physical presence a *necessity* for interaction? The answer is that is not necessity, but habit.

Most of these factors can be changed to have less of a tethering effect. There may be some that cannot – or not yet – be reformed. These can often be grouped so that physical presence at specified times does not constrain the whole of working life.

Working from a job title or from a generic term like 'mobile professional' is not adequate for designing appropriate new models of flexibility. It comes back to analysing the tasks involved and seeing how they can be made 'footloose'.

Note: using this kind of graphic, or building up to it, in a workshop setting is a valuable exercise for awareness-raising and analysis of working practices. Participants like to suggest other dimensions apart from 'Using Something' and 'Being Available'. Key ones are perhaps 'Personal Choice' and 'Lack of an Alternative'. I'm not sure 'Personal Choice' is valid in terms of a tethering factor – after all it is a choice rather than being tied down there. But not having a proper alternative is a more compelling factor for driving people to be in the office. And again one can analyse factors that make the alternative locations unsuitable: lack of (separate) space at home, house full of noisy children, and so on. I remember one person in a survey simply said, 'My husband is retired' as being a reason for not being able to work at home. I suppose you'd have to meet him to fully understand that one.

Psychological or Personality Profiling for Flexible Work

How do you select flexible workers? Are there key characteristics that should be looked for?

There are quite a number of organisations that specify a particular personality profile as part of a test for eligibility for flexible working. Many guides to flexible work make recommendations to proceed along these lines (for example, Verbeke et al. 2008, Telework Association 2003, Department for Employment 1994, Elston and Orrell 2005 – and many more). And I have seen many in-house guides work along similar lines. My advice is to approach with caution!

Most of the advice on the kind of personality required to be eligible for flexible work – in particular remote working – ranges from the banal to the plain wrong. A typical list would say eligible employees should be:

- Highly focused.
- Self-sufficient.
- Self-disciplined.
- Trustworthy.
- Flexible.
- Well organised.
- Good decision-makers.
- Proven/high performers.
- Good communicators.

While these attributes may have you nodding your head at first, it is as well to think about the corollary of this. Which of your employees do you actually expect to be:

- Poorly focused.
- Dependent.
- Un(self-)disciplined.
- Untrustworthy.
- Inflexible.
- Poorly organised.
- Poor decision-makers.
- Unproven/low performers.
- Poor communicators.

Because these are the ones that by the same token will be left working standard hours in the office. That'll be fun.

This highlights the weakness in this kind of personal profiling for flexible workers. Wouldn't it be better if all your employees had the attributes or character traits of your flexible workers? When people come through the office door – either physically or virtually – there should be an expectation that they should be wearing a professional personality that includes all these positive attributes. If they can't do this, then their problems aren't only with flexible working.

It's possible that some people who fail this kind of eligibility test might prove to be trainable. Others, under constant surveillance and occasional whippings may be dragooned into working effectively. But probably the best advice is: if anyone fails to meet these requirements, best to lose them from your organisation as soon as possible! Caging the duffers in the office is no solution.

The other main objections to this kind of approach are:

- It's invidious to make judgements on this kind of basis. It puts additional pressure on the manager, and can cause resentment between employees who (possibly rightly) perceive themselves as being treated unequally.
- It risks falling into the trap of treating flexible work options as a kind of privilege, one conferred on the fortunate as an exception to the norm of working 9–5 in the office.
- Looking for some of those attributes may just be plain wrong sometimes. For example, some people who are poor communicators are in fact absolutely great at their job. They may actually be longing to be away from the distractions of the office when it's full of other people. Johnny No-Mates may only communicate in grunts, but he's the best programmer/designer/accounts clerk you could find. His challenging but existentialist T-shirt says 'L'enfer: c'est les autres'. Working when no one else is around him may be his idea of heaven. Who are we to say he shouldn't authenticate his existence in splendid isolation?
- Conventional wisdom says flexible workers should be good decision-makers. However, for many jobs that can be worked flexibly, being a good decision-maker is not in the least relevant. As long as they decide to turn up and do the work, that's fine. Many of these attributes betray a managerial/professional bias – the same kind of bias we find in practice when surveys find managers working at home yet not trusting their admin staff to do likewise.

It's Really about *Performance*

Underlying the list of positive attributes is really the question of *performance*. To deny the option of working flexibly, when in principle the work could be done flexibly, is more or less to admit at the outset that you're not confident about managing performance. If employees 'fail' this kind of personal characteristics eligibility test, it's really an indication that their performance isn't being managed effectively when they are working standard hours in the office.

The assumptions in using such criteria for selection will undermine the transition to a new working culture and new methods of management. These criteria are saying that there is still an expectation of management by presence, and that this is both essential and the most effective form of management for a big section of the workforce. However, these are the kinds of expectation that the smart organisation needs to be moving away from, rather than reinforcing.

Interestingly, the 'right to request' legislation expressly rules out using personal characteristics as the basis for making a decision to approve or reject a request for flexible working. It has to be based on business considerations only. Past performance could be an issue if it has been flagged up as a cause for concern before, or if there is a disciplinary issue lurking in the background. But if it's just a question of thinking this person is a bit scatty and you doubt their ability to organise themselves, then that's ruled out.

To me, the funny thing about this approach is this. Lucy is presently under your watchful eye, and is undisciplined and a poor timekeeper. Therefore you don't let her work from home or organise more flexible working hours. The result is that you keep her in the office, working the same hours as you so you can keep an eye on her (assuming you are also in the office at the same times). However, her being in the office hasn't made a difference to her scatty work style so far and is a distraction to you. What makes you think that the solution is to perpetuate this?

The point is that that there is something not working here *already* that needs to be addressed. And if not, you've got a problem whether she's in the office or out of it. The real question is, does Lucy achieve results or not? If she does, and her work is not absolutely time-critical, then having some degree of time flexibility may mean that timekeeping is no longer an issue. As for being undisciplined in her style of working, allowing her to work somewhere else may reduce the intensity of the problem as long as she can deliver the results. And if she does not, then appropriate action can be taken – and that doesn't necessarily mean hauling her back into the office, which is where the problems began.

One halfway-house for discussing personal characteristics is to have a checklist that the individual and the manager both consider and then discuss. For example:

- Do you need the help of a manager or colleague to start or complete jobs?
- Can you work your own way through most problems without help?
- Are you good at absorbing and acting upon new information on your own?
- Are you able to judge the quality of your work and be motivated by a job well done without the need for someone else telling you?
- Do you draw your energy and enthusiasm from friends and colleagues?
- Do you enjoy working on your own most of the time?
- Are you able to organise your time effectively?
- Can you identify the signs of stress in yourself and others?

I think the idea of working through such questions and having a discussion is not a bad one. But I would want to question some of the assumptions about being out there on one's own, not able to draw on support from one's manager or energy from one's colleagues. A good implementation will set all the mechanisms in place for good team interaction. And in most cases, remote working will be for only part of the time, so it's possible to over-hypothesise the danger of isolation and the reserves of self-sufficiency needed to deal it.

Myers Briggs, Generation Y, Aquarius, Year of the Rabbit ...

Is it possible to do some kind of personality profiling to find aptitude for flexible working? There have been discussions around this, for example, David Lamond (Daniels et al. 2000) who discusses approaches to personality in relation to telework and concludes that it's a pretty complex arena due the different kinds of work involved, though he still makes a tentative stab at it.

And there are people who hope that some kind of Myers Briggs assessment can identify possible aptitudes for flexible work, that is, being able to identify people on a set of sliding scales of Extraversion/Introversion, Sensing/Intuition, Thinking/Feeling and Judging/Perceiving. People who go through this kind of psychometric testing will then be classified as into one of 16 possible psychological types on the Myers Briggs Type Index (MBTI), depending on the combination of positioning on these scales. You may have guessed from the subheading that I'm a little sceptical about this.

Apart from wider doubts about the method, which seems to me lacking a good evidence base and being somewhat circular in its definitions, the real point is this: flexible work is not about doing some radically different kind of work. It's about doing pretty much the same old work, only with new tools and at varying times and in a range of different places. So if you have a mix of ENTJ types and INTJ types working as a team in the office, what's the objective justification for enabling some of them to home at work two days per week and some of them not, on the basis of asking a series of questions that have nothing to do with their daily tasks or preferences?

Now there may be some interesting academic studies to be done that look at how different Myers Briggs types tend to opt or not for different working patterns. But I have seen no evidence whatsoever to suggest that it could be an accurate *predictor* of their ability to do their work on a flexible basis.

What people are doing when they suggest this is putting on their old heads and funnelling ideas about flexible work through old assumptions about work. Then essentially they are coming up with a series of personality stereotypes to match against equally artificial stereotypes of flexible work as being remote, or requiring exceptional degrees of autonomy, and so on. The result is bound to be tosh. Couched in plausible language, perhaps, but still tosh.

There are now also numerous studies and think-pieces that pigeonhole people according to generational characteristics: Baby-Boomers, Generation X, Generation Y/Millennials, and so on. I read one, for example, that said Baby-Boomers 'like face to face' and 'tend to defer to authority', while Gen Y 'is comfortable with virtual teamwork' and 'can appear to be disrespectful to more senior team members'.

When I read this I wonder:

a) Baby-Boomers deferring to authority? This must be news to anyone who was there in the 1960s and 1970s. If they can remember, that is.
b) Who invented most of this remote-working technology and first campaigned for flexible working, if not Baby-Boomers?
c) There are something like a billion people in each generational category, so how likely is it that these categories can stand up to robust scrutiny?

If we're dividing the world's population up into four categories, I think there is a good chance we may be overgeneralising a bit. We'd probably get more random hits on accuracy if we were to use the 12 categories in Western or Chinese astrological systems. So maybe Leos can be recommended for mobile teleworking roles requiring a lot of autonomy. Capricorns are most suited to home-based process work. And Sagittarius, or Year of the Monkey – better not let them out of the office at all!

That may be going over the top a little. But I hope the message makes sense. That is:

- There is no watertight way of defining personality traits.
- And there is absolutely no watertight way of matching perceived or attributed personality traits to types of flexible work.
- One can have a bit of fun with the MBTIs and other less subtle stereotypes, but in the end it's best to *stick to an analysis of the work* when planning for new ways of working.

Avoid One-Dimensional Thinking about Job Characteristics

There are also a number of tick-box methodologies doing the rounds that are intended to help make decisions about the suitability of jobs for flexible working. The ones I've seen, despite best intentions, come heavily loaded with assumptions from the old world of work.

A good example is one given in the Appendix of the otherwise excellent Acas guide to flexible working (Acas 2007). In this suitability questionnaire, people seeking flexible work have to tick boxes numbered 1 to 5. If most of the answers are 1s and 2s, then flexible working is likely to be suitable. If mostly 4s or 5s, then probably not.

By this tick-box method, if you manage more than five people, you'll score a 4 or a 5. Therefore you are not suitable for flexible working! So the assumption is basically that managers can't work flexibly: they must be based in the office.

Another question asks if the job holder has to respond to customer demand immediately, or is it longer term? If longer term, it scores 1. If immediate, it's 4 or 5. Call-centre workers need to respond immediately to customer demand, so would score 5. But they certainly can work from home, as the growing number of virtual call centres shows, and often flexible hours too for that matter. The 'tick-box suitability' approach doesn't seem to acknowledge this possibility, though.

There is an assumption in most of the tick-box approaches I've seen that those most suited to work flexibly are the solo professionals or data crunchers, people who don't need to have much personal contact with either colleagues or customers, and who can work mostly unsupervised. And these kinds of assumptions are not only wrong, but hold back the introduction of Smart Flexibility and the benefits it can deliver.

This is what I call thinking with your old head on, rather than your new head. By the standards of your old head, these assumptions are reasonable. But they are all rooted in the old ways of working.

PROMOTING A SMART COLLABORATIVE CULTURE AT BRITVIC

Britvic is one of the leading producers of soft drinks, with group revenues in the year to October 2011 of £1.3 billion. Originally famous for its range of juices and mixers, Britvic is now one of the leading branded soft drinks businesses in Europe, with a portfolio of famous brands, including Robinsons, Tango, J2O, Fruit Shoot, as well as PepsiCo brands such as Pepsi, 7UP and Mountain Dew Energy which it produces and sells in GB and Ireland. Britvic has continued to expand during the tough economic climate, with acquisitions in Ireland and France.

Since 2005 Britvic has had a focus on introducing and embedding flexible and remote working to achieve benefits across the Triple Bottom Line. And at the time of writing they are poised to move into a new headquarters building which will act as a collaborative focus for their flexible and mobile workforce.

The impetus for flexible working has come from two directions: significant investment in technology which has acted as a catalyst for change, and a recognition of the value of making Britvic 'A Great Place to Work' in order to attract and retain the best talent.

The option to work remotely applies to all staff who are laptop users, with other time-based flexible working options applying within the Supply Chain and Call Centre sites. There are also technical service staff who work at customer premises in the retail, food service and licensed trade. Their role is to install and maintain equipment in pubs, restaurants and retail outlets, so although homeworking is not an option they also have new technology that supports their being out on the road.

For other staff, from chief executive to administrative assistants, there are options to work part-time from home or work from other offices, supporting retention of those who live some distance from a Britvic site. This is particularly important for attracting talent to those roles which have scarce skills that are highly valued by the business. Regional sales staff can also use Regus offices so that they can access a professional office environment without needing to make a long drive to a Britvic site. Remote access – 'Britvic by Broadband' – is supported to give staff access to the full range of office systems and an allowance is payable to offset the cost of home broadband. Significant investment has been put into making back-office systems available electronically. Audio conferencing and messaging are used for virtual meetings, including regular use of the LiveMeeting tool. Site-to-site videoconferencing has recently been supplemented by use of Microsoft Lync which will enable more flexible use of conferencing technologies.

The changes to working practices have had both a quantitative and qualitative impact on property requirements. In 2009 Britvic reduced their main offices in Chelmsford from four floors to two. The new office in Hemel Hempstead is a similar area to the one being left behind, but is configured for collaborative working. Less than half the workspace is allocated to desks, with the remainder a variety of collaboration spaces, from a flexible auditorium that can be created by combining 4 different rooms, to small break-out spaces and privacy booths.

Sue Skinner, Head of HR, explains:

> We've tried to create an inspiring workplace so people get the most out of it when they are there. It's designed to strengthen relationships, relationships that can be built on when people are working out of the office. One quarter of the building is called 'the Hub', an area of more relaxed seating and hotdesks which we hope will be the 'heart' of Britvic in our new Head Office.
>
> With our initial drive to flexible working and our new acquisitions, there was a danger of becoming perhaps too fragmented. We needed a more accessible physical focus for the company to complement our greater ability to collaborate online.

The relationships developed are essential for the climate of trust that is central to flexible working practices. Line-manager training and induction programmes also promote and reinforce the working culture.

> It's very much about high trust and managing by results. Expectations are set for time together as a team, and individuals are clear on expected outputs, but we encourage line-manager discretion when employees look to vary their working pattern. We prefer informal arrangements rather than over-engineered policies or a bureaucratic approach. Working from home can be a great way to avoid lengthy commutes and maximises your time and personal effectiveness so you can keep those commitments outside work. And our arrangements are not just for parents, – we know everyone has commitments in their life outside work, so we also encourage people to undertake volunteering or participate in sporting and other social activities.

Helping employees achieve a good work-life balance remains a key aim for Britvic. As people have to travel to work within the congested South East of England, physical meetings are typically scheduled between 10 a.m. and 4 p.m. to allow leeway for travel and other responsibilities. Meanwhile, the focus remains on getting the job done, wherever and whenever is best for the individual and compatible with team arrangements. Sue sums up their approach:

> Flexible working is absolutely critical for the modern business. It's the way to attract and retain the best people. We've tried hard to get the balance right between the needs of the business and the needs of individual employees, and to create a physical centre for collaboration which is the heart of the company. We're delighted that our approach to flexibility has meant that we're able to retain so many of our employees during this relocation. We absolutely believe that creating such an inspiring and collaborative workspace will further enhance team-working, strengthen relationships and improve overall effectiveness.

In the Future, Flexible Work = Work

I remember hearing a paper at a European conference on 'ework'. The speaker was saying that previously in European circles ework had been referred to as 'telework'. So we had progress, he said. We'd lost the first three letters from the word, now we just had to lose the 'e'. Telework, or ework, would have come of age when we no longer talk about it. When it is just 'work'.

The same is true of the wider field of smart and flexible work. All the talk about making special arrangements for flexible work and flexible workers is predicated on the notion that there is a normal (and inflexible) thing called 'work', and flexible work is all about unusual variations to this. In this book, we are looking towards a time when flexible work is completely normal, and hopefully helping you on your way to realising this situation.

So it's imperative that we don't go down the road of setting up hurdles to leap over and hoops to jump through when creating the conditions for flexible working. We need to have arrangements where the decision about an employee's working practices are consensual and based on common sense, not box-ticking, profiling or prejudice, but instead with a clear view of the nature of the work involved and the places and times at which it can be done.

Flexible Work as Reward, Perk, Benefit or Privilege – Don't Go There!

I have often seen flexible working described as a *benefit*, or *privilege*. Certainly some managers regard flexible working as a perk – often as a perk that comes with status. It's quite common to find situations where managers and senior professionals work flexibly, while lower grades are not allowed to do so. And it can be a reward for trusted members of staff who have proved their ability.

Where companies have policies on flexible working, it is often specifically stated that flexible working is not a right. Even if not exactly called a 'privilege', careful wording of the policy often indicates that being given the option to work flexibly requires a degree of merit, and the ability to work flexibly can be withdrawn if there are managerial concerns about performance.

While there is a certain amount of common sense in reserving the right to alter working patterns if new working arrangements don't work out, I would suggest it is invidious to take such an approach. It is a recipe for arbitrary decisions, accusations of favouritism and resentment between colleagues.

Again, it is also intrinsically non-strategic. Taking a 'privilege earned' approach, on what basis are you going to plan office-accommodation needs, remote-working technology requirements, and so on? Perhaps on the basis of: 'on average each year we'll have x per cent of people trusted to work flexibly, while the rest are not'. But what does it say about a company if many or most employees are not considered worth rewarding in this way?

More importantly, taking the 'perks' approach reinforces the idea that traditional ways of working are the normal ways of working, and that flexible working is exceptional. The Smart Organisation promotes flexibility as the new normality.

New Approaches to Recruitment

Smart Flexibility should not be presented as a perk or benefit in the sense that it is a reward for good behaviour. However, it is great to present flexible working as a generalised benefit open to everyone when recruiting new staff. Survey after survey shows that people changing jobs and entering the jobs market value flexibility very highly. Some surveys also show that people would take greater flexibility in preference to a pay rise. So offering flexible working can help to make you an 'employer of choice'.

In practice, not many employers are very good yet at advertising posts on a flexible working basis. It may be that once you're in, some flexible work options may be available. But the default position for advertised posts remains regular hours, regular place.

It is quite remarkable how the approach can vary even within organisations. Department A has many people part-time, job-sharing and doing term-time working, while Department B has no part-timers at all. So Department A has, you can be sure, more working mothers while the latter has few employees with young children, and probably an interesting mix of younger and more mature workers with a bit of an age gap in the middle. Something I've found is that when this emerges through a staff survey, it's usually news to the employer. Generally, organisations do not monitor at departmental level uptake of flexible working practices or the impacts on diversity. They may monitor closely ethnicity, disability, gender and sexual orientation at the company level, but not the detailed profile of departments and how it is affected by recruitment.

As I have mentioned, in the UK we have an Employment Act that gives workers a 'right to request' flexible working. This is a help for people in eligible categories *providing they are in work already*. It does not offer any direct benefit to applicants for work, when the work is offered on a non-flexible basis.

There are two things a company can do here when recruiting:

1. They can offer jobs on a specified flexible basis, perhaps informed by particular imbalances in their existing workforce or the specifics of the role.
2. They can advertise jobs as 'normal' full-time posts, but make it clear they are genuinely open to proposals from candidates for alternative flexible working practices.

The point is that there is a huge amount of talent out there not finding suitable work because most jobs are advertised on a non-flexible basis. These people tend to fall into four categories:

- People for whom the traditional approach to workplace and working practices is disabling. That is many people with disabilities, and people with illnesses or health conditions that limit their capacity to work and/or travel.
- People with caring responsibilities – parents and carers of dependent adults.
- People with geographical challenges – that is people living in remote areas, or areas remote from the availability of their kind of work.
- People who just want to do something else as well as work for you – for example, train for the Olympics, run a part-time business, do a degree, have a portfolio career, and so on.

Some organisations like First Direct bank have really capitalised on the amount of talent that is looking for flexible work, particularly mothers looking to return to work. But it is not only large organisations. Very highly qualified people can be snapped up by smaller businesses that can offer the flexibility required even though they can't offer the wages of City firms.

Now there are specialist recruitment agencies like WorkingMums, Women Like Us and Capability Jane that work closely with large organisations and specialise in recruiting people looking for flexible work. It seems the branding of this new recruitment sector is highly gendered, though all these companies assure me that men looking for flexible work are welcome too. These companies are run by insightful and dynamic people, serving and helping to develop a real market.

From a public policy point of view, however, gender is only part of the equation. A key priority in recent years has been to reduce the large number of people who are on incapacity benefit, especially the over-50s. The government is sure many of these people could in fact work. Flexible working options are part of the equation, and at the time of writing a proposal is on the table to try to get employers advertising through government Job Centres to make all advertised posts available on a flexible working basis.

Leading Balanced Lives

From the employee side, a lot of the issues boil down to creating the best possible balance between work and the rest of life. This is not a book about work-life balance: there are many good books on this topic with a great deal of good advice for employees. This book is looking at Smart Flexibility more from the employers' side. It's about understanding how the twenty-first century employee's attitudes to work-life balance impact the new world of work, and about how employment policies can not only adapt to these demands but also harness the energy and dynamism of this trend.

'Work-life balance' doesn't describe a single phenomenon or a single strategy about balancing work and the rest of life. People have different strategies for developing the balance they want. And these strategies tend to change over time, as people develop and mature in both their work and family lives, and face different demands at different stages of life.

Christina Nippert-Eng has described the ways people view the home/work interface as an 'integration-segmentation continuum' (Nippert-Eng 1996). At one extreme is the complete separation of home and work lives, and at the other extreme is the complete integration. In practice, people position themselves, or at least their vision of the interface, at some point or points between the two extremes. And it's not simply the case that people with flexible work are integrators and people with traditional work-styles are separators, as many people who work from home like to put a clear wall between home and work activities. However, flexible working does give more opportunity for people to make mature decisions for themselves about how they want to blend home and work – or not.

Work-life conflict is a major source of stress, especially for people who have demanding roles on all fronts. Achieving a better balance is in large part about taking control of one's working life and managing the interface in one's own best interests. This is a point made by US academics Ellen Kossek and Brenda Lautsch in their book *CEO of Me: Creating a Life That Works in the Flexible Job Age* (Kossek and Lautsch 2008). Following Nippert-Eng, they set out a practical path for individuals to recognise their work-style, change it if necessary and take control of their lives. According to Kossek and Lautsch, people tend to fall into the broad categories of Integrators, Separators and Volleyers – the last category being people who ping between the other two 'flexstyles' according to the priorities of the time.

Understanding the range of work-life balance strategies is important – there is no one-size-fits-all approach. And simply having a set of work-life balance policies doesn't in itself mean that people are achieving the balance. Often there are cultural disincentives to people that prevent them opting to take up a flexible working option, because to do so makes them look the odd one out, and it can be interpreted by others as a lack of commitment. If it's the case that to get on 'you've got to put in the hours' and always be highly visible at the office, no amount of well-intentioned work-life balance initiatives are going to have a real impact:

Often managers are seeking a better balance, and according to Kossek and Lautsch can do a lot, even in the absence of top level support. By taking an approach of 'cleaning up their own back yard', and then if possible 'cleaning up the neighbourhood', they can start to influence corporate policy and culture. For managers it's a question of engaging with the aspirations and circumstances of their staff, and negotiating ways to make it happen.

And it pays off. 'Studies indicate that the availability and use of flexibility and other work-family policies is associated with higher commitment, job satisfaction, loyalty, and lower intention to turnover', say Kossek and her fellow researchers. 'Individuals who are able to use formal flexibility policies such as telecommuting and general work-family policies are likely to reciprocate with more favourable work attitudes and behaviours' (Kossek et al. 2006). We have seen examples of this in the case studies where flexible working is used to overcome recruitment and retention difficulties (AA and East Riding of Yorkshire Council).

It can also result in voluntary payback in terms of additional hours worked. A study of teleworkers from six European countries for the European SUSTEL project found that hours saved in commuting were partially paid back to the company, in a kind of 'half for me, half for you' trade-off (SUSTEL 2004). The increase in working hours is balanced by a reported increase in the hours available for non-work activities, and over 86 per cent of respondents said that teleworking gave them better control of when to work. Benefits of this include:

- Allowing parents to spend time with their children in the morning and when they return from school, and make up for it by working into the evening.
- Allowing working partners to better optimise their schedules.
- Allowing people to seize opportunities, such as taking time off on a sunny day.
- Participation in voluntary activities.

Employees recognise the value of the freedom to organise work in this way. It also promotes loyalty, as the benefits may not be easy to replicate in a new job.

Improved Health and Well-Being

Flexible working has also been associated with improved health and well-being. Making this claim risks sounding like a snake-oil salesman, but it is a finding supported in the medical research literature. A recent review of medical before-and-after studies by researchers at Durham University (Joyce et al. 2010) concluded that flexible working led to statistically significant improvements in either primary outcomes (including systolic blood pressure and heart rate; tiredness; mental health, sleep duration, sleep quality and alertness; self-rated health status) or secondary health outcomes (co-workers social support and sense of community). And no ill-health effects were reported.

According to the authors, 'The findings of this review tentatively suggest that flexible working interventions that increase worker control and choice (such as self-scheduling or gradual/partial retirement) are likely to have a positive effect on health outcomes'.

A similar finding is reported by Ellen Kossek in relation to employees' perception of their well-being in a survey of telecommuters in Fortune 500 companies: 'What seems to matter most to employee well-being was psychological constructions of flexibility regarding job control and boundary management'.

It seems the key is in being able to create working contexts that reduce the stress that comes from feelings of being not in control and facing conflicting demands. Creating such a context is actually a process of co-creation, with actions on the part of both the employer and the individual employee. Employers cannot ensure that their employees' lives are conflict-free. But they can do much to empower their employees to find solutions that eliminate the negative stresses that come from work-life conflicts. A tired, conflicted and stressed-out employee will not deliver top performance, and is more likely to seek alternative employment.

Flexible working is not a stand-alone solution to worker well-being. There are other workplace benefits and methods of engagement that have a role to play. But flexible working is certainly part of the mix.

Trust, Maturity and Autonomy

In this chapter we've looked at the people side of Smart Flexibility: roles, personal qualities, selection issues and levels of flexibility. Key principles are:

- It's not about roles, it's about tasks.
- It's kind of dumb to come up with a stereotypical personality profile for smart and flexible workers.
- The aim should be to treat employees as grown-ups, and empower them to make choices that work for them and work for the business about the times and locations of work.
- A trusted and empowered workforce will be loyal, more motivated, deliver better performance and take less time off sick.

So it's not a question of finding the well-organised and self-directing individuals in the workforce and letting them out of sight for the odd day, or letting them clock in late. It's about developing people through the application of new ways of working so that they can realise their potential as mature and loyal employees, capable of making good decisions about where and when work is done to the benefit of both the employer and themselves.

In the opening chapter we identified the quest for personal autonomy as one of the key trends in the changing context of work. Dan Pink has put forward the idea of the 'Peter Out Principle' as something that applies in corporate culture (Pink 2001). The best employees leave when the fun starts to peter out. Because while at one level work is about earning a crust and keeping the wolf from the door, for most of us this is not enough. We want work that is satisfying, psychologically rewarding, that makes us feel good about ourselves and our achievements, and which allows us some initiative and scope for innovation. In this way we authenticate our existence through our work. And this applies not only to the content of the work, but also to how we do it.

To make this happen, the organisation itself needs to mature and put more of an emphasis on trust. In Chapter 8 we'll take a closer look at this, about how to develop a culture of Smart Flexibility.

In the meantime, there are some key issues that arise from the approach I'm advocating in this chapter. And possibly I've got some senior managers and especially HR managers a little worried.

All This Autonomy – How Do You Nail It Down?

So we're creating a new workplace full of autonomous self-authenticating individuals, whom we're going to trust to do the right thing in the right place and at the right time. 'OK, dream on', says the world-weary cynic. 'Have you met some of the people I work with?'

Managing a department full of people who see themselves as 'CEO of Me' could be a bit like herding cats. There needs to be some structure, and there needs to be some policies so that people know what they can and can't do, and so they understand who is responsible for what. (I'll leave you to decide whether it's better or worse for a company to herd cats or herd sheep.)

But can these policies be created without sucking the soul out of flexible working?

If you do a quick search on the Internet for 'flexible working' and 'policy', you'll find hundreds of examples of organisational flexible working policies drawn up by HR departments. They are mostly in the public sector, as it is the public sector that is most likely to make their internal policies publicly available. Almost all of them take an approach where flexible working is granted as an exception to 'normal' office-based ways of working. It's something you apply for, and line managers can refuse it.

Creators of HR policy have a difficult line to tread. They may want their policies to be enabling, and they may want to avoid bureaucracy. On the other hand, they are the ones who will be dealing with disciplinary issues and all the ramifications when things go wrong. And when things go wrong, the documents can be subject to fine-tooth-comb scrutiny by pedantic legal eagles and people who want to sue you for every penny you have.

So the tendency is to want to nail things down quite firmly. This is how you operate homeworking. This is how you apply for it. This is the responsibility of the line manager, and this is the responsibility of the employee. This is what happens if you don't fulfil your part of the bargain.

The challenge is to be light-touch enough to enable flexibility on both sides. I've seen many policies that set out a process for establishing flexible working on an inflexible basis. The new arrangements become enshrined as a kind of immutable new set of working arrangements. Any changes to them need to be applied for and go through an assessment process, and so on.

In an ideal situation, you want both sides to be flexible and amenable to change according to circumstance. One person's part-time days are Monday to Wednesday, but the occasions may arise when it would be better to have them come in on a Thursday. It could be for a team meeting which is everyone's chance to get together, or it could be due to deadlines or peak demand. But 'coming in' need not mean physically coming in, if the work could be done remotely. Combining flexible work options as needed increases agility.

In the health sector and in manufacturing self-rostering is a form of flexible working that is becoming increasingly common. Teams can work out for themselves who is covering which shifts, and the team works together to ensure fairness. The same principle can apply to managing other forms of flexible working in teams.

It's about give and take. This kind of ad hoc team-agreed flexibility can work for the employee when there are personal and home commitments to deal with. In practice, this is what many organisations do, whether or not they have detailed flexible working policies. So flexible working policies should not be the occasion for introducing unnecessarily rigid structures to govern flexibility.

Numerous studies have found that small and medium-sized businesses (SMEs) are less likely to have formal flexible working policies, but are overall more likely to accommodate requests for flexible working practices (the latest such survey being Leighton and Gregory for Demos 2011). SMEs prefer to do so on an informal basis, perhaps essentially because they know each other and act more as one team.

This give-and-take approach requires a climate of trust and transparency. And when people are used to working this way, the actual policies matter less than the relationships within the team for managing how, where and when people work.

Smart and Flexible Retirement

At the moment in the UK people aged 50 and over are almost 30 per cent of people of working age, and 26 per cent of those actually in work. And by 2020 there will be nearly 5 million more people aged 50+ in the UK. The age balance in the workforce is shifting, and employers will increasingly depend on retaining and recruiting older workers.

At the same time, there are clear signs that many people are looking for a change in their working patterns as they approach retirement. For some, there is an aspiration to scale down the intensity of their work in the pre-retirement period. The demand for part-time work amongst the over 50s is high – though penalties on the pension front are often a deterrent from taking this up.

On the other hand, there are many older workers who want to work beyond pensionable age, though perhaps this is not on a full-time basis. Work-life balance involves leavening home-life with a little work. For some people this will be a financial imperative – and this will be increasingly the case for today's under 50s who won't be looking forward to the same level of pension as their baby-boomer predecessors.

With living longer comes the prospect for most of us of being fitter and more active in the later years of life. Later working life and retirement need no longer be seen as a 'Death of a Salesman' or 'King Lear' process of decline, obsolescence and incapacity. People in their 60s and beyond now share the same aspirations for autonomy as the rest of us, and this means working if they want to.

Part-time work is the obvious work-style that first comes to mind. For employers this means being able to retain skills and experience in the organisation. But it is not the only way. Contracting in services as needed from older employees who have become self-employed freelancers is an alternative. There are many people who have taken early retirement who set themselves up in business to sell their skills, and this often includes to their previous company. It can also be as an interim, taking skills into other organisations to manage projects or periods of transition.

For employers it also means looking out for such people as an alternative to recruitment, particularly for time-limited projects where people are needed who can hit the ground running and bring their experience to bear.

There are increasing numbers of older workers who are looking to downshift, and perhaps to set up in business using a skill, interest or hobby they've never developed commercially before, but have always wanted to. It could be that the combination of part-time work and a new 'sunset' cottage industry are the right combination for a member of staff. The mixture of employment and enterprise could be just the right balance for many older workers – in effect a move into being a portfolio worker.

There are other forms of flexibility that may suit the transition towards retirement. Homeworking, flexitime and compressed working weeks may help to take out some of the pressure from daily travelling. And these ought to be considered alongside part-time and job-share options.

At the time of writing, the UK government has just abolished the default retirement age. This will, with some exceptions, make it pretty much impossible for employers to enforce a compulsory retirement age. At the same time, the age at which UK workers can receive a state pension will be progressively raised from 65 to 68. As people live longer, and government remains mired in debt, we can expect this to rise further still. Demographics and deficits – a powerful combination.

The result is that people will be working longer, both out of choice and out of necessity. A study by the Centre for Research into the Older Workforce at Surrey University found that 58 per cent of economically active people (across the age range) would like to continue paid work after pensionable age – but that breaks down as 48 per cent would like to do so part-time and only 10 per cent see themselves doing so full time. A further 36 per cent said they would consider voluntary work (McNair et al. 2004).

This suggests a big change is on the cards, as at the moment only around 10 per cent continue working beyond 65.

While the first response of employers' organisations has been to protest about the increased difficulty in workforce planning and replacing older workers with younger ones, I have no doubt that in time this will come to be seen as the right approach. It should also bring about a new – and more honest – culture around working towards retirement. Reasons for stopping work should be based on preference and capability, not drawing an arbitrary line in the sand. And I fully expect that a new culture of flexibility will develop to inform discussions and support choices of whether and how to continue working when one reaches pensionable age.

Capitalising on Experience and Expertise

Under the new approach, those who continue to work past the state pension age have the option to draw their pension as they work, or to defer it for increased payments when they do finally retire. This should increase the capacity of older workers to adopt a flexible approach as they reach an age where they could retire.

Employers should be ready to capitalise on having access to a pool of experienced and capable workers.

ASDA, the supermarket chain, introduced a 'Seasonal Colleagues' scheme based on a permanent contract to work at peak times of the year. The 8,000 Seasonal Colleagues are mainly older workers and students (Age Positive 2011).

It may be that experienced staff have, from a work point of view, fewer issues in terms of motivation and self-discipline in working outside the office environment. And in a trust-based and empowering working environment, the more experienced workers may be just the ones to help set the standards for effective flexible working.

This is an important point. Flexible retirement options are not just a way of dealing with the new age-discrimination regulations and letting the fast-flowing careers of older workers flexibly dribble away into babbling brooks and stagnant backwaters. It's about how the skills, experience, knowledge and passion of valued staff can be retained for the benefit of the company, as well as meeting the aspirations of older staff for a change of work-style or work intensity.

This can include actively using them to mentor or buddy new recruits, involving them in training or taking a leading role in projects where their skills are of particular value.

It is perhaps no surprise that the Surrey University study we referred to found that people with higher qualifications and managerial experience are the most likely to seek to continue working beyond pensionable age. When we think about it, the people most likely already to be working into their 70s and 80s are high-level professionals like judges, bishops, MPs, Lords, company directors, and so on, and people with a skill and a passion such as artists and skilled crafts people. To a large extent these people have the ability to 'own' their work and integrate it into who they want to be, as well as often being able to regulate the amount of it they do.

It doesn't necessarily mean cutting down. It can sometimes mean the opposite, collecting new roles and responsibilities, or portfolios of work from different directions. The value brought to the work is based on experience and authority rather than the hours put in, and that is very much in the spirit of Smart Flexibility.

Age-Proofing Smart Flexibility

For the company there is a responsibility to 'age-proof' the introduction and application of Smart Flexibility. Quasi-ageist statements are often made about generational change bringing in more tech-savvy workers to the workplace, and maybe older workers struggling with newer technologies.

And yet the typical profile of the country's 3 million 'teleworkers' is of a manager or professional in the second half of their working career. What is true is that two-thirds of these are self-employed, which leads one to think that maybe it is the context of working as an employee over many years in innovation-averse environments which is the reason for any perceived technophobia, rather than the simple fact of being older. The technologies used in location-independent working and paperless offices are not rocket science, and the skills to use them fairly easy to acquire.

Our own analyses of staff surveys in organisations tend to show older workers being quite polarised between those who 'get' flexibility and want more of it, and those who are very comfortable with more traditional ways of working and are sceptical that change will be for the better.

Thinking of older workers in terms of lack of capabilities or declining capabilities is both inaccurate and patronising, and a habit to be avoided in the new world of work. The probability is that they will 'do' flexible and smart working to a greater extent than most of the rest of us in the decades to come.

Flexibility Across the Life Course

There are probably times in our life when different forms of flexible working suit us better. The focus on flexibility for parents is not wrong, though it has had a stilting effect on understanding the true nature and role of flexible working. Part-time working for one if not both of the parents for a time may be the choice when the family is young; then term-time working and part-of-the-week home-working for managing the home/work/school interface; and then other options according to preference as the kids grow up and flee the nest – all, of course, dependent on how preference can be dovetailed with the requirements of the work.

Then again, when moving forwards in one's career, other factors from personal life may come into play to affect the choice. It could be a desire to retrain or take a further qualification. Or it could be the need to be able to manage the care of a dependent relative, or deal with changing health circumstances. And in time, flexible work options and/or new entrepreneurial options can be incorporated into a review of one's working life as a mature worker, a new beginning or a phasing into retirement.

Self-Actualisation through Work

Perhaps what Smart Flexibility opens up for individuals is the possibility throughout life to become the person they want to be, whether through their work or in preventing work being a barrier to this.

Writers such as Dan Pink in *Free Agent Nation* (2001) and *Drive* (2010) and Alison Maitland and Peter Thomson in *Future Work* (2011) point to a trend where people take greater control over their work, and either are entrepreneurs or take control of their employment as if they were taking ownership of their work and career.

Smart employers will seek to capitalise on the creativity and motivation this freedom and empowerment can unleash. Their best approach is to (a) remove the barriers to this creativity and (b) create the structures in which the positive benefits of this can be harnessed and channelled into a coherent business strategy.

All this risks pulling me too far into psychology on the one hand and theories of what work is for on the other, when the aim of this book is to focus on the practicalities of implementation. But the concluding thought of this section on smart and flexible people is that Smart Flexibility is indeed about being more than a cog in a machine or another brick in the wall. The benefit to the individual – to all the individuals who work for the company – needs to be at the heart of change as much as the benefit to the business if Smart Flexibility is truly to succeed.

CHAPTER # 6 *Workplaces*

Organised crime in America takes in over $40 billion a year ... [but] spends very little on office supplies.

Woody Allen, *New Yorker*, 1970

The Historic Advantages of Concentration

There are many different locations in which people can and do work. This has always been the case, and always will be.

What happened in the nineteenth and twentieth centuries is that a particular model of workplace evolved based on concentrating people and resources together in factories and offices. Organising labour and production in this way has enabled business owners, government managers and not-for-profit managers to achieve economies of scale and greater efficiency in organising production and business processes.

We should not underestimate the impacts and scale of achievements of this kind of work organisation. It has been responsible for unleashing dynamic, creative, transformative – and sometimes destructive – forces that have remodelled the world we live in. By concentrating in one location the innovation of great minds, a disciplined labour force, and energy resources derived from fossil fuels, organisations have been able to give themselves power and influence way beyond the sum of their parts.

The psychological impacts of this kind of work organisation have also been extremely powerful. Organising humanity en masse was perhaps the key characteristic of the twentieth century. Intensified by the experience of two world wars, governments of all variations of left and right sought collectivist solutions to social problems, whether providing factory-style health care, mass transit systems or dealing with water supply issues.

It has long been noted that such solutions often depend on ignoring or deferring the external costs. Society, the environment and future generations either suffer now or pick up the tab later. That is to say, both the perceived efficiency and the desirability of this kind of work organisation have perhaps always depended on having too narrow a focus.

But what else is a business owner or manager to do? Effective management must focus on doing what is best for the business – and in strictly business terms the factory model of organisation has worked, and is still working across the world.

We have all grown up in a world where this is how organisations work, sucking people from far and wide into buildings, setting them tasks within an overall framework of processes, and monitoring them to make sure everything is done in order.

However – it doesn't have to be like this any more.

What is the Workplace For?

In the twenty-first century, it's worth revisiting the question of what the workplace is for. For many of the functions we have traditionally allocated to centralised workplaces we should ask the question: how important is it to do this?

In Table 6.1, a range of workplace functions are listed, and on the right is space to score the 'necessity factor' for each function in terms of its having to be located in a central workplace. These should be scored in answer to the question: 'How essential is it to use our workplace as a … ?' where 3 is 'essential', 2 is 'sometimes/partly' and 1 is 'not essential'.

How people answer these questions at first will no doubt reflect their personal preferences and also their awareness of the alternatives. However, it's worth running through them again, with a view as to how essential each item is in:

a) The context of using new technologies; and
b) How it works for different people and teams in the organisation.

Let's take a closer look at some of these functions, starting with the workplace as a centre of production. Production is a much-changed phenomenon in the digital age. Many products are now digital, and even where the final output is a manufactured product, relatively few people have 'hands-on' roles compared to the Industrial Age. Of course there remains a need for factories and workshops, but there is no longer a pressing need

Table 6.1   What is the workplace for?

Function of workplace	Necessity factor		
	1	2	3
The centre for production			
The centre for management/supervision functions			
Centre for administration			
Centre for specialist facilities			
IT and communications centre			
Place for individual work			
Place for teamwork			
Place to meet clients			
Place to meet colleagues			
Place for social interaction/developing personal relationships			
Centre to promote/cement corporate identity			

for the co-location of many of the other functions of the company. The manufacturing facility is something people not in hands-on roles will visit from time to time, as they need to, including people who create the programmes for automated production.

Developing software products and new media applications are examples of digital production that can in principle be located anywhere. It is factors such as teamwork that bring about an apparent need for co-location. However, it is in these fields that virtual teams are most commonly found. So physical presence face-to-face teamwork may not be a day-to-day necessity, but something for special occasions such as brainstorming new products or pitches or solutions to problems.

Is the workplace the place for management functions? If the assumption is that managers should be based at the workplace, then that is a significant constraint on them. With a mobile and flexible workforce, management needs to become more flexible too, and managers should be able to manage performance and all routine activities from wherever they happen to be.

The probability is that any discussions about workplaces not directly involved in production will focus on the collaborative aspects of work, as places to meet colleagues and possibly clients/customers. Yet of course there are increasingly many other – and possibly better – places to meet on many occasions, as well as other media for collaboration.

And of course there are organisations that are completely virtual. They really do cut back their office costs and the need for office supplies. Others have very extensive numbers of home-based and mobile workers, and the offices they retain perform a different function from the traditional office, with the focus on creating spaces that support collaboration and cater for individual work on an 'as needed' basis.

Back to the Vision

In Chapter 3, I set out some 'Smart Flexibility Principles' to underpin the vision for flexible work implementations. The key ones that apply to working environments are:

- Work takes place at the most effective locations.
- Work takes place at the most effective times.
- Employees have more choice about where and when they work, subject to business considerations.
- Space is allocated to activities, not to individuals nor on the basis of seniority
- The costs of doing work are reduced.
- There is effective and appropriate use of technology.
- Work has less impact on the environment.

For many workers, much of the work will take place outside the office for much of the time. Workplaces that remain will be smaller, and will be fit for purpose.

With the emphasis on collaboration and using spaces more efficiently, there will be an emphasis on sharing spaces. This applies both to collaborative spaces, and individual work settings.

Space Sharing or 'Hotdesking' – Myths and Realities

For most people, the idea of space sharing means 'hotdesking'. And hotdesking does not have a good reputation. I'm told that the term 'hotdesking' derives from the nautical practice of 'hot-bunking'. When a sailor came off duty he'd collapse into a 'hot bunk' just vacated by another sailor off to do his turn. An eminently sensible space saving practice – though maybe dubious from the hygienic or aromatic point of view.

Through the late 1980s and the 1990s, hotdesking appeared in a number of guises in America and Europe, also being called by names such as 'hotelling' and 'free addressing' and the like. Early implementations, though, ran into trouble due to being overzealous, people being isolated from their teams (on the 37th floor one day, in the basement the next), and lacking the right technologies to work effectively away from their own desk, let alone away from the office.

Now one can barely read an article about space sharing without someone debunking hotdesking, so to speak, on the basis of implementations from nearly 20 years ago. Time has moved on – as have technology, property prices, efficiency demands and our understanding of how to make space sharing work. Much as most of us might appreciate having our own personal territory carved out at work, the business case for space sharing is overwhelming.

First and foremost, in traditional offices with assigned personal desks, average desk occupancy rarely rises above 50 per cent, as we have seen. So employers are tying up huge amounts of money in redundant space.

Secondly, when equipping staff with the kit and connection to work from home and on the move, we create opportunities for efficiency and savings. But we also risk doing exactly the opposite, by creating multiple 'office spaces' and duplicating technology investments, if we don't cut back the facilities in the office.

Reducing the office space and introducing desk-sharing is essential to justify the investment in mobile working and homeworking. However, even when faced with a strong business case, there are always some people who don't want to share. What is also needed is to *change the culture of possession*.

At a recent workshop on culture change, one sceptic quipped: 'I only use my bed for a third of the day, but that doesn't mean I want to share it with strangers'. I had to think about that one. For me, it would depend on who the strangers are, I guess. But the point is an interesting one. Because there are two assumptions in this kind of view, that:

1.   One has a right to the same kind of 'ownership rights' that one enjoys at home.
2.   The other people one would share with are necessarily strangers.

Both of these assumptions need challenging. On the first point: in principle, one has no more rights of exclusive ownership to an office desk than one has to a seat on a bus, a restaurant table or a stall in the office toilets. And on the second point: in all probability the most likely people you would share space with are colleagues from your own team, or at least from the same department.

So a key part of the process of adjusting to space sharing is taking away the fear of change. And in particular, taking away the fear of loss of 'ownership'.

Doing work in a modern office is not about owning a particular desk, but having *guaranteed access to the right kind of facility for getting the work done*. This might be a desk, or it might be a quiet workplace in a resource area, a training facility or a touch-down space (and so on).

Achieving this more business-focused awareness should be a positive exercise, where teams analyse the way they work, and the kinds of facilities they need access to.

When teams and individuals help to redesign the way they work, they start to understand the trade-offs. And enabling a wide range of Smart Flexibility working options is a key part of the trade-off. Less personalised space is the price paid for achieving more flexibility and better team space.

Policies to Make Desk-Sharing Work

Changing the habits of a working lifetime does not happen overnight. There are always people who don't agree with it, and who will try to subvert the principles by, as far as possible, resuming old habits and re-establishing the old office geographies.

And it probably won't only be the dissidents who lapse back into old ways. After a few weeks, it's worth checking to see if people have tended to colonise favoured positions, and have reintroduced their personal library behind their favourite seat or have their family photos on the desk, or leave out that 'urgent work-in-progress' on their favourite desk whenever they go out.

Is it harmless? Maybe it seems so. But people who colonise space create a tighter ratio of desks-to-people for everyone else to work with.

So here are some principles to make space sharing work:

1. *A clear desk policy.* Absolutely essential. Establish that whenever people are out of the office for more than a certain time – say two hours – they must clear everything from the desk. Having a locker to put things in is necessary for this.
2. *Well organised team storage.* Piles of files can't be left on desks – but shutting them away in lockers can be worse. It will actually increase efficiency to accept the discipline of returning files to team storage and making them accessible to all. Shared libraries of reference materials have the benefit of reducing duplication and preventing personal silos of information.
3. *Have the same agreed compendium of essential information at each desk and/or online.* For example, key dates, fire escape routes, important telephone numbers, and so on. And ban the maverick pinning up of 'essential' information by desks to prevent 'professional personalisation' of desks.
4. *Create a beautiful environment!* Provide attractive pictures, planting, water features, and so on and this will justify the restriction on people putting their own knick-knacks on their favourite desk.
5. *Ergonomic work positions.* Achieving the best and ergonomic workplace layout will help people accept working in different positions. Chairs must be adjustable – or some will claim they have to sit in a certain place each day.
6. *Laptops or tablets are preferable to desktop PCs.* That is because they can move everywhere with one member of staff, and any specialist software installed moves with them. This will prevent people laying claim to one particular space for IT reasons and will enable more effective flexibility. When working in one position with a laptop for a long time, a keyboard and mouse, laptop stand and/or additional screen should be used.

7. *Provide ample touch-down space to cope with peak demand.* That is, places where people can connect their laptops or log into thin client terminals to work for short periods. These can be touch-down bars, or locations in resource areas, informal meeting/ refreshment areas and so on.
8. *Work in non-exclusive team areas with fuzzy boundaries.* It's good to keep the team connection and work with each other to share space effectively. But space sharing will not achieve the maximum benefits if teams become exclusive. The aim should be to break down barriers, and encourage working across teams. 'Non-Exclusive Team Space', we could call it.
9. *Have a good telephony solution.* People need to be able to log in to their extension whether in the office or out, and from whichever desk they sit at.
10. *Encourage Smart Flexibility in practice.* People working from home and on the move, and working compressed working weeks in particular will reduce the daily demand for space.

It's important to keep everything under review. Some practices may not be working too well. It may be that more training or gentle pressure is needed, or it may be that certain practices needs modifying.

But if it's done right and people feel they have a stake in devising the new arrangements, there's one thing I can almost guarantee will need reviewing. After 6 months, unless your staff numbers have increased, there'll be a surplus of space in the office again. You'll find nearly everyone loves the portable devices, loves the greater freedom to 'work anywhere', and are no longer fighting for their own personal space in the office.

Non-Exclusive Team Space

Few people these days would advocate hotdesking policies that move people all around the building from one day to the next, dividing people from their teams. Maintaining team cohesion and joint access to nearby resources is important, and space sharing arrangements agreed by colleagues in teams are more likely to work well.

However, it is a key principle that while broadly defined team 'zones' can be useful, these cannot be exclusive spaces. To increase occupancy levels and achieve the savings necessary to support new working styles, vacant desks must be open to people from other teams to use, without their being made to feel they are intruders or that they are violating someone else's personal space.

For practical purposes, when a team-based approach is taken, the units of space should not be defined around small teams. Apart from encouraging exclusivity, it is more likely to be the case that all the members of a small team will be in the office at the same time. So the smaller the level of team definition, the more acutely they will feel space pressures during times of peak occupancy, and feel that they are spilling over 'their' boundaries.

In some implementations they like to talk of 'non-territorial working', which is a useful concept for reinforcing the idea there are no exclusive spaces.

Table 6.2 outlines the main options for desk-sharing/hotdesking, and the main pros and cons:

Table 6.2   Pros and cons of desk-sharing solutions

Desk-sharing style	How it works	Pros and cons
Marginal hotdesking	Most employees have allocated 1:1 desks. More mobile staff in department or team, usually about 10–15% of total, share desks on a defined ratio: for example, 7:10, or perhaps 1:2 in bolder implementations.	Practised in many organisations dipping their toe into flexible working. Doesn't work well. Slips back to 1:1 desking in most areas, while leading to space shortages in growing teams. Doesn't address under-occupancy of desks overall.
Partial desk-sharing 1 – allocate 1:1 or flexible	An assessment is carried out of work-styles, and employees assigned to categories such as: – Fixed – Flexible (e.g., sometimes homeworking) – Partly mobile – Primarily mobile. Those in the 'fixed' category are assigned an individual desk, while others share desks. Ratios are calculated on the basis of how many are in each category, with a different formula for each category.	This is a more 'scientific' approach, attempting to align the number of desks with actual need. Significant space savings can be achieved. However, it has 3 key weaknesses: – People tend to be allocated to categories on the basis of old assumptions about how jobs should be carried out. – Allocations can be arbitrary, and vary between departments. – This categorisation risks injecting new inflexibilities into the workplace. Unless calibrated by a space audit or by activity analysis, the model and ratios are based on theory rather than practice.
Partial desk-sharing 2 – choose 1:1 or flexible	Staff are given the option of working in flexible or traditional styles. They can opt to be based at their own assigned desk in an office. Or they can opt to be flexible. This comes with the provision of kit, etc., for working out of the office, possibly an allowance for homeworking. When in the office, they hotdesk. There is a clear and explicit trade-off between personal space in the office, and the freedom to work wherever/whenever they choose.	This kind of approach has the advantage, in principle, of meeting employee aspirations, and avoids compulsion. Several large-scale implementations have followed this route. It doesn't address under-occupancy by those who are allocated 1:1 desks. It also risks being unstrategic – flexible working strategy and accommodation strategy being reactive to the changing preferences of staff.
Team-based desk-sharing	The principle is that all desks are shared, however much people are in the office. Exceptions to desk-sharing should be absolutely minimal. The expectation is that teams will continue to sit near each other when in the office, and may be allocated priority areas. In general, teams will be expected to plan for variations in occupancy, using a variety of alternative office settings to accommodate peaks. In addition there is likely to be some 'free address' space to accommodate additional demand, visitors, temporary project teams, etc.	To my mind this is the best approach for most medium to large organisations. It recognises the need for people to see familiar faces when they come into the office, people they regularly interact with. It also gives teams ownership of the sharing arrangement. It can also maintain and improve adjacencies with other teams and help to break down 'silo working' by having fluid boundaries. The main risk is in, over time, team areas becoming too strongly defined, and the people who are in the office most often 'colonising' favoured positions. There is also a risk of inflexibility with changes to team numbers – hence a need for frequent reviews to maintain agility.

Table 6.2   Continued

Desk-sharing style	How it works	Pros and cons
100% hotelling	Like a hotel, staff book ahead and check in to any available desk.	To a large extent this approach has been discredited by the gung-ho implementations of the 1990s. People do want some continuity and access to colleagues and team resources when they are in the office. However, it may still be an appropriate solution for satellite offices, flexible offices at workhubs, etc. – places with a very large turnover of touch-down or visiting staff. It may also be the most suitable options for smaller organisations – effectively treating the whole organisation as one team. And of all the options, it is most likely to achieve the most efficient use of space – though probably not the most effective.

Based on experience, the best solution to maximise the benefits of flexibility is to have desk-sharing in the context of 'non-exclusive team space'.

Desk-sharing really should apply to everyone, no matter how often they are in the office, or whether they have a personal preference for their own desk or not, and in nearly all cases, regardless of role.

It may be that there are some people, typically a receptionist or administrator, who will be in the office each day and is therefore allocated their own desk. But determining any exceptions to desk-sharing needs to be decided at a higher level than the team in order to maintain the overall viability of sharing arrangements. Otherwise, exceptions start to multiply and unfairness starts to creep into allocations, as those with the power, loudest voices, or the greatest capacity for stubbornness carve out their own nests.

What to Do with Private Offices

This democratic approach looks good – until the issue of hierarchy and its relationship to space raises its head. The question 'Should we have private offices?' can also be written: 'Where should we put the managers?' Because in 99 per cent of traditional offices, it's the managers who have their own private space.

Why? Status. An earned reward. Confidentiality. Dedicated space to hold private high level meetings. The need for quiet away from the hubbub of the open plan to think strategically and make decisions. There can be many justifications, each carrying varying degrees of weight.

It's an interesting fact that in most traditional organisations, space is allocated to people in inverse proportion to the amount of time they occupy it. The humble clerk or secretary who spends most time at his desk has the smallest space allocation. And the chief executive and chairman, who are there the least, have the most space.

To look at this objectively, it's best to go back to the space audit (see Chapter 4). Private offices invariably show average occupancy lower than open plan areas. They also typically show less desk work going on, and more meetings. Percentage occupancy levels in the low 30s are typical. If you were to take out the meetings and put them in a meeting room or break-out area, most would be well under 30 per cent.

So from the usage figures, most managers can't really justify having a personally assigned desk, let alone a personally assigned room. However, in a Smart Flexibility project, it probably needs to be put more tactfully than that, as there are multiple sensitivities to deal with. And people do get very ticklish about their hard-won personal office.

Moving flexible work from theory to practice can easily founder on the rocks of jealously guarded status. I have seen radical plans for changing working practices die the death of a thousand qualifications as one manager after another argues that their role is exceptional. I have seen HR managers campaign passionately for flexible working, then argue equally passionately to retain their private offices – confidentiality, of course, is the reason.

The simplest and most equitable solution is to get all the managers, however senior, out of their private offices and onto the shop floor to rub shoulders with the rest of their co-workers. Many senior managers and business owners like to do this anyway. It gives them a better handle on what is going on, and can create better relationships between staff and management too.

If that is a step too far, some organisations set up a management suite (or management suites within departments). This too has advantages, and can improve interdepartmental/ inter-team working while providing reassurance that there is less risk that confidences are leaking out down through the organisation. The management suite would typically contain a shared-desk area for managers and a small meeting room or two.

Another rearguard action is fought around the dual use of private offices as meeting space. Having analysed numerous space audits, I'm completely unconvinced by the argument for having meeting desks in managers' offices. They are chronically underused: 15 per cent utilisation is about top whack, even when the official policy is to let others use them if the manager is out.

So – get the manager out of the private office, put meetings in meeting spaces, and have some private spaces for confidential work if needed.

FLEXIBILITY, COLLABORATION AND SPACE SHARING AT VODAFONE

Over the past 10 years Vodafone has been on a journey into flexible working that has taken it further than most. This has involved consolidating a disparate group of offices onto one campus, transforming these into flexible working environments, enabling high levels of remote access and virtual collaboration, and achieving measurable benefits in performance and sustainability.

The initial moves were largely spurred by the needs of a fast-growing company that had acquired a disparate group of properties as it grew. The need to consolidate was driven not only by financial good sense, but by a need to promote better collaboration between different functions within the organisation. The imperative for better collaboration underpins the approach to both physical spaces and the use of technologies to support flexible working.

Vodafone moved into their new campus at Newbury in 2002, a group of seven buildings in an attractively landscaped setting. Initially there was only a limited amount of flexible working, with most work still carried out in quite a traditional way. The step-change in flexible working really began with the appointment in 2009 of a new CEO, Guy Laurence, who had introduced extensive flexible working at Vodafone in the Netherlands and who says, 'I don't believe in offices'.

The need for change was in part due to the market becoming much more competitive, and the need for the company to keep on its toes. And it was also about the need to attract and retain the best staff, including the upcoming Generation Y – people instinctively comfortable with the technologies the company was developing and selling. According to Neil Stride, Head of Enterprise Business Development at Vodafone, 'We decided we needed to eat what we sell'.

The result was a very rapid 6-week transformation to new ways of working, focusing on leadership, behaviours and organisational culture.

'This was a massive change', explains Neil. 'We moved from personal to shared space, so now there is no personal space at all. There were pockets of hotdesking before, but now this applies to everyone. The CEO does not have an office, but shares a desk like everyone else'.

Everyone has a 'home zone' – so post can reach them and IT can know where to find them. But having gone 100 per cent laptop, staff can work anywhere on site or log in remotely from anywhere. Though desks are used differently, there was not a big spend on new office furniture with a preference to reuse existing desks. There was investment in new ergonomic and fully adjustable chairs, however, to cater for most employee health circumstances.

A clear desk policy is strictly enforced. People were given two weeks to get used to it. After that, everything left behind is removed and if not claimed within 24 hours is incinerated.

Much of the focus of the design is on creating spaces for collaboration, with a multiple styles of rooms to encourage different kinds of exchanges and conversations. All the old group directors' offices were turned into meeting 'lounges', with sitting-room style furniture and fireplaces to encourage openness and sharing of ideas. Other meeting rooms are more functional to encourage speedy decision-making, and there are small 'huddle rooms' for people to pop into for up to 20 minutes. In each building there is an atrium that includes shops and facilities and a cafe where less formal and ad hoc meetings are held. The principle is that any meeting with fewer than six people should convene in one of these areas, unless it is a particularly confidential one-to-one, for example.

This approach and the design of the campus as a whole is intended to break down barriers and encourage serendipitous meetings, catching people as they walk past or having chance meetings on the walkways.

Technology is of course central to the new ways of working, with unified communications supporting mobility and collaboration. Working as virtual teams and using conferencing technologies is encouraged both for efficiency and to reduce the carbon footprint of work. One in three leadership meetings is now conducted by videoconferencing, and the company has met the WWF's target of reducing flights by 20 per cent.

Paper has been replaced by electronic processes to the extent that there is no file storage on the office floors. Incoming documents can be scanned and tagged from the multifunction printers – there are no personal or team printers now.

This 'paperless ecosystem' is supported by extensive use of Salesforce, the cloud-based customer relationship management system, and Chatter, its associated social media application that combines social collaboration with business processes.

The importance of flexible working is recognised in terms of business continuity. Floods in 2007 put the campus out of action for three weeks, and staff were able to work remotely even though at that time it was not yet the regular way of working. The value of this was demonstrated again in 2011 when the company's planning exercises were conducted on an entirely virtual basis due to snow.

There are independently measured numbers to illustrate the scale of the changes. Employee commuting has reduced substantially, leading to a net saving of 400 tonnes of CO_2 per year. And the use of conferencing technologies has led to a reduction of 12,000 tonnes of CO_2 in 2010/11 compared to 2006/7 from business mileage. This has led to cumulative savings of £40.7 million over five years. And, in conjunction with other measures of energy efficiency, CO_2 emissions from buildings have been reduced by 12,000 tonnes over the same period, with savings of £4.4 million.

At the same time, the numbers working on campus has grown from 3,500 to 5,000, in an example of 'spaceless growth'. Making this work has involved a transformation of the working culture. Enabling people to work at different times and in different places involves developing a culture of trust.

'What we've done here is create an environment for people to be brilliant, based on trust and management by results', says Neil Stride. 'Having the leadership on board is essential. Otherwise you end up with pockets of pilots, each doing their own thing but unable to translate a consistent approach to the company as a whole'.

The approach has since been extended to Vodafone's contact centre operation at Stoke, to its HQ at Paddington and is being rolled out in its overseas offices.

Desk Ratios – Is There an Answer?

For any desk-sharing solution, there are going to be fewer desks than desk-users. But there need to be enough spaces available to accommodate peak demand. However, providing accommodation to cater for the 'worst case scenario' peak is an expensive business. And it's a reactive approach. It's better to work out the reasons why exceptional peaks occur, and to see how they can be managed downwards. Is there something happening at certain times that sucks most of the staff into the office? Perhaps that can be changed, by looking at the way meetings are scheduled and conducted.

So what is the best ratio?

The answer is that it depends on the organisation and balance of activities within the organisation. In the UK government sector, the Government Property unit (formerly part of the Office for Government Commerce) deals with changing government property requirements, has highlighted examples of 8 desks to 10 people as good practice. This has been quoted out of context on many occasions and has been put up by some in the government sector as a target. It isn't. It's probably the very minimum achievable in most departments.

Each organisation has to find its own answer, based on the evidence it has captured about:

- Space use.
- Current working practices.
- The potential for increased flexibility (Chapter 4 provides more detail on this process).

In general, peak occupancy figures provide a first indication of what might be possible. So, strip out from the data any known empty desks, and find the peak occupancy figure. It's probably between 60 per cent and 70 per cent, if the company has unreformed traditional working practices. So the company could, in principle, remove 30 per cent of all desks and still have enough to go round – providing all remaining desks are up for sharing and there is a clear desk policy, with time thresholds for vacating desks and some expansion space in meeting rooms or break-out areas.

Different departments are likely to have different occupancy levels, and different levels of mobility. So one ratio does not fit all. It is tempting to say that departments must achieve 'at least 30 per cent reduction'. But there's a big risk here. A 7:10 desk ratio becomes a target, regardless of actual need based on observed data.

Maybe average occupancy recorded in the space audit is 45 per cent. Could you go as far as removing half the desks? It depends how bold you want to be, and how intensively you want to 'sweat the assets' (that is, property and facilities). In principle it would be feasible. It would mean that you don't cater for peaks by providing additional – and rarely used – standard desks. Instead there should be a range of alternatives settings that we explore in the next section, and which can be used to accommodate peaks. As long as there is somewhere to park and work, the peak is catered for.

And if there is a will to get more flexible, having people work remotely and at non-standard times, there is room to drive the ratio down even further. Many of the more dynamic firms are working on the basis of 1:4 or even 1:10 ratios. Some are even doing away with desks altogether.

Beyond Desks – Flexible Working Spaces

Desks, desks, desks. From the last few sections of this chapter, it would seem that having smart offices is all about desks. It's tempting to focus on this, as the issues around personalisation and ownership of space are so entrenched in traditional workplace culture. But it's a mistake to do so.

What makes an effective flexible working environment is not the number of desks or the sharing ratio, but the variety, range and appropriateness of the different work settings. Typically these will include:

- Flexible meeting/collaboration spaces – meeting rooms in a range of sizes, break-out spaces, cafe areas, and 'streets' or 'town squares'.
- Space for quiet and concentrated working.
- Spaces for confidential work and phone calls.
- Touch-down spaces for people working on the move.
- Resource areas.
- Special project areas.
- Larger meeting rooms.

Space designers will come up with a host of names for office work settings, but they basically come down to these.

At the theoretical level there are various ways to segment different kinds of modern office-based work. One influential model from the late 1990s (Laing et al. 1998) proposes four distinct patterns of work, described as cell/club/hive/den, each relating to the types of work to be carried out there.

Low autonomy kinds of work are the 'hive' – individual process work, with little interactivity, and the 'den' – group process work. Higher autonomy activities are the 'cell' – work involving concentrated study, with little interaction, and the 'Club' – transactional knowledge work.

These ideas have had a strong influence in taking forward new designs for the workplace, but in the second decade of the twenty-first century seem somewhat dated. They remain useful as a way in workshops, for example, for getting people to think about the kind of work they do and the settings that might be needed for them. A key problem with this kind of model, though, is the presumption that interaction is mostly about physical proximity. Those days are gone.

Any segmentation of work in these ways is likely to be a bit of a Procrustean bed when it comes to dealing with the combination of different things that people do every day, and their preferences for sitting close to team members, and the preference for adjacencies between teams. In the end, the kinds of spaces provided through this kind of analysis will be very similar to the list of spaces above.

The same is true for trying segmentations of work-styles into categories such as 'resident/internally mobile/externally mobile', and then trying to relate that to particularly suitable workplaces and technologies to provide in those workplaces. Everything is becoming much more fluid than that. I might be resident for an afternoon, a whole day even, and mobile in different ways at other times. And my being resident doesn't have to be here – it can be here, there or anywhere. It's like trying to categorise people as pedestrians, cyclists, rail users and car drivers as if it were a fixed identity, as if we're not, at times, every one of these.

At the risk of offending space designers further, and perhaps being forever branded a philistine, I would venture that in designing spaces in the office essentially the ingredients are, at root, the same: various kinds of desks, tables, chairs, soft seating, storage and enclosure. Arrange them one way, there is more scope for physical interaction. Arrange them another way, it's better for quiet work. Provide more elbow room at a desk, it's good for being there all day. Less elbow room, that's fine for touching down for an hour or two. And so on.

The skill of the office designer is then to translate that into attractive spaces that support productivity and work flow, that people want to work in, and that reflect the brand and values of the organisation. Getting the right balance and relationships between the spaces is the 'smart' bit. In the new world of work the balance and the relationships won't be permanent, however. Spaces also need to be flexible, to be able to change over time if there are significant changes in staff numbers, or new teams, or the type of work changes.

And some of the spaces need to be able to change on a daily basis too – spaces that multitask. Bearing in mind the simplicity of the basic elements, some work settings should be easily reconfigurable. For example, there's a need for a training room. But currently the training room is only used for 20 per cent of the time. So it should be reconfigurable as meeting space, and/or touch-down space to accommodate peak demand.

For the twenty-first century space designer the other crucial consideration from a working practices point of view is how the layout and furniture interact with the technologies used for new kinds of work. Getting the wiring in and having a PC and phone on a desk is no longer good enough. It's about creating the right kinds of environment (a) to enable people to use a range of portable devices in a variety of ways, and (b) enabling work spaces, and the office as a whole, to interact effectively with all the spaces beyond the office where people also work.

This is another reason too why one should approach typologies of work with caution, when trying to translate it into defined office settings. A lot of the work will increasingly be done outside the conventional office.

In the early stages of flexible work (before it becomes Smart Flexibility), this tends to be the low-interaction kind of work. Taking something home for a bit of peace and quiet to catch up or meet a deadline. And it's the low-interaction work that is easiest to manage when working on the train, or touching down somewhere between meetings when on the road. It's also usually the high autonomy work too, as in the early stages it's mainly managers and professionals who are doing it.

Increasingly, though, administrative low autonomy tasks are becoming home-based, such as data processing. More interactive low autonomy work such as call-centre work is now also being done at home – the virtual call centre.

So the office will increasingly see a focus on the more collaborative kinds of work. But even face-to-face collaboration is increasingly carried out remotely, using conferencing technologies. So the assumptions about the kinds of environment that certain kinds of work need to be carried out in are challenged by the new capacities to work anywhere, anytime.

Sometimes these spaces don't turn out to be used as much as expected. One organisation responded to staff demand for quiet concentrated space when they introduced desk-sharing in an open plan environment by setting up a very smart 'library' area. But they found in practice it was little used. Why? In part it was because the employees who were consulted overstated their need for this kind of space, out of fear of disturbance in a busier and more intensively used environment. In practice, they were able to concentrate fine in the main areas most of the time. And in part, it was because they had the capacity to shift those pieces of work somewhere else entirely, in particular to home where they had greater control over interruptions.

I've seen a couple of examples where touch-down space is hardly used. Again, there was an overestimation of the amount of these spaces they would need, out of fears around coping with peak occupancy. In practice, there were pretty much always enough of the larger 'regular' desks available if people wanted to park in the office for a while. But it was also because these spaces were not especially comfortable compared to the cafe in the lobby downstairs or the coffee shops outside, which people used for preference.

Being footloose, people vote with their feet.

The Office Beyond the Office

It's interesting how absorbing the business of creating new office environments can be in the move to Smart Flexibility. There is a danger in smart and flexible change projects that the office – as the most expensive and visible aspect of the changes – becomes the all-consuming focus. It is important, but should not become the be-all and end-all of the project. This is because with the new ways of working the office increasingly becomes the place *not* to work.

Smart work principle 1: *Work takes place at the most appropriate location.* Work can take place wherever you are, or wherever is nearest to where you need to be. At the place where you last had a client meeting. On the move. Without leaving home. The place that is appropriate for the kind of work you are doing.

In general, the places people can now work fall into four categories: company-controlled, third-party, personal and public, as illustrated in Figure 6.1.

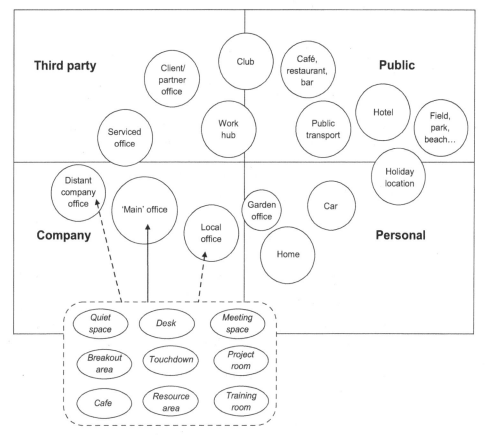

Figure 6.1   The office beyond the office

The options do not end there. Within at least the company-controlled workplaces there will be a variety of work settings (examples in the inset panel of Figure 6.1), to suit the nature of the work that you are going there for. Increasingly, the type of work done at a regular desk is the type of work that can be done in most other locations. It is the non-desk work settings that become the special attraction of the office.

Other workplaces, such as serviced offices and workhubs, will contain a variety of settings such as meeting rooms, touch-down desks and cafe/business lounge.

Broadly speaking, the workplaces on the left of the figure are more formal, while those on the right are more informal or ad hoc meeting places – though this is not necessarily always the case. Hotels and airports may have business centres, for example, that are more formal than cafes and break-out areas in workhubs or even company offices.

This is an issue for some managers and staff, who may be concerned about the professional face of alternative workplaces. Is it appropriate, for example, to meet a client in a Starbucks or a bar? Maybe, or maybe not – it depends on the context.

There are a number of factors in making the choice:

- Best work setting for type of work.
- Proximity.
- Other commitments – that is, where you want to be/could be before or afterwards.
- How different tasks can be 'bundled' to maximise the opportunity to work in one place and reduce travel.
- How the location choice impacts on others involved.
- Personal preference.
- Formality requirements.

Much work that is to be done can be done remotely using new technologies. The main reasons for going to a particular place will be for interaction with other people, or as a geographical spin-off from another occasion of interaction with other people.

The choices are not confined to 'which place'. It should no longer be assumed that a meeting has to be face-to-face. Conferencing technologies can substitute for some face-to-face interactions, so there has to be an appreciable added value in the face-to-face meeting to make travelling worthwhile (see Chapter 7)

What to Do with Other Company Offices

Where organisations have other offices apart from the main office, there are two things that can be done with them.

They can be transformed into flexible working environments as well, with shared desks, meeting rooms and break-out spaces at least. This will enable staff who live in the area to have a local base, and for mobile staff to have places to touch down.

Or they can be closed down and replaced by increased homeworking and/or the use of third-party serviced offices, workhubs or facilities exchange with partner organisations.

This is what organisations like Ofsted, the teaching inspectorate, have done. All their inspectors are now home-based. With over 1,500 staff home-based, they are the largest home-based operation in the public sector. And they have shrunk the number of local offices, going down to just three offices to support teams all over the country.

Yell, the international directories business, recently closed its 18 sales offices in favour of using Regus 'Businessworld' centres, making annual savings of £1.5 million. As their salespeople were mostly on the road and using technologies for remote working and collaboration, office occupancy was down to 25 per cent. The fixed office is replaced by the 'office as needed'.

There is a choice to be made about whether to keep a local presence in all areas, in some areas, have a regional presence or to abandon running offices away from the centre altogether.

And that is the other choice, which many companies are doing by using offices run by third-party providers such as Regus, MWB Business Exchange, eOffice, many business parks and the growing array of new wave local workhubs (Dwelly et al. 2010).

Serviced Offices and Workhubs

The 'traditional' serviced office – if they can be called traditional – is one where the third-party provider offers office accommodation, technologies (if required) and access to shared meeting rooms and reception services.

Most providers now offer virtual business services as well, so a client organisation can have a presence there that optionally includes a business address, mail forwarding, virtual PA services, access to touch-down positions, meeting spaces and video conferencing facilities, without having any kind of permanent physical presence at all.

The advantages include being able to flex the amount of office space needed to meet demand or organisational change, maintaining a foothold in areas where you don't want to establish a permanent office and having professional environments in which to meet clients and colleagues.

In Figure 6.1 (page 99), I've separated 'serviced offices' and 'workhubs' as being different categories of workplace. What are workhubs? There are many different models, but essentially they are places to touch down and collaborate, and have access to shared services. Their focus is not on providing regular office space to rent.

In fact, most serviced office providers are now also hubs to some degree, or would see themselves as such. Many science parks, business parks and business incubators also now provide some hub facilities and virtual office services as well as regular traditional office space to rent.

The field of workhubs is a fast evolving one – very much one to watch over the next 10 years. The new wave of workhubs often provides no serviced offices at all. The emphasis is entirely on shared services, virtual services and collaboration.

Some of this new generation of hubs cater primarily for home-based businesses. Some are integrated within Live/Work (see below and in Chapter 13) accommodation schemes, as at Bristol Paintworks (Dwelly et al. 2008).

Some, like the Digital Peninsula Network in Cornwall, were set up to support existing home-based businesses and provide networking opportunities. Some have a regeneration 'mission', to support home-based and micro enterprises in regeneration areas (Dwelly et al. 2010).

The government is now starting to recognise the role that workhubs can play in supporting business, particularly in rural areas (see Chapter 12), and have recommended that economic development agencies should support them.

Is that of interest to large organisations? It should be, as these workhubs can be the base for local employees to touch down if working from home is not an option, or if they need to hold meetings without travelling all the way to the main office.

It should be of particular interest to public sector employers, who are under pressure to reduce the number of offices they have, and may be inclined to enter some kind of service level agreement with local workspace providers. The hub should be happy in having an anchor client (not exactly an anchor 'tenant') or two.

The advantage of a national or international provider like Regus compared to a local independent is that an employer knows (a) that all the work areas will be specified to corporate standards, and (b) that there is a network of centres to use. One card will enable an employee to access Regus offices all over the country, all over the world even.

One interesting innovation at the time of writing is an agreement for The Office Group in partnership with Network Rail to open a network of flexible office spaces at railway stations nationwide, initially at five London locations. The first will open at Paddington station and will accommodate up to 250 people in a range of flexible office sizes. The new offices will also feature club-type services and spaces, aimed specifically at entrepreneurs and mobile workers. *

It is not for me to recommend one provider or another. But it is a significant sign that the number of workhub providers is rising fast, and new models are developing too. For the flexible organisation, this can only be good, as it means more choice, and better geographical coverage.

Client/Partner Office and 'Facilities Exchange'

On any given day there are tens of thousands of people working from offices belonging to clients or to partner organisations. They may be carrying out an outsourced function for a client, or working under a temporary contract. So they will be working in that office on a regular basis for a while. But probably not all the work they are doing is for the host company.

Others go for a meeting at a client or partner site, and then possibly later have another meeting with the same client or in the nearby area. So the best place to work is to stay in that office. Usually these arrangements are informal. The person organising the meeting will provide an empty desk for the use of the visitor. All perfectly normal.

Often, though, the set-up is not perfect. There may be a network connection that could in principle be used, or Wi-Fi, but it's too much trouble to contact IT and go through the security hoops to provide a visitor with temporary access. That's OK, though, it's what is expected, and the visitor has come equipped with a wireless dongle. They can then sit there, an enclave of one company within the territory of another. Not ideal, but passable.

Some organisations go further than this, and have dedicated areas where visitors can touch down and tune in. All that's needed is somewhere to sit and a wireless network that doesn't give automatic access to the host company's networks but gets you out onto the Internet. Setting this up does seem to challenge some IT departments who fear that the roof will fall in if they do this. But it's essentially what Internet cafes and hotels do, having one access route to the Internet for customers, and a protected network for themselves.

A more structured version of these arrangements is to set up a 'facilities exchange' agreement. This is what is happening with some public sector organisations by mutual agreement. Staff from the organisations in the agreement – local councils and health authorities, for example, can go to whichever office they happen to be nearest at any given time. Perhaps it's near their home, or perhaps near where they are working around the region.

One of the primary motivations for this is to reduce travel. Traffic patterns across the country but particularly in the south-east of England have people crossing each other's commuting journeys every day: one person from A goes to work in B, while a person living in B goes to work in A. A little bit of partnership, especially in the public sector, can cut the travel for both of them.

The issues in this kind of arrangement are not so much technical, but psychological (this is where I/he/she ought to work) and cultural (can we trust this breaching of organisational boundaries?).

The Home Office

When people talk of flexible working, discussions often end up focusing on homeworking, and I've deliberately come to it last in this review of work settings. It's not entirely wrong for people to focus on it, as we've seen how working from home one or two days a week is consistently a most-favoured option in staff surveys.

Is the home the most appropriate place to work? It can be. Deciding which is the most appropriate place involves a judgement about a number of factors – the nature of the work, any impacts on colleagues, personal preference and, quite crucially, the nature of the homeworking environment.

In staff surveys, typically around 80 per cent of people say that there is nothing in their home environment that would prevent some of their work being done at or from home. At the end of this chapter there is some guidance to address concerns about health and safety in the home office and other flexible working environments.

And there are increases in the number of homes that are specifically designed as both residential and business accommodation, or Live/Work space. We look at this in a little more detail in Chapter 13. On the whole Live/Work accommodation is more attractive to people running home-based businesses than it is to employees. However, as more of it is built around the country and as more homes are built with home offices, there is a greater scope for working from home in fit-for-purpose work environments.

The other rising phenomenon is the garden office. There is an increasing number of products on the market. In gardens all over the UK there are garden offices popping up, with all kinds of work taking place in them. One company is offering employers lease arrangements where they can have standardised pods popped into their employees' gardens. It's a cheaper option than having a dedicated desk in a centralised office, though of course not as cheap as just leaving the employees to sort out their own arrangements. But such an approach would ensure they have a separate workplace specified to a high standard, ergonomically sound and meeting H&S requirements.

Liberate the Office by Getting Rid of 'Stuff'

Now we return to the office to look at something essential that needs to be done to prepare it to be a workplace that supports Smart Flexibility.

Next time someone says that they need more office space, or that their office is too cramped or crowded, it's worth taking a close look. Is the office full of people, or full of stuff? In the pre-smart office, it's almost certain that the sense of being cramped comes from there being an overwhelming amount of clutter – on desks, around desks, on shelves, in cupboards, in drawers, maybe on windowsills and piled up on the floor.

In one smart work implementation in a local council, there was a middle manager in his early 60s, with a document archive of planning cases, decisions and guidance going back more than 20 years. Labelled, indexed and catalogued, and if anyone had cared to research it, a rich vein of social history in the borough. His small team's storage covered more than 60 linear metres of shelving, over half of which was this archive.

Each one of the team had a 'nest': a desk snuggling in a makeshift alcove of filing and reference books. One person had their own fridge in their nest, and several had their own kettles. Printers were everywhere in this office.

Moving to Smart Working presented some challenges to this team. Moving to desk-sharing involved unbearable loss. For the change team, it meant dealing with all this stuff. It had to go.

A Cautionary Tale from Academia

Storage is one of the dullest issues involved in changing to smarter working practices. Seriously, seriously boring. Clients laugh when the 'storage consultants' are brought in. 'That's really what you do for a living?' they mock. 'Can you study this in university?'

I think storage consultants have to develop a thick skin to withstand the barbs and to weather the oft-repeated jokes. For many employees involved on the client side in the storage discussions, it comes as a great relief that someone else seems to have a sadder job than they do.

Dull it may be, but it's surprising the heat that storage discussions can generate. I remember a facilities manager from an expanding university who had the task of introducing flexible working environments. One of the lecturers was berating him, feeling that his private office was under threat. 'What about all the books I need for my teaching?' the lecturer demanded.

'Well, maybe you could carry them around on your back like the students do', replied the FM.

Possibly this reply was a little too blunt. But it does raise a whole range of issues about how the working environment is managed. The students at the university, and lesser academics, work in entirely shared spaces – lecture rooms, libraries, common rooms and restaurants. And they also do much of their work from home – their parents' home, university accommodation, or grizzly rented accommodation where mice come out and dance under leaking radiators. Meanwhile the senior academics have their own offices or studies – and they need them, don't they?

I don't want to be the one leading the charge to defenestrate the professors and reclaim their studies for the commons. That's not the kind of 'cultural revolution' we're looking for. But it's worth asking: what is behind this kind of traditional allocation of space? Is it based on need? Or is it based on status and privilege?

Academics do need peace and quiet to think great thoughts and write learned articles, for sure. But if one were to do a space audit of academic offices, what kind of occupancy would we find? Below 50 per cent, for sure. Probably way, way below, given the nature of the work, the length of academic terms, and the type of homes professors tend to live in.

To be honest, if the occupancy were found to be high, we'd be justified in wondering what they were doing. Shouldn't they be out teaching – in lecture halls, class rooms and labs? At meetings and conferences sharing ideas and networking with other academics? In libraries researching?

And of course this is exactly where they are a great deal of the time. Or at home in their home offices or oak-panelled studies, where most of the writing and teaching preparation really gets done.

What is interesting about this case, though, is that the lecturer justified his need for an office not on the basis of his needing a quiet place to work, but on his need for *storage*.

Still it takes a brave man to tell them to work on the shop floor alongside their customers, and store their learning in a rucksack on their back. Could be the making of a new kind of scholar gypsy, perhaps. Like many others, I love to be surrounded by books. But having dedicated bookshelves at the office for my personal comfort, and justified on the basis of seniority, is an expensive indulgence few organisations could justify.

Where Am I Going to Keep My Pencils?

Where academics should keep their books is only one of a wide range of contentious issues around storage. Discussions and debate often go down to surprising level of details. Safety gear, samples, handbags, umbrellas – and one I remember in particular: pencils.

I was helping to run design focus groups in an organisation to help get staff involved in designs for their new flexible working environment. One of the members of the group was a designer who had a particular bee in his bonnet that day, having learned that he would no longer have an assigned desk.

'Where am I going to keep my pencils?' he asked. Quite rightly, he pointed out that these were no ordinary pencils, but were the essential tools of his trade. He asked this several times at different points in the discussion. Eventually, feeling he was not getting satisfactory answers he resorted to banging his fist on the table.

'You mean every time I want a pencil, I've got to walk across the office, go to my locker, get a pencil, return to my desk ...? It's not good enough! For the last time, where am I going to keep my pencils?!'

There was a slightly stunned silence. Then a colleague from another team said, 'If you say one more thing about this, Bill, I'm going to tell you exactly where you can put your bloody pencils!'

A more diplomatic colleague made a more helpful suggestion to ease the tension: 'How about a pencil case, so you can bring them to your desk all at once ...'

This solution, gleaned from many generations of good practice amongst primary school children, turned out to be the best one to adopt. Now we could move on to agreeing the design of the flexible working environment.

Storage Strategy

Rationalising storage needs to be dealt with on a strategic basis, with identified trajectories of reform, and acknowledging/integrating linkages to other policies. As an underlying principle, storage reform needs to work along the three trajectories identified in Figure 6.2 below.

First, personal storage will be largely replaced by team storage – as per the Smart Culture principle of there being an 'emphasis on shared rather than individualised space and resources' (see Chapter 8). Residual personal storage is not kept at desks or in a pedestal underneath, but in a separate locker area or similar.

Secondly, physical filing should be replaced as far as possible by electronic storage. This is not only more efficient, but is vital both for remote working and for facilitating effective desk-sharing.

Thirdly, as far as possible any remaining physical storage, such as files that may need to be retained for audit or for statutory reasons, should be stored off the office floor, and preferably offsite.

Removing all this storage does liberate office space. If people object, they need to be reminded of the cost of the office floor space taken up by the storage (including the circulation space for storage) and the opportunity cost in relation to introducing smart and flexible working environments. The office should be for people, not paper.

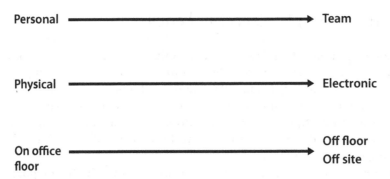

Figure 6.2   Trajectories for storage reform

Conducting a Storage Audit

A storage audit falls into three phases: Discovery, Analysis and Decision, as seen in Table 6.3. The discovery phase will usually throw up some horrors, and generate some laughs too. When asking the questions 'How much is there?', 'What is it?' and 'Who owns it?' it is surprising to staff just what is lurking in their cupboards, on their shelves and in the dark recesses of the office and basement.

'Where on earth did that come from?' 'That was so-and-so's – she left five years ago!' 'We stopped doing that in 1994 – that can go!' 'That's all online now' are the type of things people say. But that's the easy stuff to get rid of. Decisions get harder about the storage closer to home, in and around the individual desk

Table 6.3   The phases of a storage audit

Discovery phase	How much is there? Where is it? Who owns it? What does it consist of?
Analysis phase	How essential is it? How often needed How instantly needed How useful is it? Is it part of a process? Who is it for? How relevant is the format/medium of the information? Is it temporary? (i.e., draft, printed for meetings, work-in-progress, etc.) Is it available elsewhere?
Decision phase	Throw away! Cut out duplication Move to shared area/team storage Move away from floor Replace with electronic versions Reform processes to minimise passing paper around Alter storage to become more flexible

Personal Storage Entrenches Bad Working Practices

'Personal storage' comes in two forms: 'own personal' and 'personal professional'. A lot of the discussion around personal storage focuses on the 'own personal' stuff. It's about the nesting issues and territoriality involved in adorning your desk with pictures of the family, pot plants and knick-knacks, or filling the pedestal drawers and shelves by the desk with your own possessions. It spills into the computer too. The PC desktop carries an image of the desk owner's child/cat/partner/favourite band/holiday snap/naked firemen, and so on. The screen saver may be similarly personalised with floating pictures or messages.

Is there any harm in this? In one sense – not really. Looked at positively, the workers are bringing more of themselves into the office, making a corner of their environment like home and investing it with positive emotion and a sense of belonging. Who wants to work in a completely impersonal workplace?

Perhaps when you're having a terrible day at work, you can stop and look at a picture of your child (or cat, or whoever) and you feel better – more calm or more energised, as appropriate. More effective than a squadron of work-life balance counsellors, perhaps, for restoring good spirits and motivation.

So moves to desk-sharing involve a loss. Efficiency in the use of space increases, but maybe affection for the workplace diminishes a little.

This is why there has to be a 'quid pro quo' for people to consider surrendering territory. That quid pro quo may include actually seeing their child or their cat for real during the working day, rather than just a desktop image. I'm not sure how this pans out with the firemen, though.

The harm from all this nesting is more at the aggregate level than at the individual level. Once you have aggregated all that personal 'stuff' to organisational level, you may be talking about serious costs. And more than the surface space actually occupied by the personal items, it's the anchoring of people to one particular space that is wasteful. The more an individual desk and its surrounding area is personalised, the harder it is to share when the main occupier is not there.

More serious inefficiencies, though, tend to arise from the burgeoning of 'personal professional' items on, in and around individually assigned desks.

The 'personal professional' items fall into the following categories:

- Tools.
- Products and samples.
- Generic company information (company calendars, directories, and so on).
- Generic professional information (reference books, files, trade press, and so on).
- Role-specific professional information (for example, case files, decisions, and so on).
- Work-in-progress (active case files, letters, printed drafts, and so on).
- Historic information (past work completed).
- Possibly interesting information (things kept that may be read/might come in useful one day).

Discussions get interesting when people are challenged on how essential it is to:

a) Keep all this.
b) Have it within arm's length.
c) Have multiple copies across the office floor.
d) Have it in physical rather than electronic form.

These four issues are the essential ingredients of a personal storage audit. Delving into these issues usually uncovers a great deal of duplication of information across the office floor. And a great deal of clutter that many people think is unneeded. In staff surveys we've carried out, when asked how much paper could be reduced in their department, the typical response is between 25 per cent and 50 per cent. When storage of paper is actually analysed, it turns out to be a lot more.

Personal Storage: Lockers, Puppies and Hot Boxes

If personal storage at the desk is no longer an option, there is a need for storage elsewhere. Factoring in space for personal storage is important. The most common and the most obvious form of this is having a locker. It needs to be large enough to store a laptop and personal items such as handbags, change of clothes if you cycle/run to work, little bits of shopping and so on. Not to mention pencils, and other tools of the trade.

One solution is to have a kind of mobile locker, a pedestal on wheels with a handle. In the trade these are now known as 'puppies', I am told, and can be led up to the desk where you are working. Later they are packed up again with all your gear, and wheeled back to their 'garaging' space. To maintain the puppy moniker, maybe we shouldn't speak of garaging space but rather the 'dog pound', or possibly 'puppy farm'. The puppies/ pedestals are styled to integrate with desking systems, and in the brochures look very nice.

The key advantage: you don't have to carry any stuff to your desk/table – it's an intrinsically mobile solution with ergonomic advantages. You just wheel it there and have all your stuff next to you.

The key disadvantage: they take up more space than lockers – quite a lot more. Lockers will be stacked, two, three or four high. The puppy garaging takes up more space. And wheeled out onto the floor they take up more space – each desk needs some puppy-space too.

Another solution is a 'hotbox' – a box that slides into a locker and is easy to use to carry your things over to where you are sitting. Some varieties of these are lockable and have handles, and can be carted off to meetings outside, or taken home.

There is some evidence that people overestimate their need for this kind of portable storage. Use falls off over time as people get into the habit of sharing desks, clearing desks and working without knick-knacks and piles of files.

A Step Too Far?

For many organisations, changing to a purpose-designed Smart Flexibility working environment is a step too far. They feel they are just not ready for this. In reality, many do opt for implementing flexible working practices without going in for wholesale changes back at the office – at least not yet.

It's as well, though, to be aware of the possibilities, and the savings that are just waiting to happen if one goes the extra mile. And certainly worth thinking about for when the next lease negotiation is coming up, or when expansion would normally mean that extra investment in office space is needed.

The important thing to remember is: every day you don't make the saving, money is flowing out the door that could be used more effectively for something more productive.

H&S in Flexible Working Environments

When people are working more than occasionally from home, it is important that the home-working environment is set up properly, with a desk and appropriate chair. A specific homeworking or remote working policy or guidance document should provide more details of the specification. Here are some recommendations for what it should include.

It is best if there is a separate room to work in, that can be closed off from the rest of the house if needed. This is particularly the case if people are working from home frequently, and if they have to take many calls.

For people working regularly from home, a risk assessment must be carried out and training provided on the health and safety issues. There are no specific H&S regulations for homeworking in the UK: all the provisions that apply in the workplace apply wherever an employee is working. Particular regulations to consider include those that apply to:

- Using computer screens.
- Heating, lighting, ventilation.
- Having an ergonomic workplace.

- Electrics.
- Cabling.
- Working Time Regulations.
- Lifting and carrying.
- Security, including data security.
- Third-party safety.

In general, however, the evidence is that working from home does not carry substantial additional risk, and where it reduces travel it plays a part in reducing risk. Even so, it is necessary for everyone to be aware of the regulations that need to be observed and how to optimise their remote work spaces ergonomically.

Risk assessments can be carried out by a visit to the home. However, this can be seen as intrusive, and could be quite burdensome for the organisation, and somewhat over-the-top for part-time homeworkers. So most organisations manage health and safety through a combination of training and self-assessment techniques.

The employer has a duty of care to his/her employees wherever and whenever they are working. So it is probably a mistake to see homeworking in isolation. Many of the issues and the regulations apply wherever the employee is working, whether that is at home, at the airport, in a workhub or in flexible work settings in the office. So rules about use of laptops, having proper sitting positions, adjusting chairs, taking breaks, correct levels of heating and lighting need to be understood in relation to all locations.

For working for protracted periods of time using laptops the employer should provide proper equipment such as a laptop stand or a separate monitor to plug in to, plus separate keyboard and mouse. Over the next few years though we will see big advances in voice recognition technology and surface technologies that will make interacting with computers and their screens a very different ergonomic proposition – more of this in Chapters 7 and 14.

The main point is, though, that while health and safety are important issues, they should not be seen as barriers to flexible working. People resisting flexible working often put forward exaggerated arguments about the dangers and pitfalls. But for all the issues there are known solutions. It's a question of adopting good practice, just as for traditional ways of working.

The Best Working Environments – Wherever You Are Working

Having said that people should work in the most effective locations, it's up to the Smart Flexibility programme team and then the facilities and ICT teams to ensure that the new spaces and tools for work are as effective as possible. The role of these teams is therefore stretched beyond the traditional workplace. In spaces the organisation does not own, the role is more likely to be one of influencing than of directly managing.

This chapter has largely focused on making physical changes to the working environment. In Chapter 7 we will explore the ways in which technologies need to be integrated into these environments in order to maximise their utility. And in Chapters 8 and 9, we will look at the issues around changing behaviours and management techniques.

CHAPTER 7 *Technologies*

The Challenge – And a Kind of Disclaimer

Effective use of new technologies is central to a strategic approach to Smart Flexibility. Any book providing guidance about new ways of working must address the technology. But therein lies a problem. The problem is that the pace of change is such that any book that focuses too specifically on particular technologies is likely to be at least a little bit out of date even by the time it is published. And will become increasingly dated thereafter.

So in this chapter I will attempt to provide useful insight that treads the difficult path between being too specific and being too general. It's about providing principles to give guidance to the intelligent manager who is not a technology specialist about the role that technology plays in Smart Flexibility. In addition to this I'll be analysing current trends, outlining some potential pitfalls, and doing a bit of crystal-ball gazing about what's coming up on the horizon and how it may affect the increasingly smart and flexible world of work.

What Kinds of Technologies?

Technologies for supporting Smart Flexibility can be broken down into the following overlapping categories:

- Technologies that support mobility of work in the office.
- Technologies that support mobility of work beyond the office.
- Technologies that dematerialise resources used for work.
- Technologies that promote virtual collaboration and new ways of meeting.
- Technologies that support the managing and monitoring of distributed working.

Pretty much any technology for Smart Flexibility that you can think of will fall under one or more of these categories. And some, like technology for security, will be a feature of them all.[1]

---

1   Further details of particular technologies are available on the *Flexibility* website, see www.flexibility.co.uk. Here, if I mention a particular provider it will be a general reference to the brands that are already very widely available in the workplace.

IT for Mobility in the Office

Gaining the space-use efficiencies from Smart Flexibility that were discussed in the last chapter requires people to be much more mobile in terms of where they work in the office, and when they do it too. It involves desk-sharing (that is, not expecting to work at the same desk every time you're in the office) and working in a range of different work settings that are optimised for collaboration, specialist activities and brief touch-down between other activities.

In terms of IT, this has to mean scaling back on the number of desktop PCs – even to the point of doing away with them altogether. And the desktop PC as we know it will be a museum piece in five years' time, in any case. What should be taking its place?

At the moment it will mainly be laptops. When people come into the office, they use the laptops they have taken with them on their travels, or ones that they keep in their locker. They take it to the shared desk that is assigned, plug in, connect to the network and start working.

If they are to be working for more than an hour or two at that location, they should use a separate keyboard and mouse, and a laptop stand to elevate the laptop screen to eye level so the user can sit upright. An alternative or supplement to the laptop stand could be a separate screen at the desk to which you connect the laptop, so you get a bigger screen or use both screens.

I am sure screen technology will change radically over the next five years, and the option of having separate and multiple screens will become increasingly important when working in offices and working at home.

Some organisations favour having 'docking stations' for laptops, so you just clip in the laptop and off you go. I'm a sceptic, though. There may be technological arguments for this, but it's from a business point of view that I have my doubts. It locks you into one supplier, and when the time comes to change there's not only the laptop to upgrade but probably the docking station too. And it inhibits choice and variation in the meantime too. In particular, if you have people from other teams, or subcontractors or clients coming to share desks for a while, if they have different kit (and they probably do) the docking station is just something cluttering up the desk.

So it's usually better to have the simplest means possible for connecting to power supply and network. There also needs to be enough power supply and network connections at each desk for users to plug in multiple devices if required.

If laptops become the new normal, then there is a host of other portable devices that people will also be using when they come into the office, such as the various flavours of tablet devices. At the moment, many people who are mobile in the office (often managers) use a kind of tablet that is like a slimmed down laptop computer, but with a funky touch screen that can rotate and fold upwards over the keyboard so that the primary input is by touching the screen, usually with a pen. They've only been around since around 2001, and are already referred to as 'traditional' tablets. They are used quite a lot in the field in some sectors, but their use for roaming within sites or a campus has made them popular with some users.

But old hat they are already, as the iPad generation of tablets (both Apple and other operating systems) have taken consumer markets by storm. They are lighter, slinkier and have better screens for reading. At the time of writing, for all their slinkiness, they are very much in their infancy. We haven't yet seen their full capability for work usage. So far, if someone at a desk near you is using one, it's probably as an additional device rather than their main one, and is used for tasks like reading documents on the train, emailing and web surfing.

It won't stay this way, and the challenge for IT managers will be integrating a wide range of these kinds of things, probably owned by the employee and not the company, into a coherent and secure IT infrastructure. I imagine they will become the favoured style of device for use in modern paperless meetings.

Server-based computing is a must, and already is pretty much the norm in large organisations. The principle is that neither data nor systems are held locally (that is on individual user's computers) but centrally. Therefore they can be accessed from multiple locations, and by multiple users as necessary. This is important for remote access too. 'Thin client' technology is frequently talked about in this context. This refers to the amount of activity that goes on at the 'client' end of computing (that is, on the computer the user is interfacing with directly) and how much goes on at the server end (the bit that is far away and is dishing up the information and applications).

Actually there are various degrees of thinness/fatness when it comes to the amount of work being done at the client end, from having a completely 'dumb terminal' that holds neither data nor applications, to using a regular laptop for access to systems via a web browser or otherwise uses the client-server model where the server performs all the processing. Companies running thin client systems in practice combine having dumb terminals in the office, and even in employees' homes, with using laptops running thin client applications when on the move.

Basically, the non-IT manager should not get overexcited by technicalities in this area, and should probably distrust people who do. This is a fast-moving field, with a lot of fine distinctions and ambiguous terminology. And there are many options in this fast-moving field. The point is to have a system that is guaranteed as far as possible to work in all circumstances, and which can carry on working locally to a reasonable extent if remote access is unavailable. There is more than one way to achieve this, and will often depend on where technologically you are starting from.

As a general principle, people should connect by cable to the network when working in one place in the office for longer periods of time. For shorter periods, there needs to be wireless connectivity, so whether someone is working at a touch-down desk, a meeting room or project area, they have full and fast access to what they need.

Meeting rooms and project areas need to be equipped with smart display technologies that are easy to connect to, to enable collaborative work without recourse to using paper. In due course I am sure we will see all kinds of innovation in video walls, smart surface technologies and 3D applications that will augment the experience of working together – both with people physically present in the room and those beyond.

Communications for Mobility in the Office

In terms of communications, flexible telephony is a must. Nothing frustrates plans for more effective use of space quite like inflexible telephony. Traditional ways of working evolved to a point where it's each employee has one desk, one phone, one phone number – all individually assigned. Moving desk involves a call to facilities and/or IT to reassign a phone to our extension number. And that makes moves expensive.

The ability to log into a phone when you sit down at a desk has been around for many years now. Today it involves either a smart follow-me numbering system or Voice over Internet Protocol (VoIP) system. The latter is now becoming the norm.

A VoIP system (Internet-based telephony) allows the user to use a control panel to log into their phone account from wherever they are in the office – also beyond the office, though a more complicated set of issues is involved. To make desk-sharing work this kind of system is essential. VoIP can work with either a standalone handset supplied on the desktop, which looks pretty much like any other phone, and/or though softphones accessed through a computer, combined with use of a headset or plug-in handset.

The key principle is that when you log into your phone, your phone number comes to you, rather than you having to go to it. And you have access to your voicemail, 'hunt group' options and so forth. VoIP services usually include the ability to have voicemail messages delivered as sound files to email too, which is useful for forwarding them to someone else or accessing them from remote locations.

Above all it is cheaper. Calls to other extensions, including people working remotely, are essentially free.

Communication, though, is about more than phones. Phones are so twentieth century!

Instant messaging (IM) was the kind of technology banned by organisations in recent years. It was seen as a consumer technology associated with chit-chat and timewasting, and as coming with considerable security risks. Not now. Modern organisations implement IM as a productivity and collaboration tool, actively binding together the distributed workforce, whether people are in or out of the office.

An important feature that comes built in with IM is 'presence management', that is being able to flag up your availability online and set your status to say whether you are working, available to talk to, unavailable, and so on. People who use MSN, Windows Messenger, Skype, Microsoft Lync and so on will be used to this kind of IM and status-setting and how it can be combined with voice- and video-calling and document sharing. So just about everyone entering the workforce now will probably be using this kind of technology routinely outside work: it's just a question of integrating something fairly straightforward into work life.

There's more on this and other collaborative technologies in the section below on virtual collaboration and new ways of meeting.

Mobility Beyond the Office

In many respects the same principles, and same technologies, should apply to working beyond the office. Economies of scale are achieved by being able to use the same technologies wherever staff are working. One of the key mistakes to avoid in deploying Smart Flexibility is to consider mobile workers as having radically different requirements to other workers. Most office-based workers can be mobile to a greater or lesser extent.

But there are additional IT and communications kit and services that staff will need when working away from the office. Mobile phones are acquiring ever more functionality – and everybody has them. The business issue is whether the company should provide them, and if so what kind.

For road warriors there is no question but that the company should provide them. Managers tend to be provided with them as a matter of course, as they are frequently away from their desks and contact between them and their staff may be urgent.

However, it is not only voice communications that are the issue. Mobile devices are increasingly used for mobile email, for Internet access and for a range of other applications. Email, contacts and calendars can be synchronised with office systems. According to how time-critical email is, email can be set up on a 'push' or 'pull' basis.

Push email, as is standard with BlackBerrys, works on the basis of keeping an open connection between the mobile device and the mail server. The device is notified immediately when there is a new email or calendar appointment. Most mobile email systems at the moment work on a pull basis. That is, the user periodically logs in and downloads new mail. Over time, I would expect most systems would evolve to allow the choice of either method. Tablets may progressively erode the popularity of getting emails on smartphones.

Sometimes sceptical managers will argue against the need for accessing email via mobile devices on the basis that laptops can be used, and are better to work on. But it is not always practical when on the move to fire up the laptop, establish a connection (if there is one to be found) and log in either to the company systems or to webmail. The phone or tablet can provide much more instant access. And of course with phones you can also text, and on some operating systems run IM systems. I think there is no point in standing against the tide. For people leaving college and joining your organisation, not using the potential of smaller mobile devices will seem bizarre and Luddite.

However, from an efficiency and also from a cultural point of view, there are reasons to be cautious about having email constantly pushed out to you. In the office, unless your work depends on instantly responding by email to customers, there's a lot to be gained by cutting down the frequency of accessing emails. It's very disruptive to the flow of productive work, unless what you do is critically dependent on receiving and responding to them. And the same applies for the most part for people working outside the office.

Unified communications (UC) are also becoming increasingly important for virtual teamwork. UC integrates into a single user interface services providing both real-time communication (voice telephony, IM, videoconferencing) and non-real-time communication (voicemail, email, SMS and fax). It incorporates call control to route calls or messages according to the selected preference or status of users, plus speech recognition and text-to-speech software to convert messages from voice to text or vice versa.

UC can also integrate with business processes so that, for example, customer information can be called up or appropriate company experts can be flagged and brought into conversations if they are available.

People working outside the office do need effective remote access to office systems and data. There are a number of different technologies for doing this, but typically it will involve using the Internet and creating a secure, private connection back to the corporate network and accessing what is needed. This doesn't necessarily mean accessing anything that is hosted on machines that are physically in the office. The trend is towards hosting office systems on third-party servers which could be located anywhere. All the innards of this should be invisible to the remote worker, who just wants to log in and get going just as if he or she were in the office.

The remote access system needs to be fast, efficient and seamless. All too often, though, they offer a degraded working experience to the user. If the system is slow, falls over frequently, or does not allow access to all the applications needed, it will be a major brake on the uptake of flexible working.

Making it all smooth and seamless for the user can be a tough call for the IT department, who have to make it all happen. How easy it is depends on where they are starting from. Older applications need to be made accessible by grafting on 'middleware' that will make them accessible over the Internet. It may not be worth doing that, in which case it may be a case of developing new web-enabled applications that will do the job better.

If you know you have a database system that is not fit for purpose, there's little point sticking a web front end on it. Often it's the actual users who have the best take on this, and it's surprising how often they are not asked about upgrades or replacements – it's not only an issue for the IT department. So if systems need upgrading to make them accessible remotely, this is a good time to revisit how effective they are and to improve the specification.

Working outside the office, though, is not only about doing the same things as you do in the office, only somewhere else. Working more flexibly offers the opportunity to transform the ways you interface with clients and customers. People who have been stuck in the office can get out more, and they need the technologies to do it. Portable devices pitched somewhere between a mobile phone and a laptop may be what is required, and there is a range of these coming on to the market. Tablets in various sizes and, like the iPad, with inbuilt mobile connectivity are a key part of the picture.

Increasingly, field workers are using e-forms for collecting and processing information in a structured way, which can then flow back to or be synchronised with central systems. Handwriting recognition allows notes taken on the move and form entries to be processed into the format that is needed for subsequent use. Digital pens are an ultra-portable alternative, making a record that can be downloaded and processed later.

The technologies for working on the move need to be chosen on the basis of an analysis of the tasks involved in the work, and the inputs and outputs expected. The role of the IT department is to understand the business issues and advise about the possibilities. It is not to constrain the choice in accordance with what they are willing to provide and support. It may require adaptation, and costs for that need to be built into the business case for change.

What about technologies for the home office? The same principles apply about avoiding duplication and achieving economies of scale. Laptops or tablets in preference to desktop PCs, and an ergonomic set-up for working for longer periods. There has to be broadband Internet connection.

Should the company pay for the broadband? Usually there is some kind of threshold, for example if an employee is working an average two days per week or more from home or using home as a base, then the company might pay for the broadband.

Often there is a debate about whether the company should provide a printer for home workers. The default position should be 'No'. While it is true at the moment that long documents and detailed plans and so on can be hard to work through on screen, people should have to make a strong case to justify an exception to the rule, both to save costs and to save the planet. In a few years' time there will be much better screen technologies. They are already on their way in e-readers where you can comfortably read whole novels. In the meantime, having a larger additional screen can solve the problem and also boost productivity when you need to have multiple documents or different applications open at the same time.

The days are largely gone when technology can be used as an excuse to inhibit remote working and mobility. Just a few years ago people would say, 'I can't work at home because I use GIS and it won't run on a laptop', or 'I have to be in the office to work with this or that database system'. It won't wash any more. Pretty much anything done in most offices can be done pretty much anywhere now.

There are engineers working with CAD systems on the move, and people editing film and doing 3D animation from home, whizzing humungous files over the Internet to colleagues working all over the world. You just need the right tools for the job. The technology is there. When technology is used as an excuse for tethering people to the office, take a good hard look at what's really going on. It's not the technology but rather the vision, the will, or the up-front investment that is missing.

Dematerialising Resources Used for Work

In the last chapter we looked at the issue of dematerialising one of the key resources used for work – paper. There's pretty much no excuse left for generating and hanging on to tons of paper in the office. All the same, people can be hesitant about fully embracing the alternatives.

Early stage experience of using electronic systems to replace paper ones is often substandard. This will usually be because in the early stages there is often something of a hybrid – part paper, and part electronic – or because the electronic systems are not well indexed or managed, or because an enterprise system has gaps, embeds oddities or is too inflexible and that makes it hard to work with in the real world.

Such experiences should be an incentive to get it right, rather than an incentive to back-track and return to paper – the potential savings are enormous. So a properly managed electronic document management system is vital, with systematic scanning of all relevant paper-based materials that come in.

Large organisations can end up having a range of bespoke electronic systems for accounts, customer records, case management, order fulfilment and so on. Often these do not talk to each other, and are difficult to make available online for the remote and mobile workforce. So when looking to 'dematerialise' it's worth looking at completely new Internet-based systems and services (see the section below on cloud technology) which are optimised to be accessible from anywhere.

But it's not only paper. There are various items of equipment that need to be on their way out. Like fax machines. In some sectors such as manufacturing there is still extensive use of faxes, for orders, invoices, contracts, certification and so forth. In the past year I've been asked to fax documents to accountants, an insurance company and contract departments. But I haven't had a fax machine for around seven years now.

Faxes in a digital age are an oddity, a strange hybrid. This is how it goes. Someone generates a document on a computer, and prints it out. They then digitise it through a fax machine and send it over a telephone line to another machine, where it is rematerialised as a printed document, and filed. Maybe it's eventually made electronic again when it's scanned during an archiving process.

Of course this is all unnecessary, and increasingly people are using email fax services that keep the entire process electronic, unless or until there is a final printout for filing. Some people may be reading this in wonderment that this still goes on, but I do still see a lot of it. Some people consider it more 'real' as a true copy or facsimile of a real artefact, especially where there are signatures or company stamps and seals involved. The issues here are not only technical, but cultural too.

So fax machines need to go, replaced by (scanning and) emailing and email fax services. Worst case is to scan something to send through an email fax service – a single dematerialisation process at point of origin, and it should never re-enter the physical world again. And no 'fax' received via email need ever be materialised as a printed document.

Serving Up Technology from the Cloud

Cloud computing is a term currently put forward to describe a range of third-party services that will probably change the way most organisations structure their IT provision. It's probable that if you are discussing IT strategy in relation to deploying more flexible working practices, cloud computing will have been thrown into the mix as being highly relevant. But what is it?

The 'cloud' basically means the Internet, and that your organisation in the future need not host its own IT, but will outsource it to a third-party provider. This means buying the IT platform, the infrastructure and software as services. Critics say it has become rather muddled and includes too many different types of services to be meaningful as a concept. To a large extent the debates around what it is are not relevant – the point is that following a cloud computing route involves having less and less of your IT capability based within your company, or even located on your PC, laptop or other device as web-based applications are increasingly used for business purposes.

For Smart Flexibility there are intrinsic advantages to this kind of approach to technology, and it further loosens any necessary connection between the individual worker and any particular location of work. The office is available on the Internet, and as long as you can access the Internet, you can access your office systems and data.

In one sense, it's a bit like accessing online banking or using eBay or Amazon. We expect to be able to do this from wherever we happen to be, and from any device we are using, and at any time too. We expect these services to be secure and always available. As users, we don't worry too much about how it is all set up behind the scenes – as long as it works.

It's not the only approach for supporting Smart Flexibility, but it does have some advantages. In particular, it helps to move IT costs from fixed to variable – or at least more variable. Buying as much of your IT capability as possible as a service gives more flexibility to meet changes in your demand. Cloud computing solutions are intrinsically scalable, and you don't have to worry how the extra capacity is found: you simply have to order it and pay for it.

In business terms it's similar to the principle of reducing the amount of fixed office space required, and treat much or all of your office requirement as a resource to be bought in on an as-needed basis from third-party providers.

My feeling is that 'cloud computing' as a term may look quaint in five or ten years' time, like 'horseless carriage' and 'gramophone'. But the trend in this direction – to Internet-based services – is pretty much unstoppable because it makes good business sense. The point is to leverage extra value from investments in this kind of IT outsourcing by using it to enable the workforce to be more flexible, agile and location-independent. Smart Flexibility doesn't require cloud computing. But if your IT strategy team are planning migration to the cloud and are not thinking of how it can facilitate Smart Flexibility, then they're missing a trick and also a key part of the business case for migration.

BYOD – Bring Your Own Device

Forward-looking IT departments are now grappling with the issues around using employee-owned devices for work purposes. It is linked in part with the development of cloud-based services and web-based interfaces, which in principle are easier to access from many different kinds of device.

The issue is really the pace of technological change and the fact that in many respects consumer technology is setting the pace. Companies try to play catch-up, but the expense and logistical challenges of keeping up to date and issuing the latest versions to large numbers of people mean that in general they are falling further and further behind. So why not bite the bullet, reverse the traditional policy and allow people to use their own kit if it suits them, and if it meets some minimum standards?

Companies can share the cost of buying or leasing the employee's choice of device, and/or supply software to enable them to access their virtual desktop or phone account securely on their own device.

The biggest fears of course are around security. And the way forward is again to manage risk by having systems that do not leave a footprint on the device and where information and applications can be wiped remotely should the device be lost. It will require new approaches both to deploying remote access and to managing risk. There are sure to be many challenges ahead, but the old approach of banning employees' devices from interfacing with office systems seems to be on its way out.

Technology in Completely Virtual Companies

If a company has no specially designated business premises, what kind of technology should it have?

Well, there are such companies including our case study company OAC, though most of them are not very large. There are two basic models. One has a central point or home for IT infrastructure, based at someone's home or with an IT provider. Employees have remote access to this.

Each employee will probably be using some kind of 'fat client' device, whether a desktop PC, laptop or ('traditional') tablet. In this kind of implementation, the management of the applications is a more traditional process of seeing that everyone has the same kind of software on their local machine, and access to corporate systems through remote access.

The second model is one of cloud computing, where there is little processing happening on the employee's own computer. Software applications are served up on an as-needed basis. When an upgrade happens, it happens for everyone.

One of the key advantages of cloud computing is its scalability, so in that sense it seems the best way to go for the small business that wants to grow without growing any premises and keeping a tight lid on fixed costs.

THE VIRTUAL AND WIDE-RANGING ACTUARIES: OAC PLC

OAC plc is a firm of actuaries that operates on an entirely virtual basis. It has nationwide coverage in the UK providing actuarial and financial services consulting – and has no offices.

This case study illustrates the potential of businesses to grow both their business and their staff numbers without taking on extra premises – or, in this case, any premises at all. And it also shows how a company has developed techniques for managing the 'anywhere team'.

OAC was founded in 1994 as Oxford Actuaries, and was incorporated as a plc in 2003. Unusually in a sector run very much on traditional lines, OAC was set up to be a virtual company from the start. The company now has 30 permanent staff, and a further 10 contractors who work on an integrated basis using the office systems and network.

OAC has been expanding during the downturn, and currently plans to double the number of its permanent staff. This raises the question whether there are limits to the size of company that can operate virtually – so far OAC has not reached it.

Christiane Perera, Head of People and Development, sums up the advantages for OAC in operating a 'teleworking' model:

- Cutting down overhead costs
- Lower costs translates into competitive pricing, essential for the growing company in this market, to punch above their weight and compete with larger consultancies
- Ability to recruit talented people regardless of location, pulling in people who would otherwise not be available
- Easier to work with overseas clients, using electronic collaboration
- Overcoming the barrier of having to have an office to meet clients
- Ability to continue growing, even during the recession

For staff, the key advantages are:

- Greater flexibility to work at times of their own choosing
- Elimination of daily travel costs
- Being involved in a firm that offers a greater variety of work than they could do if they were geographically limited

From the outset the aim was to allow staff to be able to work from home, and to work flexible hours so as to be able to achieve a better balance between home and work. At the same time, the aim was to build a strong company identity by using systems to ensure that employees working from home did not feel isolated.

Sustainability was also among the aims, with an aspiration from the outset to eliminate the need to commute and to run a largely paperless office by using electronic documents in preference to printing. All incoming mail is scanned.

The company's IT is hosted externally by an IT service provider. Staff are equipped with laptops, separate keyboard, mouse and large screen, business line, mobile phone and remote access to office systems, which are Lotus Notes-based. There is remote support for IT, so if there are any issues their provider can take control of any staff computer and deal with the problem. OAC is beginning to look at cloud services as a possible next step.

For communication, staff make use of both IM and conferencing technologies, mainly audio conferencing and WebEx collaboration. Teams do meet up physically for project work, but now make sure it is for at least half a day to make the journey worthwhile. And staff have to meet clients. But more clients are now getting into conferencing, so OAC is trying to encourage that.

For Christiane Perera it's always been more about the people than the technology. OAC is Investors in People accredited, and assiduous attention is paid to how to develop and maintain relationships and best practice in people management as the company grows.

The company is divided into a number of practices, and practice leaders as well as managing their specialism play a key role in keeping their teams together, encouraging professional development and dealing with any possible issues of isolation. Staff use discussion boards for people to bring forward ideas and make sure work being done is as transparent as possible. Telephone conferencing is used for team projects, board meetings and any other 'team' related discussions, and people meet up for workshops. Now OAC is doing some remote training as well – a natural thing to do based on the normal way of working.

According to Christiane:

> The aim should be that everyone helps everyone else to communicate. So when we recruit people, it's not only about getting people who can fit in with the team but also finding people who are proactive. We're trying to create the atmosphere to do that.
>
> When people join, the induction takes them through the ways of working, both in terms of the technology, and in terms of the cultural expectations. We have a mentoring approach, and partner new recruits with someone who will help them to navigate through any problems and issues.

Technologies for Virtual Collaboration and New Ways of Meeting

All companies should have fewer meetings. All companies should ensure they have fewer physical meetings. All companies should ensure they reduce the miles people travel, and the time they waste, by going to meetings. At the same time, they should be open to meeting more people, and adding more value to collaborative activities. Fewer meetings, more effective interaction.

Key to squaring the circle of this collaboration paradox is effective use of technology. The use of technology falls into two categories:

1. Replacing meetings by doing something else.
2. Holding meetings without physically meeting.

1) REPLACING MEETINGS BY DOING SOMETHING ELSE

We have a closer look at how to overcome a 'meetings culture' in Chapter 8. The first step is to make the meetings you have more effective, and reduce the need for additional meetings. That can mean doing some of the stuff that is normally done in meetings outside them. One good way to do this is to follow our somewhat hyperbolic maxim:

'Never use a meeting to provide information!' Meetings are much more useful if people already have the information they need, and have had time to digest it, in order to use it effectively and make informed decisions.

That means effective use of email, IM, shared documents or online discussion forums to share information and comments in a timely fashion. Doing this can reduce the number of meetings, and/or reduce the length of them. Virtual collaboration in this way can substitute for meetings, or at least for routine parts of meetings.

Self-help online learning also falls into this category. While meeting for training can often add value, there is an increasing role for self-managed e-learning solutions. The scalability of such solutions is a particular advantage in terms of time saved in training large numbers of people.

2) HOLDING MEETINGS WITHOUT PHYSICALLY MEETING

There is a range of solutions for having meetings based on virtual rather than physical presence, or combining the two. Audio conferencing (teleconferencing) is a technology extensively and routinely used in some organisations, while being almost never used in others. There are no good technical reasons for this – it is entirely a question of familiarity and culture.

Audio conferencing is easy to set up using dial-in services, using Internet phone services like Skype, or as a feature of online meeting applications such as Citrix GoToMeeting, WebEx or Lync. Using desk or mobile phones it's also becoming ever easier to add people in to calls to have multi-way conversations.

In an audio conference all the participants may be in different places, or some may be together in a meeting room using a speakerphone while others are joining in from elsewhere.

Videoconferencing has developed more slowly than people have expected – it hasn't proved to be the revolutionary form of communications that was anticipated 10 years ago. At the high end of room-based systems it has been expensive and tricky to integrate into a normal working day, except perhaps at executive level where there are many examples of quite dramatic savings when it is introduced and reduces long-distance travel for highly paid people.

And now of course there is 'Telepresence' – high-end and room-based with huge screens that can make it seem as if the other participants are sitting on the other side of the table. This can overcome some of the missing ingredients of virtual meetings, as it captures much more of the interpersonal dynamics and body language.

Waiting to come of age have been the desk- and desktop-based systems. Videophones have been available for some time but are not widespread. What is making the difference is having video integrated into those systems mentioned above for online conferencing. Really, it's not about the video, it's about having the flexibility of interaction from the desktop to have voice, video and sharing applications – whatever is appropriate to combine during that call or online meeting.

People who work in virtual teams, working on projects together but in different countries or continents, use these technologies routinely, and throw in IM as well. This flexibility of use starts to take us to the question of 'when is a meeting not a meeting?' It can be a two-way interaction or a multi-way interaction, bringing in people as needed, even leaving the call/meeting open while people work on things and interact intermittently or reconvene. So it can end up as people more or less – virtually – working at adjacent desks, and doing away with the need to travel to a meeting at all, or even holding a specific event that is recognisable as a meeting.

When you get to this stage of using the technologies for interaction, a good headset is a must. Holding a phone handset is too constraining for working at the same time and ergonomically unsound. And ideally this headset has noise cancellation to screen out other ambient noises. And rechargeable wireless headsets are good if you are on the move or like to move about during calls. Or if you need to wander off into a confidential setting to have private conservations.

So we have swanky corporate room-based systems, including telepresence, at one end of the scale, and the local device-based systems at the other.

In the middle is having the kit in regular meeting rooms – preferably all meeting rooms – to scale up the kind of activity that happens at the low end into a more formal meeting setting. The basic meeting-room kit is to have a reasonable-size screen or screens, decent audio and Wi-Fi. A spiderphone (speakerphone) enables good audio participation. And a camera for the room is a useful though not a completely essential addition, as webcams on laptops can pick up the video. Cameras that follow voices and turn to the person speaking are good, though a little bit spooky on first encounter. But possibly it's not essential to have video for all the participants – it can be mix and match.

The prices for these technologies are tumbling, so there should not be any major technical of financial obstacles in the way of including these solutions. The productivity advantages make the business case, even before considering savings from reduced travel and staff time costs.

So what is stopping people doing it? Unfamiliarity and old habits, mainly. Some people may have had some mediocre experiences with videoconferences in the past, and that can be a constraint. People also need training in the pretty simple routines for using the conferencing technologies, bringing new participants in, passing control to each other and so forth. So it's possible to spend the first 10 minutes of such a meeting sorting out someone's missing audio, or getting a presentation up and visible to everyone. And that can get frustrating. But those are teething troubles, and once people know what they are doing it's like riding a bike. You forget there was ever a time when you couldn't do it.

Technology for Managing and Monitoring of Distributed Working

Technology also has a part to play in monitoring and managing flexible working. There are four main areas of this:

- Planning and scheduling.
- Time and/or work recording.
- Monitoring performance.
- Booking spaces.

I have already mentioned, and will cover in more detail in the chapter on Managing the Anywhere, Anytime Team, the need for being more organised when it comes to managing and being a part of a distributed team. It's partly about being a little more formal about organising and monitoring work than you might be if you were sat next to someone all the time.

PLANNING AND SCHEDULING

There is a range of applications that can be used for scheduling the times of work of flexible workers, and project management software for planning and scheduling work. Another approach is to have timetables and schedules available for all the team on a shared drive, SharePoint site or other intranet site that all the team have access to. Permissions can be allocated so that team members can update these, add new documents, and so on.

The point is less about the particular software used and more about the fact of doing something that is:

a) Coherent;
b) Always up to date; and
c) Visible to all the team.

And then there is the team discipline around making sure they keep in touch with the scheduling, understand each other's workloads and do what they need to do at the right time. It's a theme of the book that it's as much about the behaviours as any particular technology solution.

But what isn't needed in Smart Flexibility is an inflexible daily or weekly physical presence face-to-face (PPF2F) meeting to give everyone their schedules and talk about the work. There will be occasions for PPF2F meetings, but these will be about brainstorming, digging deep into complex issues, making critical decisions and so forth. So having the schedules online and having regular virtual presence face-to-face (VPF2F) contact is the way forward.

In this context, one comment that is often made to me is how little use is made of the full capabilities of standard office products, such as Microsoft Outlook. Everyone knows that they can use shared calendars, but this is often a function that is underused or not used at all, even though Outlook has been used for years. It's important to start using this when employees are working at different times and in different places on a regular basis. Similarly, using the 'Tasks' function can supplement or reinforce the systematic approach to scheduling.

TIME RECORDING

There are also numerous providers of time-recording software for the flexible and distributed workforce, and sometimes this is integrated with scheduling software. People may well need to record the time spent on projects or client accounts, but I wonder if there is a danger in putting too much emphasis on time: are we just extending presenteeism beyond the office? I would strongly discourage using time-recording systems simply as a means of clocking in or meeting requirements for core-time flexitime.

In the kinds of implementations we're talking about, management by results isn't just a measure of time spent at a desk. And in addition, there may be some duplication with other systems that automatically 'clock' when someone has logged in, for example, to their virtual desktop, remote access system or to their VoIP phone. It may simply be more efficient to derive reports from this data rather than superimpose another system requiring separate input from the flexible worker.

Bridging the gap between time recording and monitoring performance is the kind of innovative software just coming onto the market that enables automatic tracking of activity by members of distributed teams, generating timesheets without the need for additional data entry. The manager can then see detailed reports of how individuals have been spending their working day, including time spent in meetings, on the phone, using specific applications on their PC and so on. Expect more of this genre of software to come along as more and more management and monitoring tasks become automated and include increasingly intelligent features.

MONITORING PERFORMANCE

Management by results can be a challenge for managers dealing with a remote workforce. Software is available that can count keystrokes, or can tell when specified documents are being actively worked on and count that in as time on a specified project or piece of work. For tasks like data processing or virtual call centre work, the output is quite simple to count and there should already be ways to measure output in place. So what applies in the office also applies beyond the office.

There is a principle involved here – if you're finding it hard to think how to measure output if someone's out of the office, there's almost certainly something wrong with your performance management already. It indicates an uncertainty around what people are meant to be doing, and in knowing exactly what a good result is. There's more about this in our chapter on productivity.

If this is the case, then having more people working in different places and at different times should be seen as an opportunity to tighten things up and get more systematic. There is a wide range of performance software out there for measuring and monitoring output, analysing it, reporting and feeding back, involving stakeholders and so forth. These can be pretty much as sophisticated as you like, though from our point of view it is important that people can work with them wherever they are based, so it needs to be a web-based system.

And from a flexible working point of view, it's also worth noting that the organisation should be able to monitor not only the performance of individuals and teams, but also the impacts of the flexible working scheme as a whole, and of the spaces where people work.

We've mentioned the measurable benefits of flexible working in Chapter 3. So it's necessary to set in train the systems to measure them. I don't yet know of an integrated tool to pull all this together, so there's a challenge for smart working specialists and software developers out there.

In the meantime, organisations, departments or teams implementing flexible working could set up online reporting mechanisms for capturing information for example, about reduced business travel, increases in productivity, and so on.

One kind of tool that does exist already is the employee survey, to get feedback on a range of indicators; for example, work-life balance, workplace productivity and surveys can be tailored to capture staff feedback on a range of measures.

Improvements (or otherwise) in workplace occupancy can be captured through periodic reruns of the kind of space audit mentioned in Chapter 4. Or if you want continuous real-time monitoring, there are various kinds of sensor techniques that monitor occupancy of spaces and/or movements in the office. Some feel this is a bit Big Brotherish and too intrusive, but most people don't mind as long as the sensors don't extend into the toilets. Though when you think about it, throughput – in terms of people – in these areas could yield a lot of useful information for the facilities team to help planning, provision and maintenance.

Continuous occupancy monitoring can work by having sensors (not cameras) under desk positions that detect when a position is occupied, or room-based sensors that can pick up information from badges, or advanced imaging that can count people by analysing images. Information gathered from these techniques is fed back to a central server and provides real-time information and analytics. Some of this may seem a bit Star Trek, as well as a bit Big Brother, and until recently it has been a tad on the expensive side, so more the preserve of private-sector large corporations.

However, prices in this field are tumbling as techniques are improving, so expect more of this in the future. About 15 years ago I read an article in *New Scientist* about video and computing, and it prophesied something like: 'In the future everyone will be being watched by everyone else – and we won't care'. It's starting to happen, isn't it?

Or if the sensors are indeed a step too far, mining the data from room- and desk-booking systems (see below), swipe-card entry systems and logging-in systems can also yield data about how the building is being used, though is less effective in terms of reporting on actual occupancy of particular spaces (that is, booking or logging in is not the same as actual usage of a space).

Some of all this is about making your existing tools, such as your workplace information systems, work a bit harder. It's a question of thinking how they can be leveraged or adapted to yield useful monitoring of the impacts of changes to working practices.

ROOM AND DESK-BOOKING

There is a variety of technologies for booking spaces in the office, mainly meeting rooms and desks, though in principle this could be extended to any kind of space (though I'm not really sure why one would want to *book* other spaces). The reason I'm talking about booking systems in a book about Smart Flexibility is that with space-sharing coupled with more intensive use of buildings, managing the supply of space to meet demand is an important issue.

Most large organisations have some kind of system for booking meeting rooms, and systems range from a list at reception through to fully automated online systems. There are some major providers of good booking systems, and this appears to be a growing market judging by the number of new players in the field and the evolution of new products.

The best ones allow people to book meeting rooms from wherever they are, integrate with calendars, and also integrate with a control panel at the entrance to the meeting room that allows people (a) to see if it's booked and (b) allows people to terminate their booking if the meeting ends early or if the room is no longer needed.

These kinds of systems can also include the ability to order refreshments, if that's the kind of thing your organisation does.

Desk-sharing has led some organisations to implement desk-booking systems as well. Desk-sharing plus booking is sometimes known as 'hotelling', because basically you call ahead to book your stay. It can also have the advantage of letting your location in the office be visible to colleagues. On the whole, this kind of hotelling is more typically used in implementations where people sit anywhere, rather than one that has a more team-based focus. Or it may apply to locations or parts of the office that are specifically set up for a more touch-down type of hotdesking. The question is, do you need a booking system?

Unless you have an office with a very high throughput of mobile staff, it's usually quite possible to manage without a desk-booking system. Teams can work it out for themselves with peak demand met by expanding into other team areas where there is vacant space or into touch-down or break-out areas.

On the other hand, a good desk-booking system will include reporting tools which will help you keep track of how your desk-space is being used – at least in terms of bookings, though actual occupancy may be different if there is not good discipline around terminating bookings when the desk is not being used. And there are some quite funky systems around now that use interactive floor plans (like booking your plane seat) which may help users to find the best places to sit. They can also be reassuring to flexible workers in that before arriving at the office, they know exactly where they will base themselves.

A good meeting-room booking system is generally worth having. It can increase the availability of meeting rooms as long as there are protocols around not block-booking spaces. And it works better when it is supplemented by a range of non-bookable spaces, for example, smaller meeting pods and informal meeting spaces, 15-minute meeting rooms and so on. And the other technologies described above can help to manage down the demand for formal meeting space.

In general, a mixture of bookable and non-bookable spaces will give the right mix for flexibility in the office.

The Environmental Factor in IT Choices

Choices of IT and communications make a difference to the carbon footprint of the organisation. And there are campaigns to encourage companies to 'green their IT'. As we'll see in Chapter 13, there are some general principles to follow: in particular choose laptops or tablets (and other smaller devices) rather than desktops, virtualise IT where possible, and eliminate duplication. But this is a fast-moving field, and generally speaking what you buy tomorrow won't be as efficient and green as what you could buy the day after.

And in terms of the total lifecycle environmental footprint, the carbon reductions you achieve locally may be outweighed by the carbon costs of all the new production and obsolescence involved.

The real benefits come less from 'greening IT' than from 'greening with IT'. Your new servers may use less power than your old one. But far more important is the fact that it allows tens, hundreds or thousands of employees to commute less, and enables you to reduce office space as the network becomes the office. This is where the real carbon benefits are.

Bandwidth

In implementing flexible working, bandwidth is a key issue, and will remain a key issue for the foreseeable future. Available bandwidth determines how much information you get down the wire or over wireless networks, and how quickly. It's a key ingredient of efficiency in the modern workplace, and without a good chunk of it remote working practices can soon disintegrate.

There are two aspects to this: bandwidth in the organisation, and bandwidth when working over public networks. Nearly all remote and mobile workers will rely to a large degree on consumer telecommunications networks.

It is interesting to note that in the mid-1990s when people first started seriously to talk about ubiquitous broadband access, 2 Mbps (megabits per second) was seen as the minimum speed for any broadband definition of bandwidth. It is only in the last few years that broadband speeds like this have become affordably available. In the 10 year interim period 'broadband' has been promoted that is only a quarter of that speed. And it is sold mainly as an 'asymmetrical' product where download speeds (coming from the Internet to you) are fast while upload speeds (going from you to the Internet) are much slower. The assumption in the market has been that the majority of people using the Internet are passive consumers rather than active producers of content or people directly and synchronously communicating with colleagues or friends.

At the time of writing, the government is proposing a more ambitious programme including extending fast broadband to all parts of the UK. Time will tell if there is flesh to put on the bones of these proposals. BT and Virgin Media are bringing in in much faster 50+ Mbps services, but these reach very few areas right now. We've got a long way to go to catch up with Korea.

Mobile phones, too, provide a very patchy service that is a major constraint on effective mobile working. It's always puzzled me that there's a standard for mobile phone coverage of 95 per cent of the population, which the providers claim they achieve. But that is based on where people live – that is, where they are stationary rather than when they are mobile.

The actual geographic coverage of the nation is about 50 per cent. So as soon as you start moving anywhere, your mobile phone signal peters out and dies. Five miles out of Cambridge you lose the signal. On the (overground) train between Waterloo and Guildford you'll lose a call several times. There's no excuse for this – except poor infrastructure planning and weak regulation.

What the current patchy state of the infrastructure has meant is that a range of applications important to business have been stunted by this approach to the market – in particular Internet telephony (VoIP) and videoconferencing.

So we are in an age of transition. What we have now is only a fraction of the capability that we will develop for working remotely over the next 10 years. And the Smart and Flexible Organisation should be preparing now for continuous evolution.

Theory, Practice and the IT Department

In the sections above we've looked at what technologies can do and the key technologies for implementation. It is down to the IT department to see that it all happens, and ideally the IT department plays a key role as part of an integrated team.

In practice, non-IT managers are often perplexed by the language and the culture of the IT department, and sometimes find it hard to see the business benefits of new applications. Innovation is often left in the hands of the IT department, where leadership

– or the authority to lead – is sometimes lacking in terms of having a clear vision of the wider business objectives. So there's a need for a two-way process of awareness-raising so that the business understand IT, and IT understands the business.

IT managers tend necessarily to be risk averse, too. It is their job to stop business-critical systems falling over, and to add realism to the overexcited ambitions of people who want to roll out the latest technologies with all their business benefits, and do it yesterday.

One of the biggest obstacles to change can be an unwillingness or inability on the part of IT departments in large organisations to try something different. A combination of IT strategies, 3-year refresh programmes, outsourced contracts and 'not invented here' syndrome can frustrate emerging plans for smarter working. It can boil down basically to: 'We're the experts, we know what we're doing, we've got plans and what you're suggesting isn't part of it. And by the way, who the hell do you think you are telling us what to do?'

The same can also be true of the Property and Facilities departments too – any function that has responsibilities for strategy, procurement and deployment of the infrastructure that the Smart Flexibility team want to change. That's why it's essential to have that top-level support and a high-level interdisciplinary team on board at the start.

How bad can it get if the IT department isn't on side? Basically they can stop the programme in its tracks, or make it so expensive that the business case no longer stacks up.

The biggest weapon of the IT function is the ignorance of the client, backed up by a row of 0s on the cost of everything. In several implementations, I have seen way over-the-top figures come back from both in-house and outsourced IT departments for modest innovations such as having Wi-Fi in a cafe/break-out area or for a pilot in Internet telephony.

In one case, the chief executive of an organisation got a call from the lawyers of the outsourced IT provider, saying if the organisation went ahead with a pilot (using a product they had refused to supply) it was a breach of contract. In the end a kind of compromise was reached, where after several months delay the IT partner trialled its own version of the solution – at a cost of £10,000 where the proposed trial was less than a tenth of the cost. Small money, but a very big principle at stake – the supplier's monopoly position in providing IT services to the client.

I'm not an expert in writing contracts for IT outsourcing, but there are a couple of principles worth recommending:

1. No one can predict what is coming up on the horizon in terms of workplace IT and communications innovation. So it's important not to put your supplier in a position where they have an effective veto over your future strategy. It's essential to make it clear when looking for future solutions that your company will not be bound to one supplier.
2. Your supplier should not be able to put forward costings for new services unchallenged. It's important to reserve the right to test the market to see whether your supplier is proposing costs that are over the top, and exploiting its monopoly position. Proposing unrealistic costs should be considered a 'non-performance' issue.

The issues are complex, of course, but the principle is clear. When a key business objective is endorsed by the board, the IT department needs to ensure that it happens.

Innovation should not be forced into the shackles of anyone's existing preferences and arrangements.

Opposition in IT departments is best overcome by winning hearts and minds, exciting them with the challenge of innovation. If that doesn't happen, then promoting troublemakers out of harm's way is one solution. However, the bait of a good level of corporate investment in the IT department is usually enough to bring them onside.

Generally, people in the IT department are excited by innovations that depend on good use of technology. Their enthusiasm needs to be married to a good understanding of what each part of the business needs. And this is an area where other managers who are not specialists in IT really should ensure that they have a good outline grasp of the technologies and what they are good for, and a sense of curiosity that will help them keep abreast of the fast-moving changes in business technology. Later we will be looking at the essential people skills that modern smart and flexible managers need to have. In the same way, they need some core skills around understanding technologies so that they can get their teams using them to maximum effect.

8 *Developing a Smart Flexibility Culture*

Reformers have the idea that change can be achieved by brute sanity.

George Bernard Shaw

When we talk about organisational culture, we mean the way things are done, both formally and informally, and the assumptions and expectations about how things are and should be done. This covers work organisation, the way workplaces are run, leadership styles, values and language, the way people relate to each other and the rules and conventions that surround how things are done. It includes mechanisms of power, trust and control. In this chapter we are interested in how to develop a Smart Flexibility culture, and specifying what this is.

Smart Flexibility working practices require changes in behaviour. At one level, this is self-evident. Working in a different place or at a different time, in a different environment and with different tools means that we will, of necessity, behave differently.

To maximise the positive impacts of Smart Flexibility, the changes must be more than procedural or cosmetic. For the new working practices to become embedded and take root, both the behaviours and the assumptions underlying them have to change at a more profound and transformative level.

Reorganisation Rarely Brings Deep Change

In most organisations, both the way things *are meant to be done* and the way things *are actually done* largely go unchallenged. There may be grumbling and complaints, and the occasional minor reform, but the basic ways of doing things carry on.

Even apparently big organisational changes often make little difference to the way we actually work, and have little impact on the assumptions and behaviours that make up organisational culture.

Big upheavals usually take the form of restructuring, moving premises, or introducing new technologies that affect processes. But if you had a butt-kicking command-and-control culture before the upheaval, the likelihood is that you'll still have the same culture afterwards. Perhaps it is even intensified after the pain of change, as new managers exert their authority over their newly acquired teams. And if you had a long-hours coats-on-the-backs-of-chairs-at-seven-in-the-evening culture before your office relocation, my guess is that it's travelled with you. The coats are just on the backs of different chairs.

Such changes may well make a positive impact on costs, by moving offices or shedding staff. But too often they don't make any difference to *effectiveness*. You often end up with the same old problems, only in a slightly different shape.

Often one of the first acts of new senior managers is to examine the structure of the organisation, or the part they are responsible for. Then follows a reorganisation of the deckchairs, with lots of people applying or reapplying for jobs. Different departments are grouped together, only to be ungrouped and regrouped when the next New Broom arrives. Projects are paralysed mid-stream, morale slumps and paralysis kicks in as everyone's attention focuses on their job security, including thinking about whether to stay or jump ship.

Re-engineering business processes likewise often takes place without fundamentally changing how people work. They may move into new teams, and do new things. But the *where* and *when* of what they do, and their *behaviours and relationships* in the office will probably not have changed at all.

The CAN Test

Changing the culture of an organisation needs to have a practical, rather than a theoretical, approach. As I've found in many a training session, people do like to talk about the culture of their organisation, and like to talk about specifics too. Often people feel quite passionately about it, and have a lot of issues to vent.

It takes a new way of thinking, though, to relate working practices with the problems and fault-lines identified in the organisation. A good way to move conversations forward is to apply what I call the CAN test. That is, *Challenge the Assumption of Necessity* about the where, when, why and how of doing things. This involves the following questions, about any working practice:

- *Why* are we doing this (at all)?
- Why are we doing this *here*?
- Why are we doing this *in this way*?
- Why are we doing this *now* (rather than at another time)?

Challenging all assumptions is an important step when introducing new flexible working practices. Many people, accustomed to the old ways and unfamiliar with the potential of the new ones, approach conversations about change with certain assumptions of necessity. It may revolve around a type of job. 'This kind of job has to be done in the office', is a phrase I've heard many times.

But does it? Let's have a look at a couple of examples where we can Challenge the Assumption of Necessity.

What kind of job is it? It's a PA. The PA has to be in the office. Full stop.

Is this necessarily so?

In fact, I know several senior managers who have a remote PA. Thinking about the capacity for flexibility, it's important to ask the question: 'What do they *actually* do?' Our image of a PA is no doubt coloured by experience. Nearly every senior manager's PA we've ever come across sits in a private office by the door of a larger private office, as a kind of facilitator or gatekeeper.

But two-thirds of the time the boss's office doesn't have the boss in it. And the diary the PA keeps is electronic. Having letters (or emails!) dictated is now rare – and in any case can be recorded and written up anytime, anywhere.

So what is the logic of having boss and assistant co-located, or the logic of working 9–5 when these are hours the boss rarely sticks to? Or keeping dedicated space for *both* of them?

Now for the second example. 'Flexible work is OK for some', says the change-resistant middle manager, 'but *my* team has a high requirement for face-to-face interaction. So there's very limited capacity for flexibility'.

A statement like this is packed with assumptions about how work necessarily is to be done. The big underlying assumption in this statement is that the best context for interaction with colleagues or the public is at the times and in the places that I, the manager, decide.

Such a view is sometimes supported in advice about flexible working. In several of the guides to flexible working cited I've seen phrasing like the following, about the types of jobs that could be eligible for flexible working: 'Flexible working is suitable for jobs where there is a minimal requirement for face-to-face contact with other employees or the public'.

There is an assumption here that:

a) 'Face to face' means *physical* face to face.
b) 'Face to face' provides more effective outcomes than other means of interaction.

Possibly this is the case. But it needs challenging through the CAN test. When challenged, for example, it may emerge that for the public a time outside your organisation's working hours is best. In my experience customers value certainty of response more than a face-to-face meeting. And many people would prefer a transaction took place online, rather than fixing a meeting and having to travel somewhere.

On digging, I would expect to find that an exaggerated value attached to colleague face-to-face is associated with an excessive meetings culture, which most employees feel is an obstacle to productivity. Challenge the assumptions!

I was once working with an international telecoms company that was tentatively exploring the outer margins of flexible working. Given that many telecoms companies are leading exponents of flexibility, their caution surprised me at first. From a series of structured interviews with senior managers, it emerged that one of their big concerns in allowing remote working was the potential breakdown of communication between colleagues and possible negative impacts on team work.

At the same time, the interviews showed that in the R&D and operational teams there was already extensive virtual teamwork. Teams in the UK routinely worked as part of international teams, with team members from all over the world. So within the company there was extensive experience in working with colleagues without physical face-to-face contact. Several managers were obviously quite experienced in managing this. So what was the issue?

The issue was really to do with traditional assumptions about where work should be done. Face-to-face actually didn't matter as much in practice. What was of more concern was that employees should be based in, as they saw it, 'proper' workplaces where there was line-of-sight supervision. So people could work virtually if located in traditional workplaces, but doing so outside one was frowned upon.

Much of the work being done was not in the least place-sensitive. It was deadline-driven, but not time-sensitive in the sense of needing to be done within standard working hours. Or even at the same time as their colleagues, given that many of their colleagues worked in other time zones.

The issues here were really around how most senior and middle managers expected work to be. And this meant that despite its being an environment geared to technological innovation, innovation in *working practices* was going to have a hard time making its way up the agenda.

Challenging Habit and Complacency

We do many of the things we do just because we do them, and never stop to think that they could be done differently. It's not that we ever stopped to think that things have to be done this way. It's just that the possibility of an alternative has never occurred. Having eyes open to the possibility of new ways of doing things in all aspects of working life is essential for making a root-and-branch change to the culture.

One area where old habits often block change is in recruitment. Someone leaves, so by habit we advertise the same post on the same basis. Why not advertise it on a flexible working basis?

A member of staff is about to go on maternity leave. There will be a customary way to handle this in the organisation, and certain expectations will kick in based on past experience. Perhaps if work is traditionally handled on an 'all or nothing basis' and/ or there's an underlying assumption that many or most women will end up leaving for good, then that is what will happen. The rituals and stories around maternity leave will reinforce this expectation.

Yet some organisations have astonishing rates of return from maternity leave, with over 90 per cent of mothers returning to work. This doesn't just happen of its own accord. It's a combination of introducing new family-friendly ways of working and actively developing a new culture around parental leave and staff retention. If one department isn't keeping up with the high rate of return from maternity leave, that's an issue and managers will have to explain themselves.

Some leading organisations take this a stage further and have introduced 'maternity coaching'. This prepares both the mother-to-be and her manager to manage the transitions effectively and support them through the process. Options to work flexibly before and after maternity leave are worked through with both the expectant mother and her manager. Organisations like John Lewis and Accenture go the extra mile by having initiatives to support parents including supporting fathers who wish to take up paternity leave.

Similarly there will be a range of habits, reinforced by a variety of rituals, around retirement and the period leading up to it. Not only policy, but stories, jokes, leg-pulling, office banter and genuine acts of kindness and support can all combine towards an inevitable full-stop to working life. Thankfully new legislation abolishing the default retirement age will start to challenge much of this. But I don't expect that the cultural experience of being an older worker will change overnight. It will need some active help from smart employers to change it over time.

Introducing new options for phased retirement or flexible work beyond pensionable age is a necessary first step. Changing the culture may prove harder. One of the objections put forward by employers' organisations to outlawing age-based compulsory retirement is that it will be harder to get rid of older employees who may be losing the capacity to work effectively.

Here is what the UK Institute of Directors said in their advice to the government on promoting growth:

> *Drop proposals to abolish the default retirement age. Why does the Government want to make it harder for companies to remove staff who are no longer effective?* [My italics] *No sensible employer is going to get rid of someone if they are performing. By removing the DRA you are forcing employers, who will have to remove older staff at some point, to manage them out through the normal dismissal procedures (IOD 2011).*

But apart from the ageism embedded in such comments, what does it say about the existing culture of many organisations? The expectation seems to be that if an older employee is less competent this can be tolerated as they coast towards retirement – let's not do anything now, as time will take care of it. A more proactive and positive approach to older workers is a must. This should include not only opportunities to work more flexibly, but also for career progression – further training and maybe promotions too.

'Step-Up' Questions

Identifying and unpacking key cultural assumptions is crucial. That's the first step. Next is to assemble the alternatives.

Take the example above about working in virtual teams. When people emphasise the irreducible value of face-to-face interaction, ask them why all the parties in the conversation have to be in that place, at that time? Could the same or better results be achieved either by:

a) Using technology to facilitate remote communication, at least for part of the time or for routine matters, or

b) Organising systems differently so as to reduce the need for that interaction?

So along with Challenging Assumptions of Necessity there is another set of questions, which focuses on how things could change for the better. These questions focus on how working practices can 'step up' to become more fleet of foot and better targeted.

We should look at everything we do, and ask:

Are there ways of doing this that are:

> *Faster?*
> *More flexible?*
> *"Lighter"?* [that is, less heavy on resources – time, energy, physical resources]
> *More in line with customer needs?*
> *More in line with employee aspirations?'*

These questions have a strong practical focus, and may not at first appear to be questions about organisational culture. But they all have a cultural dimension, and exploring them inevitably raises cultural issues, especially when the questions are worked through in the context of where and when people work.

Just below the surface will be cultural issues involving:

* Hierarchy versus equality (vertical versus horizontal).
* Rules versus relationships.
* Centralisation versus decentralisation.
* Authority versus autonomy.
* Control versus trust.
* Collectivism versus individualism.
* Secrecy or 'need-to-know' mentalities versus transparency.
* Tradition or conformity versus innovation.
* Risk-avoidance versus risk-taking.
* Linear/sequential approaches to activities versus non-linear/interactive (that is, organising work to do single tasks or multiple tasks) – and so forth through the various sliding scales of cultural analysis.

For the most part, the Smart Flexibility working culture will identify with values and behaviours that are in the second part of each of these statements. And if we imagine each of these as being on a sliding scale, we want to slide along to the right in each case.

I doubt that many discussions in the workplace will use much of this academic language. But the issues will be in there, mixed in with the practical issues about whether this task or that task could, in fact, be done at home or whether a routine meeting could be replaced by an exchange of emails. And in trying to initiate culture change, it is important to focus on practical activities where practical changes will bring about the changes in behaviours and values that will change the culture.

People doing the work often have a good idea about where their work processes are inefficient or wasteful, where the company is missing a trick, and where changes would make a difference. And it's useful to get people from different teams together to look at these issues. A challenge can often come from outside the team: 'Why on earth do you do it like that? We do this …'.

It's also important to bring in experience from outside the organisation. While people working at the sharp end often know where the problems are, they may not be up to speed on the full range of alternatives being practised in the wider world. An experienced facilitator in the field of new ways of working can help people move rapidly up the learning curve, and provide examples from other organisations that are further along in changing the way they work.

SMART WORKING CULTURE CHANGE AT SURREY COUNTY COUNCIL

Surrey County Council's journey in Smart and Flexible Working has a longer history than most. It has included early pioneering work imitated by others, a problematic evolution, and more recently renewed progress with a strong focus on creating a strong flexible working culture.

Back in the 1990s Surrey was one of the pace-setters in the public sector with its 'Surrey Workstyle programme. Workplaces were consolidated and new working practices introduced, with higher levels of mobility and desk-sharing. But by the middle of the 'noughties', the pace of change had slackened and was followed by major restructuring exercises and a turning back of the clock to some extent.

During a short period of convulsive top-down change, Surrey went from a four-star to a one-star authority. There were high levels of unfilled vacancies, an average 13 days absence per employee per year, and very low staff trust in the leadership. Only 15 per cent of employees thought that the leadership listened to them. There was little happening in the way of staff development and manager training. All the freedoms that had prevailed since the 1990s were pulled back under a new 'command and control' style.

However, under new corporate leadership since 2008, smart and flexible working have once again moved centre stage as a way both to implement the significant savings needed in the new economic climate and to create a much more positive empowering culture for staff.

'Smarter Working' is one of several corporate programmes under the banner of 'Making a Difference'. What is distinctive about the Surrey implementation is the very strong Organisational Development approach, and the way moves to Smarter Working are entwined with the development of a 'coaching culture'.

Key to this is an emphasis on developing leadership, and 'taking the lid off everyone's talent' in the words of Carmel Miller, Head of HR and OD. 'Everyone is encouraged to take responsibility: for quality, for generating ideas, and for being a productive team member'.

The role of middle managers – often the target of criticism in change projects – is seen as essential for bringing about the new empowering culture. At Surrey they talk of 'leading from the middle'.

And this approach is delivering results. In tandem with a parallel programme called 'Office Moves', Surrey has vacated two headquarters buildings so far. Staff are being consolidated in new smart working environments in the Town Hall and are able to touch-down to use local hubs. Over 130 staff have been 'embedded' with local partners. The target is to reduce from 13 administrative buildings down to five. In the new areas, a desk ratio of three desks to five staff is being achieved.

At the same time, the absence rate has come down from 13 days per year to seven – just under the national average for all sectors. Less overtime, fewer agency staff and fewer active vacancies have led to a £4.5 million saving.

Overall the Council has saved £67 million in 2010–11 and £61 million in 2011–12 from office rationalisation and increased efficiency.

While it's made clear that Smarter Working is being rolled out, solutions are tailored to different teams according to their needs. So operational managers and staff have a strong input here, with people much more prepared to articulate their requirements. 'Buy your own device' (BYOD) is being trialled.

The Smarter Working programme has Smarter Working specialists who work with departments and teams to help them find the right solutions and to take them through the coaching process. An e-learning solution is also used. The aim is to develop a dynamic learning environment available through the web, so employees can access it wherever they are.

The scale of the changes is massive, and there is a need to leapfrog over several years of underinvestment in the right technologies and facilities, in a large organisation delivering a huge range of different services. But Surrey is moving ahead again, and making sure that employees are fully engaged and taking a leading role in delivering Smarter Working.

Defining a Smart Working Culture

After deconstructing the way work is done and the underlying cultural assumptions, it is important to develop a clear idea of what you want the new working culture to be.

Smart Flexibility is not about doing things in the old way with some new technologies and redesigned offices – it is about new ways of working using new tools, new processes and new approaches to management and teamwork. This requires different types of behaviours and different expectations about how work is done.

In essence, a Smart Flexibility culture consists of:

- Higher levels of collaborative working – between individuals, between teams, with external partners and with the wider public.
- The pursuit of continuous service improvements, in particular through the use of new technologies to increase efficiencies.
- A commitment to flexibility – being constantly open to new ways of working and delivering services, avoiding temptations to try to 'freeze' Smart Flexibility into a rigid or prescriptive formula.
- An emphasis on management by results rather than management by presence.
- An emphasis on trust rather than 'command and control'.
- An emphasis on working in shared spaces and with shared resources, rather than with territorial or personalised ones.
- An emphasis on promoting higher levels of staff empowerment and autonomy, to maximise the benefits arising from the new working styles.
- An emphasis on using new ways of working to assist employees achieve a better work-life balance, health and well-being.
- A commitment to using new technologies and new ways of working to reduce the environmental impact of the organisation's work-styles, processes and delivery of services.
- A commitment to using new technologies and new ways of working to recruit, retain and develop a more diverse and inclusive workforce.
- A culture of learning using the new technologies to help employees, wherever they are located, to develop their skills and capabilities and move forward in their careers.

It is important to recognise that developing a Smart Flexibility culture and ensuring that the changes become embedded is a collective responsibility, not one that can be imposed from above. However, strong leadership will be needed to ensure the changes are taken forward, and to galvanise teams to develop the new culture and new ways of working.

The implementation of Smarter Working at Surrey County Council is distinguished by a strategic approach to culture change. The engagement for Smarter Working is approached as part of a wide vision of developing a leadership culture and strong development of the skills and mindset staff will need to operate in a more empowering and enabling environment.

Trust, Empowerment and the Psychological Contract

Earlier in the chapter I mentioned how people can become very animated when invited to talk about their organisational culture. And one of the things they get most passionate about is the issue of trust.

People at all levels in an organisation do not want to be treated like children, as if they were still at school. But working life is often like that. Trust is a key element of working relationships. It may be competence-based trust: people are trusted because everyone knows they can do the job and will get on with it. Or it may be incentive-based trust: both sides know that there will be a reward for doing a good job. This may be expressed formally in a contractual relationship, where the inputs and outputs are defined in an agreed document. And trust is a key element of the 'psychological contract', the unwritten set of perceptions and expectations about the mutual obligations of employer and employee. It's about what the employees are expected to put in, and what they can expect to get out of it. Employees contribute their labour, their time, effort, commitment, integrity and may make personal sacrifices in order to do a good job for the company. This is rewarded not only by pay and bonuses, but also by formal and informal benefits, recognition, status, responsibility, praise, enjoyment and opportunities for personal development and growth.

Trust is also rooted in perceptions and expectations of fairness: fairness in terms of how the psychological contract is being fulfilled for the individual, but also how fair is the treatment in comparison with others. So the expectations also operate at a collective level.

The expected inputs and outputs, and fairness in how managers treat employees, are crucially important at any time when changes to working conditions or working practices are proposed or being implemented. And as we have seen in previous chapters, these inputs and outputs will change in some crucial ways.

One of the key changes is that on the input side there is probably going to be a moderately raised requirement for self-management, that is, the organisation of one's own work. On the output side there will in most cases be greater freedom, and the reward of being seen to be more responsible.

As an example, take 'core hours' flexitime, where employees are required to work core hours of, say, 10–12 and 2–4 but can vary arrival and leaving times around that, as long as they do their hours. To my mind, 'core hours' flexitime is a botched form of flexible working: flexible hours at the margins, based on lack of genuine trust. Staff surveys always show that most staff want far greater freedom in determining their own working hours, subject to the demands of the work. Do the hours of work really need to be enforced externally? Greater trust is likely to be repaid in greater loyalty, and greater flexibility in allocating hours to meet demand.

With some implementations of Smart Flexibility there may be a perceived loss of benefit, particularly in terms of unspoken benefits – like the benefit of having one's own nest in the office. Having one's own unique personal space has always just been the way things were done. There was pretty much no alternative. Unfortunately, many of the rewards associated with fulfilling the employee's side of the psychological contract have traditionally been associated with recognition and status expressed in terms of spatial reward. The bigger desk. The 'manager pod' – that bigger space in the open office with extra chairs. The private office. The bigger private office on the executive floor. The thicker carpet and paintings on the wall.

With the kind of changes for flexible working environments that we saw in Chapter 6, aspiring employees may see the much-coveted rug more or less literally pulled out from under their feet. Making such changes requires:

- Involvement of staff in analysing their existing work culture and their expectations in terms of input/reward.
- Consultation on and awareness of the new work culture that is being developed.
- Buy-in to the quid-pro-quo involved in the change – for example, loss of personal nest in exchange for greater freedom and autonomy.
- A clear statement that these changes apply to all staff – there will be no exceptions, so there can be no perceptions of unfairness or comparative gain or loss.
- A clear understanding that the new arrangements are empowering, but that empowerment is heavily dependent on mutual trust.

The evolution of a smart working culture will be easier to facilitate where there is already a high degree of trust. Trust has to become the new normality, not a privilege earned. A 'command and control' culture in effect starts with a (possibly unspoken) premise that people cannot be trusted – they have to be directed and controlled. In this kind of culture, people are more inclined to do what they should when under supervision, but break the rules as long as they can get away with it. If someone is trusted to do something but doesn't do it, the responsibility is in large measure on the manager who let them get away with it. Failure of authority is the issue more than breach of trust. It was stupid of you to trust me, wasn't it?

In a Smart Flexibility culture, breach of trust is a very serious issue.

Building the New Working Culture

There will be a three stage process for establishing the new working culture:

1. Understanding and assenting to it – agreeing it will work and buying into the concept.
2. Learning to value it, even love it.
3. Taking on the new ways of working as habit, so that operating in the new ways become second-nature.

The processes of evidence-building, consultation and involvement described in previous chapters should go a long way to raising understanding and achieving buy-in to the idea. It's worth reiterating that most people do want more flexibility – selling the concept will really not be as hard as some people are inclined to think when they focus on the potential problems or listen to the immovable objectors and prophets of doom.

Beyond that, the cultural dimension does need to be directly addressed. This is not a book to address in detail theories of culture change or to prescribe particular techniques. Different organisations will have different approaches. My recommendation is to root the culture change in the practical. This involves discussing why things are done as they are, what could be better, how the new working practices will be implemented and how they will make a difference.

It also involves direct discussion, particularly with managers, of the agreed Smart Flexibility principles and the protocols that will govern the new ways of working.

Let's take one of the principles of a Smart Flexibility culture as an example:

An emphasis on promoting higher levels of staff empowerment and autonomy, to maximise the benefits arising from the new working styles.

There is relatively little value in the workplace in addressing this in an abstract way. The conversation needs to be rooted in the real, everyday context of work. That is: how do we – our company, our team – put this into practice?

The conversation will no doubt highlight areas where staff feel they are disempowered at the moment, and where having greater autonomy, freedom and being trusted more would make a difference. It will also highlight how particular benefits are related to certain styles of working, and how behaviours such as leadership styles, transparency, team communication, and so on, will need to change to make things work effectively.

Culture change is not achieved overnight, and won't be after a single team meeting, however positive the feeling afterwards. To get first the intellectual and then the emotional acceptance of the new ways of working, and the new culture that supports it, will require frequent revisiting. So having a regular 'how's it going?' item on the agenda for team meetings is vital.

Building the new working culture does involve well-planned marketing activity. Marketeers often think in terms of AIDA – Awareness (or grabbing Attention), Interest, Desire, Action. The culture-change process has to go through similar phases. From initially becoming aware of the possibility, to interest ('That would suit me') to desire ('I want that!') to action (positively adopting the new work-style).

So there has to be a programme of communication and action that brokers this engagement, to see that staff are progressively involved and 'buying in' not only to the new ways of working but to the culture that goes with it.

Most successful smart working programmes have some kind of branding – WorkSmart, Workplace Agility, Modern and Flexible Working, Office of the Future, and so on. The branding is typically positive and progressive. But people know when they are being spun a line – so the actions in the programme have to deliver genuine benefits.

Regular communications under the brand need to keep people informed of the progress, and also of the successes. Nothing inspires like (genuine) cases of colleagues who have adopted the new ways and can spell out the benefits to them. Most people also want their company to be doing well, so reporting on benefits achieved helps to promote the emotional and aspirational involvement needed.

If there are new office environments as part of the move to Smart Flexibility, displays of the new settings can promote interest and the desire to be part of it. Importantly, they can allay fears. This is really important for bringing down the psychological barriers to change. Achieving buy-in doesn't always have to be about addressing flexible work head-on. Focusing on closely related issues such as environmental sustainability can help to achieve buy-in, for example, by showing how colleagues in another department that has embraced the change have reduced their carbon footprint. Showing the benefits and eliciting a positive response to them helps to embed acceptance of the new ways. This then becomes a story, validated by witnesses, that starts to ripple through the grapevine and permeate people's thought processes.

Overcoming Resistance

Few implementations of change can be described as plan sailing. Introducing new ways of working invariably encounters some opposition. Some of this opposition is reasoned, and some of it is not. Either way, it has to be dealt with.

There is often a link between resistance and people's vulnerabilities. They may feel exposed when required to work with new skills, particularly with new technologies and/ or new requirements to communicate more effectively. They may feel insecure in a shared office setting, and about the prospect of encountering new people who might sit next to them from time to time. Or they may just be very comfortable in the old ways, and refuse to see or accept the corporate need for change.

Middle managers are often fingered as key figures in resisting change. This makes some sense, as they are completely central to making change work. However, I think they are much maligned in this respect.

There are several possible reasons why middle managers may be resistant to change:

- Lack of trust in their staff to be responsible.
- Wanting to be liked, so caving in to stubborn opposition from below.
- Indecision.
- Fear of loss of status.
- Uncertainty about how to manage in new ways.
- 'Not invented here' syndrome – being resentful of new ideas they didn't come up with themselves. This can especially be the case in key functional departments such as IT, Property and HR.
- Dislike of change agents' perceived superiority – that is, their claiming to know what's best for their department, when the manager is actually the expert in this field.
- Feeling that it's all too much trouble – 'I'm not paid enough to care!'.
- Dislike of the senior managers instituting change.

However, it is important not to view all such opposition negatively. Scepticism about change may be reasonably founded on past experience of botched change and genuine fears that new systems may lower standards from old. Opposition may be based on a strong and genuine commitment to deliver quality and real concerns that quality may be eroded. And some organisations have a track record of 'initiativitis' – new plans and schemes come and go, while the wise manager keeps his or her head down and just gets on with doing the job.

The way to tackle middle manager resistance is fourfold:

1. Make it absolutely clear that change will happen, with or without them.
2. Provide the awareness-raising and training needed to help them understand both the principles and the corporate benefits of change.
3. Involve them as far as possible in helping to design the details of the changes.
4. Provide the necessary support and resources to overcome problems.

Analysing Resistance

There are many different kinds of resistance to change. Resistance can be:

- Overt and challenging.
- Two-faced.
- Passively stubborn.
- Talking the talk but not really buying it, so not walking the walk.
- Backsliding – starting off meaning to change, but slipping back to the old ways.

It's a useful exercise to try to analyse the opposition and put it into categories. The following figure segments the kinds of reaction to new ways of working that one is likely to come across.

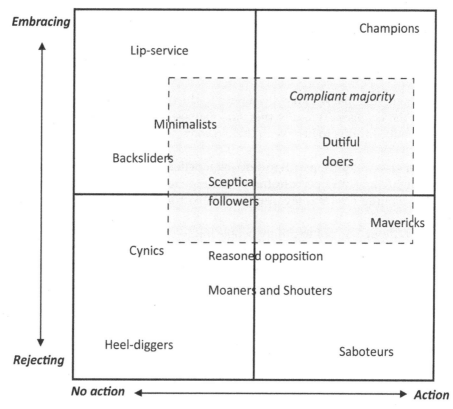

Figure 8.1   Grid of acceptance and resistance

People may embrace or reject change in principle. How that translates into action is important for analysing the different kinds of resistance to change.

The first thing to note is that in most organisations most people will fall into the category I've called the 'compliant majority'. They will do what is asked of them – even though for some their heart is not really in it. Add these to the vanguard of enthusiasts and champions, and overcoming resistance is really about dealing with a minority who express their opposition in different ways.

People who are sceptical about change may split across the compliance/non-compliance divide. Inside the camp are sceptical followers – they adopt new working habits but for one reason or another doubt that these will bring benefits. They are joined by people whom I've styled 'minimalists', that is, people who will do the minimum possible to comply. They don't really have a view on whether the change programme will work – they just don't want to make the effort to change.

These two groups will probably be the first to slide back into the old ways if the momentum starts to fade, or if the project runs into problems and seems to fail.

Opposition outside the camp will probably take a number of forms:

- Cynics, who just doubt the value of every workplace initiative.
- Moaners and shouters – the people who are disgruntled about many things, and find the change programme is one more thing to get upset about.
- The Reasoned Opposition – people who engage with the change process but are not convinced by it.
- Heel-Diggers – the people who don't make a fuss, but just won't comply. They sit in meetings with arms firmly folded and say little, thinking 'I'm not doing that!'
- Saboteurs – the small minority of negative influencers, who actively try to undermine the changes by defying the new protocols and by trying to subvert others to do likewise.
- Underminers – people who pay lip service to the changes can also, in a quieter way, sabotage the changes. Typically these are managers and team leaders who say 'yes, yes, yes', but continue to behave in the old ways.

These are terms I have come up with to describe generic kinds of acceptance and resistance. It can be enlightening, and perhaps fun as well, to create such a grid as a team exercise and without naming names categorise the different responses to change in one's own company.

The point, though, is not to pillory people but to come up with different approaches to drawing different kinds of resistor into the camp of the compliant majority. And to pull those who are on the inside upwards to be first dutiful doers and then to be enthusiasts.

This won't necessarily be easy.

Getting Over the Hump

Smart Flexibility is not about doing things in the old way, only with some new technologies and new work spaces – it is about new ways of working using new tools and processes. This requires different types of behaviours and new techniques for managing flexible workers and for being a part of flexible working teams.

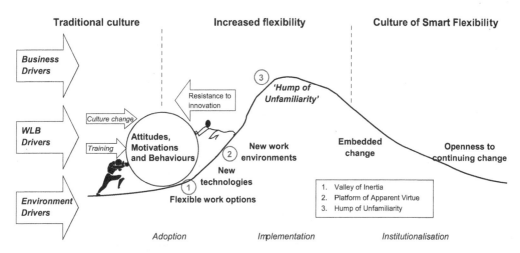

Figure 8.2 Smart Flexibility cultural change curve

The figure above illustrates the change curve for achieving a transformation of culture, moving from traditional ways of working to Smart Flexibility.

Physical changes to the workplace and the new technology tools provide the platform for change, and inevitably due to their visibility and cost these gravitate to the centre of attention during the change process. However, unless there is a process of addressing the attitudes, behaviours and relationships that make up the organisational culture, change initiatives risk becoming a Sisyphean process of uphill struggles and backsliding into previous working practices.

Without any attempt to change the culture, an organisation will probably remain rooted in position 1, stuck in the Valley of Inertia, with the traditional culture only slightly modified by the increased uptake of flexible work options. Even substantial investment in the tools and new environments may not make much of a difference.

If the groundwork is done for moving from theory to practice, there should be a good dynamic for the change programme. The arrows from the left show the business, personal and environmental drivers giving the programme momentum. Incorporating them into organisational objectives focusing on the benefits takes forward the impetus.

Consultation and involvement can bring most of the staff behind the changes to working practices. Now the culture-change programme, training and a well-focused communication strategy can take the changes forward so that the new working practices are embedded, and the new working culture takes root.

But the problem is, despite the momentum and enthusiasm engendered for change, despite all the protocols and policies, it is human nature to revert to the familiar. It may seem the resistance has been overcome, but it is a mistake to see resistance only residing in a few individuals. Adaptation to change is on a sliding scale in all of us, and it slides back and forth. On Monday, Tuesday and Wednesday on my trip to France I drove on the right, because I'm consciously thinking about it. On Thursday I got up and started to drive on the left. I can still remember the family screaming. Old habits die hard, and for me it was the most natural thing to do. Habits of one's whole life do not change overnight without a fightback. Though in the case of driving on the left in France, there are majority behaviours and compelling incentives to adapt!

Point 3 in Figure 8.2 is the dangerous point. Everyone's been working hard to get the ball rolling, but everything is still an effort. The new ways have not yet become embedded as the familiar ways. And people have other things to do apart from changing their behaviours – they have jobs to do, careers to push forward, and they are not yet comfortable in doing this within the new culture.

In a culture-change programme, much of the effort is typically put in at the beginning to get the ball rolling. Just at the moment when one last big push is needed to get over the Hump of Unfamiliarity, the energy is not there any more. The momentum dissolves as support for change unconsciously fades along with the rest of yesterday's news. And the momentum can go into reverse. Gravity takes over. Maybe not all the way back to point 1, but perhaps halfway down and rolling off onto the Platform of Apparent Virtue at point 2. People use the new environments and technologies, they do flex their work locations and work times – but not so much as to achieve the benefits.

Looking again at Figure 8.2. The contest may look as though it's between Arnold Schwarzenegger and L.S. Lowry, and the stronger one ought to win. But Lowry has the force of gravity on his side, and unless Arnie keeps the ball constantly rolling, gravity will take over.

The new technologies and the changed work environment(s) are the platform for Smart Flexibility. Many implementations don't do the 'people bit', but sit on their laurels at this point. New technology and new workplaces can give the outward impression of being 'smart'.

Building the platform without doing 'the people bit' is to adopt a 'Field of Dreams' approach: 'Build it and they will come'. Well, they did in the Kevin Costner film – but it seems the people only turned up the one time, and I guess he must have been left with his baseball stadium sitting a tad underutilised in the middle of that corn field. It's like that with Smart Flexibility. Unless conscious effort is *continuously* put into getting people to use the new platform effectively, work will slide back into traditional patterns. The main difference is that people will have the option to use some more expensive toys.

Culture change is a continuous process, and requires more than getting the consultants in at the outset for a session where they cocoon you in flip-chart paper and post-its. It's about linking change to practical measures that will help to change behaviours and attitudes and reinforce the pattern of working in new ways.

The following are examples of techniques that can overcome resistance, deal with backsliding and make the unfamiliar familiar.

Leadership by Example

If managers don't change, nothing else will. Leaving behind a private office, if they have one, is a first step. Making sure they don't sit in the same place every day will help to make desk-sharing the norm. Using conferencing technologies for meetings, rather than insisting everyone comes in to the office. Holding team meetings out of the office. Doing one-to-ones in a break-out area.

Managers can also take a lead on work-life balance practices. This is especially important in an organisation where flexibility for family reasons has traditionally been frowned upon. So being seen, as a manager, to schedule work time to fit around (say) attending a school sports match in working hours helps to set a new tone.

I was once asked to write up a case study about a senior civil servant who regularly worked at home every other Friday so he could spend more time with his family every now and then. But having seen many a near-empty public sector office on a Friday, I don't think this was exactly setting the pace. Such a gesture, however genuine the motivation of the person concerned, could easily be misinterpreted as an excuse for a long weekend.

In the end this can be perceived as a kind of tokenism and it won't wash. However, a manager who works effectively from afar, actively desk-shares, who cuts down meetings and makes a point of recruiting staff on a flexible working basis will start to make a difference. If he or she constructively discusses work-life balance during appraisals, and makes a point of associating smart and flexible work-styles with productivity, the new working culture will be reinforced.

'Management by results' is a key element of Smart Flexibility. But it is not only about management techniques, it's also about a change in values. The focus of management shifts – to the results. All the values and imperatives around presence and place take a back seat, and results move centre stage. The importance of this shift cannot be emphasised enough in terms of cultural shift. It should prompt many discussions and much reflection about goals, output and outcomes, and the whole rationale for being 'at work'.

Middle managers often come in for a bit of a bashing in discussions about smart and flexible working. They are often seen as the most resistant to change, and sometimes no doubt they are. People who are in the 'hands-on' position of directly managing teams have a strong role to play in promoting culture change.

Bearing in mind the way people are more likely to be influenced by people they like or admire, it is a good idea to choose popular and open-minded team leaders to head up any pilots and to be change leaders in new ways of working. It is also strategically sound to choose team leaders who are ambitious and career-oriented: they are more likely to want to be seen to succeed than someone who has dug in to a comfort zone and wants to see things out with minimum demands.

The success of their teams in working effectively in the new ways should stimulate a ripple effect, and exert positive pressure for change around them.

Exemplary Theatre

There are numerous tales about managers dealing with people who violate desk-sharing arrangements and clear desk policies. One is of a senior manager in a financial services company who saw things slipping back to the old ways, and decided to act. Every day at 5 p.m. he went round to each desk and swept everything left on an empty desk into a black bin bag – whether personal items or 'personal professional' ones. The only way to get them back was to go to him, ask for them back and explain why they had been left there in the first place. The clear desk policy – despite some grumbling – soon came to be accepted.

Sometimes a leader has to be prepared to be unpopular, or to behave apparently eccentrically, to make a point and to enforce an agreed approach.

Back in the 1990s a new senior manager in a department was determined to reduce the amount of paper, and encourage her staff to use email, in line with organisational policy. So she forbade the use of memos (remember them?) as a first step. One team leader steadfastly refused to do so, and kept the memos coming (and they were typed up in the typing pool – remember those?). In the end, frustrated, she went into the middle of the office and ripped up his latest memo in front of everyone. *If you put it on paper, I won't read it*, was the message. It worked: there were no more memos – from anyone.

Bottom-Up Innovation

The last two examples are of top-down enforcement. The bottom-up approach is good too. If people have said they want more flexibility, and more autonomy in their working lives, it's good to encourage their creativity with a suggestions box or an innovations board where people can post their suggestions for improving working practices and working culture.

Perhaps prizes can be given for the best ideas. But the best reward for contributors is to see their idea being taken up and put into action.

Often the most valuable suggestions revolve around the issues when people sometimes feel more vulnerable, in particular teamwork, communication and the perceived dangers of isolation. Initiatives that emerge in these areas are probably more valuable and enduring because they have developed organically, rather than being prescribed.

There are many areas where local, team-based initiatives can help to push forward a new culture. Let's take one of the items from our 'ingredients' list above of a smart working culture: 'The pursuit of continuous service improvements, in particular through the use of new technologies to increase efficiencies'. The challenge can be thrown open for teams in a department to come up with service improvements based on the new technologies and new working practices. These could then be formally or informally piloted to see if they make a measurable difference.

The point is not only about delivering better customer value. It's also about instilling a habit of thinking in terms of the new ways of working and the new tools that enable it.

Likewise one could throw out challenges on how to reduce the environmental impact of work through new ways of working, or how in practice to improve levels of collaboration. Then the lessons learned need to be internalised by sharing with other teams, adapting team charters or modifying protocols.

Some companies go further and incorporate the emphasis on innovation and creativity directly into the working environment by having areas where project teams or ad hoc gatherings can brainstorm and write on the walls, or rooms themed or furnished to stimulate innovation and service improvements.

This is the way to bring the high-level cultural principles to life, by actively involving people in working through the practicalities.

Dealing with Rule-Breakers and Mavericks

As we have explored in previous chapters, there have to be rules, policies and protocols around flexible working, so that everyone knows where they stand. These should not be heavy-handed, but they do need to be enforced. Especially at the outset.

The nature of the rules will have changed, and the balance of expectation should have shifted from external monitoring and discipline to self-monitoring and self-discipline.

For example, 'clocking in' at a set time will become a thing of the past for many. But it will be essential to let colleagues know (a) that you are working and (b) where you are.

Failure to adhere to the agreed protocols for reporting, communication, delivery of work, and behaviour in the office is not acceptable. Both line managers and colleagues need to ensure that the rules are enforced. This can be by a peer group 'nudge' or a gentle word at first, but persistent offending should not be tolerated, or else the new ways of working and the new working culture will be undermined.

The person who starts to occupy the same workplace each day instead of desk-sharing, or starts to personalise a favoured desk is acting selfishly, and is reducing the freedom of action of colleagues. The manager who starts to colonise a meeting room or quiet room 'in order to have privacy' needs to be told this is out of order. The person who pulls rank to keep an area of the team shelving for their personal work needs to be brought to book.

In the early stages this kind of discipline is needed to show that the new working culture is to be taken seriously, and there will be a break from the old ways of doing things. If not, things fall apart rapidly.

There will always be people who want to do things their own way, and flexible working should by nature be tolerant – or even encouraging – of mavericks. Mavericks can often be the pace-setters of new ways of working. Being a maverick is all about exercising autonomy. But it can also be about asserting a self-validated superior ego against the tiresome rules of lesser people. How do you draw the line?

The touchstone should be the Smart Working principles. In our Figure 8.1 (above), we have positioned mavericks as embracing their own version of smart working, rather than the official corporate version. If the maverick behaviour is a technical breach of the protocols but still in the spirit and direction of Smart Flexibility, there is room for being indulgent. One of our principles above is that it is wrong to try to freeze flexibility at a moment in time, but be open to continuous development of Smart Flexibility. New tools, techniques and practices will emerge, and the flexible workplace needs to be capable of evolution. There is a need to judge if someone is pushing the boundaries in a valuable direction, or if they are merely being capricious. Or worse still, wilfully undermining the new working culture.

Beyond the Business Case – Appealing Across a Broad Front

Experts on culture change often point out that culture change is not only about making rational appeals. There are also irrational, emotional and personal factors that can obstruct change or work towards being enthusiastic about it.

I think it's less about appealing to the irrational, but more a question of finding what are the various buttons that need to be pressed to evoke a response – and as we've seen with flexible working these are many. It's about the Triple Bottom Line. Some people will be enthusiasts for saving the planet, or at least doing their bit. It's an appeal to virtue that will gain a response amongst many people, so long as they believe the measures you are promoting are sincere and genuine.

The other side of the appeal is to do with leading balanced lives. As we've seen, parents are significantly more likely to want to work flexibly. But appealing purely on the grounds of family friendliness can alienate some amongst the other two-thirds of the workforce. So it is better to take a stance as an employer of actively supporting all aspirations to lead more balanced lives. This integrates closely with other aspects of supporting personal and professional development amongst employees. It's about being, and being seen to be, a good employer and an 'employer of choice'. People like to work for the good guys. Smart Flexibility needs visibly to take its place as a key enabler of this.

Some people, though, will say they have enough balance in their lives, thank you very much, and are not concerned about the environment. Or maybe they are tempted to be cynical about corporate pretensions to social or environmental virtue. For all staff, but for these perhaps in particular, there must also be an appeal to ambition and personal interest. This is where the approach needs to have some steel in it.

Basically, those who comply and actively support the new ways will progress. Those who do not will not progress. At the bottom of our chart of resistance are the heel-diggers and saboteurs. These people need to wake up and smell the coffee! There is no future for them in the new smart organisation and its new culture, certainly no future in management. And everyone needs to be aware of this.

The worst thing that an organisation can do is to keep on unchallenged a top or influential manager who actively undermines the new working practices. If a manager refuses to implement the new sales plan, that would be a disciplinary issue. It should be the same for Smart Flexibility. It can be a hard bullet to bite. But making the tough decisions at an early stage can quickly clear the blockages to progress.

These casualties will be the exception. Creating the conditions for people to grow as individuals and to prosper within the company by working more flexibly will create a positive working culture that most people will be able to relate to.

Embedding Change in Systems and Structures

The new ways of working have to become the new normality. This will not happen if systems and structures do not adapt to incorporate the new working culture.

Recruitment needs to adapt, so it becomes routine to offer posts on a smart and flexible basis, including enabling job candidates to suggest alternative working patterns.

Promotion opportunities need to take account of different working patterns. Monitoring how many people in senior positions have part-time or flexible working patterns will be as necessary as monitoring diversity issues: in fact the two are intimately connected. The number of women and people with disabilities working in senior positions will probably reflect the degree to which new ways of working have become embedded.

In a different way, benefits and expenses systems need to adapt too. If it is routine to offer company cars as a perk, or provide generous expenses for using one's own car, this has to be reviewed in the context of using new technologies to reduce the need to travel. (More on this in Chapter 13.)

At Ofsted, the UK government's education inspectorate, all new initiatives need to be checked to ensure that they are compatible with the principle of home-based working, and do not disadvantage the organisation's 1,500 home-based inspectors. The principle is similar to checking initiatives for their impact on equality or the environment. I would recommend extending this principle to cover all forms of flexible working, perhaps calling it 'flex-proofing'.

With a more distributed workforce – more distributed both in time and space – communications systems need to evolve. 'It was on the notice board' isn't good enough any more. This will probably mean changes to central communications, but also in a less formal sense to the ways in which managers and colleagues communicate at all levels, not only about work issues but also about social and recreational matters (doing a whip-round for someone's birthday, running a sports team or charity event, and so on).

Smart Flexibility also means redrawing psychological as well as physical boundaries. People will be working across barriers (time, location, team, organisation) to a much greater extent. Boundaries in this sense are not only redrawn, but become more permeable as well. Teams are formed, dissolved and reformed, drawing in people from different departments, different organisations and including increased numbers of temporary or freelance specialists.

For this to work, old concepts of 'us and them' need to be purged from the organisation. People within the team, whatever their original provenance, need to be treated on an equal footing. Sometimes this can be undermined by having security arrangements – both physical security and IT – that treat people differently, meaning some people are always to some extent second-class team members.

Establishing metrics around flexibility is also important. Knowing the numbers of people in each department who have different kinds of flexible working practice will highlight where the new working culture is bedding in and where it is not.

Measuring key indicators before and after change, and frequent reporting of the impact of the changes will help to reinforce good practice – levels of improvement in attendance, more effective utilisation of space, travel reduction, staff satisfaction, and so on.

Embedding Change in the Physical Environment

One way to block backsliding to the old ways of working is to make changes to the working environment that either preclude it, or make violation of the principles stand out like a sore thumb.

If desk-sharing is part of the solution, it is important not to provide too many desks. If you want people to collaborate more, then increase the number of collaboration spaces and reduce the number of desks. If you want more informal collaboration and fewer formal meetings, design the space accordingly. Reduce the number of large meeting rooms and make sure the break-out spaces are attractive and conducive to productive collaboration.

One idea is to have a 15-minute meeting room. It looks just like any small meeting room. But on the outside is a big sign saying '15 Minute Meeting Room' and a big timer that counts down from 15 to zero. Simple, and effective, and laying down a marker against a meetings culture.

In the office, having a big location board that says where people are working at the moment is a practical tool. But more than that, it also reinforces the principle that work is mobile.

Embedding change can also apply to work environments outside the office. For example, if you give staff a printer for the home office, they will use it. If the goal is to reduce paper generation and reduce the carbon footprint of the company, don't issue printers!

Large electronic display screens or smart boards in meeting rooms, plus wi-fi, provide an incentive to reduce paper use in meetings.

High Visibility Changes = 'We're Serious about This'

Having emphasised the importance of making practical changes to the working environment to embed new ways of working, it's worth thinking about the symbolic and motivational impacts of changing the work environment.

Comprehensive approaches to Smart Flexibility involve transforming the places people work. Out of the office, this is mostly about the technologies people use. In the office, this involves the layout, furniture, interior design and branding (see Chapter 6). The office should look different, and feel different. Most of all, when staff walk in for the first time they should think 'Wow!' and after that, should feel a sense of pride and ownership. It feels good to work there.

It will feel even better if staff know that they have had input into the design of the new workplace, and that it supports their aspirations for greater flexibility and for more effective working.

There's a debate to be had about how swanky the new workplace should be. A substantial upgrade to the working environment shows that the organisation is taking developing a new way of working very seriously. But there is always a danger that the change is perceived as being skin deep. It's a marvellous office – but has it really changed how people work?

The importance of the visible office change and upgrade is to gain greater emotional investment in the changes to working practices. But if the latter are not being implemented effectively, all you've got is an expensive upgrade and deepening scepticism about the value of it.

In times of economic cutbacks, pouring money into workplace redesign can be very hard to justify even when the transformation project as a whole can be shown to deliver huge savings. Some organisations have taken the approach of changing the working environment and working practices with minimal investment in new facilities by reusing existing furniture and kit as much as possible, and foregoing the investment in attractive new break-out areas, new carpets and so forth.

There is a judgement to be made. The important thing is to be aware of the cultural context and the cultural impact of making such decisions. Little visible change may make it harder for some people to adopt new ways of working. If part of your aim is to break down silo-working and excessive territoriality, an office that looks much the same may be subconsciously comforting to people who don't want to change.

You can introduce new flexible ways of working without making any changes to the working environment. But I think there is a cultural minimum that needs to be done in terms of embedding change in the environment, if you are taking a comprehensive and strategic approach. The measures needed are:

Table 8.1   Cultural minimum for workplace changes

Change in the workplace	Cultural significance
Eliminate all the private offices	Shows management are on board Changes management practice Shows the organisation is serious about wasted space Shows the organisation is serious about fairness

Table 8.1   Continued

Change in the workplace	Cultural significance
Reduce the number of traditional desks in line with actual average occupancy	Enforces desk-sharing – without this, people revert to old territoriality
Introduce smaller desks for 'touch-down' use	Emphasises mobility of work Reassures people there is expansion space to cope with peak occupancy
Introduce more informal break-out spaces	The emphasis is moving from solo desk work (which can be done anywhere) to collaborative work
Ensure there is good connectivity (wired or Wi-Fi) in all working areas	Reinforces idea of mobility of work Helps towards paperless meetings
Remove all individual storage around desks	Emphasises team work and sharing Emphasises need to reduce paper
Introduce personal storage lockers	Ensures possibility of clear desks and desk-sharing Reassures staff their possessions and equipment will be safe

This leaves open many of the questions about reuse of furniture and technology, refurbishing, interior design and branding. But these make up in my view a necessary minimum to support the culture change requirements. Without them, staff won't even reach the 'hump of unfamiliarity', let alone get to the other side.

Change Agents and Change Champions

In a formal process of change, many organisations will nominate a person to drive change within a department. Sometimes these come from a central pool, with a view to transferring skills in new ways of working. Sometimes these are people within the department undergoing change who acquire a new role of championing the change locally.

These roles are valuable, but their impact in changing the working culture as well as working practices may be limited. The will to change has to be there, and the positive relationships to inspire imitation. The people who will really make a difference are the key influencers who set the tone and set expectations, whether consciously or unconsciously.

Who are these people? They may be people with power, and the ability formally to influence the behaviour in others. Effective managers, in other words. Their behaviour makes a big difference in setting the tone. They make the most effective change managers, and also the most effective saboteurs.

There will be other people though who have charisma and are popular with their colleagues. Identifying who these are during the process of consultation is valuable, and drawing them into roles where they can represent their teams, cascade news, take initiatives and so forth will be valuable in helping to change the culture.

Recruiting new people on a flexible working basis also helps over time to change the norms of working practice. These new recruits have not experienced the old culture, and their expectations will be that the new policies, procedures and protocols are the right way to do things, and their managers and colleagues will feel a certain pressure to adapt to meet their expectations.

There are also certain practical roles that can play a part in managing and enforcing the new ways of working. Many organisations have introduced a 'concierge' role when moving to desk-sharing environments. These are the people who manage the space and see that the new arrangements work, that people do share, that the clear desk policy works, that the technologies work and that people know where everyone is.

This practical role is important, as it should prevent people sliding back into the old ways. Over time the new ways, lightly enforced, start to become habitual and are established as the new norms.

A Culture beyond Space and Time (So to Speak)

A key aspect of Smart Flexibility is that it breaks down barriers. The old boundaries become more porous – more flexible (of course!). So the working culture is not one that you simply step into in a building some time between 8 a.m. and 6 p.m. It is something that floats with you across the old locational and temporal boundaries. And it may have to co-exist with other cultures that are dominant in other areas of life.

At work, it may be that other departments have not moved at the same speed towards Smart Flexibility. And they may not understand or approve of the changes that have been made when it means that they have to rethink their expectations. It can be even more sensitive with customers, for example if they are wedded to regular physical face-to-face meetings. These may bring about some unavoidable constraints in the pace of changing behaviours.

But over time, the aim must be to help those one has to do business with up the learning curve and to share the benefits of that, for example by being persistent about wanting to have routine meetings as audio or online conferences, or at least having some participants join in a physical meeting remotely. People learn by doing. And if the benefits can be clearly demonstrated, for example, by dealing with an issue much more quickly than by convening a physical meeting, it can lead the client or partner up the learning curve while at the same time reinforcing one's own culture change.

What is clearly unacceptable, though I've come across it on numerous occasions, is to say that something critical to the business can't happen because someone is working from home that day.

The other area that will have its own rhythm and culture is the home. Changes to the time and/or place of work are likely to have an impact on home/family life – though by no means always. Mostly these will be positive impacts, as those who work from home or alter the times when they are at home are doing so in part to achieve a better work-life balance. But they may generate some cultural conflicts, if there are some conflicting assumptions, expectations and habits in the home environment or neighbourhood. Some of this is covered in Chapter 11, but for now we can just say that family and neighbours may need some informal 'training' through honest and friendly discussion in order to make home an effective location to work.

Training for Managers

Training for all managers, team leaders and supervisors is a necessary component of culture-change programmes. Management training should include:

- Understanding the organisation's strategy for Smart Flexibility and linkages to other policies.
- Understanding the organisation's aspirations to develop a Smart Flexibility culture.
- The benefits of Smart Flexibility and how to measure them.
- Understanding the flexible working options available and how to deploy them.
- Understanding the linkages between new technologies and the possibilities for new working practices.
- Understanding how to involve and motivate staff to implement Smart Flexibility.
- How to manage the smart and distributed workforce.
- How to manage by results rather than presence.
- New approaches to empowerment and trust.
- Performance issues.
- Dealing with communication issues.
- Understanding the pitfalls and issues that may arise, and how to deal with these.

Training for Teams

Staff need to be involved, trained and developed, with a view to ensuring the whole workforce is both positive about change and possess the necessary skills.

The programme of staff training should include:

- Understanding why things have been traditionally done in the way they have and the limitations of this.
- Pinpointing fault-lines and problems in current ways of working and the existing work culture.
- Being clear about the type of workplace culture that it is hoped to develop.
- Understanding roles and responsibilities.
- Taking ownership of the financial and environmental cost implications of choices around working practices.
- Developing skills and understanding in working more flexibly:
  - working with less direct supervision.
  - communicating with colleagues and partners.
  - time management.
  - monitoring and reporting arrangements.
  - health and safety in new working environments.
- Working in a 'non-territorial' environment – sharing space and resources.
- Effective use of the new technologies.

Formal training, however, is only one part of what is needed to change the culture. It is as much about the other practical day-to-day measures mentioned above, as these will turn what is learnt in training sessions into continuing attitudes and behaviours.

NEW SPACES AND NEW WORKING CULTURE AT PLANTRONICS

Plantronics, the global market leader in advanced headsets and unified communications, has recently implemented a comprehensive and integrated smart working programme for its staff in the EMEA region (Europe, Middle East and Africa). This has involved changes to 'bricks, bytes and behaviour' – that is, to buildings, technologies and the way people work.

As it has developed Smarter Working, Plantronics has reduced its property in the UK from three buildings to one, reducing floor space from 47,000 square feet (4,400 m²) to 21,000 (2,000 m²). At its new UK HQ in Royal Wootton Basset, workers now have access to shared flexible spaces based around four kinds of work activity:

- Concentration – space to go for quiet work including 'monk's cells' and 'acoustic pods'.
- Collaboration – meeting rooms and break-out areas; touch-down benches.
- Communication – vibrant areas likely to have constant noise, for example, contact centre and touch-down space for sales staff.
- Contemplation – spaces designed for creativity, refuelling and relaxation; meeting rooms are equipped with audio and video conferencing kit and wireless interactive whiteboards; identical hardware in each room ensures consistency and ease of use.

One of the striking features of the Plantronics implementation is the attention paid to improving the acoustic environment. This is in one sense natural, given the audio expertise put in their products. However, dealing with room acoustics took the project team into new and unfamiliar areas where they had to develop their own solutions. Their aims were to achieve the best possible acoustic performance for the various working spaces and to facilitate concentration, especially in open plan areas. This was based on an acoustics 'ABC':

- Absorption – The use of specialised products to absorb the sound energy that hits them and reduce unwanted reflected sound energy, for example, ceiling tiles, meeting room partitions, wall hangings, and so on.
- Blocking – The introduction of vertical barriers between the noise source and listener to block the sound from one to the other, including high-backed and surrounding soft seating in break-out areas.
- Cover – The use of a computer-generated random sound that covers or masks unwanted sound.

Mobility both inside and outside the office is supported by an enterprise-wide unified communications solution. There are no desk phones – IP telephony means that laptops and headsets are used instead, so people can work in any setting. The UC system also means that headsets can be used that pick up both calls channelled through the computer and mobile phone calls via a single headset.

Extensive use is also made of audio, video and web conferencing, instant messaging and desktop-sharing. This gives a much more flexible approach to meetings, bringing together employees from the various global locations, in the field and from home, as well as with customers and key partners such as Microsoft.

According to Paul Clark, General Manager UK & Ireland, 'One of the most interesting changes that we've found with unified communications is the way that new networks set themselves up. People work closely with the people they need to for success, rather than just with the teams they are historically associated with. The ability to build real-time teams, collaborate together and then fold down again creates a much faster response. And it's all based on the UC platform'.

Another particular feature of the Plantronics implementation is the attention given to taking forward new behaviours and culture change. Training for flexible and virtual working is a key part of this. Customised online training for working in distributed teams, both for managers and their teams, was developed by US company e-Work.com. And perhaps uniquely, all employees took part in 'speech impact training' (often the preserve of call centre staff) to improve 'voice presence'. This stems from the recognition that audio meetings can suffer from a lack of visual interaction where much of the communication picks up on body language, eye contact and emotional cues. So without visual contact, there is a need to improve use of voice and listening skills to make the most of the interaction. The benefits of this ripple through to all areas of voice communication, not only audio meetings.

Moving to Smarter Working does involve changes in behaviours. According to Norma Pearce, Head of HR at Plantronics EMEA, 'It's all about empowerment, allowing people to make choices and trusting them to make the best ones. In principle, we're happy to let people organise work to fit in with their lives. At first, some managers need help with this. In part, it's about being able to let go of things they've previously had closer control over. It's about developing soft skills – and trust is a soft skill. The role of the manager becomes more one of coaching and mentoring'.

Coupled with this is greater transparency. Plantronics uses an online solution Success Factors for setting and managing team and individual goals. This is part of the approach of managing by results. Everyone's goals are visible online, and their progress towards them. This also feeds into appraisals, professional development and pay reviews.

The shift to Smarter Working is paying dividends. Surveys before and after implementation show a 24 per cent increase in engagement. And EMEA sales results in both Q2 and Q3 were greatly increased, Q3 significantly so. Though this may not all be down to working smarter, the leadership at Plantronics is sure it has played a part. Now the programme has been rolled out in their US offices in California.

'For us, the whole idea behind Smarter Working', says Paul Clark, 'is that it makes good business sense and good people sense'.

e-Learning, Employee-Generated Learning and Knowledge-Sharing

The trend in training is towards self-help and bite-size training, where employees can (at least to some extent) set their own pace and grab smaller chunks of learning on an as-needed basis. Just-in-time training, perhaps.

At the time of writing there are a limited number of e-learning packages relating to flexible working, working in virtual teams and so forth. Some are excellent, and one or two are, quite frankly, dire. It's not for me really to recommend specific products here, as no doubt these will change over time as new products come on the market. And the ones I might label as 'dire' might end up suing.

Basically, if you find they are compatible with the advice in this book, then they would be the ones I would recommend. It is also helpful if they are customisable so that the organisation can brand them as their own and link to or weave in their own supporting policies, protocols, case studies, and so on, as Plantronics have done (see the case study earlier in this chapter).

The less useful ones are the ones those that focus on parents and work-life balance, see everything in terms of employee choice, make assumptions about people working flexibly being less contactable and so forth. In fact the ones that seem to have been written in a pre-smart era, maybe around the late 1990s.

But the e-learning approach of course applies not only to learning about Smart Flexibility, but to all kinds of training and learning in the organisation.

Flexible working has provided BT with the organisational, technical and behavioural platform to develop new ways of learning and networking. The company makes extensive use of social media technologies to encourage learning, sharing information and collaboration.

BT's intranet home page gives employees access to a wide range of internal wikis, blogs and podcasts. E-learning replaces traditional classroom learning with an online, anytime, anywhere model to deliver 85 per cent of training to its employees. Via its 'Route2Learn' portal BT has 3,000 courses available for online delivery covering everything from technical training for engineers to eye tests for drivers and new legislation around bribery and corruption.

An important part of the changing culture of work is the flattening of hierarchy, and this applies to learning too. In Chapter 7 we looked at some of the social media tools for sharing knowledge amongst workers.

BT is a firm believer in encouraging user-generated content. As an example, BT's 'Dare2Share' programme allows any employee to upload a short video, specifically geared towards teaching and instruction. This is well used and provides a corporate YouTube format that delivers a large range of short 'how-to' clips. The company believes that this is a great way of unlocking a lot of the experience that would never be shared in any other way.

When these kinds of new learning techniques are well-managed, promoted and supported, it has a transformative effect on the culture of learning. And it also encourages staff not only to take ownership of their own learning, but to recognise they have a role as an educator too.

Incentives – Recognition, Rewards and Compensation

How can changes to new ways of working be incentivised? For many people being able to have more control over their working lives, reducing the hassles of the commute and saving money are sufficient incentives. Smart Flexibility in many respects is its own incentive.

Having said that, recognition for achievement can be very motivational. Feting teams and individuals for achieving or overachieving targets set at the time of transition or for innovative practices that deliver positive results is certainly worth doing. Developing a culture of praise rather than blame has wider benefits beyond new working practices too.

Success in delivering change and working in new ways ought to be feather in the cap in terms of career progression too. Conversely, failing to adapt should be seen as blotting one's copybook. And this should be made clear in terms of KPIs and in appraisals.

The stories that arise from this kind of recognition, and indeed from sticky moments in appraisals, become part of the culture that influences behavioural change. And the most illuminating and interesting stories should be written up as case studies, and become part of the supporting material available for those implementing Smart Flexibility throughout the organisation.

Rewards – that is a more tricky area, though from what I have just said the recognition could in time translate into reward in terms of career progression. It is more tricky as particular financial incentives to change can be divisive and may in some cases lead to tax issues.

But it may be worth thinking about some kind of reward for the individual or team that comes up with the best innovation that boosts performance. Or, if a team saves a bucket-load of money in travel costs, why not reward the team collectively in some way?

It might be possible also to dovetail incentives for sustainable mobility used in company travel plans with incentives to work flexibly. For example, some employers have rewards that build up to additional holiday or pay if they don't drive to work. Some forms of flexible working can contribute to this – the incentive doesn't need to be based on using a bus or a bike instead.

Sometimes people look for, and unions might even demand, compensation for working from home. In the UK, at time of writing, the Treasury will allow £3 per week as a non-taxable expense for additional energy use for people who work most of the time at home. Some companies provide this, and some go further with additional allowances.

Apart from any set-up costs incurred, I would go along with those companies that don't provide any additional allowances. For 99 per cent of people, the savings from not commuting far outstrip any additional home energy use. And on top of this are the benefits from having more flexibility and autonomy, which most people appreciate.

Companies can also tie themselves in knots as well in working out mileage allowances for coming into the main office and travelling to client visits when people work from home. This is an area for caution, as the tax rules can be somewhat murky and their application inconsistent. But apart from that, any level of compensation mustn't turn into a reward or incentive for getting into the car and driving.

People resisting change often argue that it's all about shifting costs from the company onto the individual. But that ignores the way that employees already have costs loaded onto them in traditional ways of working from the expectation to be at a specified place at a specified time every day.

So if people are irreconcilably grumpy about this, they have the choice. They can choose to carry on spending £2,000–£3,000 per year on going every day to the office. But people who are grumpy about saving money are probably also grumpy about many other things, and it may be beyond a company culture-change process to bring joy into their lives.

CHAPTER 9

Managing the Anywhere, Anytime Team

Something Old, Something New

One of the biggest concerns for managers when moving to flexible ways of working is about managing people whom they no longer meet on a daily basis, or whom they can no longer monitor by line of sight at any given moment. These can be the biggest changes for managers to adjust to.

But the first thing to say is that this situation is hardly new. Thousands of managers have long been managing geographically distributed teams. Thousands of managers also manage teams across different shifts, when the manager clearly cannot be physically present at all times. And thousands of managers are *mobile themselves* – the assumption can't be that staff should be where managers are in these situations, or else they'd be followed by huge retinues of staff like a medieval monarch or modern dictator.

So part of managing the 'Anywhere, Anytime Team' is about translating good practice from areas where out-of-sight management is already practised. This means having a clear understanding of workloads, targets and outcomes, and monitoring performance en route, just as the manager of a travelling sales force would do.

The other part is about adapting management techniques to capitalise on the potential of the new Smart Flexibility culture that is being developed, and to make the most of using new technologies.

Most of the Core Management Competences are the Same

What kind of competences should all good managers have?

Setting objectives, managing performance, managing costs, monitoring delivery, keeping the focus on customer value, managing quality, managing risk, decision-making, communicating, coaching and mentoring, team-building, making decisions about tools and resources, adjusting objectives in the light of new circumstances – these are the kinds of skills and abilities that all managers need in addition to any specialist competences for their line of work. To these we might add a twenty-first century necessity of being able to manage change.

These competences are the same wherever and whenever the staff and their managers are working. What will change most with Smart Flexibility is the context in which the manager exhibits these competences, and some of the tools that are used.

People Skills at a Distance

Working in a trust-based culture where employees are liberated and empowered to make their own decisions to a greater extent than before means that the communication and people skills of the manager need to be sharper and well-adapted to the new situation.

It will no longer always be the case that the manager can get an update on progress by going up to team members or calling them into the office for a quick conversation. This is the kind of issue that causes greatest concern to managers making the transition to Smart Flexibility. Once again, it is worth emphasising that few people are out of the office all the time. Even so, there will be – indeed there is intended to be – a shift in the relative locations of the workforce.

To some extent, the stresses of increased mobility are already being felt by managers with a mix of more and less mobile workers. If their preference is to rely exclusively on face-to-face communication, then they are either already treating mobile workers as kind of second-class citizens or else requiring them to come into the office too often and compromising the effectiveness they can achieve through their mobility.

As with many aspects of moving to flexible working, the way forward is to get down to particular issues and resolve them at a granular level. Table 9.1 on the following page provides a way for managers to unpack the wider concept of 'people skills' and examine closely:

a) How developed these skills are;
b) How these skills are exercised now; and
c) If or how the way of exercising the skill needs to change in the future with flexible working.

As in any discussion of people skills, there tends to be a certain degree of overlapping of the categories. And when it comes to thinking about what techniques are used, one technique (like having a face-to-face team meeting) may cover several skills.

In some ways, the 'How good am I?' column is the easiest for people to complete. It's a reflective exercise with ratings on a 1–5 scale, where 5 is 'excellent' and 1 is 'not good at all', and DK is 'don't know', which can be an honest assessment of an issue one maybe has not thought about.

The two columns on the right are quite challenging, and people often think, 'How *do* I do that?' But this is useful for small group exercises, and people can learn quite a bit from each other in the process. A lot of the skills will be exercised informally and in ad hoc situations, and some people may not find it easy to express just how it is they make sure they are being understood, or what they do in a negotiating situation. Others may be clearer and have particular techniques they use, whether it's making a point of praising someone as a means of motivation, or ensuring they make eye contact when trying to make themselves understood, or using social occasions to build team spirit.

In many ways the conversations are more important than ending up with a detailed methodology for using particular techniques for exhibiting these interpersonal skills in new ways. This is because the conversations will in all probability, unless some managers are exceptionally skilled or self-assured, highlight the need to improve performance in these skills for all staff, wherever or whenever they are working.

Table 9.1   Taking forward smart people skills

People skill	How good am I?	Technique(s) now	Future technique(s)
Being understood	1 2 3 4 5 DK		
Listening skills	1 2 3 4 5 DK		
Influencing/motivating	1 2 3 4 5 DK		
Inspiring/getting the best out of people	1 2 3 4 5 DK		
Trusting others	1 2 3 4 5 DK		
Involving others	1 2 3 4 5 DK		
Building team spirit	1 2 3 4 5 DK		
Delegating	1 2 3 4 5 DK		
Assertiveness	1 2 3 4 5 DK		
Coaching/mentoring	1 2 3 4 5 DK		
Setting appropriate objectives	1 2 3 4 5 DK		
Giving feedback/appraisal	1 2 3 4 5 DK		
Detecting performance problems	1 2 3 4 5 DK		
Detecting personal problems	1 2 3 4 5 DK		
Problem solving	1 2 3 4 5 DK		
Resolving disputes	1 2 3 4 5 DK		
Decision-making	1 2 3 4 5 DK		
Persuading	1 2 3 4 5 DK		
Negotiating	1 2 3 4 5 DK		
Disciplining/having awkward conversations	1 2 3 4 5 DK		

Let's look at this more closely. The expectation is that the context for employing these skills will change. Whereas at the moment many if not most of them will be employed in real time face-to-face interaction, under Smart Flexibility scenarios there will be more occasions when they can't be physically face to face, or the interaction needs to be asynchronous as all or some of the parties involved are working different times.

The changes in context mean that there are primarily two areas where the current techniques can't be so readily used: informal/off-the-cuff exchanges and employing or interpreting body language.

So in making a transition to exercising 'people skills at a distance' there are some key things to think about:

- Can that informality I find valuable be replicated through using communication tools, whether conferencing, instant messaging or just the plain old telephone?
- … or do I have to replace some of that informality with more formal communication or processes?
- Can I gather some of that body language intelligence through videoconferencing, for example, when having virtual team meetings or in a desktop video one-to-one call?
- … and can I develop the skills and etiquette needed to pick up the cues I need from tone of voice and levels of participation in audio calls?

- Do I have to insist that particular activities where interpersonal interaction is particularly valuable takes place when we are physically present together – and if so, which ones?
- How do I ensure that I interact with my team in an inclusive way, that is, ensuring that no one is left out who needs to be included, by reason of their working in a more flexible way?

As for the most part both teams and managers will be sometimes in and sometimes out the office, it's not a question of abandoning current techniques wholly in favour of new ones. It's about building up the skills overall and adding to the repertoire of techniques for becoming a great people manager.

Building or Anchoring Team and Corporate Identity

One of the biggest concerns of people sceptical about flexible working is the potential loss of team cohesion, spirit and identity. These concerns tend to be based on both an exaggeration of the degrees of separation and an unfamiliarity with the way distributed teams operate. They may sometimes also be based on an idealistic perception of pre-flexible levels of team and corporate cohesion.

To take the last point first: co-location and cohesion are not the same thing. Expecting that it is easier to bond as a team if people are all in the same place is a fairly natural assumption. But does it necessarily happen?

Experience would tend to suggest that it does not. Repeated initiatives to break down hierarchies, silos and subversive subcultures, to team-build and build a 'one organisation' ethos tends to imply that there are existing challenges on this front in non-flexible organisations. Becoming more flexible, and developing a culture of Smart Flexibility, involves activities that can help to improve current levels of cohesion and overcome existing problems of silo working.

Good teamwork needs managing, wherever it takes place. And this comes back to the leadership skills of managers. It's partly down to the people skills, in terms of motivating, inspiring, delegating and coaching, and partly down to active measures taken to promote a specific kind of team ethic and ethos. The following are the kinds of measures used to build team and corporate identity in the context of flexible working:

- Having a Team Charter, with strong input from the team, covering collective goals and the principle of working together;
- Regular flagging up of achievements of the team and of the company; for example, how the team has contributed to corporate goals and delivered value to customers, and regular flagging up of achievements of team members, to promote a sense of pride in each other's achievements;
- Encouraging innovation within the team, and seeing that the ideas are shared;
- Use of social networking technologies to promote interaction, not only about work;
- Joint non-work actions, for example, supporting a charity, or the charitable activities of individual members; sporting or social activities, and so on;
- Team, service and/or corporate identity expressed in the new flexible working environment, for example, photos encapsulating what the service is all about, use

of corporate colours and inspirational statements. Some people may want to wax cynical (or throw up) at this point, but this kind of motivational branding can be tastefully done as part of an overall refresh and improvement of working space. It's about incorporating a sense of identity into good design.

Ofsted is the UK inspectorate for standards in education, children's services and skills. It became the largest home-based organisation in the public sector just after the turn of the millennium, with more than 1,500 home-based inspectors, when it took over the role of Early Years Education inspections from local councils. At that time it was decided to move all inspectors, including all the existing schools inspectors, onto a home-based working basis, in an early example of 'spaceless growth'.

Over the following decade, Ofsted has developed and refined its home-working operation, radically reducing its office network while investing in technology and in developing the support structures for remote workers.

The national network of offices has been shrunk to three – in Bristol, Nottingham and Manchester – with a small headquarters building in London. These are all set up on a desk-sharing basis, without personal offices. Most middle and senior managers are also home-based. At first, administrative staff remained office-based, but now most work from home two to three days per week.

One of the most striking features of the Ofsted implementation has been the support given to home-based workers. From the earliest days, Ofsted have channelled support through a dedicated Home-based Working Coordinator, Caroline Oldham. As well as supporting the practical implementation, Caroline's role has been to support and encourage team-building. A range of techniques has been used both for carrying out remote teamwork and management, with training, coaching and mentoring, clear target setting and monitoring, plus monthly face-to-face team meetings and social events.

This has now been supplemented by effective use of Microsoft OCS (Lync) for working on shared documents and being able to work with each other face to face. They also use this for 'lunch and learn' sessions, mixing work and social interaction.

Ofsted also has a process for what would have to be called 'flexible working-proofing' for new policies and initiatives. So any new initiatives or policies have to be checked through to see that they are compatible with the flexible working approach.

According to Caroline, much of the reason for the success is because 'Ofsted is genuinely trying to make flexible and home-based working a really good experience. HR has been producing great policies, the senior leadership team are totally behind it, and the IT provision is very responsive, checking everything through with the remote workers to arrive at the best solutions'.

The technology for home-based workers includes:

- Lightweight encrypted notebook PC.
- Broadband.

- Unified communications solution – the separate landline phones are now being removed as the UC solution makes them redundant.

Ofsted provides an allowance for heating and lighting, and initial allowance at the outset for ergonomic home office desk and chair. This expenditure is justified on the basis that employees are full-time home-based, and the need to provide a professional working environment – though at a fraction of the cost of maintaining a national network of offices.

Recent changes have meant that the early years inspectors service has now been outsourced. They do, however, remain home-based.

'Communicate, Communicate, Communicate' – But Don't Do It All Yourself

All the guidance that's out there about remote working says that for managing remote working and virtual teams you can't communicate enough. At one level this is true, but there are dangers too. Remote working employees may come to dread an obligatory stilted phone call from a manager who is just going through the motions or who really wants to bond but hasn't really got the social skills to do it.

The way I'd put it is like this. The manager needs to encourage a two-way and multi-way flow of interaction, by whatever media are appropriate. And it should be almost exclusively work-focused. Social interaction should be a marginal extra, but over time all communication should have a framework that is socially pleasant and fulfilling – because ideally all work is like that.

Where there are good workplaces, we enjoy the experience of human interaction, whether it's work or social. It's too artificial to start to think, 'I've talked about our objectives for the week now, let's talk about last night's TV'. Instead, all the conversation has to have a credible social envelope.

It's about staying on top of what the Anywhere, Anytime Team is doing. And this means not only whether they are meeting objectives and on track for hitting deadlines, but also getting candid feedback about any difficulties they might be having. This could be directly to do with the tasks in hand, or it could be to do with the tools, or more widely with the experience of working remotely. It could also be about wider issues in life where they are encountering complications or problems.

There are also issues around personal development that will be of concern to the team, especially in terms of training and career progression, or in the case of freelancers and contractors, opportunities for continuing work. These are all topics where there is a need for interaction.

While the manager needs to be on top of all this, a key principle is that it doesn't have to be the manager who runs all the conversations. This would be an intolerable imposition. So delegation – one of the most important leadership skills – is essential for communication and team-bonding.

This doesn't mean having a particular trusted lieutenant to do this. It's more about getting other team members involved in promoting positive interaction, such as:

- Coaching and mentoring.

- Buddying new recruits.
- Having responsibility for seeing that particular projects or kinds of work are on track, and doing the chasing and getting the feedback on these.
- Getting other team members to initiate and run any social or extra-curricular activities.
- Getting people to liaise in sub-teams on work, either with shared responsibilities for delivery or to ensure that people are not left flying solo, and that another person can deputise or cover if they are ill or not around for any reason.

The manager's role is as a facilitator here, and keeping on top of things enough to see that the right kinds and levels of conversations are taking place.

Different Strokes for Different Folks – Different Kinds of Anywhere, Anytime Teams

There will be different kinds of relationships, different kinds of communication and different kinds of things to watch out for depending on the makeup of the team. Table 9.2 below gives some examples of the different ways in which a flexible or virtual team might be made up.

This is just a selection of possible patterns for flexible teams, showing a number of different combinations of locations, times of work, nationality and employment or organisational relationships. There are also quite different types of work and different levels of complexity involved in the work, as well as varying levels of autonomy and possibilities for self-organisation. So there is clearly not going to be a 'one-size-fits-all' approach to how they should be managed, or for building team identity, or for promoting communication.

Table 9.2   Examples of types of Anywhere, Anytime Team

Team type	Main locations			Times		Nationality		Relationship		
	Home	Mobile	Office	Reg hours	24/7	One country	International	Employees	Contractors	Ext partner
Data processing	✓			✓		✓		✓		
Contact centre	✓		✓		✓		✓	✓		
Civil engineers		✓	✓	✓			✓	✓	✓	✓
Design team	✓	✓	✓	✓			✓	✓	✓	
Medical researchers	✓		✓ lab		✓		✓	✓		✓
Product dev team	✓	✓	✓	✓		✓		✓	✓	✓
Schools inspectors	✓	✓		✓		✓		✓		

Our home-based data processing team here looks to be quite straightforward in terms of working pattern, compared to many of the other kinds of teams. However, it doesn't necessarily mean that managing them will be straightforward, as the work may poses challenges in terms of motivation. And though it's not a 24/7 operation, often this kind of routine work is not only home-based but also may include people on part-time or term-time-only work patterns. So seeing that everyone is included in the loop may have challenges in that context.

Some types of work may require 24/7 cover, involving shifts of people, whether to be available to customers in different countries, for emergency response or to keep equipment or experiments going or to provide round-the-clock observation. This may or may not involve people in other countries. But when people in other time zones are involved (which could indeed be within a single country), then the operation of the team usually has to extend beyond the regular hours to enable the team to communicate at times. People may all be working regular hours in their own time zone, so there is no objective 24/7 operational requirement. It's just that as the team includes people from Australia, Singapore, USA, Turkey and the UK, someone, somewhere in the team is always working. So when it the best time to be communicating? Who gets up early and who stays up late, and what are the ground rules for varying this in the interests of fairness?

When there is more than one nationality involved, then there may well be cultural issues to consider in terms of communication, etiquette and team dynamics.

And if there are contractors, freelancers, agency workers and/or external partners involved, there will be additional issues around the team dynamic and communications. For example, is it reasonable to expect non-core employees to share in the same goals for the organisation as a whole, or just the goals for the team? To what extent can they be expected to 'go the extra mile' for the project out of loyalty rather than for additional payment or other incentive? Are there issues of confidentiality – both ways – to consider?

Where is the Manager?

Against these kinds of possibilities, there is no hard and fast rule about where or when a manager should work – except to say that sitting in the main office 9 to 5 can't be expected to be the default position. With these kinds of patterns of work, it's fairly certain that he or she will not be working in the same place as most of the team members, and possibly not at the same times as many team members.

The argument for the manager having visibility in the main office comes down to the fact that in many of the types of team models, people do spend quite a bit of time or even the majority of the time working in the office as a base from which they operate. Full-time home-working or full-time on the road are not the norm for most people in distributed teams. And there will be times when all the team are together for face-to-face meetings, or the manager wants to have appraisals or review meetings in the flesh. So there remains a kind of compelling logic to the manager having a presence and good visibility at an agreed base. Unless the organisation has given up its office, of course.

But there are reasons why this is not such a good idea as well:

- If there are team members who are never, or only rarely in the same office as the manager, they may start to feel like second-class citizens.

- The temptation to fall back on line-of-sight management for those who are more readily in line of sight will be great.
- Managers are often highly mobile people to start with. This mobility is there to be built upon as an exemplar of smart and flexible practice. The manager should not start to feel himself/herself chained to the office as a kind of symbolic anchor now that others are acquiring greater mobility.
- The office will probably be a less productive environment, and more will get done using a range of other locations as appropriate.

So that 'compelling logic' I mentioned may be a little too much thinking with one's old head on, and not with the new, smart head. The touchstone should be going back to the first principle of Smart Flexibility: 'Work takes place at the most effective locations' and 'Work takes place at the most effective times'. So the manager has to make decisions about where these are. For the team, it is important that the manager is contactable and responsive, not that he or she is in a particular location.

There are challenges here. One of them is a hierarchical issue that tends to come up in reorganisations quite a bit. Should the manager be co-located with the people who report to him, or the people to whom he reports? And how does this issue translate to smart working environments?

To me, there is a problem with the approach of executive suites where senior managers congregate or special management zones where heads of department share desks and meeting rooms. Ideally, the organisation should walk the talk all the way up to the top. Having a set place within the office, a management ghetto, is to be halfway down the slippery slope that leads to meeting rooms being turned back into a private offices. So the answer is that whenever the manager is in the office, he or she should be able to work in whatever activity-based setting is appropriate for the work in hand. On a practical basis, and to be best informed, this is more likely to be with his team than with those who are the next level up.

Those who are in the higher levels of management need to be prepared to be more mobile and to work in whatever area is best for the tasks in hand. They are likely to have several managers reporting to them, and it may be a case of ensuring that they migrate around the various team zones so as to be equally visible.

But bearing in mind that their immediate reports will be much more footloose than before, the same principle applies. It's about being contactable and responsive and being 'visible' through the collaborative technologies that is important, not identification with a particular place.

The End of Command and Control and Presenteeism … or Is It?

Almost no one in the world of management studies or manager training would recommend traditional 'command and control' techniques for management. Yet it's what tends to be the default position in practice in many organisations. This doesn't just apply to 'line-of-sight' management. Sometimes the most controlling are those in charge of nomadic staff, not least in sales where in many companies a target-driven 'butt-kicking' culture prevails. Some experienced managers working the traditional way are sure that there will always be staff who want to bunk off or shilly-shally, and need to be kept on a tight leash.

Smart Flexibility, though, is much more about creating a trust-based and empowering culture, and management by results. However, I think there is too much wishful thinking about this, and much of it is based on a false, or at least outdated, premise.

There is a pervasive myth that command and control management and presenteeism are not possible with flexible working practices. The false premise here is that when people work somewhere else or at different times it is not possible to know if they are working. This is increasingly no longer the case, and in a few years' time will hardly be the case at all. This is because of the technologies described in Chapter 7 for registering presence and status, and for recording time spent on different tasks.

Arguably, these techniques for monitoring presence and inputs could actually make matters worse. They will yield a rich vein of data which can be analysed with reporting software to make it seem like managers have really got their fingers on the pulse of the work being done by the team. Foreseeing the totalitarian possibilities of new technology, Tolstoy once said, 'Imagine Genghis Khan with a telephone!' So the new technologies, wrongly used, could provide the basis for command and control on steroids.

But just as watching people in their seats and gathering timesheets is a poor proxy for productivity, so are these kinds of more sophisticated techniques. These technologies may be helpful for other purposes, for example, billing clients and knowing people's availability to be contacted, but for the most part fall a long way short of measuring output or assessing the quality of output.

What does this mean for the manager of the Anywhere, Anytime Team? The point is that developing a trust-based culture should not be based on the (apparent) lack of rigorous mechanisms of control. It has to be based on a much more positive foundation – a commitment to trusting the team.

Setting the Foundations of Trust

Good teams will have a strong basis of trust wherever they are based. Trust is based on personal and professional relationships within a shared history, on shared achievements and on expectations met. People in a relationship of trust don't have to love each other, or even like each other. But there has to be a mutual respect for abilities. This may be qualified in some cases by reservations people have about each other's abilities, but a good working relationship can nevertheless be based on awareness of what can and can't be achieved.

So it may be that people are turned loose from the office as a proven functioning unit, and carry on performing because they trust each other and know what to expect from each other, are mutually supportive and know how to deliver the goods. But distributed teams may include, as we've seen above, a diverse group of people who don't necessarily have an existing relationship to build on. So what is needed is a good framework in which to operate, one that provides a practical basis in which people can be empowered and trusted to get on with whatever they should be getting on with.

These are the ingredients of such a framework:

- A clear and agreed idea of what success is, both for the team as a whole and for discrete tasks.
- Clear and understood objectives.

- Clear and agreed roles and responsibilities.
- Clear and agreed processes for reporting progress.
- An agreed process for feeding back difficulties in good time.
- Mechanisms for supporting and coaching when needed.
- Routines to have work in progress available in shared areas.
- Agreement to be contactable and to keep presence status updated.
- Encouragement for team members within this framework to do what they need to do without any attempt at micromanagement.

These are key ingredients of the Smart Flexibility culture set out in the last chapter. The essence of the trust is basically that people can work wherever and whenever they want, as long as they get the work done.

'Wherever and Whenever' – Does That Mean a Complete Free-for-All?

Having said that, there may be operational constraints that limit the choices available to individuals. 'Getting the work done' may often involve working at specific times or at specific places.

People may have work that is largely time-critical, for example, if their role is to deal with and process calls from the public. Some degree of employee control over this might come through team self-rostering arrangements, but at the end of the day the team has to take ownership of delivering the required work, and that means the work must be done at specific times.

Other work may be place specific – for example, for hands-on work at the employer's site, whether for complex lab work or routine maintenance work, or the need to be at a client site at specific times or even all the time (for example, to deliver outsourced work or to work on a particular project).

These are issues covered in more depth in the section on selecting for Smart Flexibility in Chapter 5. So the principle of Smart Flexibility, working wherever and whenever is best to get the work done, needs to start by clearly defining where is the best place and what is the best time. Sometimes, it is the only place or only time, but more often there are a range of options for some if not all of the work.

Figure 9.1 on the following page sets in a simplified way the basic choices for where and when work should take place. It may have to take place at a specific time and a specific place ('That place' and 'That time'). The time of work or the place of work may be varied, and in some cases both.

Around the outside of these time/place combinations in Figure 9.1 is a range of 'critical choice factors'. These are the factors that managers and teams should apply when making judgements about where and when work should take place. It's not simply a question of work being time/place dependent or independent. The factors illustrated will have varying amounts of weight when it comes to deciding the preferred work-style.

Priority has to be given to business factors – being able to work effectively and to deliver the goods. One thing that doesn't feature here as a separate factor is 'Manager's preference'. As employees, managers can throw their personal preference into the equation when they have the opportunity to flex their own time and place of work.

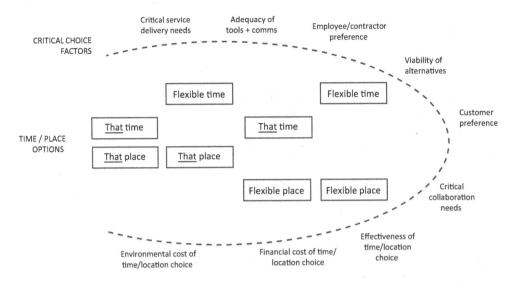

Figure 9.1   Factors affecting choice of time and place of work

But as a manager, 'preference' has to be based on objective business considerations like delivering the service, effectiveness and the potential to minimise the financial and environmental costs of work.

'Customer preference' is an interesting one. In many cases, particularly for work that is traditionally office-based, changes to time and location should be invisible to the customer. But in other cases it may be a compelling factor, if for example they specifically need or request a service to be carried out at their site or at certain hours. Sometimes their reasoning may be outdated, and working with them might feel like entering a time warp. In that case the aim should be respectfully to bring them up the learning curve. But in the end, it may be a case of he who pays the piper calls the tune.

Of course the 'Other time' and 'Other place' may be plural. The same critical choice factors apply. When real options are being considered, often there may not be a huge difference between some of the alternatives in terms of efficiency and effectiveness. There may be several viable choices – and that's what flexible working is all about.

This is not a rigid template for coming up with prescriptive solutions, but a way to encourage a smart approach to the choices for flexible working. Once the team gets into the habit of making choices with this kind of mindset, the manager can relax a bit, and trust that the team members are making the appropriate choices.

Managing by Results – How Do We Measure Results if People Are Out of Sight?

Different kinds of work have different kinds of results based on different kinds of output – there is no one-size-fits-all prescription for measuring the output that is to be managed.

So this is very hard to encapsulate in a book aimed at a wide audience covering all kinds of work rather than a single discipline. But it is one of the most critical areas, and one of the things raised most by managers when we run conferences or deliver workshops. It is further complicated by few managers being ready to say that they don't already manage by results. In which case, what's the problem? It must be always other managers who will struggle. Often questioners want clarity about some of the more high-level, fluid and reactive areas of work where outputs and results may be hard to pin down.

In setting out to take Smart Flexibility from Theory to Practice, though, I think one has to go beyond the single-bullet-point generalities often found in guidance on flexible work. What is meant by results? How do we measure them? How do we keep track of work in progress that leads to the results? As with all these complex issues, the key is to break it down into the component elements.

Step One is to think about the kind of work that is involved, and the kinds of measurements that can apply. Note we are focusing on generic types of work, rather than any kind of distinction between different sectors, or occupations, or types of end result, or the nature of the input, and so on. A suggested typology which can be applied across sectors and occupations is as follows:

Process work – What I mean by this is all kinds of work that forms part of a regular well-defined process, and where the output at any stage is usually clearly countable. This includes most forms of production, data processing, volume telephony work, finance, and many aspects of sales. Something comes in to you, you deal with it (by adding something to it, shaping it, analysing it, fulfilling it, and so on) and you pass it on. There should be workflow management systems in place already, and the main issue for us is around being able to track the progress, completion and quality of work wherever it is carried out.

Project work – Project-type work encompasses anything that can be seen as a one-off collection of work tasks that lead to a well-defined budget, purpose, scope, timescale and result. In contrast to other kinds of ongoing work, it has a clearly defined beginning, middle and end – a story in its own right. This kind of work can include projects to deliver a product or set of services to clients, bidding for work, building something, creating marketing materials or running a campaign, delivering change projects, and so on. For this kind of work, outputs are not only the outputs at the end, but all the defined deliverables en route. This is also an important principle for many of the kinds of work that people struggle to know how to measure – turn it into projects.

Case or account work – This is work where people work with a particular client to deliver a service, solve problems or monitor the delivery of a service. This could be on the one hand a social worker working with vulnerable people or offenders, or on the other a commercial account manager. In either case they will be delivering or monitoring a service of value to the client. A characteristic of this kind of work is that it often contains a mix of more routine work and unpredictable work that may need a fast reaction. In some areas, it may need long periods of work with a client or prospective client before a desired result is achieved – and may even be unsuccessful. These are the kinds of uncertain results that some people may feel are intrinsically unmeasurable. But while the final outcome may be uncertain, the various activities that make up the output have to be monitored and managed to see if the right amount is being done and that it is of good quality.

Innovation work (coming up with new things) – Innovation isn't only about inventing the next iPad. Innovation is an essential component of many roles. It is about coming up with new ideas, insights, designs or tweaks to designs. It can be about creating new policy, writing an article or a speech, making a presentation or producing marketing material. On a day-to-day basis, much innovation work is of a routine nature. Behind an innovative end-product may be a fair amount of research, analysis or experimentation. This again holds the prospect of negative results – things that are produced but don't quite cut the mustard in the end and are dropped. It doesn't mean the work is unmeasurable, just that there are different kinds of results. For example, if people are coming up with a range of ideas for an advert, most must fall by the wayside but hopefully contribute to creating a strong final result. There is clear output to be achieved, but the results may be uncertain in terms of winning the bid.

Support work – is about supporting the work of other people. A lot of the work may be quite reactive, that is, dealing with what other people request or expect to be done. Much of the work done by some people considered as support or admin workers may really be process work: for example, filing things or printing things as part of a well-defined process. Reactive support work appears to be more challenging to measure. The final results (outcomes) of reactive support work may be hard to quantify in isolation, but the outputs are not. Are the tasks set being done in a timely and accurate way? Are diaries being kept up to date? Are phone calls handled well?

Managerial and coordination work – Managers, team leaders and supervisors also have an obligation to achieve results that have to be monitored and measured. Some of these will be their individual performance (for example, in producing reports for managers higher up, meeting financial targets, and so on) and some will revolve around the output and outcomes of the parts of the business they manage. And there may be metrics around staff satisfaction within their teams, ability to retain staff, absence levels that indicate comparative performance with other managers.

Step Two is to apply *measures of quantity and quality* for the outputs (see Table 9.3), and on the basis of this apply appropriate targets for the individuals and teams. While some people will be engaged almost entirely in one kind of work, many will be involved in a mix of types, for example, a mix of case work and process work, or support work and process work, or project work, innovation work and case work. Understanding the mix is the key to being able to set realistic and fair workloads and being able to monitor and measure the output by applying the right kinds of measures and quality standards.

Step Three is to consider what, if any, additional issues arise in measuring the amount and quality of work when (much of) that work is carried on at different places or times, and where the manager doesn't have immediate line-of-sight access to it. This is why initially the focus should be on 'outputs' rather than 'outcomes'. The manager has to see that the output is managed well in order to achieve the desired outcomes. If one waits for the final outcome before assessing the result of a piece of work, it may already be too late. The manager needs to be able to step in to make sure everything is on course, and to set it back on course if it's going off track.

It is important to remember the context here of Smart Flexibility. After the discussion of technologies and techniques for managing the Anywhere, Anytime Team, hopefully the view of flexible working is no longer that people and their work are out of sight and out of mind. So the manager should have confidence that people are contactable and their work is viewable.

All the same, managers have concerns about work in progress – they do need to know if employees are keeping on top of their workload and are meeting targets. Generally this is easier to manage within the well-defined structures of process work. For other kinds of work, the way forward is to think of work as consisting of components that are within themselves projects with mini-deliverables, and clear lines of workflow so that work is delivered on time for colleagues to add their input.

Table 9.3 Segmentation of types of work for management by results

Type of work	Characteristics	Examples	Measures of output (examples)	
			Quantity	**Quality**
Process	Work that is part of a regular well-defined process, and where the output at any stage is usually clearly countable	Most forms of production Data processing Volume telephony work Many aspects of finance Many aspects of sales Customer fulfilment work	Number of items produced Amount of information processed Number of calls handled Number of transactions Number of items delivered	Meeting required standards Accuracy Customer satisfaction with process
Project	Project-type work – encompasses anything that can be seen as a one-off collection of work tasks with a well-defined budget, purpose, scope, timescale and result	Delivering a product or set of services to clients Bidding for work Building something Creating marketing materials Running a campaign Implementing change projects	Production of deliverables to time and budget Number of component deliverables handled per person/team	Quality of deliverables Quality of contributions of project team members Degree to which project meets objectives Value for money
Case	Work with individual clients to deliver a service, solve problems or monitor the delivery of a service	Working on commercial client account Social work case work Legal case work Resolving employee disputes	Number of services or products delivered to client Number of elements delivered by each team member or case worker Number of cases handled overall Balance between straightforward and complex cases in workload	Customer satisfaction with service in the case Efficiency and effectiveness of case/account handling Meeting objective standards (for example, legal standard; government-set targets) Success in meeting or exceeding billing targets Success in resolving problems

Table 9.3   **Continued**

Type of work	Characteristics	Examples	Measures of output (examples)	
			Quantity	*Quality*
Innovation	Coming up with new ideas, strategies, insights, designs, modifications to designs	Creating new policy Writing an article or a speech Preparing a presentation Producing marketing strategy Designing new product Scoping smarter working	Number of articles, speeches, presentations produced Contribution by team members to producing new strategy, product, and so on Amount of research, analysis, evidence gathering, reporting as contributions to innovation	Speed of response to requests for new materials Quality of materials delivered Ability to take new idea or new product/prototype forward Robustness and insightfulness of evidence and analysis
Support	Supporting the work of other people, more in a reactive and as-needed way rather than as part of a process or project	PA/secretarial work Technical support Reception work	Number of people supported and with what services Number of sites or equipment supported Number of requests responded to	Speed and efficiency of response Accuracy Being proactive in spotting issues Ability to coordinate functioning of team Organisational skill
Managerial	Managing, coordinating and supervising the work of others	Managing or coordinating teams Managing people (effectiveness, collaboration, skills development) Managing resources and budgets Managing results Mentoring, coaching	Output of individuals and teams managed Personal output as individual, if applicable Amount of people management work Contributions to meeting corporate objectives	Success in managing workloads and setting and meeting targets Quality of output of teams Quality of reporting to senior management Success in resolving problems Quality of people management Feedback from 360° appraisals Quality of resource management

Results-Only Work Environments (ROWE)

One high profile approach that firmly focuses on results rather than presence is Results-Only Work Environments (ROWE). According to the team behind this approach, 'In a ROWE, people focus on results and only results – increasing the organisation's performance while creating the right climate for people to manage all the demands in their lives ... including work' (www.gorowe.com).

The methodology was developed at BestBuy in the USA, with significant results in terms of improved performance, elimination of wasteful processes and employee retention. One central and challenging feature of it is the emphasis given to individual autonomy. People are not bound by schedules or place so long as they deliver the results. They don't have to attend meetings if they decide they have something more useful to do. It's the results – only the results.

In many ways I agree with the outlook and philosophy of the originators of ROWE (Dressler and Thompson 2011). They have a kind of 'shake 'em up' approach to what I would call Smart Flexibility, and come down hard on any half-measures. But is the world ready for this Results-Only approach? The US Government's Office for Personnel Management (OPM) is not. In February 2012 they announced the scrapping of their ROWE pilot in which 400 federal workers participated. Because of 'mixed results': some teams up, some down.

The main reason cited was lack of clarity around goal-setting and metrics, which they seem to feel was an insuperable problem, or at least a problem that could be better overcome in other ways.

People do have problems with the goal-setting and metrics. And I think that people can get the wrong ideas when you talk about 'results'. Because for the manager, getting results is not like setting homework and marking it out of 10. Managers don't just set tasks and judge the results, they have to manage the process of achieving the results.

The Inescapability of Time

Many commentators in this field, in the effort of breaking free from presenteeism, emphasise very strongly that *time* should not be a factor in measuring work. When we are clear what results are, then people should be paid only by results, not by the time spent in work. While agreeing with the thrust of this approach, I have some reservations about it.

The first is that if we do go down this route, all work in the end becomes piece-work. And there have been 150 years or more of campaigning on the lines of 'a fair day's work for a fair day's pay'. Piece-work is historically associated with exploitation of those who do not have much leverage in the labour market.

An argument might be that if you have two people doing data processing, for example, and one is able to complete the work in half the time, they should be able to use the time they have freed up however they want, whether for leisure or doing something else where they can be paid for results. But that runs into my second reservation. In allocating work and coming up with reasonable work schedules, a manager must have a clear idea about what can be accomplished over a given time. If someone exceeds expectations, that is good but there are always more tasks to be done within a team. Usually people's workloads will consist of a mix of tasks, and are shared out amongst colleagues to get the most efficient balance. The amount of time that a task should take is an objective standard that the team as a whole can work with. It is an indicator of performance, and also an indication that work may need to be reallocated, or that someone is struggling, or that in the light of new efficiencies we can rethink the notional time-budget for a task when scheduling workloads.

Time is also embedded within the concept of productivity. Being more productive is about producing more per unit of time. And when it comes to weighing up the comparative efficiency of team A and team B, or last month's work and this month's work, knowing how many widgets per hour, how many calls per person per day or how many cases per team per month are essential metrics for planning future workload and future output.

And there are some kinds of work where time is actually embedded in the output. Take the example of a lifeguard. The role involves constant vigilance to ensure people are not drowning in the pool. The output, really, is the vigilance itself. It's not the number of saved lives, which could presumably be increased if an unscrupulous colleague were to throw hapless children in the deep end for rescue. And there are many other monitoring roles of a less life-and-death nature that work on similar lines. It's *being there over a duration of time* that is crucial to achieve the desired outcome.

Management by Outputs or Outcomes?

In Table 9.3 I've focused on managing outputs. However, when looking at 'management by results' overall, it is also important to focus on the outcomes of work activity. The reason for making the distinction is that the outputs have to be worthwhile putting out. Too often people working in large organisations fill their days with internal activity that is ultimately of little value. So an outcome is where the overall value of the contributing outputs is weighed and measured.

It does seem that some commentators try too hard to distinguish between managing by output and by outcome. There often isn't much difference between 'quality of output' and an assessment of 'outcome', and there is a danger of trying to be too precise in a way that might be interesting in the abstract but is of little practical value.

And in some cases, there is not much to say about a piece of work activity in terms of its outcome, if it is a small cog in the wheel of a larger process. It's done, and it's of good enough quality to contribute to the whole. The output of the whole process or project after a series of micro-outputs is where the significant outcome is to be found.

At the end of the scale there are types of work where the final outcome is uncertain, and may be so for some time as in many kinds of case work or innovation work. In the meantime all the individual bits of output have to be managed well, as do the processes that support them.

An example of this might be a complex child-protection case. The outcome that is aspired to is that a vulnerable child is protected, or that an abusing adult is removed into custody. The activities involved in the case will cover many agencies and a wide variety of different kinds of actions, all of which have to be closely monitored as the case proceeds. For the manager, keeping track of all the activities of the people contributing to the case is the challenge. The job is to make sure that all the outputs are of the best possible quality to raise the probability of a successful outcome.

Call handling, by contrast, is one kind of work where at one level the output is easy to measure. The number of calls handled, time taken to answer calls, speed of dealing with the call can all be measured automatically. Calls are typically recorded, so there is a base of data for assessing the quality of calls.

Most of us, though, as consumers, experience enormous frustration in dealing with call centres. The mechanical parameters of the call handling service often fail to provide a satisfactory route to getting the real issue resolved. If managers simply focus on output measures to check that work is being done, they risk missing a significant point about the outcome: did the customers get a satisfactory resolution to their request or problem? So a real assessment of 'results' would have to encompass on the one hand the experience of the customer (outcome) and on the other the performance of the service responsible for solving the problem (quality of output).

So the outcome is about the value of the activity to customers and to the organisation and its mission. The outcome may also be seen in terms of making money and contribution to other corporate objectives.

As an example, the outcome of delivering an outsourced IT support service to a client is that the service is provided successfully and the client's equipment and networks are kept running to an agreed level. At a more granular level, the service reacts through the process of a help-desk which escalates work into a series of cases each with its own outcome: a happy and satisfied individual. And as a result of these individual outcomes, the overall outcome is that the client is happy and renews the contract.

Smart Flexibility Inputs, Outputs and Outcomes

The manager of the Anywhere, Anytime Team and the managers of the Anywhere, Anytime Organisation should also be actively monitoring and measuring the outputs and outcomes deriving from a Smart Flexibility approach to work-style choices. Figure 9.2 on the following page pulls together an approach to inputs, activity, outputs and outcomes in the context of Smart Flexibility.

The manager's role includes:

- Managing the inputs – time, effort, resources (money, materials), skills, motivating people to do their best and work effectively together.
- Seeing that the work is being done – not by micromanaging but through effective delegation and empowerment and the right level of collaborative involvement.
- Making or supporting Smart Flexibility work-style decisions about the most efficient and effective times and locations of work for those involved.
- Seeing that there is measurement of the impact of the work-style choices.
- Seeing that outputs are achieved, and assessed in terms of quantity and quality.
- Assessing the outcomes of the new ways of working in terms of their impacts on the business, employees and the environment.
- Ensuring that all this can be managed while people are working in a range of places and at a range of times, as appropriate.

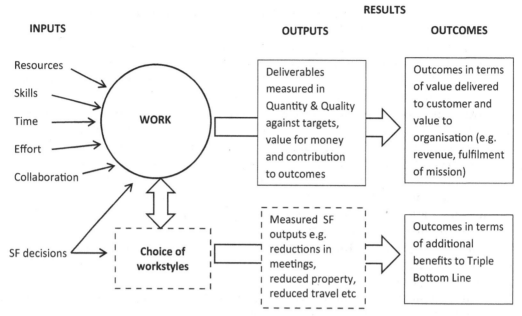

Figure 9.2   Management by results – the 'Smart Flexibility' approach

Note: SF = Smart Flexibility.

'Managing by Results' is not only about looking at the results. It also involves having a good grasp of the inputs and seeing that they are used wisely in order that the results can be achieved.

That doesn't necessarily mean doing everything oneself as a manager. One of the key competences for managers is delegating effectively. In the context of Smart Flexibility, this means getting others involved in coordination and keeping teamwork on track.

And some of the routine monitoring and measuring tasks will increasingly be automated. This delegation and automation should leave the manager with more time to focus on the people aspects of managing the Anywhere, Anytime Team.

A New Kind of Management?

Managers in the coming years will be looked to more for their creativity, leadership and emotional intelligence, managing a more diverse workforce on a more individualised basis. Managers will also have a role in supporting employees as work-life balance evolves into work-life integration for many of us, according to a Chartered Management Institute report *Management Futures: The World in 2018* (CMI 2008).

So management becomes a more varied, creative and subtle art, as managers work across boundaries, business models and work styles, inspiring rather than controlling:

> *In 2018 more organisations will be virtual. There will be a greater polarisation between the number of organisations that are virtual and large global corporations. Organisations that*

maintain physical premises will be run by managers who demonstrate genuine competence and create a sense of calm. People will feel motivated and valued …

Leaders and managers will be accountable, well informed and anticipating. They will act with humility and at the same time have drive. With highly tuned inter-personal skills, they will avoid distractions, cope with different work principles and manage conflicts and emotion. They will know how to manage complex relationships and use their political and partnership skills while operating across organisational boundaries. They will be risk-takers constantly challenging current practices. There will be more people spending time 'thinking' as well as doing. Playfulness and creativity will be encouraged to unlock new ideas and will be rewarded accordingly.

With the increase in remote and virtual working, managers will be able to lead from afar, balancing out a sense of social isolation and a lack of internal relationships. There will be more flexibility in working structures. People will come together in teams for specific projects, complete them, disband and then reform as new projects arise. (CMI 2008, 22–3)

This was a blue skies futures exercise, based on consulting captains of industry, futurists and academics. Possibly the world will be a little more mundane than this playful, creative, risk-taking future of virtual project teams. I think that the experience of living in a technology-rich environment will have a big impact on what we see as 'internal relationships' and be a large factor in how we see social isolation and connection. But the manager's role in building relationships and teams across organisational and geographical boundaries is very much part of Smart Flexibility and the coming world of work.

Smart Flexibility is Only Part of the Context of Change for Managers

There is an interesting point here about context. When we think of the skills that managers will need we tend to think of the context from which new ways of working are developing – that of traditional office-based working. And we think of this rather than seeing the changes in working practices in relation to wider changes in business and society, the kinds of trends highlighted in Chapter 1 (plus several others, which I'll return to in the final chapter).

The problem with a narrow and backward-looking approach to the context of change is that we may still be thinking of the new flexible ways of working as somehow exceptional, and that a few additional skills have to be grafted on to existing styles of management. Instead *we should be thinking of the type of management as a whole that we will need in the future.*

So do we want managers to have better people skills because they are working with remote workers – or do we just want managers to have excellent people skills? Do we want our managers to be better able to deal with flexible and fluid situations because they are managing an 'anywhere team', or because the world as a whole will be throwing up more flexible and fluid situations that they will need to deal with?

The way the world is changing, with more older workers, greater aspirations for work-life balance and for more choice and autonomy, more pervasive technology, more freelancers, and more connections in a globalised economy – all this means that the old methods of management will increasingly be the exception, rather than the smart and flexible styles described in this chapter.

So, having the capability to manage the Anywhere, Anytime Team is not a bolt-on: it's set to become the new normal.

10 *Smart, Flexible and Productive*

Teach everyone to touch-type – this could prove to be the single most effective investment to improve productivity!

Senior manager in a local authority moving to Smart Working

Where's the Evidence?

In this chapter, I will refer to a range of studies that show evidence of increased productivity from smart and flexible working. But the main purpose of the chapter is to show how and why Smart Flexibility can support greater productivity and how to make the most of this.

I'm often asked questions at conferences and workshops about where the evidence is that flexible working is more productive. There is quite a lot of evidence now to show that flexible working is more productive. But I'm not going to overdo the evangelist role here, because I don't believe that flexible work is *necessarily* more productive. What I think is true is that the greater choices of work times and locations enabled by Smart Flexibility create the conditions where people can be more productive. And as long as it's well managed and the people are well motivated, it should be.

Most of the evidence comes from organisations that have implemented new ways of working. Sometimes the evidence is in the form of hard measurement. More often it's based on feedback from staff and managers, which will of course contain some subjective elements.

At the same time, we need to remember that organisations don't rush out and tell the world about their failed transformation initiatives.

Academic studies of new ways of working by their nature tend to be at least five years behind the times. Researchers are people who observe trends rather than innovate, and by the time a trend is detected in academia, it is often already being superseded in the workplace. To add to the time lag, it can also take two to three years for a study to be published after completion. So there are many studies about work-life balance kinds of limited flexibility, but few around the large scale technology-enabled transformative implementations where flexibility becomes the new normal.

Studies, however, have been finding positive impacts on productivity and performance from flexible working since the 1980s. Digging deeper into the studies, one of the key factors is the ability to have greater choice over work schedules (for example, Kossek et al. 2006). Interestingly, similar factors also arise when looking at positive health impacts from flexible work. For a good summary of the impacts of work-life balance measures on performance, see the article by Beauregard and Henry (2009).

These kinds of studies focus primarily on implementations where the employee is making a positive choice to work differently, and usually could be expected to have good motivation for making the new arrangements work. That tells a story in itself about part of the value of introducing flexible working – but it doesn't necessarily reach all parts of the organisation.

One of the most extensive surveys looking at self- and colleague-reported performance was carried out by researchers at Cranfield University (Kelliher and Anderson 2008). A total of 3,580 respondents from seven large companies (Centrica, Citi, KPMG, Lehman Brothers, Microsoft, Pfizer, and the Defence Aerospace business in Rolls Royce) were asked about the impacts of flexible working on the quantity and quality of work.

From these, 61 per cent of individuals said flexible work had a positive impact on the quantity of work, with 33 per cent saying it had a neutral effect. Managers are mostly positive or neutral: 45 per cent said there was a positive effect, with 43 per cent neutral, and 12 per cent saying the effect was negative. Co-workers were less willing to give credit perhaps, with 27 per cent noting a positive effect, 63 per cent a neutral effect and 10 per cent saying there was a negative effect.

These figures are very striking, providing clear evidence of a positive or neutral impact in around 90 per cent of cases.

The picture for quality of work is similar, with all the figures for positive or neutral impacts up a point or two, and negative impacts reported by only 4 per cent of managers and 6 per cent of co-workers.

These responses are from people in leading companies who presumably would put the resources into getting it right, and hopefully had systems in place for performance management. Unfortunately, it wasn't enough to prevent Lehman Brothers going down the pan a short while later and taking the global economy with it, but the others are still here and have indeed been taking smart forms of flexible working further since the time of this study.

A survey by Microsoft of employees in 15 European countries in 2011 found that 56 per cent of those surveyed said they were more productive working away from the office, with 24 per cent saying about the same and 10 per cent saying they were less productive.

These are examples of self-reported and manager or co-worker reported impacts on productivity. These inevitably include some subjective elements (though hopefully based on some hard evidence). What about more objective measurements of productivity improvement?

In 2006 the UK Government Audit Commission published some case studies of home-working in local government. At East Riding of Yorkshire Council home-working was introduced in 2001 as a means of retaining staff and improving service levels. By 2004, time to assess new claims was reduced from 103 days to 26 days, with complaints reduced from 56 per month to 26 per month. At the same time, staff turnover was reduced from 35 per cent to 10 per cent, and sickness absence reduced from 8 per cent to 3.4 per cent.

At Salford City Council, home-working in the revenue and benefits service led to a 15 per cent increase in productivity and the benefits service improved from a zero-star to a four-star rated service between 2002 and 2006. As a result of the scheme, the department has made substantial efficiency savings, with the net cost of running the benefits service reduced by £250,000 (Audit Commission 2006b).

In the private sector, BT report (BT 2011) an average 20 per cent productivity increase from home-based workers (it varies according to function) and Vodafone report 24 per cent productivity improvement amongst flexible sales and service staff (Vodafone 2010).

I could run through a long list of industry case studies showing productivity improvements to prove the case that Smart Flexibility (or Agile Working, and so on) consistently reports significant productivity benefits compared with traditional office-bound ways of working.

However, I would urge a degree of caution. These productivity improvements are striking when you compare old and new ways of working. Once these new ways have shown the benefit, one of two things should happen. Either everyone moves to the new ways of working, or the weak points of traditional working practices are shown in a sharp light, and other measures are taken to close the gap.

Productivity benefits, in terms of improved output or quality of output, are only one of the kinds of benefits achievable. There may well be cases where existing working practices are exceptionally well geared for productive work, and working at different times and places may make productivity improvements marginal. Even so, the range of other benefits is such that modernising working practices is the right thing to do. And the range of cost savings contribute to overall productivity gains. More on this below.

What Do We Mean by 'Being More Productive'?

At this point, it would be useful to step back and reflect on what is meant by 'increased productivity'. At a basic level, productivity is the ratio of outputs produced to the inputs used.

Some studies indicate that people who work remotely do a kind of trade-off with their employer. They divide the time saved by not commuting between their family and their work, so both sides benefit. An extra hour per homeworking day in that way might be given to the company. But it is a mistake to see the extra hour worked as in itself an increase in productivity, as it is focusing on an input measure: the hours worked.

If those extra hours result in increased output and more value being produced for the company, then that is no doubt to be welcomed – but is it being more productive? The answer is probably no, as there has been no change in the ratio of outputs to inputs. Both inputs and outputs have gone up according to the existing ratio.

In fact, it could be worse than that. Home and work may be more comfortably balanced and the remote worker may be less stressed, but if he's getting the same amount of work done as before but now takes nine hours instead of eight, he's actually being less productive. His foot is off the gas and he's coasting.

If, however, remote workers are able to handle 20 per cent more forms in the same amount of time, or answer 20 per cent more calls in their regular hours, they are clearly being more productive. We will explore in the next section some of the reasons why this kind of increase in productivity for these kinds of functions is often reported.

There are factors other than time that have an impact on productivity for the smart and flexible worker. When technology replaces travel, the resource input to work as well as the time input (from travel) decreases. So the output can be achieved with less input.

An example of this would be a mobile worker who can gain access remotely to work systems rather than return to the office. This enables an increase in productivity by:

a) Eliminating unnecessary return trips to the office;
b) Saving time from not re-keying information, which can now be done one time only while at the remote site; and
c) Creating the space in the day for more client interaction.

Peace and Quiet: The Connection/Disconnection Paradox

Again and again in interviews and staff surveys I've come across the recommendation for homeworking that it 'gives a chance to really get on with work by getting away from all the distractions of the office'.

It clearly works. But at some point we've got to unpack this statement and ask:

1. Is something else lost by this disconnection?
2. Is this really consistent with 'Smart Flexibility'?

One of the reasons why working from home tends to be – at least in the early adoption phase – the chance to get on with things is because the workplace is full of interruptions and distractions, both welcome and unwelcome.

To understand what is actually happening here, we need to break down 'distraction' into its component parts. To do this it is useful to put distractions under three headings:

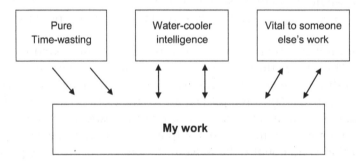

Figure 10.1 Unpacking 'distractions in the office'

1. Distractions that are just plain time-wasting (in terms of the work getting done): basically of two kinds:
    - People: Social chit-chat, food preparation, eating (by self and others).
    - Environment: 'Noises off': bells and alarms, machinery; also factors such as poor lighting and temperature control can damage concentration.
2. Distractions that relate to the informal sharing of office information – work-related chat or 'water cooler' conversations. This is in three kinds:
    - In the end, just office gossip.
    - Valuable information, but of no value to you.
    - Intelligence of either direct or indirect (potential) value to your work or to your career.

3. Distractions that come from colleagues' work, and this we can divide into two:
   - Their work causes a visual or noise distraction to you, but is unrelated to your work.
   - They interrupt you/demand something from you because it is essential to their work being done.

To get work done that requires high concentration or is up against a deadline, it is indeed helpful to get away from distractions. Traditionally this is done by either taking work somewhere else (usually home, probably after hours), or getting to the office early or staying late, when most of the noisy and demanding colleagues are not there.

So, taking work home, away from all the distractions, has a role in increasing productivity.

But, looking again at Figure 10.1, how valuable is it to oneself, and to the organisation as a whole, to do this? As an exceptional activity this kind of disconnection may be fine, but it can't be an intrinsic feature of Smart Flexibility.

In fact, it goes to the heart of the fears expressed by sceptics and opponents of flexible working:

- How can we run an effective team when no one's here at the same time and people can't be contacted?
- Won't we all be isolated and out of touch when we work remotely?

People tend to have these fears because they are based in part on their own experiences of 'getting away from it all' and doing disconnected home-working.

Some of the 'distractions' do have value: the social interaction that leads to team bonding, or that leads to finding out vital intelligence that can help one's work and career.

The productivity value of 'interruptions' also needs to be looked at from both sides. I remember working many years ago in an organisation where they sent all the female managers and team leaders off on assertiveness training courses. Some of them thereafter would always assertively rebuff anyone who asked them a question, telling them firmly that they were too busy right now or to come back at a certain time. Fair enough, to some extent.

But on the other hand, a 20-second interaction might give their colleague all they need to get on effectively with their job. Delaying all interaction to suit your priorities can damage other people's productivity, when you single-mindedly progress down your tick-list for the day. It's a question of balance, and screening out all interruptions has wider impacts.

Here we reach the 'Connection/Disconnection Paradox' in homeworking. Disconnecting yourself from the office and from colleagues can bring some productivity (and possibly some sanity) advantages for certain tasks. However, the whole direction of Smart Flexibility is to *stretch the office and its systems to wherever you are*.

Using the right kinds of technology and telephony, people working flexibly should be *just as contactable as ever* (see Chapter 7). Their computer desktop at home should replicate that at the office. It can be the same laptop that you're using in all locations, or a virtual desktop served up wherever you are. Office files and systems should all be accessible remotely, including of course all electronic communications systems (email, messaging, conferencing). The remote telephone should act seamlessly as an extension of the office system. Unified Communications mean there is no escape – you'll get the message somehow.

More methods of interacting with remote workers and virtual teams are on the way. Some companies have already set up various kinds of online communities and social networking for their distributed employees, and we're sure to see more deployed in the future. There'll be greater use of desktop videoconferencing and in due course telepresence to replicate the experience of being in the office and in meetings.

But that kind of takes away the advantages of remote working, doesn't it?

Going back to the diagram in Figure 10.1, what it's all about is choosing or agreeing the types or range of interruption and distraction that you are open to. In the office, there's often no escape from the phone-call yellers, office bores and mouth-open munchers.

But by working remotely there is the capacity to slide a barrier across so you can screen out the pure time-wasting distractions, while leaving it open to various degrees to facilitate useful business and business-social interaction.

Though, of course, the alternative location of work may have its own unique set of distractions, whether it's in the home, on a train or in a cafe.

The Impact of Smart Process Change on Productivity

In Chapter 6 on working environments and Chapter 7 on technologies we looked at issues around moving towards a paperless office: de-cluttering, rationalising storage and investing in the systems that can take you towards an e-culture of electronic processes.

Working effectively in a context of Smart Flexibility presupposes that one is working with primarily electronic processes, and ideally with seamless and frictionless end-to-end processes that enable you to enter and access information without travelling and also eliminating the need to duplicate or re-key information. This in itself should be a boost to productivity. And the effects of this should be felt as much in the office as beyond the office.

In this sense I worry about people straining to prove or disprove the productivity effects of flexible working. Once flexible working becomes normal, where will we find the productivity bonanzas? We should then be equally productive wherever and whenever we work.

It's just that at the moment we have a lowest common denominator benchmark, in traditional ways of working. This is the baseline from which we measure improvement. But when improvement is ubiquitous, it will be hard to record year-on-year improvements in productivity stemming from changing work-styles.

IMPROVING PRODUCTIVITY THROUGH 'MODERN AND FLEXIBLE WORKING' AT FIFE COUNCIL

Modern and Flexible Working (MFW) is Fife Council's programme for modernising working practices. Key features are a strong emphasis on increasing productivity, creating a new working culture to deliver the benefits and a flexible approach to deploying technologies for mobility and collaboration.

MFW at Fife runs closely alongside a concurrent office rationalisation programme (ORP). This has the aim of reducing the number of offices from 90 down to 30 over 5 years. This is set against a backdrop, as with all councils, of reducing staff numbers as part of wider efficiency measures.

Although the two programmes are clearly interdependent, the business case for MFW is predicated on productivity gains and the real estate savings sit in ORP. While there are to be £12 million savings in terms of capital receipts and 2.6 recurring revenue savings from ORP, there will be at least £19 million of productivity benefits from the change to MFW over the life time of the programme.

Measures for productivity vary according to role, with targets set at the outset when MFW is adopted. The 26 full-time home-workers working in Finance, mainly processing applications, are already showing a 20 per cent productivity increase. Mobile workers are achieving a 15 per cent increase in the number of jobs, inspections, assessments or reviews they carry out per month.

For other flexible workers who have more fluid types of work, a 7.5 per cent increase in productivity is sought in terms of reducing the amount of downtime. Carrying out meetings in different ways is a key part of this. All this is part of a drive to move towards managing by outcome and output, rather than by presence.

The new approach to offices is not just about reducing the number, but about remodelling them to support greater flexibility and mobility for staff across Scotland's third most populous region. The former Amazon building in Glenrothes has been acquired and the office accommodation has been kitted out as a flexible working environment. The Fife House Complex (the main council building) has been remodelled on the same basis. Around the region the remaining offices are focused on customer service with 'back office' team zones for patch-based staff plus touch-down facilities for use by any council staff.

Social workers at Fife were amongst the first to embrace this mobility. Their main challenge is to be able to access all the systems they need, and with high levels of security. But this is a challenge they have risen to and they are making the most of being able to do more when out of the office. This has meant changes back in the office, where their main base operates on the basis of one desk space for every two social workers. Elsewhere, the overall desk ratio is 8:10.

Change to these new arrangements has not been all plain sailing. As elsewhere, there are some who have been unwilling to move to desk-sharing arrangements. According to Jill Pritchard, Business Change Manager for Mobile and Flexible Working, some people have been uncomfortable with the changes. One person even claimed that taking away his personal desk 'violated his human rights'. One isn't sure whether the European Court would support that claim if it ever got that far. 'People are at different stages', says Jill, 'and all life is here'.

A great deal of attention is being given to supporting cultural change. This involves a mixture of workshops, one-to-ones and e-learning. All staff have to attend engagement sessions. New guidance, policies and protocols (such as a clear desk policy) have been introduced.

On the technology side, desktop virtualisation is being introduced so staff can access their desktop from anywhere. The mix of tools provided depends on the role being undertaken and the nature of the employee's flexibility. Those who work full-time from home are provided with broadband, home PC and office kit. But the number of these is small, and MFW is not at all predicated on working from home.

Essential to achieving the new ways of working is a programme of 'e-enablement'. That is, getting the ICT in place, plus a big push to replace paper with electronic processes. And it isn't all about knowledge workers. Handheld devices and scheduling tools are being used by a wide range of people with 'hands-on' tasks, such as the people working in building services: electricians, plumbers and gas engineers. This is now being extended to include all field inspection staff.

'We're aiming to create an environment of self-reliance and self-service for people who work remotely, and provide the right tools for whichever job they are doing. We're building up the available toolkit, and trying to get to the situation of enabling staff to be able to use any device, anywhere – in the office, in the field, at home, in a cafe – to do their job', says programme manager Linda Robertson.

Every job is profiled against one of four work-styles, and that decides the criteria for the range of tools that can be deployed. This is a very fast-moving field, driven in many ways by the consumerisation of IT devices. 'Bring Your Own Device' is on the agenda, but is not in place yet. There are big security issues involved, which also overlap with issues around sharing information with partners. There is close liaison between IT and individual services to get the right tools in place, and to take the opportunity to modernise business processes.

'One of the biggest challenges in reducing from 90 buildings to 30 is that everyone expects to bring all their paper and storage with them', says Linda. 'And of course that can't be done. So we've had to address all the issues of records management, document management, what point do you scan back to, and how to deal with legacy systems. Some of these don't lend themselves well to web-enabling. So some are being replaced, and any new ones will be completely web-based. We're very much in a transitional phase with the technology'.

At Fife they recognise that introducing new ways of working is a journey. It's mainly about business change and modernising management approaches – technology is secondary to this. And it has a purpose, to deliver better services to customers, whether internal or external.

Teach People to Type – or Throw Away the Keyboards!

Teach everyone to touch-type – this could prove to be the single most effective investment to improve productivity!

This was the suggestion, said partly tongue-in-cheek, of a senior manager in Children's Services in an interview I was conducting as part of an evidence-gathering exercise in a local council that was starting to implement Smart Working. We were discussing the issues with social workers being able to work remotely and the technologies they might need. And it is an important point that he raised.

Since the demise of the typing pool and secretaries for every team, professionals and managers have been expected to be their own secretarial and admin assistants. And it's very time-consuming. Arguably, professionals being paid £35,000+ per year and managers being paid £70,000+ to do admin is not a good use of resources. Especially when they are hopeless at typing. And clueless at filing, for that matter. And an immense amount of professional and managerial time is spent typing and wrestling with knowledge-management systems.

So actually, if they could type at 100 words per minute as my mother used to do, wouldn't they be a lot more productive? The same for me too, as it happens!

In fact, we bought my mother her first-ever computer, a laptop, for her 80th birthday. And – here's one in the eye for Generation Y, perhaps – she took to it like a duck to water, as many of her far-flung family and friends were doing too. And, once she had got used to the flatness of the keyboard, she was rattling off emails and letters in a fraction of the time that I would take.

However – this observation has an onrushing sell-by date. Within the next 7 to 10 years, we will see the demise of the keyboard. And his little pal the mouse, too. Keying in information is actually a barrier between the originator of information and its destination. We will soon be seeing genuinely intelligent artificial intelligence that will oversee speech recognition, and intelligent processes that will routinise many of the things we currently crank by hand through our electronic systems.

So these advances on the 'smart' side of Smart Flexibility will take us to new levels of productivity. And our work practices will have to evolve again – probably our work environments too – as we preside over much of our work rather than slog it through as slaves to the machine.

Work Intensification Is Not the Same as Productivity – but There's an Overlap

Some studies of flexible work have noted that flexible workers experience intensification of work – they work harder or longer. This has led a few such as Timothy Golden (2011) to see teleworking in particular as likely to lead to increased work-family conflict and to (some) teleworkers experiencing greater levels of exhaustion than they would have experienced working in an office.

Others, such as Claire Kelliher and Deirdre Anderson (2010) at Cranfield University dig a bit deeper into the nature and causes of work intensification which can be divided into three types – imposed, enabled, and reciprocal trade-off.

Imposed intensification may occur, for example, when someone moves onto a reduced hours schedule but doesn't find that the work actually reduces on a pro rata basis.

Enabled intensification, which I think is much more common phenomenon, happens because the new way of working allows the individual to get more into the work. This is because the workers are away from the distractions, conventions and confines of the office and can work in the way that suits them best. Being less stressed and without the strains of the commute may also mean that workers have more energy and enthusiasm for the work.

The reciprocal trade-off effect refers to the situation where the employee experiences the flexible hours as a significant benefit for which they are willing to go the extra mile for the employer. In the case of home-based working, this can mean sharing the saved commuting time between the individual and employer (SUSTEL 2004, Glogger et al. 2008).

One element of this reciprocity is that early adopters of flexible working, or those adopting in the face of scepticism from managers or other colleagues, feel an obligation to show that it works.

Kelliher and Anderson did find evidence of the various kinds of work intensification. The 'enabled intensification' was mostly associated with remote workers, some of whom reported finding it difficult to tune out of work. See the next chapter on problems and troubleshooting for further discussion of this.

What is interesting is that Kelliher and Anderson found little in the way of negative outcomes associated with this work intensification. Really this should come as no surprise when we look at the reasons why people seek flexibility, which is usually so that they can do their job better. Apart from part-time work, flexible working has a proportionately higher uptake amongst managers and professionals, who are perhaps the people more likely to show strong commitment.

What does surprise me, though, is that 'work intensification' in the academic literature is almost always seen as a negative rather than being viewed objectively. Whether work intensification is experienced as good or bad depends on your starting point and your outlook. Some people can't bear a slack working pace or work that involves a lot of wasteful practices, and welcome some intensification. A slack work intensity is often mediated through organisational cultures and subcultures: Smart Flexibility (or even un-smart flexibility) can be the occasion for the more committed or ambitious worker to break free.

If it moves towards exploitation (which is what lies behind the negative presumptions) then that's a problem. And equally, it's a problem if it's a sign of work spiralling out of control due to the way an individual interfaces with his or her new freedoms to work wherever and whenever. But on the whole, research studies don't report this happening. Usually, any additional input is freely and willingly given.

But this is the thing: focusing on the intensification of work is all about the inputs. More effort and more time input. It doesn't tell you anything directly about the output.

Having said that, however, the evidence of people working harder to deliver what they have to could be a factor in achieving more or higher quality outputs. And thinking about it in reverse, the evidence of increased productivity may well reflect something back about more care and effort being put into the input.

Reducing the Costs of Labour Inputs is a Factor in Productivity Increases

In the last chapter on managing the Anywhere, Anytime Team we looked at the responsibilities and competences of the manager. Part of a manager's role is cost control. And in Smart Flexibility this includes managing down the costs of working practices.

By shifting some of the previously fixed costs of overheads to variable costs, the costs of doing work can be managed down. If the resources required for doing work are reduced, producing the same outputs at reduced cost is a productivity increase. The effects of this may be measured more at a team level than an individual level, and may include a number of diverse elements.

The costs of property, facilities and travel are the stand-out items in most implementations. But reducing the amount of paper and the number of times information is handled as processes go paperless also reduces costs. And there may be a bullet to bite here, as elements of some people's work becomes redundant. Part of reducing the costs of work can be reducing the amount of labour input – the same output achieved by fewer people overall.

That leads to the familiar challenge brought about by productivity increases. Do you move forward with fewer people, or do you make use of this new spare capacity to do more things, which will in turn be done with lower labour cost?

Smart Flexibility should have the impact of increasing effectiveness on the frontline while reducing the internal costs of doing work. That reduction of internal costs may well involve job losses, or people being reskilled and redeployed to where they can deliver more value. While this principle may seem to have a tough edge to it, it is one of immense significance during a period of tough economic challenges.

The Productivity Impacts on Non- or Less Flexible Co-Workers

One of the fears often expressed before flexible working is introduced is possible impacts on colleagues. These fears boil down to two main issues:

- Will productivity suffer because colleagues no longer in the office at regular times will be uncontactable?
- Will those in the office end up picking up extra duties such as office cover, answering the phones, even emptying the recycling bins more?

I am quite sure that badly organised or badly managed flexible work implementations could have these impacts. When you have reactive flexible work policies, insufficient technologies and don't have a team charter approach, then those people who work standard patterns may feel put upon and feel that they are covering for an absent colleague, an effect that perhaps increases as more people in a department or team start to work away from the office (Golden 2007).

When flexible work is seen as a privilege that some have and some don't, jealousy, frustration and anger can be added into the mix of feelings – of some staff.

But how widespread, really, is this impact? I've been back through all the results from staff surveys that I've been involved in when flexible working is being introduced. Most people are actually pretty level-headed about the potential impacts. When we asked 'If you worked more flexibly, what would be the impact on your colleagues?' in each case the largest number – between 42 per cent and 60 per cent - anticipate that the effects would be neutral. And in each case more people expect the results to be positive than negative, by a ratio of about 1.5 to 1. And the numbers of people who anticipate negative impacts are roughly the same as the numbers who are against introducing flexible work in the first place.

I did a 'deep dive' into the minority who expressed negativity towards flexible working in one organisation (about 15 per cent of the total sample in that organisation). They split into two camps:

- Those who thought their job role unsuitable for flexibility.
- Those who were really angry or deeply cynical about change, and who peppered their responses with a wide range of grievances, many of which had nothing to do with the changes to work practices being proposed.

So when analysing feared or reported negative impacts, it's important always to contextualise. If 85 per cent of people can get on with this OK, what's up with the 15 per cent? Is something going wrong in these cases, and if so how can it be remedied?

The evidence is not there that substantial problems are generally caused after implementation. A detailed study by Gajendran and Harrison (2007) analysing 46 observed studies of teleworking in the US concluded:

Telecommuting has a clear upside: small but favourable effects on perceived autonomy, work-family conflict, job satisfaction, performance, turnover intent, and stress. Contrary to expectations in both academic and practitioner literatures, telecommuting also has no straightforward, damaging effects on the quality of workplace relationships or perceived career prospects. However, there is a downside of higher intensity telecommuting in that it does seem to send co-worker (but not supervisor) relationships in a harmful direction.

What that downside means is that people doing full-time home-based ('higher intensity') teleworking do tend to lose touch with people in the office. Are these substantial problems? In the case of high-intensity remote work, relationships will necessarily be different. In the next chapter I take a close look at the issue here about who you want to connect with.

With reference to the productivity impacts on colleagues, there is absolutely no reason why there should be a negative impact.

Take the issue of 'office cover'. The question to ask is what exactly is office cover for? If it is the place where there is high footfall from the public, then cover is needed. But most offices do not fall into this category. When the office is on the network, the concept of 'office cover' changes meaning – if it has any residual meaning at all.

Or take a comment like this in one of our surveys expressing a common fear in a pre-Smart organisation:

It would mean that members of the public trying to contact me would be referred by my voicemail to other colleagues which would interrupt their work.

This is what we call thinking with your old head on. Smart Flexibility means that staff should be contactable wherever they are. This can mean being more contactable than under the old ways of working. In a sense we can forgive studies before about 2005 that failed to have a vision of effective communications in distributed working. But there is no excuse now

... But Why Are Colleagues Less Flexible?

There is a continuing problem with continuing to take the traditional office environment as the norm for working practices. The *principles of Smart Flexibility have to apply to all workers*, regardless of where or when they are working.

There will be people, whether by necessity or choice, who will find themselves working something akin to their old working pattern of regular hours in the same place as before. But it's no longer the case that these working patterns can be the norm. Not being mobile should not mean being inflexible. For example, expecting everyone to be available for face-to-face meetings just as before is not compatible with the new ways of working. It violates the Smart Flexibility principles.

So maybe there is a misreading of the situation where office-bound colleagues feel their productivity is being damaged by their 'missing' colleagues. It may well be their intransigence in not adapting to new work methods that is the real source of the problem.

The evidence points to this being a minor effect, and one that can be remedied. Better deployment of communications technologies, developing smart teamwork protocols and keeping on working at cultural change are all part of the solution.

Design for Productivity

Working environments need to be designed to support greater productivity. Doing this is of course not at all new. But how you do it changes in the context of the new possibilities derived from working smarter and more flexibly.

The usual principles apply of good ergonomics, lighting, temperature control, building services and so on. What is new is the need to design a range of activity spaces that support different kinds of work. These spaces need to support the tools of twenty-first century working, and they need to do it on a plug-and-play basis.

Our Smart Flexibility principles (set out in Chapter 3) say that work takes place at the most effective times and locations, and it is important that these different locations are designed to facilitate productive working. The principles also refer to allocating spaces to activities, not to individuals, and that there must be effective and appropriate use of technology. The mix of spaces then has to reflect the different types of work being done, and they need to be set up with the appropriate technologies or facilities to use the technologies that users bring to them.

Let's take the example of collaboration spaces. The mix needs to be there that reflects the styles of work needed: break-out spaces for short meetings of two or three people, confidential spaces for one person making sensitive calls, one-to-one spaces for appraisals and dealing with confidential issues, project spaces, rooms for brainstorming, and so on. The first consideration is easy availability – hunting around for the spaces you need saps energy and harms productivity.

The second consideration is the functional design of the space. This may include setting up all the collaboration spaces with wi-fi, and the enclosed collaboration spaces with screens or smartboards and cameras and phones for conferencing. Having walls that you can write all over or stick things on can also be valuable for brainstorming, training and project spaces. The acoustic environment needs also to be thought through, with the right levels of sound-proofing according to the nature of the activities likely to be conducted.

The third consideration is the visual design. It is beyond the scope of the book to go too far into this. And though there are always hard-bitten sceptics ready to snipe at anything they consider too luxurious or pretentious, there is overwhelming evidence that the visual design of workspaces impacts on productivity. Many organisations theme or decorate rooms to motivate staff and to get them to think of the needs of their customers of the nature of the services they deliver and the products they sell, and to reinforce company identity.

In the context of Smart Flexibility I think it's well worth making the effort to aim for excellence in visual design. Apart from the intrinsic aesthetic value of doing this, there are two particular reasons. First, in moving to a new shared working environment, employees feel they have given up something: their desk and their personal stake in the office. If the new environment has a 'wow factor', then people can be quickly won over as something has been gained in return. In particular, a new shared identity will be reinforced, and the message comes through that 'this is our space' as opposed to 'this is my desk'. And secondly, if people are coming to the office less often, then it's worth creating an inspiring and motivating environment to make their coming together more of a special occasion.

The range of spaces is covered in Chapter 6 on Smart and Flexible Workplaces.

11 *Home Alone, Disconnected and Tripping over Wires*

This chapter is about problems and pitfalls, and how to deal with them. Problems can arise, but often the fear of problems is greater than the experience. People unfamiliar with flexible working may express fears of the unknown. Opponents of flexibility may try to make the problems appear insurmountable.

The first step to understanding the risks is to contextualise the conversations, and put the issues in perspective. Too often discussions start from the basis of assuming all-or-nothing scenarios. We'll be home alone, disconnected and tripping over wires.

Home Alone

Discussions often conjure up the lurking spectre of isolated, atomised workers who rarely or never meet. Isn't there something dehumanising about this? After all, we are social animals. We need the social contact. If work is only about getting the work done, then we become distributed cogs in a distributed machine. This may be worse than the old factory model as the prospects of developing relationships and having fun with colleagues is diminished.

I remember at one meeting someone protesting that home-based working would undermine society. Work was very important socially. In fact his parents, like many others, had met at work and subsequently married. Without the traditional workplace, he said, he would not be here today.

I'm not sure how far one should extrapolate from the serendipitous context of one's parents' meeting. My parents met as part of the occupying forces in Germany in 1946. So without Hitler, I guess I wouldn't be here. I'm sure many couples meet as a result of conflict and chaos too, but it's not something we ought to promote.

It's also true that many people meet their lovers at work – the ones they don't tell their wives, husbands or partners about. So it cuts both ways. The truth is that although work is a social setting for meetings, we've reached a sad place in life if it's our only place. And the dominance of going to work in our lives can cut out the possibilities of a wider social life too.

Here's the thing: the fact is that in most cases flexible work is not an 'all-or-nothing' set-up. People who work a four-day compressed working week are still around at work for those four days. Someone who works at home two days a week is still around for the other three. And so on. From the point of view of interaction in the office, this is not a lot different in principle from the experience of mobile workers who spend relatively little time back at base. They do survive, and sometimes even marry.

The other thing that needs to be written in big letters about Smart Flexibility – *it's not all about homeworking.* It's about working at the most effective time and places to get the work done.

Analysing Isolation

Working away from the office and away from daily contact with colleagues can be isolating. But whether isolation becomes a problem depends on a number of factors:

- *How often are you working away from the office?* 1–2 days per week is typical for homeworking employees.
- *What kind of work you are doing?* In particular, the amount of interaction involved with colleagues and clients by phone, conferencing, site meetings, and so on, makes a big difference. The big growth area in homeworking is in work using home as a base – that is, skipping the visits to the office before setting off for more mobile tasks.
- *What's your domestic and community situation?* One can have a more or less active family and community life, and this can make a substantial difference to one's perception of isolation.

To understand the phenomenon of isolation, we need to dig into it a bit. The key issue is: by working away from the office, what are you being disconnected from, and what are you connecting or reconnecting to?

The following grids (Tables 11.1 and 11.2) are a useful way to assess the pros and cons of an individual's situation. The individual can look at each factor, then see whether he or she is disconnected from them or not, putting in a 'Y' for Yes, 'N' for No or 'S' for 'somewhat'.

Disconnection isn't necessarily bad. You may actually value being less connected to some things or people. So individuals can assess whether the situation is on balance a good (G) or a bad (B) thing for them, or tolerable (T).

Table 11.1 Disconnection analysis grid

Disconnected from?	Y/S/N	G/B/T	Remedy – if needed
Good colleagues			
Unbearable colleagues			
'Office buzz'			
Vital information/systems			
Team working			
Interruptions			
Opportunities to share problems			
Training opportunities			
New work opportunities			
Promotion opportunities			
Office gossip			
Office politics			
Recreational opportunities			

After that, you can look at what the key issues are for you, and whether a remedy is desirable or possible. Some remedies may be technological – like good remote access or one-number telephony that links you in seamlessly to the office networks and exchange.

Other issues may be more to do with management or communications – ensuring that remote workers are always included in briefings and team activities, for example. It may be necessary to formalise previously ad hoc communications, for example, with electronic newsletters or via an intranet. And ensuring regular face-to-face interaction takes place is vital.

For balance, a similar grid can be worked through to find out the value of home-working. To whom or what are you *re*connected? Reflecting on the positives, or finding where the fault lines are, helps to overcome feelings of isolation (people can add additional lines for things they feel disconnected or reconnected to).

Table 11.2   Reconnection analysis grid

(Re-)Connected to?	Y/S/N	G/B/T	Remedy – if needed
Spouse/Partner			
Children			
Neighbours			
Pets/natural environment			
Time for concentrated work			
Time to relax/reflect			
Local shops and services			
Opportunities for recreation			
Self-development opportunities			
Outside interests			

Some things can be hard to face up to. Being with the family more – essentially by eliminating the commute and being there at lunch-time and when others come home – is in principle a benefit. But, if it causes stress by making working difficult or exacerbating emotional conflict, this needs to be recognised as a negative impact. Remedies could include ensuring there is a clearly separate workplace at home, or reassessing the occasions for homeworking, or working at a local workhub.

Changing the location of work necessarily changes our 'activity spaces' and the range of daily interactions. Understanding what has been lost and what has been gained in our daily activities helps to put feelings of isolation in context, or to understand how enduring problems of isolation can be overcome.

What makes one person feel isolated is not necessarily the same for the next person. So analysis like this is important to be able to tailor appropriate solutions.

24/7 Working – Curbing It or Embracing It

The concept of 24/7 working should be about the economy. It's not a requirement for your daily life. This is something that twenty-first century flexible workers may be inclined to forget when the office is on the network and work can be wherever they are. This is one of the main concerns expressed when we run *Flexibility* events – that taking work home, or taking the technologies for work home – can mean that you never switch off. There's always the temptation to check the emails last thing at night to see if you got that urgent reply, or to start on the report over breakfast to make a flying start to the working day.

Mobile phones, BlackBerrys, tablets and laptops go everywhere with you – to parties and on holiday too. The world will fall apart if you're not on the end of the line, it seems.

And when you put down the work and should be relaxing, you find there are two extra members of the family party accompanying you everywhere – Stress and Guilt. Guilt that you're not working, plus guilt that you're not giving family life your full attention. So stress on both fronts.

We know that one of the benefits of Smart Flexibility is increased productivity. Increased productivity from greater flexibility should be about working more effectively, not about working longer. However, Smart Flexibility has been a developing trend at a time when there is another dominant trend in the workplace – the Long-Hours Culture.

British workers apparently work the longest hours in Europe – 4 million of us work more than 48 hours per week, with 1 in 6 working more than 60 hours per week. The average is 43.5 hours: 4 hours more than German workers, and 5 hours more than the French. But there's no indication that we're doing anything especially useful with these extra hours. Are we any more productive? Not according to official figures.

Now we have the tools to bring the long-hours culture home with us. We have the opportunity of finding a genuine work-life balance by eliminating wasteful travel time and creating an efficient working environment away from the office. We don't do it. Instead, we bring bad habits home with us.

Apart from the 'long-hours culture', another key driver of 24/7 working is information overload. We seem to have far more information at our fingertips, largely due to the ease of making it and sending it to everyone we possibly can.

Of course a lot of it is useful, and where would the 'Knowledge Economy' be without it? But a lot of the information we receive and share is of no or minimal value. And getting through it is so time-consuming! So we tackle the email mountain at midnight for the same reason as people climb Everest – because it's there. The difference is that unlike the email mountain, Everest doesn't get higher if you don't climb it.

Often it is guilt that is driving overwork. Guilt is the spectre at the feast, the ghost holding out the laptop to you, saying 'You didn't finish that report!', 'The whole team is waiting for your input', 'You're the only person who can deal with these customer queries'.

Here are some ways to deal with it:

- *Make rules, and let people know about them.* For example, you can be called at this time, but definitely not at these times. You won't *ever* switch on your computer or check emails on a Saturday/after 7 p.m./before 8 a.m., and so on. And stick to the rules, without sounding churlish or unhelpful.

Of course, if you want time out during core hours, you need to allow for some work being done at other times. But not at all time.

- *Enable/empower other people to do your work.* This is key to having a good holiday, and it's also useful in dealing with work crises. It's amazing how many people work on holiday simply because they are deemed to be the only person who can do often quite routine tasks. Why feel guilty about not doing work when someone else could cover for you?
- *Do something fun instead.* When you feel the demon work-guilt approach, have another glass. Well, it doesn't have to be a drink. Sometimes one has to make a conscious decision not to cave in as you travel on the upward slope of the anxiety curve. It's about letting go, and letting any thought of work act as a spur to have some fun. The options are many.
- *Manage your regular working time more effectively.* Improving time management is also important for combating long hours. This is often less about managing your time 'after hours' than in managing your regular working hours more effectively. As we tell our kids: get as much work done at school as you can, and you'll have more time to play in the evening.

Why do we let work spill over the boundaries and upset the balance? Partly it's down to high workload, for sure. But that's not 100 per cent of the reason. A key part of it is because time 'at work' during regular hours is not used as productively as it could be.

Key timewasters at work are:

- Constant interruptions.
- Pointless meetings.
- Unnecessary travel (especially to pointless meetings).
- Chit-chat (including moaning about difficult journeys to pointless meetings).
- Needy colleagues.
- Constantly checking emails as a distraction from irksome work.

No doubt everyone can add to the list. The point is that the solution to work spilling over its designated hours is mostly about tackling wider productivity issues.

Alternatively, it may be time for a true confession and embrace the long hours. Many people actually work long and additional hours because they want to! But it can be hard to admit it. You really want to bury yourself away in the den and not play with the kids? Yes! You'd rather burn the midnight oil than climb into bed with the one you love?

Well possibly on occasions you might make this choice, or bring your laptop to bed for a threesome. If people do this because they love their work, or they're committed to delivering the highest quality product, they should celebrate it! Their loving partner will understand, and hopefully will still be there in the morning. Everyone will be able to handle it better if they know what the deal is, and the stress levels will go down. Unless it's every day, in which case expect the divorce papers soon.

The perfect work-life balance is what works for the individual, not some objective standard handed down from on high. And if at times in one's life it makes one happy – or pleasingly wealthy – to put in some extra work, then one should go for it.

Flexible work helps work-life balance as long as there truly is a balance. Working late hours becomes more reasonable if you've taken time out in the day to do what you have – or want – to do: attending school sports day, carrying out a caring responsibility, going hang-gliding, being a board member of a charity and so forth. And it's also more acceptable when you know that you have earned some time out through your commitment and output. So employees should be ready to ask for it, and managers ready to agree so long as the work is getting done.

There's also the phenomenon of 'binge working' – working flat out for a while, to be balanced by longer periods of chilling out. And why not, if it works for the individual? The key principle is to take ownership of the hours on and the hours off, and not become a slave to the machine.

Finally, there is the off button. Switching off the computer and the communications gadgets can be psychologically challenging – traumatic even. But mechanically, it remains simple. Click. The American telework guru Gil Gordon offered exactly this advice in his book 'Turn it Off: How to Unplug from the Anytime-Anywhere Office without Disconnecting Your Career' (Gordon 2001). The title sums it up nicely.

Many of these remedies may sound simple, but they are often overlooked. Managers need to be aware of these issues and help their staff to deal with them.

Psychological and Physical Well-Being

Can flexible working damage your health? The evidence is overwhelmingly in the other direction. A review of medical studies covering 16,000 people found that flexible working led to statistically significant improvements in health (Joyce et al. 2010), as outlined in Chapter 5. But whatever the benefits at the statistical level, our own experience is at the individual level, and general levels of well-being are not always reassuring for people who are struggling in one way or another.

Problems such as isolation may occur for people who end up with little interaction with their colleagues. And overwork is a possibility for anyone who has the tools to bring work home with them. Both of these may lead to problems of psychological well-being, or exacerbate existing issues.

It can't be assumed, though, that such problems would not arise if the person was working in a traditional way in the office. The main issue is really about the capacity of managers and colleagues to spot and deal with any problems that might arise, if the person suffering is working mainly in different places and/or at different times. Out of sight, out of mind – perhaps in more ways than one.

We noted in the chapter on Managing the Anywhere, Anytime Team how over the next decade or so routine management tasks will become increasingly automated, and the key management skills will be the softer ones. An esssential skill that managers and colleagues need to develop is what might be called 'distributed empathy'.

Some people are naturally better than others in picking up vibes from other people in the office, but it's largely about knowing what to be looking out for and what to do then. The manager and colleague who is well engaged with the team and communicates well are more likely to pick up the signals.

And what are those signals?

- Declining performance – non-delivery, late delivery or poor quality of work becoming increasingly common.
- Avoidance of contact.

- Inappropriate levels of communication, for example, silence in (virtual) meetings – or garrulousness.
- Defensive or volatile behaviour.
- Increased neediness – for example, always looking for help in tasks that you know they can do; requiring affirmation of their abilities to do tasks, and so on.
- Coming into the office more than they need to. This could be people with relationship problems, wanting to avoid partners, parents or children at home – and even people with money problems wanting to avoid debt collectors.

It can be a range of what doctors call 'non-specific symptoms', like that headache and those aching bones could be symptoms of a hundred different ailments, some serious but mostly not. But here the combination of declining or erratic performance and behavioural changes may well indicate that there is something to be explored.

The manager noticing these behavioural changes is of course a manager and not a counsellor or mental health professional. So there may be a point of handover to qualified others if the situation demands it. But in the meantime and probably in most cases there is a range of low-level actions and remedies to put into practice:

- Talk to the person who you think is struggling. This sounds obvious, and it should be part of the routine process of being a manager. Sometimes, though, the habits of conversations and sensitivities of broaching unfamiliar subject matter can be a barrier to openness. Focusing conversation initially on performance should help to open doors to finding out what factors are making a difference.
- Reassess the form of flexible working being undertaken. It does not necessarily mean coming back into the office, just rethinking what are the most effective times and places for that individual to work.
- If the person is struggling with outputs, it may be a case of breaking down the tasks into bite-size chunks so both he and the manager are more on top of how the workload is being dealt with. Having a series of small successes in delivering good work can be motivating and energising while the person is getting back on track.
- Without revealing confidences, encouraging another team member to buddy, mentor or just be a sounding board for the person who is struggling. Keeping the focus on work, it is a deliberate way to increase social contact in the team at the same time.
- Where appropriate, involve the team in reallocations of work tasks.
- If the sources of stress are coming from outside work, supporting some time-out could be valuable. They may need a complete break, but the model of asking to be able to keep in contact about key work issues on which they have expertise can help to support self-esteem. Remote working makes this a more viable possibility.

A key factor is recognising what it is in one's power to fix, and what is beyond that. A relationship breakdown or serious family illness can't be fixed by the employer. But it should be possible to create more supportive working arrangements to help the individual cope with the situation.

It's worth noting that, while I and others working in this field always extol the benefits of a trust-based working culture, there can also be a down side for those who are struggling. While it can be satisfying to leave work and blow off steam at a traditional command-and-control manager – even if you are in the wrong – it can be psychologically and emotionally hard to be letting down someone who trusts and empowers you.

For genuine and committed people who happen to be struggling, there is a danger of spiralling down in a vortex of self-blame and self-loathing. The feeling can be, 'I'm letting down myself, my colleagues and my manager'. This is that unwelcome spirit of Guilt emerging again – and all the more unwelcome in that it may be hitting the nail on the head. Anxieties like this feed back negatively into performance, and is often the reason for people who have got into this negative cycle avoiding contact.

This is where, in the trust-based culture, the successful manager – and colleagues too – need to combine perceptiveness and empathy with a practical approach to organising work in a way that builds the opportunity to succeed, within a context that is socially supportive. And be prepared to call for outside help if necessary.

Career Progression

One of the most common concerns amongst flexible workers is the possibility that working flexibly – or being seen to want to – may damage career progression. This applies to those working part-time as much if not more than those who choose to work remotely.

This was recently confirmed in a survey of 1,400 working parents by My Family Care (My Family Care 2011). Their annual survey of working parents found that while flexible working patterns are central to working parents being happy with their work-life balance, those who have flexibility are often concerned that it may have a negative impact on their career.

That's not surprising in the context of a traditional working culture, with its emphasis on inputs rather than outputs, workplace visibility, presenteeism and the long-hours working culture. To get to the top, you have to put the hours in and be seen to be doing it. And those who do put the hours in feel they have earned a right to get to the top. After all, as a consequence of putting in more hours, they have perhaps also made sacrifices in terms of family and social life in order to be successful. And they may have a lead in terms of outputs too – billing more, selling more, hitting higher targets because they have put more hours into doing it. Why should they give way to people who've opted for a less work-intensive lifestyle?

The point in terms of career progression though, should not be about time inputs but about skill levels, productivity, commitment and managerial potential. These characteristics may well apply to the corporate warriors who live at the office. But in today's extended workplace and diverse workforce, they also should apply – and be seen to apply – to the range of workers with alternative working patterns.

Addressing the Progression Gap

So how can organisations address these fears? The solutions do not apply only to remote or home-based workers. They should be for everyone, and there should be no feeling of remote workers either missing out or getting special treatment.

In terms of training, we've already had a look at the need to keep everyone posted on training opportunities and the need to sometimes formalise communications that previously might have been informal. But it is not only that: it is also about doing things differently. While there always remains value in getting people together for learning, the nature of training is changing. It is becoming more footloose, flexible and smarter just like most other kinds of work.

E-learning and webinars are the best ways to make learning available to distributed teams, saving on unproductive travel and also, in the case of e-learning, available more in bite-size chunks for self-help. A good e-learning system will enable trainers and managers keep abreast of what courses employees are taking and their progress.

And in an age of developing social media, it's important not to think of learning as being a one-way street, from expert to student. Many organisations are 'crowdsourcing' corporate knowledge and intelligence, using wikis and forums to pool knowledge and send out requests for help from other people in the work community who have the wisdom and experience to help. As well as facilitating personal development, perhaps people's contributions to this knowledge-sharing and informal training can be captured as a factor to be recognised in career advancement.

And in terms of career development, it's important again to make sure that people are notified of available opportunities and not have to rely on looking at a physical noticeboard. Even posting jobs on the corporate intranet is too passive an approach. As organisations become flatter and work becomes more project-based, the opportunities of interest to members of the distributed team may be less about promotion and more about finding a place on the next interesting project. People need to be able to register their interest in types of work before the opportunities come up.

One trend we have noted is for employees to become more entrepreneurial in developing and taking ownership of their careers, acting more like a freelancer in some ways. The term 'entreployee' has been coined to describe this (Pongratz and Voß 2003). In this respect, organisations should be prepared to run an internal 'LinkedIn' style of business networking, where people can post up their experience and interests, form interest groups and 'sell' themselves. It's a way of saying, 'I'm here, this is what I can do, and this is what I'd like to be doing to take the company forward'.

The value of this goes beyond the progression of the individual. By opening up new channels of collaboration, new avenues of innovation are also opened that can help to inject energy into the company.

There's a debate to be had about whether to open this up to the contingent workforce – regularly used freelancers, interims, agency workers and contractors. Some may be concerned about this, but it's worth thinking about why these people are working for the organisation in the first place. It's primarily to bring in skills that the organisation doesn't already have amongst the permanent workforce. So their contribution to corporate learning and innovation is, in my view, often an untapped or at least underused resource.

Tripping over Wires

The other most commonly expressed fear about home and remote working is to do with health and safety. Smart Flexibility increases the prospect of using all kinds of workspaces outside the traditional workplace, and so in theory raises the prospect of encountering new kinds of risk.

Back in Chapter 6 we explored the regulations about H&S for remote and home-based workers. To recap, there are no particular regulations in the UK specifically pertaining to working from home and other locations. All the regulations that normally apply still apply wherever the employee is working, and the employer has the same duty of care and of managing risk.

While there are important issues around ergonomics and working in the correct posture, taking screen breaks and so forth, I don't think many people think that working from home or in an airport lounge or cafe constitutes a significant increase in risk of injury compared to working in an office. In fact, when you think about, the most dangerous thing that most people do every day unless they work for the military, in a mine or on a construction site, is to travel to work. Every time you don't travel to or for work, you are making yourself safer at a statistically significant level.

I've been working at least part of the time from home since the mid-1990s and though there are many wires round here, I've yet to garrotte myself with them or trip over one.

Actually, what most people are concerned about is not so much the health and safety of the individual flexible worker, who by all accounts should be healthier and safer at home, but about complying with the legislation in new contexts. And this isn't rocket science. People make a fuss either because they are unfamiliar with the situation, or because they want to put barriers in the way of Smart Flexibility.

Many organisations have come up with perfectly acceptable H&S solutions based on organisational guidance, training and doing self-assessment risk assessments. And apart from checking out Chapter 6 for an introduction to the issues, the thing to do is check what other organisations are doing and take professional advice through your usual routes.

12 *Smarter Government and Its Impacts*

This chapter focuses on the development of Smart Flexibility in the government sector in the UK. The issues though are applicable to government anywhere, and to much of the wider public sector too. As well as having an impact on how government organises its own working practices, the practice of Smart Flexibility also has impacts on areas of public policy such as economic development and planning future settlements – in other words how we live and work now and in the future. So later in the chapter we look at how smart approaches can make a difference in these fields and how government working practices can interact positively with wider social benefits. Government also has a role in promoting environmental sustainability, and this is dealt with in detail in the next chapter.

For the public sector in the UK – and indeed over much of the world – the recession has brought very severe financial constraints, and the start of significant reform in the way public services and government are run. Major change against a background of funding cuts is the name of the game. The imperatives to achieve greater efficiency, to do more with less, are greater than ever. There has never been a more urgent time to work smarter. And necessity is concentrating minds as never before.

To be fair, many public sector organisations have over the past 15 years or so made very significant strides towards implementing flexible or Smart Working practices. I would identify the following as the most common practices:

- Flexitime and time off in lieu – these are almost ubiquitous in the government sector.
- Work-life balance programmes or policies – a menu of primarily working-time policies, mainly aimed at supporting female staff with caring responsibilities. These have often been strongly supported by people in Equal Opportunities and Diversity roles.
- Limited/ad hoc homeworking – with some notable exceptions, homeworking in the public sector has tended to be small scale. Usually it is part of a work-life balance initiative, or occasional homeworking by managers and professionals to get work completed without interruption.
- Marginal hotdesking – hotdesking introduced in a small way to support a small number of workers from partner agencies, mobile staff or visitors. This is usually a failure.
- 'Non-territorial working' – the introduction of widespread desk-sharing, but without necessarily a strategic approach to including the range of flexible working options.

Some organisations have gone a fair bit further. Hertfordshire County Council has through its 'The Way We Work' programme brought about a major transformation in working practices and working culture to support greater flexibility and mobility, and in the process has reduced the number of offices from 51 to three.

Ofsted, the Office for Standards in Education, Children's Services and Skills, has become the largest home-based working operation in the government sector. All its inspectors are home-based, as are many managers, and office staff have a range of flexible working options. The adoption of home-based working was taken for strategic reasons at the time they absorbed inspectors of early years education from local councils.

And it made sense to do so. Schools inspectors have a highly mobile work style, and have a limited need to be based in an office. The strategy involved looking again at the areas in which inspectors operated. In many ways this is a good example of using Smart Flexibility to get closer to 'customers'. At the same time, the process was begun of rationalising office space.

Islington Council in London began its Smart Working programme in 2005, and has ramped up from departmental initiatives to have an integrated framework that guides Smart Working throughout the Council. Around 2,400 staff are now set up to work more flexibly, working on a desk-sharing basis.

Starting from a portfolio of around 40 office buildings, the council has now released 12 of them, and refurbished 13 as Smart Working environments, where the focus is on collaboration rather than working at fixed desks. By 2010 this had led to a 10 per cent reduction in accommodation running costs as well as capital receipts from selling off surplus property.

Moving away from organisations based in London and the South-East of England, two of the most advanced implementations of Smart Flexibility are in Scotland, at Fife Council and Aberdeenshire Council. At Fife they call it Modern and Flexible Working and at Aberdeenshire it goes by the name of Worksmart.

These are examples from amongst the most progressive 10 per cent or so of government bodies.

Rearranging the Deckchairs – and Sending People to Coventry

Given the progress that the leading-edge governmental organisations are making, it is always depressing to find how often change is a question of shuffling the pack and drawing new organisation charts. New Chief Executives love to do this, as do new political leaders. They can see the fault lines, and rearrange things (in their view) more logically. They can bring functions together that need to work more closely together. They can create big new directorates, or break them down to eliminate a layer of management.

For fun one could track the organisational clumping together and de-clumping of departments in the UK Government dealing with Environment, Planning, Local Government, Transport and Rural Affairs over the past 20 years. Grouped this way, then that way, then all pulled together in one bloated ministry, then separated out and rearranged several times more.

The waste involved in doing this is absolutely enormous. All the rebranding is just the tip of the iceberg. Below the surface is constant movement between posts, often with people having to reapply for posts in newly made-up departments. Paralysis and demotivation can be the order of the day, and many of the best people jump ship.

How is all this relevant to Smart Flexibility? The point is that this traditional kind of change in fact changes very little about *how organisations actually work*. It often amounts to rearranging the deckchairs with the maximum of fuss. At the end of the day, people still come into offices and work at the same times, and pretty much the same jobs are there to do, even if they're being done by different people under a different department head and a different logo. There are still the same services that need to be delivered – only they've been delivered pretty badly during a period of convulsive introspection. Our Surrey County Council case study is partly set against such a background.

If I were prime minister, I would bring in legislation to ban all changes of organisational boundaries and rebranding in the public sector for 20 years. Instead, the focus needs to be on changing working practices to introduce greater agility in delivering services and greater flexibility to improve efficiency, cutting the cost of government and managing public services, and improving the working lives of employees.

The other efficiency red herring that swims to the surface at regular intervals is to move government services out of London to another part of the country. In practice, this means uprooting agencies or departments with little political clout or weak management and sending them off to Manchester or Bristol or Sheffield or somewhere else similarly impractical for the existing staff.

One ill-starred government agency a few years back was uprooted and, literally, sent to Coventry. It was also seriously shaken up and rebranded just for good measure. Understandably, not many people wanted to uproot their families and make the move. Commuting there from their existing homes was simply not practical. So why would they want to go there if it could be avoided? New York, Paris, or Barcelona, maybe. That might be worth the upheaval for the employees and their families.

Sure, property is cheaper outside London and the South-East. But the point is, in the twenty-first century giving up desk-space in London doesn't require buying lots of desk-space in a lower-cost city elsewhere in the UK. Few of the people working in central London live there. With Smart Flexibility working practices, it doesn't matter too much where their official base is. They can work from home, or from the nearest government/ government-approved workhub (see below). And, of course, the principle of relocation does little for organisations already located outside the South-East and London.

Many of these relocation measures are political rather than practical. In large part they are about reducing the impression of government being too London-centric and about bringing jobs to other parts of the country. There are obvious local benefits to having central government departments in other regional centres. Should we stand in the way of this decentralisation?

Smart Flexibility means that we need to look at this the other way round. Flexible working should be used to overcome the geographical barriers to people in other parts of the country working for government agencies based in London, or based anywhere. Decentralisation needs to be replaced by non-centralisation.

So my second act as prime minister would be to veto all the old-fashioned (and mostly arbitrary) relocation projects. If the head of a department or a government minister is in love with a move to Coventry, he or she can go there. But the rest of the staff should have the option to stay put.

The government agency that went to Coventry was cited as one of the worst examples of waste by Sir Philip Green in his 2010 Efficiency Review of government spending (Green 2010). It was abolished 9 months after its move, after signing a 20-year lease with no break for 15 years, committing to rent of £1.2 million per year. Relocation costs for 400 staff were revealed to be £24.5 million. This illustrates the potential impacts of both poorly conceived relocations and government restructuring.

The New Approach in Whitehall

There are welcome signs that central government here has begun to take a more coordinated and strategic approach, with a strong emphasis on efficiency and reducing waste. Working smarter is taking a more central role and is being recognised as being necessary for the delivery of the programme to rationalise government real estate.

A new approach to efficiency in government IT and in reducing the costs of procurement are starting to take more tangible form not only in re-evaluating long-term IT contracts, but also in the new explorations into cloud technology. At the time of writing, the government has just launched its 'CloudStore', a catalogue of tested and approved cloud applications within the Government Cloud (G-Cloud) Framework. As we noted in Chapter 7, use of cloud technologies is strongly associated with the capacity for Smart Flexibility working practices.

At the moment, the structures do not exist to bring together effectively the property, HR and IT functions as a whole. So to a large extent moves towards Smart Flexibility have to be driven by common acceptance of standards and imitation of the leading examples. The demands for modernisation and cost reduction as a whole are driven by the Efficiency and Reform Group of the Cabinet Office, and of course by the need to implement very large savings, and do more with less.

Interestingly, we don't have any centrally driven measures towards flexible working like the United States' Telework Enhancement Act, setting out both obligations and a process for federal government. Several other governments, including most recently Iran's, have set out similar regulations. All the same, the achievements of the UK Government are in some respects pace-setting when you look at comparators across the globe. In the end, the will to change and the awareness of the benefits and possibilities are probably more effective than trying to legislate or regulate people into working smarter.

According to Richard Graham, Head of Property Performance Improvement at the Government Property Unit, the aim is to achieve a much more integrated approach to change. Reshaping the government estate is essential to improve efficiency, but to do that there needs to be an integrated approach bringing in new uses of ICT and a new approach to engagement and culture change. The recently published Civil Service Reform Plan (HM Government 2012) sets the context for fundamental change in central government and represents a major new programme of workplace change requiring the engagement and support of departments as well as dedicated leadership, management and resources. The Efficiency and Reform Group, of which the GPU is part, is designed to bring these issues together. But to succeed, it's not only about addressing the internally facing parts of government departments. It's also about addressing the operational side. According to Richard:

> It's really important to take the lead from the top of the organisation and the Civil Service Reform Plan provides strong strategic direction. At the same time we need to engage with the

business side: for example the people dealing with roads, and railways, and public services. They are the ones who want to know what it means for how they do their work.

The Olympics has provided us with a kind of 'enforced pilot' for trialling new ways of working across the civil service. And we need to ensure there is a legacy from this, and take on board the lessons learned about the way we work.

On the property side, shared spaces are central to the new approach in central government. In the five postcode areas around Westminster, there were in 2011 over 170 government offices. That is being reduced and the plan is to reduce that to less than 30 over the next couple of years. Plans are developing for the range of offices in Whitehall to become the 'Whitehall Campus', based on shared spaces and mobility.

Some 80,000 civil servants work within the M25 (the motorway that encircles Greater London). Most of them live outside London. In the future, as well as working on an as-needed basis in offices in London, they will be able to work in a proposed network of campuses around the country. Some are already being co-located with local government, and we can expect to see more of this.

Richard Graham believes that there is a 'perfect storm' developing, of financial pressures to reduce costs and increase efficiency, technologies that now really do the business, employees who are up for change, and government ministers and senior civil servants who understand the role of smarter working in delivering the benefits.

The Civil Service Reform Plan – amongst many other reforms – envisages 'Creating a decent working environment for all staff, with modern workplaces enabling flexible working, substantially improving IT tools and streamlining security requirements to be less burdensome for staff', and will have a 'much less hierarchical, pacier culture focussed on outcomes not process' (HM Government 2012, 27). In principle, this is on the way to Smart Flexibility.

Having said that, central government is not a single entity, but a complex collection of departments and agencies that have a history of managing their own budgets, holding their own property, running their own IT and HR, and generally doing their own thing. What is needed are some stunning exemplars of Smart Flexibility to show the way and to encourage imitation. On the whole, these tend to be found more at local government level than in central government at the moment.

There are ministries that have moved to desk-sharing and towards flexible working environments in recent years, like the Home Office and the Department of Business, who have presented their achievements at Flexibility conferences in recent years. However, the time is here for more radical and thorough-going change, in part because of significant reductions in headcount, but mostly because it is possible to do so much more in terms of using new technologies and changing the culture of work.

Local Government – the Hydra Organisation and Its Challenges

In many ways, the issues facing public sector organisations are the same as those facing other larger employers: using resources efficiently, delivering services effectively, being an employer of choice. So all the measures detailed in the previous chapters for the implementation of Smart Flexibility equally apply. But in some ways government bodies can be different.

Many public sector organisations – particularly local councils – carry out a far greater range of services than any sensible private sector employer would ever attempt. Encompassing child protection, running car parks, running housing estates, making planning policy and collecting rubbish within a single organisation might strike a disinterested observer as an eclectic or even eccentric mix. If a company tried to do all this (and much more) the first advice would be to decide what you are good at and sell off non-core activities. But of course for the council, they are pretty much all core activities. And in challenging times when money is tight, leaders of such organisations face impossible choices about which services are more and which are less important. Cut children's services, or cut adult social care services? Or should they cut grants to local charities that carry out many essential local services at a fraction of the cost of the council doing it?

These are the kinds of choices that public servants and elected members overseeing them are often presented with. Elected politicians often have little or no expertise in dealing with company finances and organisational change. The choices they make can have profound implications, but their grasp of the complex organisations they believe they are in charge of is nearly always, at best, superficial.

Within such multi-headed organisations, there are competing demands, with internal empires growing and being cut back, and probably several different kinds of organisational culture. Not a single entity, but a federation of entities, in practice. Some of the departments may in fact work much more closely with external partner organisations working in the same field than with another department in the same organisation that has a vastly different function.

The commonality is often provided by the internally facing functions such as property, facilities, HR, IT, procurement and legal.

All this poses additional challenges when looking to introduce Smart Flexibility in the strategic way advocated here. However, although any change programme may have to recognise some distinctive work patterns and work cultures, it remains important not to give in to any special interests but rather to persist in taking a strategic and integrated approach. There will always be people who oppose a corporate approach to Smart Flexibility on the grounds that 'one size does not fit all'. While there is always some truth in this, it's also often a coded way of saying 'we're not changing – because we're special'.

The real truth is that no one's work is so special that it can't be done more effectively and consume fewer resources by being done smarter and more flexibly.

What is up for change is the way people work – not the mission, the nature or value of the service, but the working practices. Despite the range of services involved, there can only be a limited number of working practices. In every service, there will be people who are more office-based, more mobile, working at specific sites, working at certain times, and so on. The types of work may be process work, knowledge work, case work, highly interactive work or flying solo, externally facing or internally facing.

Breaking down the work styles and the tasks that people do means that the infrastructure and appropriate range of workplaces can be developed that allow people from different services to work effectively in many more locations than they do at present, and at more appropriate times for the people they deal with, while at the same time having access to all systems and information.

A STRATEGIC APPROACH TO CHANGE AT HERTFORDSHIRE COUNTY COUNCIL

Since 2005 Hertfordshire County Council has transformed the way it works, through its 'The Way We Work' (TW3) programme. New flexible and remote working practices, new technology and new working environments have combined to deliver annual operational cost savings of £3.8 million, property disposals totalling around £40 million, plus reduced travel and increased staff satisfaction.

The new working environments are open plan, with no individual offices for managers, and team-based desk-sharing for all staff who have some degree of mobility. Touch-down points have been set up across the county to provide staff with the opportunity to 'drop in and plug in' to pick up emails, access their systems and documents. These enable staff to work from a range of locations including libraries, fire stations, partners' premises and NHS sites to help reduce travel time and costs.

According to David Robinson, Programme Director for TW3:

> There has been a shift of thinking. We have moved from flexible working being an HR policy document to becoming a recognised means of achieving business objectives and personal commitments. We see the implementation of flexible working as a catalyst to help us achieve the vision and objectives of transforming the way we work. Flexible working combines with the modern office bases, the right ICT equipment and document management to form a joined-up solution.

There has been significant investment in technology, accelerated by the initial experience of difficulties experienced by staff when working remotely. As well as portable IT equipment, there has been a major investment in enterprise systems and document management to support effective remote working.

The impacts of this have been felt back in the office with a concerted programme of paper reduction. There has been a 50 per cent reduction of paper files, and an 85 per cent reduction in paper usage as a result of moving to electronic document management. This has led to a major reduction in storage available in offices, coupled with archiving moved off site. 'Bin it days' or 'Tidy Fridays' were organised which meant 36 tonnes of paper were sent for confidential recycling. Overall, the council has reduced over 13 kilometres of storage down to less than 4 kilometres.

As well as being good for productivity and for the environment, this has also contributed to the scale of property reduction. Around 4,500 staff have been moved from 51 offices to five main offices. This has encompassed all staff in central support functions, administrative support staff and front-line staff like social workers.

Managerial buy-in has been key to implementing a successful change programme. This included a clear vision endorsed from the top, with heads of service leading the changes and early line manager engagement. Clear expectations for managers were set, with training and support on hand to help them through the changes.

Throughout the programme there has been a strong emphasis on staff engagement at all levels. Focus groups identified the advantages and how to overcome any identified barriers. It wasn't all plain sailing, as some managers and staff were resistant. So people were encouraged to share their experiences and concerns, and to think positively how to deal with the issues. At the same time, the top-level vision and support made it clear that the changes would be happening.

According to David Robinson:

> *There has been a move away from managing by input to managing by output, with a strong emphasis on Performance Management and regular supervision sessions. With flexible working, trust is fundamental and there is a strong link between performance management and trust. To achieve this we've had to ensure that there are good communication processes in place which help maintain the cohesiveness of the team and ensure no one is excluded from important information or feels detached from the team.*

> *Any culture change takes time to embed into an organisation. We have approached flexible working as a journey, and recognised that teams will all be at different stages. Flexible working cannot be a one size fits all approach. We have to look at the needs of the service and staff preferences within each team.*

What about Teachers, Doctors and Firemen?

The argument is sometimes put that while the office-based functions can become more flexible, most functions in services like education, health, the emergency services and also low-skill manual work, just can't be flexible. A teacher has to go to school. You can't have a home-based teacher.

Actually, I know many home-based teachers – mainly in post-16 education, specialist subjects like music, and tutorial kinds of teaching. But for mainstream teaching it is true there are premises to go to and that isn't going to change. So where does the flexibility come in for the regular teacher, and what are the benefits of introducing it?

Few teachers in the UK have more than 20 hours contact time with students. So what are they doing the rest of the time? There are some supervision duties, cover for absent colleagues, clubs to run perhaps – but this does not add up to many hours. The truth is that for a substantial chunk of their contracted hours, their presence at the site is not strictly necessary.

What they are doing with their remaining non-contact time (and often well beyond) is planning, preparing, marking, timetabling, budgeting, writing reports and winding down from the stress of classroom performance. These are all things that in principle can be done from anywhere. And of course increasingly this is what teachers are doing. It's quite traditional in fact to take piles of work home. Now in many cases it can all be smarter, a bit more electronic, with students emailing assignments to teachers or uploading it to shared online areas. Teachers are producing electronic learning resources, which students access from their homes. One of my daughter's teachers prepared a series of excellent podcasts to help his students' exam revision, something which I'm sure was prepared in the quieter environment of his home. So the boundaries of time and space in education are becoming more blurred.

Distance teaching is also on the increase for specialist subjects, with one teacher able to run lessons in several schools without having to race from one to the other. Of course, remote teaching has been the norm for a long time in far-flung places with sparse populations. We are only just beginning to see these techniques coming into play in 'normal' schools.

Schools have also long been making considerable use of family-friendly employment patterns such as part-time working, not least because it is a profession dominated by women (at least below secondary level). 'Term-time working' in other sectors means having unpaid leave during school holidays. All teachers have term-time working, only with the considerable advantage that the holidays are also paid.

There is great interest in smart and flexible working in the health service too. Family-friendly employment practices are seen as essential in many hospitals as a way of enticing nurses back into employment, and the traditional command and control approach to rostering is giving way to self-rostering and self-organising teams.

But it is a mistake though to see the health service as being all about hands-on medical care. There are many doing office work, managerial work, IT support, research, diagnostic work, plus cooks, cleaners and maintenance people. A lot of jobs, in fact, just like any large employer. Some are quite site-specific and some are time-critical. But many are not.

A survey a while back for one large hospital in the context of developing a hospital travel plan found that 80 per cent of its employees worked regular hours between 8 a.m. and 6 p.m., Monday to Friday. The government currently is pushing health services to offer more services at evenings and weekends. This has the twofold aim of providing services at more convenient times for working people, and also 'sweating the assets'. Operating theatres and consulting rooms that are used during 'office hours' are, in fact, lying underused for most of the time.

How flexible can firemen be, though? The South Wales Fire and Rescue Service has consolidated a number of disparate premises into one new headquarters building. But what was initially conceived of as a traditional property project became a strategic exercise in implementing Smart Working with the aim of promoting and supporting location-independent working, with desk-sharing in the headquarters and touch-down desks in local fire stations.

Putting out fires and cutting road-accident victims out of wreckage is the visible end of the fire service's work. But just as essential is the fire prevention work, inspections, training and all the support activities behind the service.

Blurring Private and Public Sector, Employment and Self-Employment

In the public services there is already substantial use of staff with flexible contract arrangements. In professions such as nursing and social work, use of agency workers is very common. Alongside this there is increasing use of independent professionals such as physiotherapists and others offering specialist services. A great many health workers work for more than one organisation, across both the public and private sectors. And of course most general practitioners – at least the principals and partners – are self-employed and are running a small business that provides services to the National Health Service.

Whether services are undertaken by employees within the health service or not tends to reflect their historical evolution and funding exigencies, rather than any compelling strategic rationale. Independent contractors and private sector services are now often used to plug gaps and to deliver new services in a cost effective way.

Beyond anything that might be prescribed by a doctor, there is an increasing range of personal care services on the market. Most of these are undertaken by independent practitioners, and are often home-based. Some practitioners have bought or rent live/work premises, so they have a purpose-built practice room or salon within or attached to their home.

At the risk of running roughshod over sensitive ideological toes, it is clear that this is the future of healthcare: a mixed market, characterised by loosening boundaries between organisations, with growing numbers of 'free agent' professionals and new enterprises. Health professionals will in the course of a career cross the boundaries of private and public sector health providers, and flex between employment and self-employment. The health sector will become more entrepreneurial, and the health 'consumer' will be offered more choice.

For some people this is a horrific vision – the steady erosion of the principle of free health care from cradle to grave, and the increasing privatisation of the National Health Service, not to mention a weakening of the collective bargaining power of the health unions.

We probably passed the point of no return on this some time ago in the UK, and the trends and drivers mentioned in Chapters 1 and 2 (not least the requirements of an ageing population) are all pointing in the direction of increased flexibility and choice. The challenge now is to extricate the health services from the haphazard muddle of current approaches and the never-ending 'restructuritis', and to embrace the opportunities provided by new ways of working and new kinds of contractual relationships.

The mixed market is also spreading throughout the government sector. Most government sector bodies use consultants not just for the special projects, or for their outsourced IT operations, but also for many core functions. It's increasingly common to find external consultants sitting alongside regular employed staff working on the same projects. And why not?

One advantage is to be able to draw essential skills and experience into the organisation. The traditions of a career civil service mean that people working in a government department are unlikely to have much in the way of 'real life' experience running the kinds of private sector operations or delivering the kinds of complex projects that they have responsibility for. Having seasoned professionals on board who may also want to maintain a private practice has advantages. Having more porous boundaries so that it is easier for people to move between sectors has advantages too.

Of course there are all kinds of concerns about independence and not gaining particular advantages in tendering processes and so on. But the evidence is that current public/private partnerships with the strict division between client and contractor don't necessarily work all that well. The spate of government IT and defence procurement disasters in the decade up to 2012 has provided evidence that there is often a serious lack of expertise and market wisdom on the client side in specifying and overseeing projects.

Actually, a quick perusal of networking websites such as LinkedIn will show that there are already many managers and skilled professionals in the public sector who are also offering consultancy services. Possibly they are preparing an exit route from public service in doing so. In recent times, there are many who have accepted early retirement or a redundancy package, and have now set themselves up as consultants in their field of expertise. In due course many do work again as contractors or possibly interim managers within the public sector.

We are here at a transitional stage in terms of flexible contract work in the public sector. The recession is increasing the number of ex-public sector consultants, but there are some signs that, for a while, at least, political considerations and short-termism are behind some dodgy decision-making as regards temporary workers in the public sector.

The Cull of the Consultants

Many public sector organisations are doing what appears to be the logical thing at the moment. They are shedding staff, and the first instinct of self-preservation is to start by ditching consultants, contractors, interims and agency staff.

Big voices on all sides of politics have their teeth into government consultants. So many millions can be saved per year by ditching consultants. After all, consultants are people who borrow your watch and sell you the time, aren't they? And isn't the first duty to protect the permanent staff? Unions and management tend to agree on this. But is this approach correct?

First of all, it depends what they are doing. The reason for many of the temporary/ project workers being there in the first place is that they are providing skills and expertise lacking amongst the core staff. Who will do their work after they are gone? Replacing a consultant with a member of the permanent staff who has the wrong skillset but whose post would otherwise disappear can end up being a very costly exercise.

Secondly, there's something wrong in principle here isn't there? At a time when the organisation needs *more* flexibility and agility, the *people on the variable payroll are being ditched while the people on the fixed payroll are being entrenched*, regardless of whether they are doing anything useful. The organisation's freedom of action to respond to changing market conditions has taken a hit.

The right course of action is to retain whoever is delivering a vital service, regardless of employment status, and to introduce new flexibilities rather than eliminating the existing ones.

What we are looking at here is the question whether the way forward for government, like other organisations, is to become more of a network of relationships, with many functions – and not necessarily only 'non-core' ones – being done with trusted partners and greater use of the contingent workforce. Can government be more flexible in the sense of being a 'virtual organisation' in the Charles Handy sense as well as being more virtual in terms of technological collaboration?

The Paperless Bureaucracy

I think most of us have at the back if not at the front of our minds an image of civil servants as people whose *raison d'être* is to push lots of paper around, gathering information, shovelling it on to colleagues and eventually storing it in dusty files. We're not sure why, but there will be many occasions in life where, baffled, we have to comply and fill in forms so that we can be efficiently regulated and taxed within some arcane and musty continuum. We have visions of this from Dickens through Kafka to Terry Gilliam's *Brazil*. Bureaucrats need paper like fish need water.

Or so it used to be. Paper-dependence is a particular problem in the public sector. Most if not all public sector organisations have programmes in place to replace at least some paper processes with electronic ones, but the scale of the dependence is often so great that it seems initiatives barely make a dent in the problem.

However, all the issues and solutions detailed in Chapter 6 apply equally to the public sector, and probably more urgently. Nothing tethers people to the office quite like the paper trail, and it is a major obstacle to effective Smart Flexibility.

In my work in public sector organisations I have observed a culture of extreme caution about disposing of paper documentation. It is true there are particular statutory duties that apply and the need to hold on to records for a set period has legitimate roots. However, new standards about keeping files electronically are working through the system. There is also an ingrained fear of litigation or complaint, of investigation and scrutiny that also feeds the squirreling tendency. But even if we concede the need to hoard, there is no good reason to hoard it *in the office*. An old salt mine is a much better option.

There is also an understandable caution about making documents and systems accessible from anywhere. Paper is solid, and if you know it's in the office and that's where it should be, the paperwork is safe. It's easy to be broad-brush and be critical of 'bureaucracy'. The information concerned can be highly personal and sensitive, about people's health or finances, legal cases, or about agency responses to situations involving very vulnerable people.

All this is true. But it's worth looking at the examples of banks and the financial services sector. They hold very sensitive information about all of us, and it needs to be very secure. At the same time, though, we need to be able to withdraw money from any cash machine anywhere in the world. We want to use online banking to manage our finances. We want to be able to call the bank and expect the person at the other end to have all our details and records at their fingertips. If they had to go off to fetch a paper file every time to find the information, the services we expect would simply not be viable.

If banks can do it, and if we can accept this way to handle our money, then there must be ways to deal with other sensitive information across networks. High-profile security leaks have mostly been due to data being stored inappropriately on laptops or even on CDs. There are issues to be resolved and protocols to observe about where, when and how data and systems are accessed. But there are solutions, and many public sector organisations are already using them to support mobile workers in fields such as social services and policing. When you think about it, some of the most mobile workers in the public sector – spies and the military – need secure access to highly sensitive data wherever they are. And they have ways to do this.

A particular imperative that affects many parts of the public sector is that to work effectively there is a need to work in partnership with other agencies, and to share information. This creates problems about data security and permissions, but it also highlights the need for greater flexibility in how information is handled and shared.

The current passion for joined-up working perhaps begs the question why intimately related functions are divided between different agencies in the first place. But effective partnership working does depend on both sharing information and on creating common records, accessible by all parties. In cases of child abuse, for example, where doctors, police, social workers and educational welfare officers may all be involved workers from each agency need to know about all the contacts that have been made with the family concerned. And they need to have that information at their fingertips, not wait for case meetings where they can hand paper to each other.

There are security issues to address. But there are also opportunities for gains in efficiency and cooperation that must be taken. It's about managing risk, not preventing effective activity.

Meanwhile, back at the office, the real world of funding shortfalls continues, and the scanning and archiving project your mobility depends on is going to take three or four years to get round to your department. What is the answer? To be bold and look to the future. Establish the systems you need to work with and which will support greater mobility. Access to old cases and decisions will be increasingly rare as time goes on.

This does require a culture change. I remember one council whose planning department, in compliance with government recommendations, requested people seeking planning permission to submit applications online. That's great, and to be encouraged. What applicants didn't know was that when online applications were received, at least 5 copies were immediately printed – one for the case file, one for the public inspection file, and the rest for statutory consultees, including in-house ones such as the highways department. A physical post box was simply being replaced by a virtual one, and behind the scenes the council had given itself more work to do and more expense as it sought to give the impression of being modern.

The goal has to be end-to-end online processes, enabling staff and customers to access all materials online, wherever and whenever they need to.

Bureau-Less Bureaucracy

We're getting rid of the paper – perhaps! Can we get rid of the offices too? The government sector owns huge amounts of property – £370 billion worth, of which around £240 billion is held by local government and around £130 billion by central government and public corporations. Around 72 per cent of the central government estate is offices (HM Treasury 2009).

Currently the government intends to reduce the government estate through disposals by £20 billion over the next 10 years, and save £5.6 billion per year in running costs.

How is this to be done? In the studies emanating from the Treasury up to mid-2010, there was very little mention of the role of smart or flexible working in achieving this (except in appendices and footnotes), though there is considerable emphasis on the sharing of properties. Further relocations out of the expensive London and the South-East have been high on the agenda.

However, in 2008 the Office for Government Commerce did publish a fine study called *Working beyond Walls – The Government Workplace as an Agent of Change*, produced in conjunction with workplace consultancy DEGW. In the foreword, Sir Gus O'Donnell, then Cabinet Secretary and Head of the Home Civil Service says:

Work is what you do, not a place you go. The next generation of workforce will know that and be ready and able to work anywhere. Work has migrated beyond the conventional boundaries of time and space into a wider environment and those who manage the government estate need to be prepared. The office is rapidly becoming just one of a network of workplace options, and for many people their work and personal lives are becoming more integrated. Technology now allows people to communicate virtually anywhere in many different ways, and members of the next generation are learning from birth to use this technology as second nature. They are already highly mobile, highly connected and comfortable mixing the real and virtual worlds. (OGC and DEGW 2008, 5)

What could be a clearer call for Smart Flexibility in government? The final chapter is called 'Reimagining the Government Workplace'. It looks forward to how the government workplace ought to be in 2020. It is lean, green and decentralised. Whitehall is now a campus centre for policy initiatives and knowledge working. It is a place where:

High-tech serviced working and meeting spaces have brought together both Internet and baby-boomer generations to work and meet in team neighbourhoods, non-territorial ICT labs and airline-style club-lounges. Full-immersion room displays and computer animated virtual environments (CAVES) support communication between remote teams. Life size, standup telepresence enables people to meet and speak in real time across the globe using hologram video technology. (OGC and DEGW 2008, 99)

This is complemented by a network of similar campuses around the country:

Away from London and centred on each UK region, alongside each campus headquarters is a shared service centre (SSC), which enable economies of scale to be achieved through centralizing administrative and transactional functions across branches of government. Where cost and space permit, family friendly reception areas allow parents access to childcare facilities. (Ibid.)

Extensive use of contract staff and consultants is expected to be part of the mix. Homeworking will be a natural way of working for most staff who want to do so.

One of the authors of *Working beyond Walls*, Bridget Hardy of the OGC, has recently written (Hardy 2010):

I can see a time where the virtual place becomes the constant – 'the office'. It will be the place we go to meet our colleagues and customers, where we know and are known by others, where we have our place, our work and identity. Meanwhile the physical places we choose to work in will become more diverse, more distributed and our occupation of them more transient. This combination of virtual and radically transformed physical workplaces makes up the government office of the future.

This is a powerful vision. But how close are government agencies to achieving this?

Making It Happen

Some implementations are well on their way, as we have seen. But overall the connection between Smart Flexibility and the savings that can be achieved are not well understood at the policy level, and the new Smart Working environments envisaged in *Working beyond*

Walls seem a long way off, even with the broad statement of principle in the Civil Service Reform Plan.

As yet, there isn't an integrated programme within government to make this happen, though there are clear signs it is beginning to emerge. There is no overall programme that successfully integrates property, HR and IT – at least not so far.

Introducing Smart Flexibility is interdisciplinary, and it involves bringing together a coherent policy on a broad front. What it needs is clear statements of intent from the highest level, some exemplars, and then an existing body with sufficient clout to drive it along.

As you can see from the case studies in this book, there are some very good implementations in the government sector. Pretty much all the issues involved have been tackled by one organisation of another. And it clearly works. Perhaps the essential first step is to have a very clear statement from Whitehall that 'This is going to happen. Now design your solution on the basis of these principles. And make sure the implementation is underway within three months'.

Facilities Exchange and Shared Premises

In Chapter 6 I mentioned initiatives to enable government sector employees to touch-down and work at the nearest government building, belonging to any participating organisation. Public sector organisations need to plan to have more of these.

In some areas several different government bodies are sharing premises already. The real value comes when they slim down their portfolio of offices overall, and achieve high occupancy rates at the shared premises. Some of the examples I have seen of different bodies sharing the same building are not very encouraging. The staff sit in separate areas, and have their own IT and telecoms systems which can make it difficult to be flexible.

The new generation of shared premises will need to have desk-sharing as standard, and a much greater emphasis on spaces for touching down and for collaborative work, rather than fixed desks apportioned to each organisation.

Merging and Pooling

Currently the vogue in the UK is for the government to look to allocate funding to the public sector on a locational basis rather than on a purely agency by agency basis. Public bodies are encouraged to pool resources to prevent duplication at the local level, and provide more integrated services. In many areas this is leading to a pooling of property, and in some areas to the effective merging of some services, such as property, HR or customer services, and in some cases to the merging of organisations such as local councils and health services.

Such initiatives will undoubtedly be even more cost effective if they also include Smart Flexibility working arrangements as standard.

There are big challenges here. More than ever the need is to be able to work and especially to make decisions across boundaries: adopting the same protocols for working in the office, reducing paper, and above all to adopt the same or at least compatible Smart Working culture(s).

The biggest challenge though is to reach agreements to share property, services and resources *and then stick to it*. Nothing undoes good public sector initiatives like the compulsion to restructure.

In 2011 two 'Leaner and Greener' reports were published by the Westminster Sustainable Business Forum. Their recommendations included both increasing the uptake of flexible working practices to achieve 20–30 per cent reduction of office space in local government, and setting up joint property vehicles between public sector bodies to manage asset rationalisation and occupation more efficiently.

The recommendations are on the right lines. But they underestimate the potential benefits from adopting new ways of working, and suffer from classic traditional thinking when looking at new mechanisms for managing property. A 20–30 per cent reduction in space could be achieved tomorrow by better workspace design and desk-sharing, without getting particularly smart about Smart Flexibility.

The report does, however, highlight the potential for £8 billion per year savings by a mixture of productivity increases from flexible working and using workplaces more efficiently. And this is on top of an identified reduction of £7 billion in reduced property costs per year.

Leaner and Greener also proposes – as have others – setting up new entities such as Local Strategic Property Forums, Local Property Boards or other joint venture companies to coordinate or take over the running of property services of public sector property. Versions of these are already happening in some areas – or are at least on the drawing board. And those that work are profiled as achieving significant savings.

It is, however, a somewhat public sector solution to multiply new bodies, and what is proposed here would create a few hundred new bodies, each reporting to multiple public sector stakeholders. Business transformation going along these routes will certainly be expensive, extremely slow, riven by politics and turf wars, and ultimately delivering few benefits.

Public sector property ownership and tenure is very complex, and efforts at collaboration tend to increase rather than decrease the complexity. It's fine to pursue the aim of working together to produce results, but in the meantime, the best thing to do is to forge ahead with changes that are within the remit of each organisation, and that means going ahead with the introduction of Smart Flexibility practices. Every public sector organisation can rationalise its own property as a result. And after that, with fewer properties to manage, it may even prove easier to join forces and manage them collectively.

Use of Local Work Hubs

Back in Chapter 6 we noted the growing importance the new phenomenon of workhubs. Use of workhubs is going to be increasingly important to smarter government, as it is to all large organisations looking for flexible use of space.

Though there are a number of different models, essentially a workhub is a third-party provided work centre that has hotdesks, touch-down spaces and meeting facilities to access on a flexible as-needed basis. The 2010 Workhubs study for the UK Government (Dwelly et al. 2010) focused on the interaction between these new-style flexible working premises and home-based enterprise. Several of the case studies were supported during the start-up phase by local or regional government as economic development initiatives.

The true potential of these is not yet being tapped by government bodies. Local government and other public sector services have many mobile staff who have little need of a permanent office base. What they need is touch-down space, professional meeting space and access to services such as videoconferencing.

There are two main reasons why not much of this is happening yet:

1. Lack of awareness of a new sector of facilities provision.
2. Fear of sharing premises – partly stemming from security concerns, but mostly stemming from traditional territorial working cultures and silo mentalities.

Most of the discussions about and early implementations of public sector space sharing have been predicated on co-location of public sector services in government-owned premises. The model is one of offices more intensively used with some fringe touch-down space. It is a model of concentration rather than dispersion.

Local workhubs provide the opportunity to have flexible bases out in the communities served, rather than concentration in special campuses. The model for the future will surely be a mixture of both. That is, slimmed down and shared corporate campuses, shrunk down even further by extensive use of homeworking and local/community workhubs.

Business Continuity and the Sink Hole Fable

The value of flexible working, in particular home-based working, has been demonstrated in times of extreme weather and natural disaster. Increasingly, it is now built into business continuity and disaster recovery plans. However, if employees are not used to remote working, the experience may be more Business As Unusual than Business As Usual. But what if the Unusual were as effective as the Usual, if not more so?

It's time to carry out a conceptual experiment. Imagine you're working for a local council, or a government department, and overnight a huge sink hole opened up under the town hall or main administrative buildings. The building(s) collapsed into the hole, falling down 80 metres or more. Everything inside is crushed, shattered or swept away through underground caves. When employees turn up in the morning, the council is gone. But the work has to go on.

Where would you start the recovery process? It would have to start online, with the backups of all your data that is held off site, away in remote servers.

Would you set in place a plan to rebuild your old buildings according to the old pattern (preferably on more stable ground)? With the same kinds of environments, the same kind of systems and storage? Almost certainly, you would not – and should not either.

And what would happen in the meantime – how would staff deliver critical services? In the immediate aftermath they would have to improvise. They would use phones and whatever online technologies they could muster to rebuild the essential core of their services, and to carry on as soon as possible dealing with their customers and clients.

They would meet wherever they could. In cafes, employees' homes, workhubs, in other government offices – but for collaboration rather than desk work.

Some serviced office space might be rented as a central administrative point, but would probably be a fraction of the space previously occupied.

Would there be a big reinvestment in filing cabinets and systems to rebuild paper processes? If people kept their old heads on, it might happen. But it would be a huge mistake and a lost opportunity. Instead it should provide the impetus for a huge migration to (almost) entirely paperless systems.

Systems would be not so much rebuilt as remodelled, based on cloud technology. There would be little time to sit down and conceptualise bespoke systems for each service. People would have to get going as fast as possible with more or less off-the-shelf customer relationship management (CRM) systems and case records systems to replace extensive paper records. Working with suppliers, these could be adapted over time.

But it is a besetting problem of the sector that every service exaggerates its uniqueness. Everyone demands a host of bespoke features in their applications, when in fact there is a limited number of useful ways to hold records about the people you work with, and flag up appropriate actions that need to be taken.

So what has happened here in this hypothetical situation? The disaster has concentrated minds on the essentials of running services and delivering value. The old platform for delivery has proved to be far less essential than previously thought. And a kind of Occam's razor has been applied to the ramshackle Babel of incompatible information systems that were a brake on efficiency, and were costing a fortune to reform. A principle of simplicity is long overdue in specifying these systems.

The disaster effectively pulls the council out of the limbo the public sector finds itself in, one of 'wandering between two worlds: one not yet dead and the other powerless to be born' (to misquote Matthew Arnold). It is the legacy of traditional ways of doing things that makes change so hard.

The central point of our Sink Hole Fable is a question: do we really need a catastrophe to happen in order to make the changes? One can't help feeling that these changes would be self-evident if we didn't have the weight of historical practices and mindsets upon us.

Smart Public Policy for the New World of Work

We've looked at how the new world of work is (or should be) changing the way government operates as an employer and how it organises its working practices.

Government also needs to take on board the wider social impacts and potential benefits from new ways of working. There need to be new approaches to public policy if the benefits are to be realised. The rest of this chapter looks at the main issues in policy that arise.

New Ways of Working Mean New Approaches to Economic Development

As well as being a major employer – in many areas by far the largest employer – the government sector also has responsibilities in the field of economic development. They have a role in stimulating local economies, supporting business and innovation, and in determining land uses and transport policy.

The UK, like many European economies, has become over-reliant on the public sector as an employer and a provider of contracts for the private sector. This is an imbalance that needs to be corrected.

There is indeed an urgent need to promote the growth of new businesses. And this needs to be done in new ways. The old days of big inward investment – plonking a large production, warehousing or distribution facility down on designated land and creating thousands of local jobs – are gone. Any future occurrences will be exceptional, and we ought to be wary of them too. Many that landed in the 1980s were gone a decade later. Industry has become much more footloose, and automation means that even large facilities bring far fewer jobs than in the Industrial Age.

The new model is of smaller, networked enterprises, coming together with each other or larger enterprises in non-permanent relationships, and offering all kinds of services both to businesses and to the public.

In this new world of work there will be many more 'free agents', many more part-time businesses, and most enterprises will not have the same requirements for space as the typical twentieth century small enterprise. Most businesses start-ups are already home-based, and this trend will continue. Increasingly, growing businesses will not require additional premises as they grow. A key aim for many will be to expand into smaller space. For most companies, the norm will be 'spaceless growth'.

How should Smart Government respond to this changing world of work? The first thing is to recognise that there is a need for significant changes in enterprise policy. Two key assumptions underlie enterprise policy: that successful companies (a) must have premises and (b) will increase the number of their employees. Expanding premises and expanding staff numbers are embedded in policy as indicators of success.

There is a certain traditional logic in this. All the big corporate names have large amounts of property and thousands of staff. However, new forms of organisation and new ways of working are changing this for the majority of enterprises. The old assumptions no longer apply.

For the past 30 years or so government at all levels has promoted the development of science parks, innovation parks, business incubators and various kinds of themed business parks (digital clusters, media villages, and so on). These provide space to rent plus some shared facilities. Usually, they are on the edge of town and require commuting to get there. Except in really hot areas (such as hi-tech and biotech parks around Cambridge) many of these are struggling, if they have not become white elephants already. At the end of the day, those running them have spaces to rent, and ideals to create innovation hotbeds give way to just filling the space with whoever can be found to pay the rent.

There is no need to build any more of these. The ones we have will be sufficient for many years. And in terms of overall business support, their impact has arguably been negative. Support gets focused on a very small number of very visible companies at the science park, while the majority of businesses have been operating unsupported, 'under the radar' of government awareness (Dwelly et al. 2005). Those that succeed mostly do so in spite of, rather than because of, government activity.

Over the past 50 years or so, government regulation has acted to inhibit the growth of home-based businesses. All kinds of regulation in principle restricts domestic enterprise: planning and business rates in particular. Until recently, social landlords, including council housing, had a blanket ban on their tenants working from home. The good thing about most of this regulation is that it has been largely ignored by home-based entrepreneurs, and probably most of it is unenforceable.

The new approach to business growth needs to start with new attitudes:

- Home-based enterprise is good.
- Community-based enterprise is good.
- We need to do all we can to encourage these, and only intervene if operating a business causes a local nuisance.
- Microbusinesses are good – they do not need to grow into corporate giants to be valuable.
- A network of microbusinesses can be as or more valuable economically than a few larger businesses with employees.
- Businesses that wish to grow turnover but not take on premises and additional staff are still valuable contributors to the economy.
- Part-time, lifestyle and 'sunset' businesses should also be welcomed and encouraged.

Most microbusinesses act on a larger stage through networking and collaboration, not through employing more people. This is just as valuable as employing people. A network of 12 freelance associates is just as valuable as a company with 12 employees – probably more so as it will probably be a more dynamic arrangement in terms of creating new business opportunities and spin-off value to support services (accountants, IT and telecoms providers, and so on).

These new kinds of less resource-intensive businesses contribute to 'Smart Economic Growth'. Smart Economic Growth is about using Smart Flexibility ways of working and smarter land use to support continued growth, while at the same time improving the quality of life and the environment (SEG 2009).

The one thing the new types of business do not want is overbearing fixed property costs, and this brings us back to the need for local flexible workspace, or workhubs.

There is a *convergence of interest* here between the needs of local home-based and microbusinesses and the needs of smarter government. Both need more in the way of flexible workspace. For small property-less business it is the need for touch-down space and collaboration space, a place to drop in to when working at home is impractical or when out and about between meetings, and to meet colleagues and clients.

For local government, it is much the same. The difference is that local government employees are part of a larger entity, and their use of a local workhub may need to be on different terms. They may also want part of the space for confidential meetings, or with a visible front-of-house as the delivery point for local services.

Such a combined approach, with government sector as anchor 'tenants' using the workhub, may help to provide the financial security for workhubs to run as a business in areas where building up the client base of home-based businesses may take longer, for example, in more dispersed rural areas.

By doing this, government can cut the cost of its working practices while at the same time enhancing its local delivery of services. And in the process, supporting local business growth.

Planning and the New World of Work

The planning system that emerged in the UK in the twentieth century is based around the separation of different land uses. Policies and planning decisions have created and reinforced in particular the separation of work and home.

In the Industrial Age, when much work was dirty, smelly, toxic, dangerous or noisy, this is understandable. But in an age when most work is clean and quiet and large parts of it can be carried out anywhere and anytime without causing a nuisance, the old planning assumptions and policies need to be relegated to the waste-paper basket of history.

We have a world where most new homes are built without adequate space to work in, and where hundreds of houses are built in new communities that have no local services or local workspace. Commuting is the only option for most people, and those people who do work from home have no nearby facilities.

When drawing up local planning documents, planners designate large areas of land as 'employment sites', and vigorously protect them from being used for other purposes. In these planning documents, assumptions are built in about the number of jobs these designated areas of employment land will support. These assumptions are now way, way out of date in the Information Age.

Offices with Smart Flexibility working arrangements will be more intensively used than the numerical assumptions expect – but these are likely to be in central business districts, rather than the industrial land designated as employment sites. Factories, warehousing and distribution centres these days employ far fewer people than in the last century, due to automation and just-in-time processes. The fact is, that if many of these employment sites were used for live/work accommodation – spaces designed for both living and working – the small businesses located there would probably generate more jobs than would more industrial uses.

In the planning system, the big growth sectors of health and education are treated differently from the industrial and business jobs that are eligible for location on employment sites, even though such uses may create more sustainable employment. The whole process of allocating land use is riddled with archaic ideas and practices that tend to ignore how the real world of work has changed and is continuing to change.

Poor planning causes both blight on the one hand and inflated land values on the other where supply of land to meet demand is artificially constricted. It also enforces situations where work premises are built in locations away from where people work, and which are left unused for most of the time (that is, those times outside 8 a.m. to 6 p.m. Monday to Friday).

To counter this, the government has encouraged more 'mixed use' development, trying to locate houses closer to work, retail and leisure facilities. This may be a step in the right direction. However, the concept is one of *adjacent* uses rather than genuinely mixed uses, integrated in the same premises.

There has been some encouraging wording in national and regional planning policies in recent years, and some local authorities have local policies to guide and regulate integrated work and business use. But several local authorities have introduced policies to oppose live/work homes and even (as in the case of Hackney Council in London), to take away live/work permissions. Other local authorities have bizarre restrictions on live/work, for example, saying that it should be for individuals or childless couples only. Most try to restrict the business use of live/work to office work or a studio for artists and craft workers. Old ways of thinking prevail.

Back in Victorian times, if you wanted to turn your front room into a small shop or workshop, you would just do it, knocking out the front wall to make a shop front, perhaps. Are there compelling reasons for not dropping most of the industrial-age restrictions that were brought in and allowing much greater mixes of use? How radical could we be?

There could be great gains both for enterprise and for sustainability, as we will see in the next chapter.

New Ways of Interacting with Government

Most governments in the developed world are in the process of embracing new ways for citizens and businesses to interact with government and indeed the public sector as a whole. I have been applying for my vehicle licensing tax disc online for several years now, and submitting VAT returns online as the e-services move beyond the informational to transactional. There are all kinds of things you can do through web processes as well as interact with officials and politicians by email. A number of countries, though not yet the UK, have online voting too.

Most government agencies have been consolidating telephony interaction into contact centre processes, behind which are back-end systems that should make it easier to capture information and requests from citizens and extract the appropriate responses. There is good and bad practice in this respect, but the interesting issue in a book about modern flexible working is that these new ways of interacting ought to be challenging the 'where' and 'when' of government working more than they are.

Some serious thinking needs to be undertaken about where and when the work takes place, as the choices are much greater than they used to be. Not many councils or government departments are following the examples of utilities, telephone companies, and telephone banking in offering telephone contact and web-chat interaction way beyond the nine-to-five. Is there a good reason why not?

One good thing about the gradual roll-out of e-services, though, is the reduction of a requirement for people to queue up as supplicants at the municipal offices. How can this change be built upon in terms of Smart Flexibility? Some obvious ways are with:

- Video interaction from (customer's) home – it would be very helpful to see the person you are dealing with in terms of getting a feel for personal service.
- Video interaction from a local centre: and in the new age probably not a council-owned local centre but a workhub, or even a local store.
- Using web collaboration to go through form-filling processes and to explain procedures.
- Meeting with officers when they take up (temporary) residence at a local workhub or even a local cafe.

And for the first three of these ideas above, where should the government worker be located? The answer is as per the first Smart Flexibility principle: 'wherever is most effective to get the work done'. Having all these electronic processes in place and then expecting staff to commute into a central location every day is nonsensical. So they may work from the central office (assuming there still is one), from the nearest public sector office, a local workhub or other 'third space', or from home. It's a question of having the right systems and protocols in place to enable the employee to make a mature choice.

And a side-effect of this will be relocating government officials and their work back into the local community, but without a massive property overhead. Over time, I would expect this, along with the growth of other locally based businesses, to transform the way we think about and interact with government.

One Foot in the Future

Now it's time to pull together the two strands of this section on Smart Government. First we have, as our case studies show, some clear momentum and good examples of Smart Flexibility emerging in government working practices. The focus on making savings is giving a strong impetus from the property side. There's some good thinking around too, about how we need to start thinking not only about the physical workplace, but the workplace as both a physical and virtual working environment.

The danger is that those organisations focus on delivering great workplaces will find themselves behind the times already just five years down the road, as the possibilities shift increasingly towards virtual collaboration.

Secondly, we have the wider changes that are happening in society and the need to modernise policy in line with the opportunities that arise from everyone being able to be more flexible.

I feel these ideas are still too much on the margins of public policy thinking. There needs to be much more intensive exploration of the opportunities, and what it means for how government and society work and interact.

At the moment we have one foot in the future. That future is going to one of much more blurred boundaries, and between home and (government) workplace, local and central, private and public, with spaces shared much more by multiple organisations, and infrastructure that works both for business and for government.

It's not time to sit on any property reduction and 8:10 desk-sharing laurels, but to engage positively with opportunities for delivering more with less, and use techniques of Smart Flexibility to enjoy a closer and more accessible relationship with citizens and with partners, and to make government an integral partner in new forms of smart economic growth.

13 Smart Flexibility and Sustainability

In this chapter I will be taking you beyond 'motherhood and apple pie' statements about the environmental benefits of Smart Flexibility. My aim is to offer a practical approach where decisions can be taken that will integrate sustainability benefits into decisions about changing the way your organisation works. It's not rocket science: just a question of taking decisions with a conscious awareness of the impacts, and encouraging maximal uptake of options that reduce energy and resource consumption from our working practices.

Beyond that, in the later part of the chapter, I will offer some thoughts on the wider impacts on work and society, and how the new ways of working can be leveraged to create a more sustainable world.

Smart Flexibility and Sustainability – the Theory

Back in Chapter 2 I said that the environmental benefits of smarter working come in three main areas:

- Reducing the amount of work space needed by each worker, and therefore resources required to build and service this space. Aggregated, this means over time a reduced requirement for society to build more offices.
- Reducing the amount of travel of each worker – both commuting travel and business travel.
- 'Dematerialising' processes and products – doing things electronically rather than physically.

In Chapter 6 we looked in detail at the potential for reducing space, travel and paper. The question is – by how much? In the following sections I will attempt to put some numbers on what can be achieved, and examine the factors that make a difference.

Environmental Savings from Property Reduction

What evidence is there that flexible working (a) reduces property requirements and (b) produces an overall net saving when the impact of alternative work locations are taken into account?

On the first point, there can be no doubt. Throughout this book there are examples of organisations that have made property savings through implementing new ways of working. Essentially this operates at three levels:

1. Implementing desk-sharing and increasing internal mobility with activity-based (rather than individually assigned) work settings. A 20 per cent space saving is quite achievable without any additional move to towards Smart Flexibility.
2. Having a positive but reactive approach to a basket of flexible working measures, as well as desk-sharing. A 30 per cent property saving should be achievable.
3. Having a strategic approach to smarter working, including an aim to maximise property rationalisation. Clearly it depends on your starting point and your ambition, but reductions of 50 per cent or more should be in order. For small and especially micro businesses, the right option may be to dispense with fixed office premises altogether.

But how does this translate into resources and energy savings?

The Environmental Impacts of Office Working ...

The typical carbon footprint per office worker from their office working ranges between 1.5 tonnes and 4 tonnes of CO2 per year, a finding both by James (2008) and Goodall (2007). This does not include transport energy from car commuting, which in the UK is around 1.2 tonnes CO2 per year, based on average commuting distances.

The average space that a worker occupies varies considerably. Recent surveys show variations between 9 m² and 22 m² per worker (calculated by dividing the net usable area by the number of people who work there). A survey by the Royal Institute of Chartered Surveyors (RICS 2008) suggests an average of around 14 m² per person.

Running an office consumes a lot of energy – heating, lighting, air conditioning, ventilation, and power for all the other services such as IT and telecommunications, lifts, kitchens, printing, hand-drying, cleaning, and so on.

And for the office building and all the building services *just to be there* also requires a huge input of energy and resources – a massive initial investment borne by the landlord and developer in the construction, fit out and transportation of materials that add to the whole-life environmental costs of the office. Having fewer offices is better for the environment, so long as the occupants are not simply displaced into alternative and equally environmentally unfriendly accommodation.

... Compared with the Environmental Impacts of Homeworking

The environmental impacts of home-based working has been the subject of considerable research in recent years. Most of the research has focused on the transport impacts, but there is a developing field looking at the total energy costs of homeworking as compared to working in an office separate from the home. Though individual circumstances will vary, the overall findings show a significantly lower environmental footprint for homeworking (for example, Lake and Cherrett 2002, Cairns et al. 2005, Banister et al. 2007, James 2008).

Table 13.1 Carbon cost of offices and home offices per person

Building type	(kwh/m²)	CO$_2$/m²	@ 10m² per person	@ 14m² per person
Office – naturally ventilated, cellular (2003 average)	205	103	1030	1447
Office – naturally ventilated, open plan (2003 average)	236	119	1190	1665
Office – air conditioned, standard (2005 average)	404	203	2030	2850
Office – air conditioned, prestige (2005 average)	568	286	2860	4004
Dwelling (UK 2005 average, all stock)	261–368	132–186	1320–1860	1841–2597
Dwelling (built to 1998 Building Regs)	128–216	65–109	650–1524	903–1524
Dwelling (built to 2005 Building Regs)	75–124	38–63	380–630	532–875

Source: James 2009, adapted.

Although of course there is a great variety in building stock both for homes and for offices, the carbon footprint per square metre of homes is significantly less than for offices. Only when you compare a poorly performing house with the best performing offices does the home fare comparatively worse. So a homeworker may consume more energy if they move out of an eco-office and work from a draughty cottage in the Highlands, but in a typical move to home-working the opposite will be the case. The table above shows indicative energy consumption in different kinds of homes and offices.

Somehow it seems counter-intuitive that shifting people out of a single building to go and work at home (that is, multiple buildings) reduces the carbon footprint of work. People do expect that the additional home consumption of energy will cancel out any savings back at the office. Often people ask for – and sometimes receive – financial compensation for taking this on.

While people are often concerned that working at home will cost them a lot in additional energy costs, the reality is perhaps reflected in the maximum non-taxable allowance set out by tax authorities that employers can pay to home-working staff. In 2012 this stands at £3 per week (£156 per year). This isn't just HM Treasury being mean – it has some basis in actual usage.

A study back in the 1990s (Wright 1997) identified reasons why offices do not usually deliver the expected economies of scale in terms of energy usage. It's because of the tendency to have 'everything on'. Large buildings are heated and lit from before most workers arrive until after most have left. All the systems – air conditioning, printers, computers and so on are all on even when people are not present at their desks. This tends not to happen in the home office.

Ten years later the finding is supported by another study by David Banister at the Transport Studies Unit of Oxford University (Banister 2007). Analysing data to find a 'full costings approach', Banister calculates that a room at home used for working with a computer and telephone has a carbon cost of 865 kg CO2 per year (based on 5 days per week working at home). That is around half the carbon cost of a space in the office – 58 per cent in the case of a better performing office. Of course the *saving is only realised if there are consequent reductions in office space*. At one day per week Banister finds the CO2 reduction negligible – but it depends how many people are doing it.

That homeworking typically has half the carbon cost of office working is an interesting finding. And that is before factoring in transport energy saved. For a typical commuting roundtrip in the UK it is 5.43 kg CO2 per day, which translates to around 1,200 kg when working a five-day working week over the year.

For the average case, then, around two-thirds of the energy savings from homeworking are in terms of transport energy. So even when the home office does not perform as well as the office, there are still overall net savings.

The calculations here are based on a move to full-time homeworking from a traditional kind of working, with assigned 1:1 desks. The real opportunity for the employer once people spend more time out of the office is to reduce the amount of property overall, and optimise it for the new working styles. At a simple level, if today 1,000 employees occupy 14,000 m^2 of office space, and tomorrow 2,000 occupy the same space, the space per worker supported has reduced from an average 14 m^2 to 7 m^2, and the carbon cost per worker would seem to be halved.

In fact, the effects are more complex. In the building that is occupied by double the number of workers, the overall energy requirements of that space have increased, as it is being more intensively used. Although not everyone will be there at the same time, average occupancy will probably have increased from below 50 per cent to over 70 per cent, putting extra demand on the IT and building services. But on the other hand, there will be a massive energy saving from having given up the other office space that the additional 1,000 employees used to be based in.

Meanwhile, some of the energy consumption and costs have been displaced to the other locations at which staff are working – home, coffee shops, and so on.

In a study under the umbrella of Smart 2020, BT has been measuring the carbon impacts of homeworking in the organisation, with smart meters installed in the homes of 30 home-workers. The net annual saving per home-based employee is 1.4 tonnes of CO2 as a result of reduced commuting-travel emissions (primarily) and reduced office energy use, counting in an increase in home energy use (Smart 2020 2009). Our estimate based on the Banister study would be in the region of 1.8 tonnes per home-based worker (1.2 tonnes from transport plus 6.3 tonnes from reduced office energy). So I think we are homing in on a credible ball park figure for what is achievable in terms of raw energy savings before factoring in energy use in third-party workplaces and some of the more complicated rebound effects, which we'll take a look at later in the chapter.

A Note on the Impact of Work Hubs and Other Third-Party Spaces

One of the alternative places where people can go to work is the local workhub, if one is available. In Chapter 6 we looked at the nature and role of this growing phenomenon. But what is the environmental impact of using a workhub – the 'office as needed'?

Clearly there is an environmental cost to using any workspace, and something to be factored into any overall calculation of the environmental impact of work. And as the location of work becomes more variable and complex, so do the possible impacts. Take the following scenarios:

- Someone who is already a full-time home-based worker now uses a workhub that has opened in the area a few times per month. The environmental footprint of their . work increases (that is, increased transport energy, energy use at workhub, offset by reduced energy at home office).
- Someone running a small business has for some time wanted to work from home, but has felt the need for having premises available for customer and colleague meetings as a reason for keeping an office. Now membership of a workhub for all the employees means that home-based working is possible. The environmental footprint of work goes down considerably (that is, office energy costs and transport energy go down, offset by home energy use, hub use and travel to hub).

The way we look at the impacts in these cases can be looked at as a kind of 'fortunately/ unfortunately' environmental story.

Fortunately, John kept the environmental footprint of his working practices low by working from home. *Unfortunately* (from John's carbon-reduction point of view, that is), a workhub opened in the area and he worked there on average three times per month. *Fortunately*, it was near enough to cycle to. *Unfortunately*, this was in England and as it rained most of the time (and there was sometimes a lot to carry), John usually drove there. *Fortunately*, John found the videoconferencing facilities there excellent, and began to reduce the number of physical meetings he travelled to. *Unfortunately*, this increased the number of times he used the workhub. *Fortunately*, the presence of a workhub meant that the total number of people working from home grew. *Unfortunately*, many organisations enabling their mobile staff to use the workhub carried on with otherwise traditional working practices, and had mixed benefits from using workhubs. *Fortunately*, the majority of organisations that embraced using the workhubs switched over to smart working practices, and radically cut both their buildings energy requirement and transport energy too.

And so on. In the snapshot study in Workhubs (Dwelly et al. 2010), the transport impacts reported (by an admittedly small sample of) home-based workers who used workhubs was generally positive. Most reported substantial reductions in their travel compared to when they had worked previously in a workplace separate from home. The distance to a workhub was on average around half the distance to the place they previously worked.

Furthermore, there was a greater likelihood that users of workhubs would walk or cycle to a workhub, compared to the national average for travel to work. The mix of home-based working and occasional walking or cycling to a local workspace makes for a very attractive proposition.

However, until there are more thorough studies it could be wise to sit on the fence with this one. This study looked at home-based businesses in particular, and how they are impacted by the new phenomenon of local workhubs.

Large organisations at the moment are more likely to buy into workhub-type or 'business lounge' services provided by organisations like Regus, which have locations all around the country and around the globe. These locations tend to be on business parks and in central business districts, and people touching down to work there (as opposed to their core clients who rent serviced offices) are for the most part mobile employees of companies who may well have a desk in a workplace somewhere else.

The savings in this case are probably more in terms of business travel – being able to touch down and work somewhere between meetings rather than returning to base. These types of facilities may be many miles from the worker's home and/or office. However, the business case for using the Regus-type solution is strongly connected with wider moves to Smart Flexibility: the costs of using these centres is in principle part of the investment in being able to radically reduce the company's property requirement overall. And when homeworking is introduced as part of the mix – as it is for Regus' own staff – then both the environmental and financial savings can really start to stack up.

It is worth noting that workhubs themselves ought to be first class examples of flexible working environments. They will have many more members than work positions, on the basis that members will use the facilities on an occasional basis. So a hub that has, say, 30 work positions for 300 members is operating an effective 1:10 desk ratio. Commercially, they will aim for the highest ratio possible that is consistent with not deterring customers by reason of being too often full. This is good news on the environmental front.

To be able to calculate the overall environmental footprint of work when work takes place in so many different locations, it is necessary to think on the basis of per capita carbon footprint rather than in terms of area or building. Understanding the carbon footprint per square metre is a first step, but then this has to be related to the number of people that the building serves, and the time that individual workers spend there.

The Environmental Impacts of Time-Based Forms of Flexible Working

I've made the point elsewhere that all temporal forms of flexible working have spatial impacts. When you flex the times of work, you also affect how space is used and the impacts of movements between spaces. Let's take a look at this in practice.

Example 1. Someone changes their pattern of work from a regular 9–5 to start at 10 a.m., and leave at 6 p.m. Their motivation is:

a) To miss the worst of the morning and evening rush hour;
b) To be available to take their child to school; and
c) From a work point of view, as a manager they want to have a clear time after most of the staff have gone home to get on with work uninterrupted.

What are the impacts of this? Spatially, it gives a chance to use the office more effectively after 4 p.m. when occupancy declines rapidly. The office is being used differently – this is the basic spatial impact. The environmental impact may be minimal in the case of one person making the change. But if by shifting the times of people's work the spikes in occupation can be levelled out, and set against a background of reduced overall office provision, the cumulative impacts will be significant.

Travel to work will also be different. By creating a clearer journey, it reduces the time and energy used, with less time in congested traffic.

Example 2. Instead of relatively minor adjustments to working hours, our worker moves to compressed working hours. Now all the week's working hours take place in 4 longer working days. The spatial impact back at the office is similar to working from home one day per week – there's one whole day when someone is not there. But it's not exactly the same. If a significant number of people move to this pattern, space will (in principle) be occupied for longer in the office than previously on any given day. As long as they are not all opting for the same day out of the office (Friday or Monday are favourites!) then demand can be managed to increase overall occupancy rates.

And the non-work day for the individual is a day with no work travel at all, so 20 per cent of the weekly 'carbon bill' for commuting is saved. Arguably that may be offset by some additional non-work travel (see below on rebound effects) – but we are talking here in the first instance about the environmental impacts of work. And it's the company's responsibility to deal with that.

Changing Behaviours Can Achieve More Than Changing Buildings

There are three ways to reduce the environmental costs of office work:

- Engineering solutions – changing the way the office building itself, building services and IT are designed and function.
- Organisational change – providing less space per person, and moving to shared space solutions.
- Behavioural and cultural changes – getting people to work in new ways, and in new locations.

The environmental literature focuses almost exclusively on the first of these. Smart Flexibility encompasses the second and third, and is at least as important as physical changes in reducing the carbon footprint of work.

Where environmentalists do focus on behaviour change, it tends to be around issues like recycling or catching buses and cycling to work. While these are valuable, to me they seem to tinker on the edges of unsustainable work practices rather than addressing the fundamental issues of why traditional working practices have such a high environmental footprint.

Applying the practices outlined in this book to reduce property, reduce travel, reduce the number of physical meetings, reduce resource consumption and dematerialise processes and products are the key ingredients of making work more sustainable. Against the new framework of work that this creates, we can green the reduced platform of work with eco-offices, green IT, more sustainable travel modes and increased recycling. But the key is to have a much reduced resource-base to green in the first place.

Reducing Travel – Business Travel

Reducing business travel depends not only on technological change, but changed culture and behaviours as well.

CULTURAL CHANGE

It's important to stress at the outset that it's not the case that all business travel is bad. This is a point where a Smart Flexibility approach to environmental benefit will differ from the approach of someone who is purely interested in environmental outcomes. For Smart Flexibility to be successful, it has to deliver business benefits. It can't adopt the approach of a moralist or a zealot. Travel is necessary to succeed in business, especially if you are sourcing and selling.

All the same, not all (physical) travel is equally necessary. The trick, the smart part, if you like, is to know which travel is essential and which is less essential now that we have effective substitutes for travel. It is typically cultural, rather than technological, factors that make us slow on the uptake about this.

I once suggested in Telecommuting 2000 (HOP Associates 1998) that every car should be fitted with a device so that when you opened the driver door it asked: 'Is your journey *really* necessary?' No doubt this would be *really* irritating, and prompt a cottage industry in disabling it. However, by getting us to think about our travel behaviours, it might do more than any public information campaign could.

Some companies do a similar thing when, in times of crisis, they impose a travel freeze. When this happens, any decision for business travel has to be actively justified. And often useful travel can be blocked in an indiscriminate or panicky freeze.

So stage 1 is deciding what kind of travel remains essential, and what kind can be replaced by virtual mobility or some other substitute activity. There is a fair amount of academic and commercial literature about how to make meetings more effective, and on the productivity of meetings and impacts on information flow (and so on) – but much of this perhaps misses a fairly basic point. Most people, especially managers, are up to their ears in meetings, and few people regard time spent in meetings as more than 50 per cent productive. So, in many cases, the best meetings are the ones that don't happen.

Travelling to pointless meetings is doubly unproductive. Funnily enough, though, the 'face time' with colleagues en route or the chance to catch up on work if you're a passenger may often be more worthwhile than the meeting you're going to. Just a shame you have to be travelling to a pointless meeting to find these benefits!

So getting behind what's going on in meetings and what the meetings are intended for is important for deciding what is essential and what is not.

In Table 13.2 on the next page, the main purposes of meetings are set out. The list is adaptable, but I would venture that in fact most types of meetings can be slotted into one or other of these categories. A training exercise could get people to come up with their own list. And in the following columns are potential answers to the question 'How much should meetings be conducted physically face to face?'

In your company, you could start by asking 'How often are meetings for this purpose face to face at the moment?' This is the kind of exercise to engender lively discussion and debate that will highlight the existing culture and different assumptions and prejudices.

The second step is to run through the exercise again and ask whether, using the range of new technologies – email, audio conferencing, videoconferencing, web conferencing, instant messaging, e-learning, and so on – it is possible to reduce the frequency with which these meetings are held on a face-to-face basis. This would be displayed in the table as a movement of ticks from the left to the right. And the final column is for suggestions

Table 13.2 How much should meetings be physically face to face?

Meeting purpose	Always/mostly	Sometimes	Rarely	Never	Alternative?
First meetings					
Selling					
Customer support					
Setting strategy					
Making key decisions					
Consultation					
Project review/updates					
Brainstorming					
Presentations					
Team work					
Team-building					
Appraisal					
Training					
Key underlying activities					
Exchanging information/reporting					
Decision-making					
Socialising/developing relationships					
Learning					
Monitoring performance					

of what alternative technologies or methods would do the job just as well, or sufficiently well, or even possibly better.

At the bottom of the table are some key underlying activities that go on in meetings. While a meeting will have an up-front purpose, there are underlying activities that are valuable, but may be better or worse served by being part of the meeting format.

For example, a meeting may be held to take some key decisions, but what actually happens is a process of information sharing and questioning which results in further meetings. Is there a big chunk of this that can be done by email and a few phone calls or audio conference? I would expect so. Properly managed, this new approach can mean that people are better informed before making decisions, and that the eventual process of decision-making is altogether sharper and shorter.

People often have a very jaundiced view of regular team meetings. They mostly cover what people already know, but there is a bit of learning that goes on, especially for new team members, and the occasional coffee and cakes before or the pub lunch after are valued for social reasons and opportunities to network informally. Identifying what is actually valuable in the meeting could lead to a different approach, with a focus on the face-to-face for its social aspects, and reducing the less valuable time accordingly.

Can this approach be taken with external meetings and relationships too? To me, the answer is obviously yes. We are all familiar with selling approaches that insist on face time and pressing the flesh, 'it takes seven meaningful contacts to make a sale', and all that. And it may be true to some extent, in some fields. But in an increasingly globalised world with customers far and wide, other methods are routinely used. For building an initial relationship, meeting in person has huge value, although this is often a second or third step in building a relationship rather than the first. However, in a world of telephone and Internet selling, with relationships built using social media too, these personal meetings may be becoming increasingly cost-ineffective compared to other ways.

So it's always worth 'Challenging the Assumption of Necessity'. The results of past performance are not necessarily a guide to future performance, as the financial services salesmen always tell us. Especially in a changing, and smarter, world.

Meetings, as we know them, as well as being physical events, are also social and psychological constructs. Our experience of them and our status within them suggest a limited set of 'action possibilities' for us. These limitations are also often reinforced by formal processes such as agendas, chairing formalities and minuting, and even by well-meaning guidance on 'how to conduct effective meetings'.

One effect of taking meetings out of the meeting room and breaking up its components over different media is that other dynamics and other action possibilities may emerge, for example, flattening of hierarchies, more interactive presentations, new decision-making processes, more careful consideration of minority viewpoints rather than domination/domineering by authority figures or the loudest voice.

Can you set targets for this? I think you can. Why not set a target of reducing the number of physical meetings by 50 per cent over a set period of time – two years at most?

TECHNOLOGICAL CHANGE

I would hazard that 20 per cent of meeting time could instantly be eliminated by the kind of culture change approach I've just outlined. More, if your company is particularly dedicated to the task. In the public sector, with its intensive and ubiquitous meetings culture, I would say this should be doubled. The inability to take clear decisions at the appropriate level is crippling for public sector efficiency, and generates swathes of time blocked out for additional meetings to revisit ground that's already been covered many times over. But it's so ingrained in the nature of the beast, I would not be too optimistic that it can be achieved.

Beyond that first 20 per cent of waste-elimination, it's about being productive in different ways. And here are some examples of travel reduction through carrying out meetings using new technologies:

- The UK Department for International Development (DfID) introduced video conferencing with the specific aim of reducing air travel. An independent study found that their videoconferences eliminated 2 million air miles per year and generated savings of £700,000 in costs and 230 tonnes of CO_2 emissions (DfID 2007, James 2007).
- A study by the same team found that audio conferencing at BT eliminated 338,600 trips in per year, saving 1.5 million return journeys over the year and an average 288 miles and 40 kg of CO_2 per call (all participants), leading to £81 million of avoided costs and £54 million of time benefits, and 54,000 tonnes of CO_2 emissions avoided (James 2010).

- Deutsche Telekom and its subsidiary T-Mobile calculated that 40,260 videoconferences between 2004 and 2007 saved 7,000 tonnes of CO_2, mainly from air travel, and 200,000 hours of people's time.
- Analysis of videoconferencing by the SusteIT project found that virtual meetings at the University of Swansea had an average of 9.7 people spread over three or four sites; 46 per cent said their last meeting had replaced a physical meeting. Of these, the virtual meeting avoided an average 206 miles travelled at an average cost of £83 (James 2010).

Most of the measured examples in case studies focus on the use of more high-end conferencing, with the exception of the BT study here. In the next few years there will be a range of solutions coming on to the market that will make instant remote meetings, with or without video, the kind of activity that we no longer give a second thought.

Increase Positive Contact by Reducing Meetings

Though it's somewhat counter-intuitive, I have found in my own working life that reducing the number of meetings can in fact increase and improve positive contact with clients and partners. What I mean by this is that in the pre-Internet age, working on projects would include periodic meetings where plans are made and where deliverables – pause for fanfare: ta-dah! – are unveiled to a hopefully appreciative audience (sometimes with a bit of smoke and mirrors at prototype stage). Feedback is noted, and off you go again to carry on to the next deliverable.

We made a feature of our approach to involve clients much more closely in the development process as projects proceed. This involves making work-in-progress more available online, in secure project areas. And this is quite normal now for many companies.

It has two key advantages:

1. All parties are better informed, and can feed in their input on a continuous basis.
2. Physical meetings when they happen are much more valuable for making purposeful decisions and progress towards next steps.

The interesting thing is that technically, this is not at all hard to do. It's the cultural part that is challenging.

Reducing Travel – Commuting

I've already outlined above the savings that can be made in commuting, based on average travel distances. People who work from home or work a compressed working week save on average 17.4 miles every time they don't go into the office.

In fact, people who work full time will be saving more than this, as people with full-time jobs tend to travel further for work than people with part-time work. And people in senior roles travel further still. It's the travel cost/pay packet trade-off at work, a question of inconvenience and cost versus reward.

- Of the people working full time, 29 per cent have long journeys (defined as more than 60 minutes), compared with only 14 per cent of part-time workers.
- Of the people working in high-skill jobs, 36 per cent have long journeys, compared with only 12 per cent of those in low-skill jobs (ONS 2011).

And all the studies of early adoption of home-based working show that it is people with longer journeys who are most likely to find flexible working attractive, as we saw in Chapter 5 on selection for Smart Flexibility.

The kinds of mileage savings reported include:

- 90 miles saved per home-based call centre worker per week at the AA (Hopkinson et al. 2001).
- 43 per cent reduction of commute trips by teleworkers in the Greater Munich area (Glogger et al. 2008) and 19 per cent reduction of all household trips.
- Teleworkers working for the National Science Foundation in the USA save on average around 1,600 miles of commuting resulting in savings of 795 kg of CO_2 emissions per year (Olsen 2008).

In fact these kinds of savings have been reported consistently in both in-house evaluations and academic studies since the early 1990s. The savings ought now to be beyond question: the issue is how to maximise them and how to 'normalise' low carbon working practices.

The early stages of introducing flexible working, where managers and (senior) autonomous professionals work from home from time to time, will tend to show the largest per capita reduction of mileage and carbon. As lower grade workers do likewise, then the overall travel reductions will move towards the average.

From analysing smart working staff surveys, I've also observed another effect. This is that where large numbers of staff live close to the workplace, the option of splitting the day between home and the office becomes more popular and the number of days working full time from home reduces in popularity. This will erode most of the carbon-reduction effect of working from home, offset only by the benefit of travelling in less congested time. It may also impact on the amount of space that needs to be provided in the office, if those who do this expect to be provided with a regular desk rather than just touching down for a short while.

So while there may be some benefits to doing this, it needs to be addressed at a cultural level by challenging people's need to be in the office. And it can also be addressed from the sustainable transport angle. If they live close enough to travel in for part of the day, then walking, cycling and buses should be a more viable option.

Complex Effects

When looking at the impact of new ways of working on travel, it is usual to distinguish between commuting travel, which is the responsibility of the employee, and business travel which is under the control of the employer. It is a practical approach, and one that broadly reflects the way things are. But for some kinds of transport replacement activity, it can be difficult to tell the difference.

For example, if an employee comes to work and then has a videoconference, there is no doubt that it is business travel that is being replaced. However, say this person – Joanne in Figure 13.1 below – occasionally works from home, and usually does so on the day she visits Customer A. Starting from home, she travels less in total than if she starts from work. This reduces the business travel from 25 miles to 20 miles, and eliminates her commuting travel altogether.

Sometimes, though, she needs to bring in her colleague Jeff, and occasionally a colleague from their research centre in Toronto. The best way to bring all these together is via videoconference, which is at this stage only available from the workplace. This eliminates 25 miles of travelling for both her and Jeff, and in principle 3,500 miles for their Canadian colleague. But as she's gone in to the office, it has incurred 15 miles of commuting, so perhaps there is only a net saving of 10 miles for Joanne on this occasion. Or is it a net saving of only 5 miles, as she would normally have travelled to the meeting straight from home? And again, in the real world, if Joanne and Jeff had both travelled from the office to the customer's site, they would have travelled together – one trip to be accounted for rather than two.

When in time the company sets Joanne up for videoconferencing from home, she now saves 20 miles of business travel, compared with her usual car journey to customer A. Or is it 25 miles, which is the figure previously used to account for the trip from the

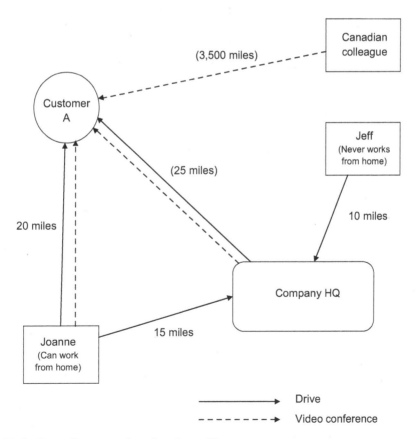

Figure 13.1 Complex travel reduction effects

office to the customer? If Joanne starts to work from home full time, then every trip to the office now becomes a business trip. So by videoconferencing from home, she is arguably saving both a trip to the office and a trip from the office to the customer.

There's a further consideration too. Some of the savings are notional rather than real. In reality, Joanne's Canadian colleague would not actually fly over for a physical meeting as often as he joins in videoconferences. Before videoconferencing, if the customer brought up an issue that needed his input, Joanne would have to make a note of it and call Canada later, then get back to the customer with a response. So his input from Canada via videoconference doesn't replace a flight on every occasion – in this case it's replacing a couple of telephone calls. But his availability instantly via video has a productivity bonus.

This is a small vignette of the impacts of conferencing technologies. They can, and should, be used strategically to reduce unnecessary travel. But they also transform the nature of other communications too. A telephone call, if you have the right service, can be transformed at the touch of a button into a multi-way audio conference. So if you want to count the number of miles replaced, you need to factor in some way of distinguishing between conferencing that actually replaces meetings, and conferencing that is really 'augmented telephony', that is, adding value to a call that would otherwise have been taking place, and in the process replacing multiple back-and-forth phone calls. That's efficient, but it doesn't necessarily take the miles off the road.

What is the moral of this story? Really it's to highlight the complexity of measuring the impacts, and perhaps a warning not to get too hung up on the detail. In the days when everyone came into the office, and travelled from there to meetings, then measuring the distances replaced was quite straightforward. Now, with people working all over the place, it's more tricky. And it's not going to get any easier.

However, the way forward is to have a mindset that focuses on every opportunity to reduce travel through Smart Flexibility. And this extends not only to the team as well, but beyond. Changes to behaviour at the individual level can be an influencer, and can influence not only colleagues but also customers and suppliers as they get used to new methods of interaction.

Do 'Rebound Effects' Cancel Out the Benefits?

In the academic transport research world there is a fair amount of concern about possible 'rebound' effects of virtual mobility. These are unintended side-effects of changing behaviours or modes of transport that lead to an increase in travel elsewhere in the system. This revolves around questions such as:

- To what extent will additional new trips be made by the flexible worker during the course of the day, or by other family members using the car now that it's available?
- How proportionately will transport substitution affect different traffic modes (for example, will regular public transport users become occasional car users if they work at home)?
- To what extent will latent demand be realised by other road users taking advantage of 'liberated' road space?

- Will work using ICTs in due course affect location decisions so that people will tend to live further from their places of work, and therefore make fewer but longer trips and possibly contribute to urban sprawl?

These are all sensible questions that are often voiced by sceptics in organisations who remain unconvinced by the environmental arguments. Measured (rather than speculative) studies almost always show significant net savings on travel, when other household trips are taken into account. A small number show *additional* household travel savings, reflecting a cultural change in the household about how they travel.

There is almost no evidence one way or the other about wider transport effects, though there is no lack of speculation. It's quite common to find academic studies that show clear measured savings, but then speculate on what rebound effects there might be. These speculations are often cited in other more general studies as evidence that there are limited savings or no clear benefits from flexible working practices, in particular telework (or telecommuting).

One line of speculation has been around whether people will tend to relocate further away from their workplace once they can work from home. This will lead to fewer but much longer commuting journeys. In recent years there have been a few studies that have started the process of settling this debate.

David Ory and Patricia Mokhtarian have analysed data collected from more than 200 State of California workers who telecommute over a 10-year period (Ory and Mokhtarian 2006). They found little evidence that the ability to telecommute is a significant factor in relocation. It is more often the case that telecommuting results from a move that happens for another reason. Comparison between telecommuters who had moved and non-telecommuters showed that overall they were not travelling further. And several telecommuters moved closer to their workplace during this time.

There have been similar findings in two further studies of a large dataset in the Netherlands covering variables relating to residential location (Muhammad et al. 2007, Ettema 2010). Telecommuting is not found to be a key factor in relocating: with respect to relocation probability, the modelled estimates 'for all commuters and for telecommuters only are remarkably similar, and telecommuting is not found to be a significant factor for relocation. This suggests that telecommuters are not more likely to relocate than regular commuters'. The ability to telecommute was not found to be central to relocation decisions: '… traditional factors like household type, number of children in the household, and especially the stages of life cycle still play a dominant role in residential locational preferences'.

One further interesting conclusion is that 'telecommuters cannot be treated as one uniform group, but instead show considerable heterogeneity'. Perhaps this should have been obvious to us all at the outset, as much as that the ability to work from home could theoretically increase commuting distance.

But a further observation about this relocation debate is that it is a bright shining example of 'thinking with your old head on'. Let's start to deconstruct the assumptions in the hypothesis that 'telecommuting' will lead to longer commuting journeys. The key assumption is that remote workers will still need an umbilical cord connecting them and nourishing them from one fixed, immutable place. New forms of organisation mean that that is not at all the case.

Organisations that have gone to a homeworking basis, like Ofsted or OAC, or location-independent/work-anywhere like Vodafone or BT effectively dissolve the ties with one particular office. Regular commuting trips disappear, meetings happen online or at the nearest hub or third-party space, and a trip to the 'main office' (if there is one) is now occasional and classed as business travel rather than commuting.

Travelling by Not Moving

The trouble with most approaches to 'sustainable transport' is that the experts are experts in *managing* physical mobility, rather than finding *alternatives* to physical mobility. They are overwhelmingly engineers, and focus on engineering solutions – public transport solutions, new kinds of infrastructure, less-polluting vehicles (electric cars, and so on) and passenger information systems. Worldwide, billions of dollars annually are poured into research, government initiatives and subsidies aimed at getting people to travel by different methods, with most of the effort directed at boosting public transport uptake.

In one sense it is a changed behaviour to travel by bus rather than by car. But in terms of carbon impacts, buses are about 75 per cent as polluting as cars per passenger km, and rail around 50 per cent (based on normal levels of occupancy). So these are not intrinsically environmentally friendly forms of transport. They are intensely polluting, but have the relative merit of not being as polluting as cars.

I look at it like this. In terms of the benefit, moving people from cars to public transport is like trying to move people from throwing their garbage in the river every day to only doing it three or four times a week. At a statistical level it might be an improvement, but it's not something you'd really hail as a great advance. And it's a touch misguided to make this kind of marginal shift in behaviour a central plank of environmental policy.

Moreover, those billions of dollars spent are really not making much of a difference to uptake. More than 80 per cent of people don't choose public transport, and their reasons are both practical and common sense. They choose to use cars because cars provide:

- Autonomy.
- Convenience.
- Comfort.
- Carrying capacity.
- Speed of reaching destination.
- Flexibility in combining trip purposes.

Generally speaking, the public transport alternatives cannot compete with these characteristics of cars. Buses and trains are collectivist solutions in an age where individualism is growing, and people want greater autonomy. They only compete in major urban centres like London where congestion makes driving comparatively less convenient, and the costs of driving are increased by high parking charges and road pricing.

Policy needs to respond to a sustainability hierarchy of:

- Lowest carbon modes:
  - Walking.
  - Cycling.

- Low carbon modes:
  - Virtual mobility, including homeworking/teleworking, teleconferencing, online shopping, e-services.
- High carbon modes:
  - Rail.
  - Bus.
  - Other public transport.
  - Car-sharing.
- Highest carbon:
  - Car: driving alone.
  - Plane.

The first of these groups, the lowest carbon modes, are those that replace motorised mobility with a non-motorised alternative.

The second virtual mobility group also replace mobility with a non-motorised alternative, but have a higher resource intensity than walking or cycling. E-shopping incorporates a motorised component on the delivery side, unless the product or service bought is a non-material one (for example, music, book or film download, software, insurance, online gaming, lottery ticket).

The third group are the collectivised motorised solutions. Their carbon impacts are variable, but outside large urban areas and inter-urban travel the mass transit options are rarely financially viable and, due to low occupancy, have a carbon cost that can be higher than a car with passengers.

Arguably electric vehicles could fit into this third group. Vehicles powered by fuels other than hydrocarbons cannot really be classed as low carbon, as there is so much embedded carbon in their production, distribution and maintenance.

The fourth group are the highest carbon modes, and are the modes where the use of virtual mobility has its highest value as an alternative. This is not only because of the carbon saved in any individual instance of travel substitution. It is also because the modes in groups 1 and 2 are not viable on most occasions to replace car trips and plane trips. Nor is virtual mobility able to replace trips on every occasion. But the difference is that good use of virtual mobility can reach many of the parts that buses, trains and bikes cannot reach. This is because with virtual mobility you don't try and replicate the trip by a different mode, but you try to achieve the *purposes* of the travel without having to travel.

Hence the term 'virtual mobility'. And virtual mobility does replicate some of the advantages of the car, in particular speed (instantaneous), convenience, comfort and autonomy.

The other massive advantage it has is scalability. The carbon costs of developing the infrastructure and rolling stock for public transport systems would take generations to claw back, not to mention the impacts on land-take and on public finances. Though additional broadband infrastructure will help, scaling up the impacts is not critically dependent in building more infrastructure.

So what I am arguing for here is to move virtual mobility up into a much more prominent position as a sustainable travel option. And if just a fraction of the spending on public transport support was spent on improving the broadband and telecoms infrastructure and on awareness-raising, I believe it could make a very big contribution to creating a more sustainable world.

Dovetailing with Travel Plans

Now I can step down from my soap-box, and follow the theme of the book by exploring how we can take virtual mobility from theory to practice.

The preceding chapters contained detailed advice about implementing Smart Flexibility, and virtual mobility is an added value component of this. However, organisations can go a bit further by explicitly promoting virtual mobility within company ('Green') Travel Plans.

In the first decade of the century most public sector organisations and a handful of larger private sector organisations have developed Travel Plans to promote sustainable travel amongst their staff. And a sizeable niche of consultancy organisations, public sector-funded campaigns, networks and academic projects has grown up to support this. The focus has been on getting people within a company to change their mode of travel, usually focusing on commute travel. Some companies have in fact made substantial achievements in driving down both commute travel and business travel.

Typical methods have been supporting 'quality bus' and other public transport initiatives, taking measures to encourage walking and cycling, promoting car-sharing and for business travel 'greening the fleet' and changing the way mileage is recompensed. Some Travel Plans also have some words around supporting flexible working, but without clear ideas on how to make this make a difference. To support changing to more sustainable travel modes, organisations typically undertake research and consultation to find out where employees live in relation to public transport provision, and consult staff to find out their preferences and the barriers and constraints they face. This is then used as a basis for developing infrastructure, service and facilities solutions (cycle lanes, new tailored bus services, car-sharing clubs, workplace showers for those who cycle, and so on). And it is also used as a basis for designing new information and awareness-raising programmes and solutions to promote the alternatives and make them easier to understand and use.

Some of the same techniques can be used to support Smart Flexibility solutions that actively promote virtual mobility. For example, the postcode plotting of employee home locations can also be used to identify the best locations for hubs and touch-down centres, whether they are owned by the company or by a third party.

Including preferences for flexible working in travel surveys can identify opportunities for reducing travel, for example via homeworking or a compressed working week. These have more impact in travel reduction than car-sharing clubs, for example. But in some areas a car-sharing scheme and homeworking may have benefits for each other. One of the current barriers for some people taking up homeworking is the inflexibility of public transport season tickets. There is no financial saving from working at home one or two days a week if you are a season-ticket holder. But being able to car-share on the other days when you do go into the main workplace would bring about a saving of thousands per year if you could abandon the season ticket altogether.

Travel Plans can also be one of the means of actively promoting the uptake of conferencing technologies. And it will be better still if people are encouraged to engage with targets for business and commuting travel reduction. The Travel Planning process can also be the means of monitoring and measuring the impacts of virtual mobility.

Some leading organisations are also using incentives to reduce travel – for example, giving staff a swipe card with a points credit. Points are deducted every time they use the car park, and at the end of the year remaining credit can be exchanged for cash, or additional days' holiday, or some other employee benefit. Flexible workers can also benefit from such a system, or adapted versions that reward working from home or a location closer to home.

There is scope to be imaginative and innovative. In any case, the aim is to link Smart Flexibility explicitly with reducing travel and, over time, to make this a psychological and cultural reflex.

Dematerialisation

Dematerialisation is an important concept in sustainable production and consumption. It is also a key principle within Smart Flexibility.

The concept is essentially about using less in the way of physical resources to do what you do. According to the United Nations Energy programme, it's about 'the reduction of total material and energy throughput of any product and service, and thus the limitation of its environmental impact'.

This has been going on around us for decades now. It's evident in the replacement of physical objects by downloads for music and film, the replacement of answerphones with voicemail services, the shrinking of newspaper circulation and the falling sale of books as they are available for download online. It's also evident in the high street where shops are closing as more is bought online. In this case the product may not be changing, but the physical infrastructure that mediated the purchases is being dematerialised. Services that provide products like insurance are now largely bought online, and a physical infrastructure of shops, local offices and door-to-door salesmen and collectors has dematerialised into history.

Similar dematerialisation is also what is happening with organisations that embrace Smart Flexibility. The shrinking of the office physical infrastructure and its substitution by a technology-enabled network of relationships is a dematerialisation of the office.

The main current challenge for many organisations is to dematerialise their paper resources. We explored this in some detail in Chapter 6. From the environmental point of view, the aim should be to dematerialise the methods of interacting with suppliers and customers, and all internal records and communications. Again, this is an area where targets can be set. Often, taking a baseline measurement of current consumption and expenditure on paper and printing is enough of a jolt to prompt action. Many organisations now record their paper reduction and other resource consumption achievements in their annual Corporate Social Responsibility report.

We have also been witnessing the partial dematerialisation of ICT resources too. With trends to convergence and miniaturisation, we have witnessed over the past 30 years a migration from big bulky boxes and separate devices to smaller portable devices that can multitask.

Over the next 5 to 10 years we will see the demise of the mouse and keyboard, which will largely be replaced by software for speech recognition and response and for sensing movement. We are probably only at the beginning of the changes that will transform the way we think about the 'stuff' we need for working.

Greening with ICT Rather Than Green ICT

Just as we noted that the mainstream environmental movement tends to focus on making offices environmentally friendly rather than completely rethinking the role of offices, the same is true of technical/engineering-focused approach to 'greening IT'. To be sure, there are significant savings to be made by adopting new and more efficient equipment, capturing the heat from servers to heat office buildings, and so forth. But there are even greater benefits to be achieved by 'greening with ICT'.

There's a great introduction to this in a report produced by the Worldwide Fund for Nature (Pamlin and Pahlman 2009). The authors look at the potential to reduce carbon emissions through changing IT and how we use it. They calculate that across the decade to 2020, 'greening IT' would provide 2 per cent and 'greening with IT' the remaining 98 per cent of the carbon savings that can be achieved. And the potential emissions reductions are enormous: around 50 million tonnes of CO_2 per year. Of this, earlier calculations indicate that 22.17 million tonnes could be saved by flexible workers and 2.1 million tonnes by audio conferencing to replace 20 per cent of business travel.

A recent report by the US-based Telework Research Network on the Bottom-Line Benefits of Telework (Lister and Harnish 2011) calculate that telework at 2.5 days per week for 30 per cent of the workforce would reduce greenhouse gasses by 6.2 million tonnes of CO_2 per year, equivalent to taking 2.5 million cars off the road in the UK.

Now, there are always questions about (a) the assumptions underlying the aggregation of the measured effects of savings to a national or international scale, and (b) the cumulative carbon impact of producing, distributing, using and disposing of all the ICT kit produced. This is an embryonic area of research, and it's well worth taking a look at these studies which have a credible methodology and decent baseline data for working up to aggregate effects.

Early indications from this new field are that the net benefits are substantial and are already contributing to achieving economic growth at a lower environmental cost. The question is more about how to maximise the benefits, rather than whether there are benefits.

At the practical level, the choice is about how to maximise one's own contribution to sustainable working practices, and how your organisation can do so.

Impacts on Families and Household Activities

Flexible working has long been associated been associated with family-friendliness and having greater work-life balance. Having the ability to have more control over your use of time and where you are located enables people to do things like take the children to school and pick them up, attend school events, accommodate medical appointments for the family, and so on.

There is a certain amount of evidence from measured studies that being able to work from home can lead to further alteration and rebalancing of activities. The SUSTEL project found evidence that home-based workers were more likely to become involved in community activities, and some evidence of shifts in household activities, for example, the teleworker taking on escort duties for the school run (SUSTEL 2004).

This is an area where we should not be surprised if we find that flexible workers become more tightly integrated in family life. In Chapter 11 on the dangers of isolation we explored the question of being disconnected from work colleagues and being reconnected to family and friends.

Impacts on Communities – Making Them More Sustainable?

Does this (potential) re-engagement or tighter integration with family life ripple through to the local community?

Many suburbs, market towns and villages across the western world suffer from being dormitory communities, with thousands of their inhabitants commuting out of the area for work and being rarely seen in their neighbourhoods during daylight hours. Some communities have seen the collapse of all the local services – shops, post office, pub – and the only option is to jump in a car to get access to services.

Smart Flexibility offers the potential to put some economic clout into the localism agenda, and help revitalise local communities. Here I pick up on some of the themes set out in the latter parts of the last chapter on Smart Government about economic development and changing the way we plan communities.

Over the past 15 years or so there has been much discussion about 'sustainable communities' and 'eco-settlements'. I have described these elsewhere as fig leaves covering the nakedness of business as usual (*Can Homeworking Save the Planet* at www. flexibility.co.uk/savetheplanet). It's actually worse than that, as the official Sustainable Communities programme of the last government was essentially about concreting over swathes of the English countryside. It was the odd bus route, better insulation and (rarely) some rainwater harvesting that threw a sop to making them 'eco' or 'sustainable'.

Government policy favoured high densities, as this is meant to help support public transport and locate more people within walking distance of local facilities – if there are any, that is. Until 2007 this was a goldmine for developers, who were encouraged to cram more homes into less space. Unfortunately, in many cases this has designed out the option to run a business from home, or even have a garden large enough to grow your own fruit and vegetables.

Despite this, and despite poor or non-existent broadband infrastructure in many new-built as well as existing rural communities, there has been a growth in home-based working. And there is evidence that flexible workers – both home-based workers and part-time workers – are more likely to spend their money locally, if there is anywhere to spend it.

We also found, during the Workhubs study, that well-located workhubs attracted local home-based businesses, with users much more inclined to arrive by foot or bike.

In the parlance of social geography, home-based workers tend to have 'contracted activity spaces'. In other words, they do more stuff nearer home. Or at least, their natural inclination is to do so – if only the opportunities are there to do so. I remember a few years back working on a project looking at the ageing society. We had a meeting at the home of the regional director of a national charity that was a partner in the project. As we were discussing working from home as a retirement option, she pointed from the window towards several of her neighbours where people worked from home, as both she and her husband did also. The problem was that planning rules prevented people running the kinds of businesses that could provide a service to the local community. So if you wanted a newspaper, any groceries, or pretty much anything at all there was no alternative but to get in your car.

But where there are more local facilities, people working from home tend to use them. A study of telecommuters involved in the State of California Telecommuting pilot found that on telecommute days around 30 per cent of activities (including shopping and leisure) are performed closer to home than on non-telework days, and that destinations on telecommuting days are more evenly distributed in all directions around the home, whereas a majority of destinations on commuting days are oriented toward the work location (Saxena and Mokhtarian 1997).

So the social and environmental context of flexible working can make a big difference to how sustainable it can be in terms of second order effects. It can reduce commuting and business travel as a direct result. But to maximise the social and environmental benefits in the wider world requires a whole batch of new thinking from developers, infrastructure providers and government agencies.

I look forward to a time when the Smart Flexibility approach is embedded within how we design and develop the communities we live in. These will be designed as essentially 'walkable' communities, with a range of flexible housing types including a good supply of live/work homes (that is, designed both for living and business uses), the freedom to change uses during the life course, local workhubs, most homes with gardens big enough to grow much of your own food, inclusive design throughout to be an enabling environment for people with disabilities and age-related conditions, local markets, zillion gigabit broadband infrastructure and all wrapped up in the highest standards for zero-carbon living.

In terms of taking this from theory to practice, I have to concede that achieving this is beyond the scope of most organisations as they implement Smart Flexibility. And it's certainly the subject of another book.

But there are factors embedded in this vision that may influence how far organisations wish to go in devising solutions to have a social and environmental sustainability impact. Table 13.3 sets out a range of impacts from different levels of (Smart) Flexibility.

So the ideal approach would be to encourage Smart Flexibility at a corporate level, with Virtual Home-based Businesses and Total Live/work to promote smart economic growth.

And I hope I live to see the day.

Metrics and Targets

So now it's time to narrow our gaze and home in again on how we can enable organisations to consider how they can, in a practical way, set targets and measurements to be more sustainable.

In looking for an overall account balance of the environmental impacts of flexible working, we encounter a complex set of interactions. To try to find a path through these, I put forward a conceptual model that I call the Environmental Equaliser, which can be

Table 13.3 Relative sustainability impacts of smart and flexible working options

	Building impacts	Commute travel impacts	Business travel impacts	Community impacts
Employee homeworking with no change to office provision (Dumb flexibility)	Increase in home energy use	Travel saving depending on number of days worked away from the office	May be savings by skipping initial trip to the office	Minor impact, depending on days worked at home
Employee remote working with office transformation and collaborative technologies (Smart Flexibility)	Increase in home energy use offset by reduction in office space per person	Travel saving depending on number of days worked away from the office	Potential for substantial reduction through use of conferencing and other collaborative technologies, plus ability to work from any site	Variable impact, depending on days worked at home and degree of virtuality of the company
Home-based business (Traditional HBB)	Higher than average home energy use, offset by absence of external office build costs and energy use	Major savings from absence of commute	No impact	Significant impact
Home-based business (Virtual HBB)	Higher than average home energy use, offset by absence of external office build costs and energy use	Major savings from absence of commute	Savings through high use of virtual technologies	Significant impact
Live/work scheme (Basic/No frills)	Higher than average home energy use, offset by absence of external office build costs and energy use	Major savings from absence of commute	No impact	Significant impact
Live/work, hubs and high virtuality (Total live/work)	Higher than average home energy use, offset by absence of external office build costs and energy use	Major savings from absence of commute – location of hub may impact transport savings + or –, and may increase uptake of home-working	Savings through high use of virtual technologies Savings through shared services and close access to more local businesses	Substantial impact

Source: Adapted from *Tomorrow's Property Today*, Dwelly et al. 2008.

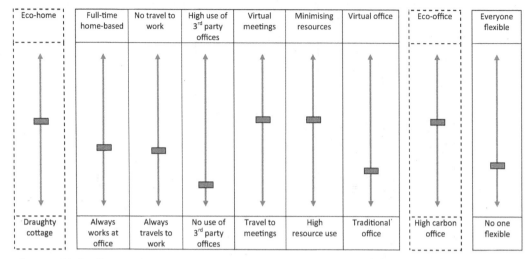

Figure 13.2 The Environmental Equaliser

portrayed on the lines of the old graphic equalisers that we all used to have on our hi-fis, back in the days when people used to care about the audio quality of their music.

So we have a set of sliding scales, some of which interact with each other, while others depend more on separate decision-making. Sliding the control towards the top of each scale has a positive environmental impact. But by sliding some to the top of the scale, for example, by using third-party offices or workhubs, could have the effect of sending the control downwards on the 'no travel to work' scale.

The overall impacts would also be affected by the relative sustainability of the home and office work locations, shown in dotted lines. And the final scale on the right has a multiplier effect to assess the overall sustainability of working practices.

Let's look at an example. Starting at an individual level, if someone works at home for a couple of days per week, this will have an impact on their travel to work, which at a basic level will reduce in proportion to the number of full days they don't go into the office. They may also use conferencing technologies to reduce travel. But if they have to go to a third-party office to use the technology, this will increase their work-related travel and also take the edge off their home-working capacity.

This kind of model can be used to stimulate discussion about how far the organisation has progressed in Smart Flexibility, and how far it aims to progress. How much does it want to shed real estate and embrace virtuality? How far does it want to go in dematerialising its resources and in reducing travel on all fronts?

It is possible to work this through and attach targets, in terms of numbers of people capable of working remotely, how much they should do it, use of collaboration technologies to reduce meetings and business travel, environmental performance of the office(s), and so forth. Organisations may wish to go a stage further, and work with employees to assess the environmental performance of home-working environments to set a comparator with the (residual and improved) main office. A responsible organisation might even want to incentivise and support the upgrade of the home environment as an employee benefit.

CHAPTER 14 *Smart Flexibility – Now and Into the Future*

The Story So Far

Up to this point in the book, we've covered:

- The trends that are the context for change.
- The particular business drivers for businesses to implement change.
- How to move from theory to practice in an integrated way, covering:
  - Developing an evidence-based business case.
  - People issues and culture change.
  - The platform for change: property, facilities and ICT both in the traditional office and beyond it.
  - Measured examples of benefits, and how to set targets.
  - How to integrate sustainability principles in a real and measured way.
  - Special considerations for the government sector.
- Some of the wider impacts and potential benefits for society.

On the way I hope I've provided some practical techniques to help both managers and other employees to understand what it's all about and how to make the transformation.

So now it's time to ask: where is your organisation on the path to Smart Flexibility?

The Smart Flexibility Maturity Model

There are thousands of companies, public sector bodies and third-sector organisations out there who are at different stages of the journey, and probably all of them coming at it from different angles and starting points.

So I hope it will be helpful to set out my thoughts for a Smart Flexibility Maturity Model (Figure 14.1 on the next page), so that you can see where it is that your organisation slots in, what progress you have made so far and what else might be needed to move to a position where flexibility is the new normal and the benefits can be maximised.

There are four stages in this Maturity Model.

ISOLATED INITIATIVES

The organisation has started to think about getting a bit more flexible, or allowing some limited flexible work practices. The examples on the left in Figure 14.1 are of typical early

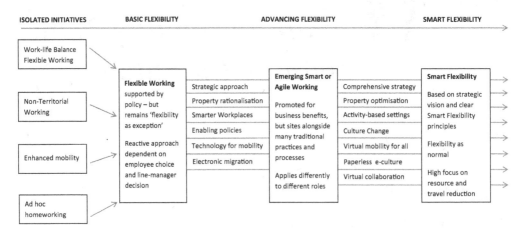

Figure 14.1 Smart Flexibility Maturity Model

initiatives or emerging practices. One would be a good set of work-life balance initiatives, with policies that include flexible working alongside other family-friendly measures (for example, paternity leave), but which don't go so far as to make flexible working a regular option for many people.

Or perhaps there's been some tightening up of space through desk-sharing, with the development of 'non-territorial working' to encourage the link to be broken between the individual and a personal desk. But the capacity for this has not been expanded by greater flexibility in working practices.

Or possibly – and maybe combined with limited desk-sharing – the most mobile workers have had their technology upgraded so they have some remote access capability, and can spend more time out of the office.

These kinds of initiatives, along with tolerance of occasional ad hoc home-working, can often sow the seeds of more integrated programmes by demonstrating some of the benefits.

BASIC FLEXIBILITY

This is where there are now policies and procedures in place that enable staff to apply for flexible working. It meets the statutory minimum, and goes beyond that to make options available for all staff. But there are various tests to be eligible, and line managers effectively exercise a veto. The result is that flexible working is applied reactively and unevenly across different departments in the organisation.

Really, in the twenty-first century this should be the minimum position, but I know many organisations are still more 'old school' and inflexible than this.

ADVANCING FLEXIBILITY

This is the stage that many progressive organisations are getting to now. It is a more strategic and business-focused approach, and is often referred to by those doing it as Smart Working or Agile Working. Sometimes this terminology is a deliberate attempt to avoid the preconceptions that some people have about 'flexible working' as being all about families and caring.

In the current climate it is often closely associated with property rationalisation and the higher levels of homeworking and mobile working needed to support it. It is also closely associated with a focus on improved customer service and improved productivity.

New smart or flexible working environments are introduced, with an emphasis on more collaboration areas and fewer desks. At the same time, there is still a strong focus on desk work and an emphasis on achieving specific desk to people ratios, typically 7:10 or 8:10.

Technologies have been significantly upgraded, with an emphasis on portable devices and remote access, but probably limited progress has been made on upgrading legacy systems and paper processes, and this acts as a constraint on flexibility.

The platform for Smart Flexibility has made significant progress, but probably the cultural side is more wished-for than delivered. Many managers and employees continue to think in traditional terms about work, so Smart Working still seems a novelty and something that applies much more to some roles than to others. This is sometimes reinforced by categorising work as fixed, flexible or mobile.

Typically at this level while logging in remotely to work grows fast, 'meetings cultures' remain unchallenged and there is comparatively little use made of conferencing and collaboration technologies as a normal way of working.

SMART FLEXIBILITY

This takes the 'Advancing Flexibility'/Smart Working/Agile Working stage to the next and more comprehensive level. The Smart Flexibility principles will be fully implemented, and particular investment and care has been given to transforming the culture of work. Flexibility is seen as available for all – in one form or another, and is seen as applying to tasks rather than whole jobs or roles. Desk-based work is seen as something that can for the most part happen anywhere, and the other activity-based work settings are more numerous and acquire increased importance.

The significance of the main office decreases, and becomes more equal as a venue for work alongside other spaces where people can work, both physical and online.

Enabling all this is a strong drive to have seamless electronic processes, use of cloud-based services, greater freedom in choice of ICT devices and extensive use of unified communications, conferencing technologies and social media applications.

There are strong targets for resource reduction and travel reduction, and meaningful targets are set for performance in all aspects across the Triple Bottom Line, at every level in the organisation.

Contractors, freelancers, interims, agency and other temporary workers as well as partner organisations are included as far as possible within the Smart Flexibility culture, and may be selected because of their own track record in being smart and flexible.

The impacts of Smart Flexibility spill over into wider social, environmental and economic benefits and have the potential to make a substantial contribution to 'smart economic growth' and to the quality of life.

These four stages form part of a continuum, with each stage building on the best elements of the previous stage. Connecting the latter three stages in Figure 13.2 are some of the key enablers or principles that define the difference between the stages. As you look through to see where your organisation has got to so far, it's possible that you're straddling a couple of stages. The main thing is to see that you're going in the right direction and not doing anything to entrench the half-measures of an earlier stage.

And What of the Future?

You may notice that our Maturity Model here doesn't end with stage 4: the arrows point forward to something beyond. The model of Smart Flexibility should contain an openness to future change and I hope that it can evolve to encompass the range of changes that one can see coming over the horizon, and even those you can just about see when standing on tiptoe.

And what are the trends and changes coming over the horizon that are likely to be making an impact over the next 10 years or so?

Let's jump forward 10 years to the year 2022. For the sake of nostalgia, you've plucked this book from the bookshelf, or reloaded it into your e-reader, and you are looking back on what has come to pass, and what the new challenges are.

Over the intervening years there's been a major increase in what this book calls 'Smart Flexibility', but is now just a normal way of working. Most organisations no longer seem to feel the need to concentrate their workforce together in one place. Home-based working is now commonplace for around 40 per cent of the workforce. Most self-employed people now work mainly at or from home, but the big breakthrough is in the number of employees who now do so.

There's been a big increase in the number of 'workhubs' – the third-party office providers providing ad hoc office space for home-based businesses and mobile employees. This has proved to be a somewhat volatile sector over the decade, with many new companies and new concepts coming and going – but the underlying trend is upward, as the market finds what and where works best.

All this has in turn had a big impact on (a) how we use space and (b) how we use time.

Office space – in fact any productive space – is now understood as a mixture of physical spaces and online spaces, with fluid boundaries between the personal/company/customer/outsourced/public/virtual elements of the mix. Managing activities and communications across these boundaries requires new kinds of skills, though many aspects of this are now automated.

The ability to work 'in' another country without having to spend large amounts of time there is intensifying many aspects of globalisation, as well as redefining commercial and contractual relationships, as people work across both organisational and national boundaries.

Immersive telepresence technologies, new 3D and holographic communications and remote manufacturing capabilities are adding new dimensions to how and where work is done. Many people work virtually co-located with continuously open communication channels.

For many the need to work internationally with minimal travel is leading to a restructuring of working time, which is necessarily more fluid. Working in (sometimes multiple) foreign time zones is also a driving factor for many people to work from home. Part-time work for many now means working in the middle of the night, virtually present in a foreign country, yet still being able to take the kids to school.

Despite the increasing affordability of the technologies, not all companies are buying in wholeheartedly to the new world of work. A minority are dragging their feet. But the world of work will not wait for those lagging behind. Next generation workplace innovations are creating a new momentum for change.

Big advances in artificial intelligence (AI) are starting to make significant inroads into business processes, into how work is managed and also into working practices. Smart Flexibility in 2022 involves new ways of interfacing with technologies, and these in turn will impact both on the workplace and on work relationships.

The most noticeable impact of AI in the workplace by 2017 was in speech recognition – people interfacing with computers through talking is much more common. Keyboards were already on their way out. The mouse is giving way to other pointing and sensing/tracking technologies. The RSI generation is being succeeded by a generation of workers who dialogue with their technologies through gestures and voice.

AI is also making big inroads in work and non-work environments with ever-increasing capabilities of ambient computing, bringing surrounding intelligence to the spaces in which we live, work, shop and play. Recognising patterns of behaviour and preferences, they are starting to anticipate our probable needs in a given context and set up with a head start in what we want to do, or at least start off with the first question based on our past choices and patterns of behaviour.

It is also enabling us to transfer electronic work easily between devices, screens and surfaces, and whistle it between different locations. Most of the bandwidth problems we had in 2012 will have been overcome, though the new applications are themselves very bandwidth-hungry and generating new challenges that the authorities and infrastructure providers are being slow to address.

What has this meant for the design of workplaces? The prospect of an open-plan floor full of people talking and gesturing to screens at first sent some people scurrying back to cellular offices. Or at least asking for one. In the end, it has prompted further rises in the level of home-based working. Use of a noise-cancelling headset at least is now a must for interaction with computers, wherever one is working. However, it is also the case that many of us just get used to workplaces with higher levels of ambient noise, like working in an ancient or medieval library where most people used to read aloud, and those who did not were marvelled at.

The most significant change that is happening in 2022 is the demise of the desk. An office without a desk – who would have thought this possible? In a paper-free office, with no keyboard or mouse, or paper, and an established 'clear desk' mindset, what use is the desk except as a place to put one's coffee, or possibly one's feet?

Office designers have been going to town with new concepts and furniture solutions. The cutting-edge office has become more like a lounge, or possibly like the bridge of the Starship *Enterprise*, where we can sit in big armchairs and interface with technologies by voice or by swinging screens into a position where we can touch them or point at them. Touch-down alcoves protected by noise-cancelling techniques are an ever more popular part of the mix of activity-based work settings. But working somewhere else, far from the madding crowd, is the most appropriate option for much of the time.

This has accelerated the trend for offices to be smaller, and to function almost exclusively now as centres for collaboration on those occasions when people do actually want or need to meet in the flesh.

In 2022, we haven't got to grips yet with the wider ripples of impacts from this rapid pace of change. The commercial property market has never recovered from the recession, and workspace providers are still struggling to get a handle on the community-based alternatives. And the government is commissioning experts to come up with ways to tax the 'office on the network' to make up for their revenue from property-based business rates, which continues to nosedive.

Smart, Flexible, Boundary-Blurring and Just-in-Time

The trends that take us through to 2022 look set to be ever more smart and flexible. There'll be more blurring of boundaries, more choice and more innovative technology.

Trends to just-in-time will be intensified, with the platform for work increasingly made up of just-in-time offices and just-in-time (cloud) technology infrastructure and services.

There is one area of blurring boundaries which really takes me to a point where I dare go no further in scanning the horizon.

We looked at the increasing role of speech recognition, but this only represents the foothills of the ascent to the smarter ways of interfacing with technology that may become commonplace by the middle of the twenty-first century. Over the next two decades we will see the arrival in earnest of the neurochip.

Already neurochips that allow the direct interface between neurons and external devices are being used in the field of neuroprosthetics, to overcome disability. Direct interface between the brain and (other) computing devices offers the prospect of not only rethinking the way we work, but rethinking the way we think.

This is blurring boundaries with bells on, and possibly work-life balance will never be the same again.

Though we may baulk at the thought of implants for work purposes – unless there are big rewards involved – the point is that we are just at the beginning of direct human-machine interaction, by one means or another. And that will, in the lifetime of most people reading this book, enable or require continuing transformations to the way we work and the places we work. Making them smarter and more flexible for sure. The question remains, how well will we be able to capture the benefits for the Triple Bottom Line and see that, as a result, we live in a better world?

Further Trends That Will Impact on the Directions of Change

Throughout the writing of this book, I have been aware of a key shortcoming – a cultural bias towards Western, developed world methods and expectations of working.

It's interesting that we in the West still expect that other nations will tend to adopt our ways of working and the social, ethical and cultural standards that go along with it. There is something plausible about that, with the dominance of Western management ideas and literature, and of the English Language as the international language of education and business.

All the same, the rise of the emerging economies of Asia, the Middle East, South and Central America and Africa is going to create many changes in the world of business. Just in terms of sheer numbers and volume of business, this is bound to make a difference. Different sets of values, not only about doing business but also about hierarchy, equality, networks of family and social relationships and the interface between home and work will make a difference to how ideas of Smart Flexibility pan out internationally. Uneven rolling out of infrastructure will also be a factor.

What difference will it make? Barring catastrophe, we will be looking at a more integrated and globalised world. The concepts of Smart Flexibility – however described – are already taking root around the world. They have a compelling business logic behind them. And some of these emerging countries will make faster progress without the legacies of traditional ways of working and institutional conservatism to hold them back.

But given the scale and dynamism of the emerging economies, I am sure it will not be a one-way traffic in ideas and new business practices.

How Smart Flexibility is transformed through this global interaction will be a key – and very exciting – part of its story in the coming years.

CHAPTER **15** *Top Tips*

I asked contributors to the case studies for their top tips to pass on to others implementing Smart Flexibility.

It makes for interesting reading, and you may notice some interesting themes emerging – like the need for leadership buy-in – which endorse the approach in this book.

Here are their tips in their own words.

Neil Stride, at Vodafone

- Decide what the business wants to achieve, what the priorities are and how everyone in the business should be performing.
- There must be strong leadership from the top.
- Keep it simple and consistent.
- Make the transition but be prepared to keep reinventing as new opportunities to do so arise.

Jill Pritchard, Fife Council

- Get buy-in at the highest level.
- Get the right governance in place to make sure issues are swiftly dealt with in implementation.
- Make sure you have a fantastic comms team – you can't communicate enough.

Adrian Rathbone, Birmingham City Council

- Carry out a space utilisation audit: it gives the ability to challenge people's assumptions for how work needs to be done.
- Get the buy-in, through quick wins and engagement with all stakeholders, and a first-class communications programme.
- Ensure that the occupiers have some influence over the solutions, and so they don't get any surprises.
- Have a skilled delivery team.

Sue Skinner, Britvic

- Have regular reviews to ensure that you're achieving right balance between business requirements, individual preferences and team contribution – all three are equally important for high performance and should be regularly evaluated.
- IT support and stable systems are critical to maintain effectiveness when out of the office/working from home – if not in place then this will create more pressure and frustration as people can't get the job done!
- Create a culture of openness with calendars visible to all – it makes it much easier for others to respect existing commitments.
- Reinforce this by 'role model' leadership for commitments outside work/visible support and encouragement for those who 'flex and deliver'.

Caroline Oldham, Ofsted

- Have someone in the kind of role that I perform, to coordinate health and safety, ICT and HR.
- Keep in touch with home-based staff to find out what they want and don't just make assumptions.
- Invest in good IT equipment.

David Robinson, Hertfordshire County Council

- Do not under-estimate the importance of ownership of the cultural change journey; if you can establish 'Change Champions' early on the journey then there will be greater buy-in to new ways of working.
- People are not all technically competent, and if you can establish trust and honesty at the outset, supporting people when they admit they cannot understand ' VPN', 'Secure log-ons', and so on, then all change is possible.
- The reduction of the 'Paper Mountain' is not only satisfying in terms of space saving but the physical process of 'De-cluttering' certainly clears the mind and starts people thinking in quite a different way.
- Remember to highlight the advantages of new ways of working and the best way is to get people who have made the changes to tell the story, far more powerful than any consultant or Change Management Team.

References

Acas. 2007. *Flexible Working and Work-Life Balance*. London: Acas.

Actium Consult. 2012. *Total Office Costs Survey 2012*. Actium Consult.

Age Positive. 2011. *Good Practice Case Studies: Managing without a Fixed Retirement Age*. Department for Work & Pensions, London.

Audit Commission, UK. 2006a. *Case Study: East Riding of Yorkshire Council: Home Working*.

Audit Commission, UK. 2006b. *Efficiency Challenge Case Studies*.

Banister, D., Newson, C. and Ledbury, M. 2007. *The Costs of Transport on the Environment: The Role of Teleworking in Reducing Emissions*. Transport Studies Unit (Ref. 1024), Oxford University.

Beauregard, T.A. and Lesley, L.C. 2009. Making the link between work-life balance practices and organizational performance. *Human Resource Management Review*, 19, 9–22.

BERR. 2007a. *Annual Small Business Survey 2006/7*. Department for Business, Enterprise and Regulatory Reform, London.

BERR. 2007b. *The Third Work-Life Balance Employer Survey*. Department for Business, Enterprise and Regulatory Reform, London.

BIS. 2010. *Phasing out the Default Retirement Age: Consultation Document*. Department for Business, Innovation & Skills, London.

Bridges, W. 1995. *Jobshift: How to Prosper in a Workplace without Jobs*. Reading, Massachusetts: Addison-Wesley.

BT. 2011. *Agile Working in BT South Tyneside & South Tyneside Council*. Presentation at Flexibility conference, Smart Working: The Way Ahead for the Public Sector, Edinburgh.

Cairns, S., Sloman, L., Newson, C., Anable, J., Kirkbride, A. and Goodwin, P. 2005. *Smarter Choices: Changing the Way We Travel*. Department for Transport, London.

Carter, Lord Stephen. 2009. *Digital Britain*. Department for Culture, Media and Sport and Department for Business, Innovation and Skills, London.

CIPD. 2011a. *Annual Survey Report 2011: Resourcing and Talent Planning*. London: Chartered Institute of Personnel and Development.

CIPD. 2011b. *Annual Survey Report 2011: Absence Management*. London: Chartered Institute of Personnel and Development.

CMI. 2008. *Management Futures: The World in 2018*. London: Chartered Management Institute.

Daniels, K., Lamond, D. and Standen, P. 2000. *Managing Telework: Perspectives from Human Resources Management and Work Psychology*. London: Business Press.

Department for Employment. 1994. *A Manager's Guide to Teleworking*. Department for Employment.

DfID. 2007. *Annual Report 2007*. Department for International Development, UK.

Dressler, C. and Thompson, J. 2008. *Why Work Sucks and How to Fix It: The Results-Only Revolution*. New York: Portfolio.

DTI. 2007. *The Third Work-Life Balance Employee Survey*. Department for Trade and Industry, London.

Dwelly, T. and Lake, A. (eds). 2008. *Can Homeworking Save the Planet?* Smith Institute. [Online]. Available at: www.flexibility.co.uk/savetheplanet.

Dwelly, T., Lake, A. and Thompson, L. 2008. *Tomorrow's Property Today*. Live/Work Network.

Dwelly, T., Lake, A. and Thompson, L. 2010. *Work Hubs*. Department for Communities and Local Government & Live/Work Network, London.

Dwelly, T., Maguire, K. and Truscott, F. 2005. *Under the Radar: Tracking and Supporting Rural Home-Based Business*. Commission for Rural Communities & Live/Work Network, London.

DWP. 2004. *Building a Society for All Ages*. Department for Work & Pensions, London.

Eaton, S. 2003. If you can use them: Flexibility policies, organizational commitment, and perceived performance. *Industrial Relations*, 42(2), 145–67.

EHRC. 2007. *Enter the Timelords: Transforming Work to Meet the Future*. Equalities and Human Rights Commission.

Elston, C. and Orrell, S. 2005. *Teach Yourself Flexible Working*. London: Hodder Education.

Ettema, D. 2010. The impact of telecommuting on residential relocation and residential preferences: A latent class modeling approach. *Journal of Transport and Land Use*, 3(1), 7–24.

Fawcett Society. 2009. *Sexism and the City: The Manifesto*. London: Fawcett Society.

Gajendran, R.S. and Harrison, D.A. 2007. The good, the bad, and the unknown about telecommuting: Meta-analysis of psychological mediators and individual consequences. *Journal of Applied Psychology*, 92(6), 1524–41.

Glogger, A.F., Zangler, T.W. and Karg, G. 2008. The impact of telecommuting on households' travel behaviour, expenditures and emissions, in *Road Pricing, the Economy and the Environment*, (ed.) C. Jensen-Butler, B. Sloth, M.M. Larsen, B. Madsen and O.A. Nielsen. Berlin: Springer, chapter 21, 411–25.

Golden, T. 2007. Co-workers who telework and the impact on those in the office: Understanding the implications of virtual work for co-worker satisfaction and turnover intentions. *Human Relations*, 60, 1641–67.

Golden, T.D. 2011. Altering the effects of work and family conflict on exhaustion: Telework during traditional and nontraditional work hours. *Journal of Business and Psychology*.

Goodall, C. 2007. Carbon Emissions and the Service Sector. [Online]. Available at: http://www.lowcarbonlife.net.

Gordon, G. 2001. *Turn it Off: How to Unplug from the Anytime-Anywhere Office without Disconnecting Your Career*. London: Nicholas Brealey Publishing.

Green, P. 2010. *Efficiency Review by Sir Philip Green: Key Findings and Recommendations*. Cabinet Office, London.

GSA. 2001. *Implementation Manual for Telework*. US General Services Administration.

Hardy, B. 2010. *The Future of Work in Government: Workplace 2020*. [Online]. Available at: http://www.flexibility.co.uk/issues/modgov/government-workplace-2020.htm.

Hawksworth, J., Dobson, C. and Jones, N.C. 2010. *Working Longer, Living Better: A Fiscal and Social Imperative*. London: Public Sector Research Centre, PricewaterhouseCoopers.

HM Government. 2012. *The Civil Service Reform Plan*. London: HM Government.

HM Treasury. 2009. *Operational Efficiency Programme*. London: HM Treasury.

HOP Associates. 1998. *Telecommuting 2000: The Future of Transport in the Information Age*. HOP Associates, Cambridge. (Archived at www.flexibility.co.uk/telecommuting2000).

Hopkinson, P., James, P., Mayurama, T. and Selwyn, J. 2001. *The Impacts of Teleworking: A Study of AA Employees*. Bradford University and UKCEED.

IOD. 2011. *IoD Freebie Growth Plan*. London: Institute of Directors.

James, P. 2007. *Conferencing at DFID: The Economic, Environmental and Social Impacts*. Peterborough: SustainIT.

James, P. 2008. Homeworking and carbon reduction: The evidence, in *Can Homeworking Save the Planet? How Homes Can Become Workspace in a Low Carbon Economy*, (ed.) T. Dwelly and A. Lake. London: Smith Institute, chapter 10, 86–96.

James, P. 2010. *Flexible Working, Conferencing and Carbon Reduction: The Evidence*. Presentation at Flexibility conference, Save Money, Save the Planet! London.

James, P. and Pamlin, D. 2009. *Virtual Meetings and Climate Innovation in the 21st Century: Can Offsetting CO2 Emissions from Flights by Investing in Videoconferencing Be a Way to Support Transformative Change?* Gland: WWF.

Joyce, K., Pabayo, R., Critchley, J.A. and Bambra, C. 2010. Flexible working conditions and their effects on employee health and wellbeing. Cochrane Library. 2010, Issue 2. John Wiley & Sons.

Kelliher, C. and Anderson, D. 2008. *Flexible Working and Performance: Summary of Research*. Cranfield University School of Management and Working Families.

Kelliher, C. and Anderson, D. 2009. *Flexible Working in Organisations: The Perspective of Co-Workers*. Paper at International Industrial Relations Association World Congress, Sydney, 24–27 August, 2009.

Kelliher, C. and Anderson, D. 2010. Doing more with less? Flexible working practices and the intensification of work. *Human Relations*, 63(1), 83–106.

Kossek, E.E. and Lautsch, B.A. 2008. *CEO of Me: Creating a Life that Works in the Flexible Job Age*. Upper Saddle River, New Jersey: Pearson Education.

Kossek, E.E, Lautsch, B.A and Eaton, S.C. 2006. Telecommuting, control, and boundary management: Correlates of policy use and practice, job control, and work–family effectiveness. *Journal of Vocational Behavior*, 68(2006), 347–67.

Laing, A., Duffy, F., Jaunzens, D. and Willis, S. 1998. *New Environments for Working*. London: BRE Publications.

Lake, A.S. 2008. The impacts of e-Work and e-Commerce on Transport, the Environment and the Economy, in *Road Pricing, the Economy and the Environment*, (ed.) C. Jensen-Butler, B. Sloth, M.M. Larsen, B. Madsen and O.A. Nielsen. Berlin: Springer, chapter 19, 373–93.

Lake, A.S. and Cherrett, T.J. 2002. *The Impact of Information and Communications Technologies on Travel and Freight Distribution Patterns: Review and Assessment of Literature*. Department for Transport, London. [Online]. Available at: http://www.virtual-mobility.com.

Leighton, D. and Gregory, T. 2011. *Reinventing the Workplace*. London: Demos.

Lister, K. and Harnish, T. 2011. *The Bottom-Line Benefits of Telework*. Telework Research Network.

Live/Work Network. 2012. *Live/Work Business Briefing 2012*. Live/Work Network. [Online]. Available at: www.liveworknet.com.

Maitland, A. and Thomson, P. 2011. *Future Work: How Businesses Can Adapt and Thrive in the New World of Work*. Basingstoke: Palgrave Macmillan.

McNair, S., Flynn, M., Owen, L., Humphreys, C. and Woodfield, S. 2004. *Changing Work in Later Life: A Study of Job Transitions*. Reading: Centre for Research into the Older Workforce, University of Surrey.

Monks, J. 1994. Trade unions and new ways of working. *Flexibility*, 2(2).

Moynagh, M. and Worsely, R. 2004. *The Opportunity of a Lifetime: Reshaping Retirement*. London: CIPD.

Muhammad, S., Ottens, H., Ettema, D. and de Jong, T. 2007. Telecommuting and residential locational preferences: A case study of the Netherlands. *Journal of Housing and the Built Environment*, 22(4), 339–58.

My Family Care. 2011. *Working Parents & Carers Flexible Working Survey 2011*. [Online]. Available at: www.myfamilycare.co.uk.

NEF. 2010. *21 Hours: Why a Shorter Working Week Can Help Us All to Flourish in the 21st Century*. London: New Economics Foundation.

Nippert-Eng, C. 1996. *Home and Work: Negotiating Boundaries through Everyday Life*. Chicago, Ilinois: University of Chicago Press.

OGC and DEGW. 2008. *Working beyond Walls*. DEGW/Office of Government Commerce, London.

Olsen, L. 2008. *Telework under the Microscope: A Report on the National Science Foundation's Telework Programme*. National Science Foundation and Telework Exchange.

ONS. 2010. *Social Trends*. Newport: Office for National Statistics.

ONS. 2011. *Commuting to Work – 2011*. Newport: Office for National Statistics.

Ory, D.T. and Mokhtarian, P.L. 2006. Which came first, the telecommuting or the residential relocation? An empirical analysis of causality. *Urban Geography*, 27(7), 590–609.

Pamlin, P. and Pahlmann, S. 2009. *From Green IT to Greening with IT in 2009*. Gland: WWF.

Pink, D.H. 2001. *Free Agent Nation: How America's Independent Workers Are Transforming the Way We Live*. New York: Warner Books.

Pink, D.H. 2011. *Drive: The Surprising Truth about What Motivates Us*. Edinburgh: Canongate Books.

Pongratz, H.J. and Voß, G.G. 2003. From employee to 'entreployee': Towards a 'self-entrepreneurial' work force? *Concepts and Transformation*. 8(3), 239–54.

Purcell, K., Hogarth, T. and Simm, C. 1999. *Whose Flexibility? The Costs and Benefits of 'Non-Standard' Working Arrangements and Contractual Relations*. York: Joseph Rowntree Foundation.

Randall, C. 2010. e-Society. *Social Trends*, 41, ONS, UK.

RICS. 2008. *Property in the UK: A Digest and Review of Key Data and Statistics*. Royal Institution of Chartered Surveyors.

Saxena, S. and Mokhtarian, P.L. 1997. The impact of telecommuting on the activity spaces of participants and their households. *Geographical Analysis*, 29(2), 124–44.

SEG. 2009. *Smart Economic Growth, European Interreg Project*. [Online]. Available at: www.segproject.eu.

Smart 2020. 2009. *BT Agile Worker Energy and Carbon Study*. Climate Change Group. [Online]. Available at: http://www.smart2020.org/case-studies/.

SUSTEL. 2004. *Is Teleworking Sustainable? An Analysis of its Economic, Environmental and Social Impacts*. Final report of the SUSTEL (Sustainable Teleworking) project. European Commission.

Telework Association. 2003. *The Teleworking Handbook*. 4th Edition. London: A&C Black.

Verbeke, A., Schulz, R., Greidanus, N. and Hambley, L. 2008. *Growing the Virtual Workplace: The Integrative Value Proposition for Telework*. Cheltenham: Edward Elgar.

Vodafone. 2010. *Flexible Working at Vodafone*. Presentation at Flexibility conference, Flexible Working Environments. 2010, London.

Westminster Sustainable Business Forum. 2011. *Leaner and Greener: Putting Buildings to Work*. London: Policy Connect.

Wright, A. 1997. Saving Energy through Teleworking. *Flexible Working*, 2, January 1997. Eclipse Group.

Index

Note: Figures and tables indexed with bold numbers.